KU-261-534

THE WORLD BANK AND THE POOR

INSTITUTE OF SOCIAL STUDIES

SERIES ON THE DEVELOPMENT
OF SOCIETIES

VOLUME VI

INTERNATIONAAL INSTITUUT
VOOR SOCIALE STUDIËN - 'S GRAVENHAGE

THE WORLD BANK AND THE POOR

Aart van de Laar

KLUWER·NIJHOFF PUBLISHING

BOSTON/THE HAGUE/LONDON

Distributors for North America:
Kluwer Boston, Inc.
190 Old Derby Street
Hingham, Massachusetts 02043

Distributors outside North America:
Kluwer Academic Publishers Group
Distribution Centre
P.O. Box 322
3300 AH Dordrecht, The Netherlands

Library of Congress Cataloging in Publication Data

van de Laar, Aart J. M.
    The World Bank and the poor.

    (Series on the development of societies; v. 6)
    Bibliography: p.
    1. International Bank for Reconstruction and Develop-
ment. I. Title. II. Series.
HG3881.V333   332.1'532   80-12011

ISBN 0-89838-042-1

QUEEN MARY
COLLEGE
LIBRARY

Copyright © 1980 by Martinus Nijhoff Publishing. Second printing 1982.

No part of this book may be reproduced in any form by print, photoprint, microfilm, or any
other means, without written permission from the publisher.

Printed in the United States of America

For Hanneke, Marjolijn
and Katinka

ACKNOWLEDGEMENTS

Many people have helped me in the writing of this book, among them my former colleagues at the World Bank who contributed to my education. The functioning of that institution did not entice me to stay long, but my colleagues were not to blame for that and I can only hope that they will not see this book merely as an indication of my disenchantment.

At the Netherlands Ministry of Foreign Affairs various officials have given me access to recent internal Bank documents, for which I am grateful.

At the Institute of Social Studies, present and former colleagues have commented on drafts of this thesis, and this has been appreciated. With their help, I hope to continue to move away from standard neo-classical economics, which I found to be so unhelpful when trying to understand the realities of underdevelopment.

My thanks are due to Hans Linnemann, my promotor, who supported and encouraged me at critical points on my lonely journey through subject matter that made me feel increasingly depressed.

Wouter Tims was willing to act as co-referent notwithstanding the fact that he disagrees with much of my analysis and with many of my conclusions. His comments have saved me from making a number of errors and I am thankful for that help.

Inèz Zwager and Tonnie Schenk typed most of the drafts and redrafts. Jean Sanders did a splendid job as editor and Netty Born faultlessly typed the final copy.

My greatest thanks go to my wife, Hanneke, for her courage and resilience which I have come to admire in the last three years. Our daughter, Marjolijn, gives us much happiness.

FOREWORD

The authors of a recent textbook on the *Economics of Development* (P.A. Yotopoulos and J.B. Nugent, 1976) chose as the title of their first chapter 'The Record of Economic Development and Disillusionment with Development Economics'. It is striking that dissatisfaction with this young branch of the tree of economics has become so strong that a textbook treatment of the subject matter takes Disillusionment as its point of departure. True, the Disillusionment chapter is followed by many other chapters — there is, after all, something to be said on development economics that is worth saying — but the wording has changed, and frequently the focus as well, in comparison to the development economics of the 1950s and 'sixties.

Dissatisfaction and disillusionment may be interpreted optimistically as an inevitable stage in the coming-of-age process of development economics. Others may say that the search for a new paradigm is the core of the problem. At any rate, there is no room for complacency. It cannot be denied that at least part of the 'early' development theory came into being as a justification *ex post* of policy measures that, for a variety of reasons, were judged desirable or essential. And when it was found, in the course of time, that such policy measures had failed to produce 'true' development — in terms of the then current definition of the concept — theories or parts of theories were discredited and discarded. This process still continues, but slowly and gradually development theory is trying to reduce its subservience to development policy. This has created a relatively new situation for policy makers whose activities meet with more criticism than in the past — criticism coming this time not from the side of political opponents but from academic quarters.

Due to the present state of dissatisfaction within the discipline, development economists at universities cannot address policy makers with too loud a voice. Yet they should not refrain from speaking-up if they are convinced that there are good grounds for doing so. The present study by Dr van de Laar is a case in point. The World Bank is undoubtedly one of the leading policy makers in the development field, and its professed policy to reorient its activities in large measure towards the poor and the poorest in the developing world is an issue of major importance in designing an international development strategy for the years to come. But will the Bank be able to implement such a poor-oriented policy successfully, or are there good reasons for serious doubt in this respect? That is the question to which Dr van de Laar addresses himself in the following pages.

A discussion of the appropriateness and adequacy of Bank policies has to cope with two problems — problems that are interrelated and which seem to have a common cause. The first, as Dr van de Laar points out in his introductory chapter, is that relatively little information about the Bank Group's internal functioning and decision-making processes is available in documents and reports that are accessible to the public. Attempts to evaluate the Bank's performance in identifying, formulating, modifying, approving and executing development projects are hampered all too often by lack of relevant information — as distinct from information on how the Bank would like to do it in principle.

The second problem is that the Bank — as any large bureaucracy — is inclined to react rather negatively to public criticism. It either ignores such criticism as much as possible, or starts to contradict it vehemently. This is regrettable, as then no discussion or dialogue is possible. The Bank should realize that as a development agency it is far too important to be left alone by those in the academic field who try to think critically but constructively about the development process. And why should constructive criticism always or nearly always be seen as a threat or a nuisance? Avoiding an open dialogue creates the impression of weakness rather than of strength.

The present study will hopefully provide a starting point for a discussion of the Bank Group's future role on the international development scene. This will be, in all probability, an important role — but let us try to be explicit about what the Bank can do and cannot do. This book is an attempt to achieve greater clarity on this point — and in spite of its limitations (see the first problem mentioned above), I think it is a very valuable attempt. I hope that people in Bank circles will read it with open minds. Not only in Bank circles, however, because the issue at stake is equally important to other members of the U.N. family and to the development profession at large.

In the first paragraph above I have referred to the dissatisfaction and disillusionment with development economics. In Dr van de Laar's analysis, dissatisfaction and disillusionment are also present. They may represent a good point of departure, however, from which to ask the proper questions and to deepen our understanding about what is and what is not possible. The author is to be credited for doing exactly this with regard to the World Bank as an agent to help the poor.

Hans Linnemann

Free University of Amsterdam
November 1979

CONTENTS

THE WORLD BANK AND THE POOR

I

INTRODUCTION

The theory of, and the public policy recommendations for, international development efforts seem to have been in a state of confusion since the late 1960s. Although the developing countries have experienced growth rates of Gross National Product that were high by historical standards, there is evidence that that growth has been distributed rather unevenly between and within countries and among socio-economic groups. Growth seems to go hand in hand with growing unemployment, growing inequality and growing poverty.

At the theoretical level it seems useful to discuss two principal modes of viewing development. One may be termed the conventional, traditional, neo-classical approach; the other the political economy or radical approach. These two paradigms or world-views start from different value assumptions, have different operational criteria for defining the 'good society', and formulate strikingly different strategies for attacking the problem of economic development.

At the public policy level we find a flow of sometimes contradictory recommendations that seem to succeed each other at two-year intervals. Though the Pearson Committee (1969) was not unaware of the patterns of development that had emerged, its recommendations may be summarized briefly, but not perhaps unfairly, as 'doing more of the same'. The ILO sponsored Employment Mission to Kenya (1972) advocated a strategy of 'redistribution *from* growth'. Two years later the World Bank formulated elements of a strategy of 'Redistribution *with* Growth'. In 1976 the ILO formulated a 'basic needs strategy' (ILO 1976). In 1978 Adelman, among others, advocated a strategy of 'redistribution *before* growth'. Though the report of the Brandt Commission has not been published, some sceptics suggest that its recommendations may add up to '*no* redistribution and *no* growth'. No-growth for ecological and environmental reasons, and no redistribution because the reality of world power relations does not permit it.

If, indeed, there is a growing body of evidence which indicates that the past pattern of economic growth has been accompanied by growing unemployment, more pronounced income inequality and continuation of mass poverty and disease, there is then a clear need for a different pattern of future growth and development which will alleviate social and human problems and improve the living conditions of the lower income strata of the populations of developing countries, and theorists and policy makers should re-direct their efforts towards finding ways and means to achieve it.

This book deals with the response of the World Bank to the new challenge. It attempts to investigate what the Bank may be able to do and can achieve in redirecting its activities towards the poor.

Why focus on the response of the World Bank? The answer must be in part because Mr McNamara, its president, has been speaking out eloquently about the lot of the poor. His address to the Board of Governors on September 25, 1972, was specifically devoted to Social Equity and Economic Growth. It focused on the low-income strata — roughly the poorest 40% — of the total population in all developing countries who, despite their country's gross economic growth, remain entrapped in conditions of deprivation which fall below any rational definition of human decency. Subsequent speeches have reiterated and elaborated this theme. More relevant, however, is the fact that in 1973 Mr McNamara, to redress this imbalance in past patterns of growth, announced a plan of action which, at first sight, seems more focused than the exhortations of other United Nations' agencies. Most important, however, is the fact that the World Bank is the *only* UN agency which has substantial financial resources at its disposal with which it could back up any envisaged change to the scope and orientation of its activities. Most UN bodies have to confine themselves, willy-nilly or not, to providing technical assistance and to devising and presenting policies to forums which do not generally have the authority to enforce compliance even if concrete and specific proposals are adopted, which is rarely the case.

The World Bank Group of institutions: the International Bank for Reconstruction and Development (IBRD), the International Finance Corporation (IFC) and the International Development Association (IDA), has of late become the major actor in the context of international development cooperation. Yet the number of serious evaluative studies of the World Bank is very limited. In part this has to do with the nature of much of its activities. The major activity of the Bank Group consists in the (co-)financing of specific development projects. But such projects are prepared and negotiated with governments or agencies of member countries under conditions which often evoke an analogy with secret diplomacy in order to protect the interests of the immediate partners. A second range of World Bank activities is to advise governments on general and specific economic policies at macro and sectoral levels, and the same desire for semi-secrecy often applies. A third group of activities, and for some of the Bank's staff its sole activity, is to produce studies and reports which contribute to the international debate on development, be it in academic circles or in more public opinion-oriented periodicals or books. They are best evaluated in public debate. These contributions deal with issues of development in general, however, and many of them lack operational significance for the Bank's other activities.

Given this nature of the 'output' of the World Bank, major problems can be expected to arise in evaluation. Each Bank-financed project has its own history. It is shaped in interaction between Bank staff and various officials and agencies in a country, often with one or more consultants advising one or all partners. To disentangle the contributions of the various parties would be nearly impossible. Up to mid-1978, the Bank had been involved in some 1600 projects and IDA in some 950 projects. There must be a bunch of 'bad eggs' in so large a basket. Similarly, there will undoubtedly be some very successful projects. Bad or successful, but by what standards and criteria? Even assuming that it were possible to produce 2500 project histories, what could one possibly 'generalize', especially when it may be assumed that most of the projects approved since 1970, nearly 1600 of the total, are still 'ongoing', i.e. are not yet completed in terms of disbursement or of subsequent benefit? Questions to ask and to be answered would be: In what ways would projects have been shaped differently if other staff had been involved in their preparation and execution? In what ways have projects changed because of changing Bank policies and procedures over time? Project decisions are made in response to challenge and issues in the light of the perceptions of those responsible at the time when decisions had to be made. Can one avoid the dangers of 'hindsight' reasoning in an area where conventional wisdom changes frequently, often rapidly and sometimes drastically?

Albert Hirschman, in his *Development Project Observed* (1967), studied only 11 Bank-financed projects. This sample was selected on the basis of two criteria: as a group they had to be well diversified with respect to economic sector and geographical area, and each project had to have an extended history including, if possible, several years of operation. The latter condition, in particular, limited the sample in practice to projects to which the Bank had given support at an early stage of its own operations, i.e. mostly during the 1950s. Hirschman then used these projects to make a broader and often brilliant analysis of project behaviour. Such and analysis makes it difficult to assess the precise role of the Bank in each specific project, however, and it is not clear how general the lessons of the Hirschman analysis really are.

Two other volumes dealing with Bank-financed projects are by-products of the teaching activities of its Economic Development Institute. John King's: *Economic Development Projects and their Appraisal* (1967) deals with a number of projects (sometimes including more than one loan per project) in the fields of electric power (17), transport (9), and industry (4); and J. Price Gittinger's book: *Economic Analysis of Agricultural Projects* (1972) deals with projects in a more recently developed field of Bank endeavour. These volumes contain teaching materials and focus for the most part on technical problems in the appraisal of projects. So much for the readily available published studies.

During 1973-74 the Bank's Operations Evaluation Department made about 25 so-called Project Performance Audits (PPAs), reviewing all projects on which disbursements were completed one year earlier. Typically, these reports review the process of project preparation up to the appraisal report as a basis for the lending decision. A realization versus appraisal report forecast was made, including an analysis of the causes of discrepancies between these two sets of figures. Where appropriate a new rate of return on the project was calculated.

This format is more helpful in an analysis of the role of the Bank than the studies mentioned earlier. Yet, allowing for regional and sectoral diversity, the sample was still very small. These recent studies, like nearly all Bank reports, were written under considerable time pressure, but were relatively unbiased despite their in-house publication status. Internal clearance procedures were minimized. The Operations Evaluation Department (OED), together with the Internal Auditing Department, were at that time placed under a Vice President who had no other operational responsibilities. Thus, some 'arm's length' assessment was possible.

These PPAs were made available to the Executive Directors on a confidential basis, limiting access to outsiders, but have now been discontinued as too costly. A Project Completion Report (PCR) is now produced as part of the regular supervisory function of the Bank's project staff. By the end of 1975 reports on about 170 completed development projects had been issued (Willoughby 1977: 30). Some role conflict may occur if the same personnel bears supervisory as well as evaluative responsibility. In practice, it is rare for the same Bank officials to be directly involved throughout the whole history of the project, from identification, preparation, appraisal and execution to completed disbursement. Nevertheless, early project officers may become the superiors of those charged with writing the PCR.

On the basis of the PCRs, the OED produces an internal *Annual Review of Project Performance Audit Results*, the third of which was published, after editing, in February 1978.

Most PPAs and PCRs do not try to assess the impact of completed projects on incomes, employment and distribution. There is not necessarily a close relationship between adherence to negotiated project agreements and project impact. Rates of return feature prominently in project appraisal, and thus also in project evaluation. Yet they are quite inadequate as major evaluation instruments in approving and reviewing loans.

Similarly, how is one to evaluate Bank macro or sectoral policy advice of the past in the light of constantly changing perceptions about the nature of the development process, the stress laid upon factors which are deemed critical levers, and improved awareness of the side effects of alternative sets of policy proposals? Countries differ greatly and policy advice has to take account of different and changing environments. More parties may be affected by policy advice than by project work, and the contribution of each participant is almost impossible to isolate.

Country Economic Reports and other studies of individual countries made by the Bank must be cleared by the governments concerned prior to publication, and can be obtained only by special written permission. Because they are printed in limited editions they are often unavailable. More sensitive material is not published at all, understanding being reached in face-to-face contacts.

Insofar as it is now realized that 'something has gone wrong' with development, those who attempted to influence past policies must take part of the blame, including the Bank. But with much past advice proving inapt, recipients may tend to be wary of accepting future advice from similar sources.

In addition to problems of access to the various types of Bank work and of finding yardsticks by which to evaluate them, due to the complexity, specificity and time perspective of each piece of Bank output, problems are created for any analyst by the nature of the information that is available to outside researchers. Official publications by the Bank provide a great deal of factual information about its activities. There are, however, limitations with respect to their usefulness for understanding the inner workings of the Bank. The Bank, like any large bureaucracy, has an institutional interest in presenting a picture of its activities which avoids touching upon issues thought to be controversial. For instance, U.S. Senator Ernest Gruening complained at one time: 'Publications by international organizations were virtually useless. Filled with euphemisms in order not to offend anyone, they become so bland and obfuscated as to be virtually meaningless. Congressional hearings provided only a few tantalizing clues... Thus the bits and pieces from published sources furnished only fragmentary insights' (*United States Foreign Aid in Action: a case study*, submitted to the Subcommittee on Foreign Aid Expenditures of the Committee on Government Operations, U.S. Senate, Washington 1966: Preface, vii). One might add: insight from a U.S. perspective. Analogous information from other countries is rarely available because their style of governmental and parliamentary operation is different. The issue, of course, is whether such publications by international agencies could be any different in view of the often deep conflicts between the numerous member states.

The major analytical study of the World Bank overall is that by Edward Mason and Robert Asher: *The World Bank since Bretton Woods* (1973). The authors have intimate knowledge of the Bank, having been associated with it as consultants or observers for many years. The preface to the book shows clearly that nearly everyone of any importance in the Bank has provided an input. Notably absent from that list is Irving Friedman who, from October 1964 to May 1970, was Economic Advisor to the Bank President. In reviewing the book, Friedman was tempted to add his own version of subjects in which he was deeply involved, and found it a pity that the authors had not expanded their work to two or even three volumes to provide an even more systematic and comprehensive study (Friedman 1974: 36-37). Yet this monumental 900-

[handwritten margin notes: "→ Don't underestimate the complexity of / Bank work", "→ significance of developing countries' projects / situations!"]

page volume comes as near to being an official history of the Bank as is feasible, but with the independence, objectivity and academic tradition which the Brookings Institution required before accepting the commission, as well as part of the funding, from the Bank. It is, however, mostly a history of the Bank, from the Bank's perspective. The book covers the period 1946-71, leading up to the time when McNamara began to embark upon his policy to revamp the Bank to serve the needs of the poor, the focus of the present study. Despite its bulk, the complexity of the Bank's work is such that it is inevitably a bit thin in the treatment of certain issues.

Another useful and relatively recent book is Escott Reid's *Strengthening the World Bank* (1973). In particular, it has interesting things to say about the future organization of the Bank. Reid advocates a thorough decentralization of the Bank. As he was a Director of the Bank's South Asia and Middle East Department in 1962-65, his book is in several respects that of an insider, and thus interesting for a study of the organization.

A much more publicized book on the Bank is Teresa Hayter's: *Aid as Imperialism* (1971): the publicity stemming more from attempts to suppress its publication than from the value of its content. Hayter is too ambitious in trying to analyse the activities of the International Monetary Fund, the World Bank, the United States Agency for International Development, the Inter-American Development Bank and the Inter-American Committee for the Alliance for Progress in Colombia, Chile, Brazil and Peru. She should have realized that international agencies, like national agencies, are subject to various types of pressure by national governments and private interest groups. Allowance should be made for the fact that institutions may be structured in such a way that they have to behave in ways that are abhorrent to some. To portray them merely as villains overlooks the fact that they can also be victims — undergo pressure from some as well as put pressure on others.

Hayter's book is dated since it deals with her findings and assessments of the situation studied in 1967-68. As far as the Bank is concerned this is the pre-McNamara era. Yet it is useful in parts in that it looks at the Bank more clearly from the perspective of some member countries, and thus adds a perspective on which the Mason & Asher volume is rather weak.

There may be studies in developing countries which relate to projects or situations in which the Bank has been involved, and it would be worthwhile to collect them (both the Mason & Asher and the Hayter book provide a number of references). But whether it would be possible to validly and meaningfully generalize from such facet studies is open to doubt; such an analysis has not yet been attempted with the exception of the Colombia study by the Bank's Evaluation Department (1972). An undertaking to make more detailed case studies of countries' relations with the Bank would clearly be a major job.

Finally, a number of papers published by present or former Bank staff may shed light on a variety of issues in revealing within-Bank thinking as opposed to

Bank-thinking. Some 40% of the individually authored publications listed in the Mason & Asher book (pp. 884-890) are by people who at one time or another were or still are employed by the Bank. This material has to be used with caution. Some staff members may be prolific writers, but it does not follow that they have much impact on Bank policy. The contrary conclusion could also be drawn: they have time to write so much because they have so few other responsibilities within the Bank! On the other hand, and under certain conditions, it would be good policy for management to allow individuals other than Bank presidents or vice presidents to do some 'stumping': to parade a few 'in-house radicals' to pacify criticism from the left, and a few 'in-house conservatives' to pacify critics on the right. Moreover, it is often a popular line of defence for the Bank to point to its involvement in projects that could comply with every conceivable set of criteria: it has a project to please everyone and a project for all occasions! But the analyst must look for major trends and not for incidental occurrences. Literature on bureaucratic behaviour (Downs 1966) teaches us that the more complex and controversial an organization becomes, the more it tends to guard itself against attacks from diverse groups. And the Bank has become quite complex.

To supplement any written material that might be available, it would be helpful if it were possible to interview Bank staff members. In general this has to be prearranged and needs authorization by senior bank officials, because staff members are prohibited from communicating on their own to any person or agency outside the Bank Group. Such authorization has occasionally been granted for specific and limited purposes (White 1967; Weaver 1965). But even then problems may arise as, for instance, those encountered by Teresa Hayter (1971, especially 193-214). Prior authorization is also required before staff members can communicate with the Bank's Executive Directors. Much internal policy making escapes the control of the Board: the Bank's Executive Directors. The fact that staff are periodically reminded of this obligation, indicates that indiscretions in this respect do occur. After all, how can Executive Directors perform their function of supervising management, if they only have the information which Management decides they should have? Nor is senior staff and management above such practices as the 'planted leak' to trusted journalists and other forms of lobbying in attempts to influence public opinion on certain issues.

But even if authorization to interviews is obtained, it is still necessary to evaluate conflicting views. Key personnel are often no longer with the Bank or are unavailable. Others, sufficiently informed to be valuable resource persons, are reluctant to co-operate for a variety of reasons. Some may fear that anything that is not written in praise of the Bank will harm it, reflecting a complete lack of a sense of proportion. Others may have become dependent upon Bank patronage for contract research and/or future employment prospects. Regretfully, this patronage system extends deeply into the academic world.

All this information adds up only to the Bank's view of certain problems and issues. It would be necessary to check with the counterpart government or agency to hear the 'other side' of the story. Such an approach would obviously be financially costly and time consuming. The same problems of access, bias and perspective would arise, multiplied by the number of countries or projects which one wishes to study.

All these factors may help to explain why so little serious evaluative material exists on Bank operations over the first 25 years of its existence which could help in a judgement of whether and how the Bank can respond to the new challenge of assisting the poor.

From what has been said so far, it might perhaps be concluded that a comprehensive study of the response of the Bank is impossible. Also, the present study has had to be confined to a limited range of issues.

For better or for worse, the present is largely determined by the past: while the new rhetoric emphasizes change, new directions and new strategies, there is also a great deal of continuity. Hence, this book can be divided into two parts. Chapters II-IV deal largely with that past, and explore how the past has shaped the present, from which a search for a different future must start. Chapter II sketches the evolution of the functioning of the World Bank proper, the International Bank for Reconstruction and Development; the focus is on its main characteristics, financial resources, growth record and major operational policies as they have shaped up in the course of a 30-year history. Chapter III similarly treats the International Development Association, in existence since 1960, and the 'soft loan' window of the World Bank Group. Together these two chapters provide background material on the external environment within which the World Bank has to function and on the pressures with which it has to cope if it is to stay assured of its finances and thus of its survival.

Within this structural context, the various forms of Bank output are a function, *inter alia*, of the potential and capacity of its staff and their accumulated store of experience and knowledge, but also of the limitations resulting from background, status and attitudes. The World Bank staff differs in several respects from that of other UN agencies. It has not been subject to much public scrutiny, and hence it is now given more attention in chapter IV – perhaps more than is strictly necessary.

Together, finances and personnel determine the resources which the Bank Group may envisage employing in response to the new challenge of the 1970s and beyond.

Part 2, chapters V-VII, deals with various aspects of what a new deployment of Bank resources may entail. Chapter V attempts to document major trends in the post-war growth of developing countries and shows that there is considerable substance to the concern about this record expressed at the beginning of the chapter. The analysis attempts to find indications of the incidence of poverty as criteria for future reallocation of World Bank financial resources, and discusses the likelihood of such a reallocation. Chapter V thus examines whether a re-employment of Bank financial resources means a re-allocation to poor countries.

The Bank has chosen the small farmers as its major target group among the poor. Small farmers do not comprise all the poor, nor do they necessarily represent the poorest of the poor. For present purposes it is sufficient that they feature prominently among the poor. The question is whether the Bank can execute 'small farmers' projects in line with its intention to develop target group approaches. The emphasis in chapter VI is on project-related policy issues and on developments seen as a process in time and space. Attention is given to the comparative empirical impact of past projects that were oriented towards the small farmers.

Chapter VII focuses on institutional issues. If the record of international development has proved disappointing in a number of respects, there is an obvious need to re-examine premises and practices of past development efforts by UN agencies. The question then arises of whether the institutional environment in which development agencies have to work is conducive to self-examination and experimentation. While the Bank Group has grown considerably in the last decade, a number of institutional issues have become more acute.

In this book little will be found on development theory. No new paradigms will be constructed, nor will existing paradigms be contrasted and compared. These have already been extensively discussed in the literature (a particularly lucid and concise analytical review is that by Weaver & Jameson 1978). Similarly, many Bank activities will not or only summarily be dealt with. Yet such activities may be important. A dialogue on policy matters may yield more significant results than variations in the volume of project loans. But general policy advice is often just that: it is *general*. The critical issue for the Bank is to lend or not to lend. It does lend to a very large number of countries representing a wide range of policy settings. Only when Bank policy advice is linked to project lending, and its acceptance is preconditional to a loan, has policy advice any bite, because it then links carrot and stick.

The problems of international development show a complexity that is increasingly realized, requiring much solid research. Judgements about the value of research may differ, but it seems reasonable to ask whether the premises of such research are realistic. The Bank is *not* a university. Output should not primarily be evaluated in terms of the internal consistency of the theory employed given chosen premises, but in terms of the reality value of its premises and the usefulness of the results. In addition, it might reasonably be asked whether some activities that are undertaken are really necessary for a better functioning of the Bank in terms of contributing to its output in ways that could not be obtained by other and more simple means. It may seem obvious to require that activities should not be undertaken in duplication of activities elsewhere in the UN. When so many basic issues of development are still unexplored, it seems inefficient use of scarce resources to devote them to the duplication of activities better performed elsewhere. Central to the pursuit of Bank activities should be the question of choice and of comparative advantage. Not only in terms of which activities are best undertaken by what agency, but also in terms of the most appropriate level of organization: global, regional or national, and through what channel, official or non-governmental, can certain issues best be tackled.

It would seem that the Bank does a number of things which have only limited significance towards making it a more effective project lending agency, which it is by its charter. No attempt will be made, however, to review the research programme in this light.

II

GROWTH AND EVOLUTION OF THE INTERNATIONAL BANK FOR RECONSTRUCTION AND DEVELOPMENT

INTRODUCTION

The IBRD is by far the largest component of the Bank Group of institutions. Between 1964 and 1978 cumulative gross Bank lending to developing countries was 2.8 times the cumulative amount of credits provided by the International Development Association (IDA). The cumulative gross investments of the International Finance Corporation (IFC), founded in 1956, totalled one-third of Bank lending in fiscal year 1978 (the Bank Group fiscal year runs from July 1 through June 30). From this it will be clear that what the Group as a whole can do, in terms of lending money, is largely determined by the scope for IBRD activities.

IBRD MEMBERSHIP

The membership list of the Bank is characterized by the absence of most East European socialist countries. Yet there is nothing in its Articles of Agreement which excludes the membership of socialist countries (see Oliver, 1975, for the prehistory of IMF and IBRD, and Bitterman, 1971, for negotiations on the Articles of Agreement of IBRD).

The Russians, who participated in the Bretton Woods Conference, at that time set great store by the reconstruction objectives of the Bank (Bitterman 1971: 71). They, together with delegates from many of the less developed countries, were in fact far more interested in the Bank than in the International Monetary Fund. Eventually, however, the Soviet Union decided not to ratify the Articles of Agreement. Bank and Fund are twin institutions in the sense that IBRD membership is only open to countries which are members of the IMF. Fund membership would require that the USSR make available a substantial amount of information hitherto usually undivulged, while borrowing from the Bank involved exacting investigations. This the Soviet Union was not

Notes to this chapter may be found on p. 54.

prepared to accept. At a meeting of the UN General Assembly in 1947 the Soviet representative charged that the Bretton Woods institutions were merely 'branches of Wall Street', and that the Bank was 'subordinated to political purposes which make it the instrument of one great power' (Mason & Asher 1973: 21-22, 29 note). When the Soviet Union did not join, this accusation became indeed a self-fulfilling prophecy in practice though not in design.

The Soviet Union thus never was a member of the Bank, unlike other socialist countries. Poland and Czechoslovakia were members but left in 1950 and 1955 respectively for political reasons. Yugoslavia remained a member and Romania joined in 1973. Cuba and the Dominican Republic withdrew in 1960, but the latter rejoined in 1961. Indonesia joined in 1954, withdrew in 1965, and was readmitted in 1967.

In Bretton Woods it had been considered logical that subscriptions to the Bank should be the same as the IMF quotas. The practical application of this principle, however, proved less simple than anticipated. Whereas many countries attempted to obtain high IMF quotas, the same eagerness was not shown with regard to equal subscriptions in the Bank, probably because of the liability deriving from the subscription. The US, and to a lesser degree Canada, agreed to a Bank subscription that was higher than their IMF quota. This more than offset the reduction in Latin American subscriptions, which were only 70% of their IMF quotas, and those of some other countries (Basch 1949: 798; Bitterman 1971: 73-74).

In consequence, the voting superiority of the US became larger than initially negotiated. Under the terms agreed at Bretton Woods, the member countries with the most shares were, in order, the US, UK, Soviet Union, China and France. Since the Soviet Union failed to ratify the Articles of Agreement, however, India moved into fifth place. In 1947 only three countries could produce a majority vote: the US, with 35.07%; the UK, with 14.52%; and France, with 6.03%, controlled 55.62% of all votes at that time (Mason & Asher 1973: 29, 800).

Quite apart from formal voting power, the US was the only country after World War Two which was in a position to provide capital for reconstruction and development purposes on any large scale. It was then quite unthinkable that the Bank should be able to tap the US capital market if the US did not have a strong position in the Bank. Precisely because of the importance of the US capital market, then and now, Bank presidents have always been Americans. With the exception of McNamara they have all been close to the Wall Street Bankers fraternity prior to their Bank presidencies. (Eugene Meyer, 1946, had been the head of a successful investment banking house, Eugene Meyer and Company, before World War I; John McCloy, 1947-49, was a member of a New York law firm and counsel to several banks; Eugene Black, 1949-62, was a vice president of the Chase National Bank of New York; George Woods, 1963-68, was chairman of the Board of the First Boston Corporation. In contrast,

Robert McNamara was for a long period a motor industry executive, and for seven years US Secretary of Defence, prior to his appointment as Bank President in 1968.)

Contrary to current practice in the UN General Assembly, formal voting by the Bank's Executive Directors (EDs) who reside in Washington, rarely takes place, despite the growth of Bank membership over time.

With control firmly in their hands and the main operating principles well established through years of experience the major Western powers can block any proposal that is not to their liking. The major shareholders — at present US, UK, Germany (FR), France and Japan (the latter having obtained a capital share larger than that of India) — appoint one ED each; all other countries together elect the remaining fifteen EDs, who thus may represent up to 19 countries each. (The Dutch ED represents Cyprus, Israel, Romania and Yugoslavia, in addition to The Netherlands.) Each Director must cast *all* his votes one way. To reach a compromise among so many LDC members who are served by one ED is not easy, and makes a forceful representation on the Board difficult. Moreover, present management aims at consensus, which often means that lending proposals which are likely to be controversial are simply not presented to the Board. Confrontations in the Board may arise on major policy issues, however, which sometimes results in amendments to major operational policies.

EDs are frequently not re-elected for a second term of two years in order to make room for someone from another represented country. It takes time to master all the complexities of the Bank's procedures, and the new EDs are at a disadvantage in terms of experience and accumulated knowledge vis-à-vis management, where continuity at the top echelons is much greater. In practice, until recently, the Bank was management-dominated (Mason & Asher 1973: 739).

The EDs receive instructions on policy issues, as distinct from routine matters, from the Governors of the Bank, i.e. the Minister of Finance or his equivalent of the countries they represent (Articles of Agreement, Article III, Section 2). This fact, together with at best uncertain re-election prospects, tends to imply that EDs often maintain strong loyalties with their home country base. This limits their effectiveness in lobbying on behalf of the Bank for changes in policy back home — and of whose necessity they may have become convinced through their daily contacts with the practical work of the Bank.

The growth and geographical distribution of Bank membership is given in Table 2.1, from which it is clear that the big spurt in membership occurred between 1961 and 1964 following the political decolonization of most of Africa.

Table 2.1 *Growth in IBRD membership*

Region	August 10, 1947	June 30, 1957	June 30, 1967	June 30, 1978
Africa	2	2	34	44
Asia[a]	3	13	17	20
Australasia	1	1	2	5
Central and South America	18	20	22	26
Europe[b]	14	16	20	21
Middle East	5	6	9	14
North America	2	2	2	2
Total	45	60	106	132

a. includes Israel
b. includes Cyprus and Turkey

Source: Mason & Asher (1973: 65); *Annual Report* (1978: 146-47).

GROWTH OF LENDING COMMITMENTS

Up to and including June 1978 the IBRD had made cumulative loans totalling $44.7 billion. In the early period, lending was largely for reconstruction efforts in Europe and this need not concern us here: lending to most West European countries has been phased-out since the mid-1950s. Similarly, the last Bank loan made to Japan was in 1966. Lending to 'past borrowers' totalled $3.1 billion, leaving $41.6 billion in lending to 'current borrowers'. From the late 1950s through most of the 'sixties, annual lending levels increased only moderately. In contrast, they doubled in 1969-73 over the previous five-year period. Since then growth has continued to be rapid, although considerable allowance should be made for the high rates of inflation in recent years. The growth of IBRD lending is shown below in Table 2.2.

Table 2.2 *IBRD loan commitments, disbursements, net transfers and numbers of operations*

Fiscal years	Through 1963	1964-68	1969-74	1975-78
Commitments ($ mln.)				
Past borrowers	2378	709	24	—
Current borrowers	4744	3588	12111	21154
Total	7122	4297	12135	21154
Annual Averages	419	860	2023	5289
Disbursements	5426	3395	6326	9888
Net transfers	2758	789	1523	3300
No. of operations	348	202	479	561

Source: Mason & Asher (1973: 219); Programming and Budgeting Dept. (May17, 1974); *Annual Reports*.

In comparison to the growth of new loan commitments the rate of disbursements has lagged behind since the expansion began under McNamara. That disbursement lag behind new commitments is not due to greater inefficiency in Bank lending since McNamara took over, as the US General Accounting Office has alleged (1973: 17, 19-21), but to a number of other factors, including: a shift in lending away from developed countries; a shift to project lending from programme lending which contributed to the high level of early disbursements during 1948-60; the limitation of retroactive financing; increased administrative delays in declaring loans effective; increased complexity and changing sector mix of projects; and a shift from older countries and traditional borrowers to newer countries and first-time borrowers.

A large-scale statistical analysis of disbursements on past loans was conducted by the Bank in 1971-72, when it was found that between the late-1950s and mid-1960s the average rate of disbursement on IBRD loans had slowed down appreciably. While 67% of the loan amounts signed in FY 1957 was disbursed in the first two years, only 24% signed in FY 1964 was disbursed within two years. Since FY 1964, about 30% of the loan amounts has been disbursed in the first two years, without noticeable trends. A comparison of the IBRD/IDA disbursement experience with that of other agencies, in particular the Inter-American Development Bank and the US Agency for International Development, shows that the overall disbursement rates of these agencies were much the same (*Review of Disbursements* R72-205 [August 21, 1972] 1-2; *Technical Paper on Review of Disbursements, Programming and Budgeting Department* [January 22, 1973]).

More recently, disbursement levels have been lower than expectations. A review by the Bank in 1978 of the causes of the slow growth rate in disbursements shows that the implementation of many Bank-assisted projects has been adversely affected as borrowing governments have tried to adjust to inflation, to balance-of-payments difficulties, and to rising budgetary deficits. As a result, counterpart funds are in short supply and this obviously affects project implementation. The review also shows that disbursements in certain major sectors, particularly agriculture, will for several years be somewhat lower than might be expected on the basis of past disbursement activities. The Bank points out that 'new-style' projects are not only technically complex; they also involve new agencies and institutions carrying out new activities to benefit groups of people who were previously considered outside the reach of most government programmes (*Annual Report* 1978: 9). But even before the Bank reoriented its lending activities towards the poor, agricultural projects were disbursing slower than projects in other sectors. This slower rate reflected considerable implementation difficulties in agricultural projects 'old style'.[1]

A characteristic of sustained Bank lending is that net transfers, defined as gross disbursements minus repayments of principal, interest and other charges, are bound to become negative over time and more quickly as the terms of the

the loans harden or the rate of increase of new commitments slows down. The only ways in which negative transfers can be postponed is by increasing the rate of increase of new commitments, by softening the terms of Bank lending, and by debt renegotiation. We shall return later to the Bank's position on these three issues.

DISTRIBUTION OF BANK LENDING BY COUNTRY

The proliferation of Bank membership has not led to such a massive reorientation of Bank lending to new members as might have been expected.

The country distribution of Bank lending to current borrowers is shown in Table 2.3, in which large borrowers are grouped according to major changes in lending patterns between the Woods and the early McNamara era. The analysis has been made for periods which correspond broadly to the regimes of successive Bank Presidents. The dates of appointments do not coincide with the beginning of the fiscal year of the Bank; moreover, new presidents would presumably refrain from interfering very much with projects that have reached an advanced stage of preparation. The lending programmes thus cannot be fitted directly to the responsible presidencies. Nevertheless, a broad classification of lending programmes by Bank presidents seems useful in order to see whether different presidents made substantially different judgements in lending decisions within the broad structural context within which the Bank has to operate.

The last four years are shown separately in order to see how the Bank has responded in its lending programme to the New International Economic Order, the oil price increases, and McNamara's Nairobi speech in which he announced the new focus of Bank Activities (see further Chapter V).

It will be seen that since the early 1960s through 1974 as few as 20 countries have received about 75 per cent of total Bank loans, the rest being shared by the remaining 65-odd currently borrowing countries. It is these 20 countries which by and large have been the important customers of the Bank.

The most remarkable feature of the first group of six countries in Table 2.3, comprising countries with declining shares of Bank loans received, is the near eclipse of lending to India and Pakistan. The second group of seven countries comprises the big winners; their share in new lending rose from 16.8 per cent under Woods to 37.9 per cent under McNamara between 1969 and 1974. The third group includes the seven countries which have more or less maintained their relative position, even though their combined share in new lending declined from 29.8 per cent under Woods to 26.2 per cent under McNamara's first six years as president.

The breakdown of the category 'others' by region shows that nothing much occurred in 'other' Africa and 'other' Asia. The share of 'other' Latin America has declined in favour of (Southern) Europe, the Middle East and North Africa.

Table 2.3 *IBRD lending to current borrowers (in %, fiscal years)*

	Black Through 1963	Woods 1963-68	McNamara 1969-74	1975-78	of which Third Window 1976-77
India	18.5	5.3	2.2	4.8	22.7
Pakistan	5.7	3.3	1.8	1.1	8.6
Bangladesh	0.6	1.2	0.2	–	–
Malaysia	0.8	4.6	2.6	2.0	–
Peru	2.5	3.2	0.9	1.1	–
Venezuela	0.9	5.6	1.1	–	–
Spain	–	5.2	2.0	0.2	–
Subtotal	29.0	28.4	10.8	9.3	31.3
Brazil	6.2	6.1	10.8	9.7	–
Iran	4.1	3.9	6.8	0.3	–
Colombia	7.1	4.5	5.2	3.8	–
Turkey	1.3	0.3	5.6	3.5	–
Korea	–	0.1	4.1	7.1	5.7
Morocco	0.3	1.3	3.1	2.1	3.6
Zambia	1.3	0.6	2.3	0.9	–
Indonesia	–	–	–	8.1	–
Romania	–	–	–	3.9	–
Subtotal	20.4	16.8	37.9	39.4	9.3
Mexico	8.8	10.3	8.9	6.6	–
Thailand	3.8	3.7	2.9	2.5	3.7
Nigeria	0.9	4.0	3.3	1.5	–
Argentina	3.0	2.0	2.6	2.3	–
Philippines	1.7	1.9	2.4	5.7	5.0
Yugoslavia	3.3	4.9	4.3	5.1	–
Taiwan	–	3.0	1.8	–	–
Subtotal	21.5	29.8	26.2	23.7	8.7
Others, of which in					
Africa	9.1	6.6	6.8	8.0	30.5
Asia	1.9	1.9	2.0	0.3	–
EMENA *	8.7	6.2	10.4	12.0	10.6
LAC **	9.3	10.3	6.0	7.2	9.6
Subtotal	29.1	25.0	25.2	27.5	50.7
New lending ($ mln)	4744	3588	12111	21154	700

*   (South) Europe, Middle East, North Africa
**   Latin America and Caribbean

Source: Annual Reports.

There have been several major changes in the pattern of Bank lending during the last four years. Lending to Venezuela and Iran has virtually disappeared, as these OPEC countries have become relatively flush in investible funds. Indonesia, a major oil producer, has emerged as the second largest Bank borrower, after Brazil. Before the oil price increase in 1973 Indonesia received no Bank loans but only IDA credits. Romania, which joined the Bank in 1973, is becoming a significant borrower with a lending programme, at 3.9% of the total during 1975-78, which is beginning to approach that of Yugoslavia, a country of similar size and per capita income. In 1973 Romania had 20.8 million inhabitants and an estimated per capita income of $890 and Yugoslavia 21 million and $1010 respectively (*World Bank Atlas* 1975). Since the Peoples Republic of China joined the UN, the position of Taiwan has become somewhat sensitive and Bank lending has ceased. Lending to Korea and the Philippines has increased substantially over the last four years. The four largest borrowers in 1969-74 were, in order, Brazil, Mexico, Iran and Turkey; they received 32.1% of all loans. In 1975-78 the four largest were Brazil, Indonesia, Korea and Mexico; they received 31.6% of all loans.

Table 2.4 summarizes all loans held by the Bank per June 30, 1978, i.e. after repayments on older loans and sales of loans. Confining ourselves to current borrowers who are in debt to the Bank for more than $400 mln, we see that Latin America, with Brazil, Mexico, Colombia, Argentina and Peru, accounts for 32% of the Bank's portfolio; Asia with Korea, Indonesia, Philippines, India, Thailand, Malaysia and Pakistan accounts for 34%; Africa with Nigeria, Kenya and Zambia accounts for only 7%; and (Southern) Europe, the Middle East and North Africa, with Yugoslavia, Turkey, Romania, Iran, Morocco, Egypt and Algeria, account for the remaining 26%.

The five largest borrowers account for 32% of the Bank's portfolio, and the ten largest for 51% of the total loans held by the Bank in 1978. This gives another indication of the way in which IBRD activities are concentrated in relatively few countries. This is not to deny, however, that relatively small amounts by Bank standards may loom large in the external capital flow of small developing countries.

FINANCING THE BANK

Introduction

The Bank was conceived at the Bretton Woods Conference held in July 1944, when it was realized that the requirements for international finance in the postwar era were likely to be enormous. Large sums were required for the reconstruction of productive activities that had been destroyed during the war. Large sums were also required to enable developing countries to increase their productivity and to improve their living standards. The sums required and the

Table 2.4 *Summary of loans held by the Bank, per June 30, 1978*

	$ mln	%	Per capita Income 1974	Population 1974 (mln)	Loans per capita $
Japan	399	1.2	4070	110	
Other Part I (10 countries)	569	1.7			
Subtotal	968	3.0			
Brazil	3014	9.3	920	104	29
Mexico	2387	7.3	1090	58	41
Korea	1846	5.7	390	33	56
Yugoslavia	1589	4.9	1310	21	76
Indonesia	1567	4.8	170	128	12
Colombia	1305	4.0	500	23	57
Philippines	1292	4.0	330	41	32
Turkey	1237	3.8	750	39	32
India	1219	3.7	140	596	2
Thailand	1014	3.1	310	41	25
Romania	857	2.6	1100	21	41
Iran	850	2.6	1250	33	26
Malaysia	838	2.6	680	12	70
Nigeria	797	2.4	280	73	11
Argentina	766	2.4	1520	25	31
Morocco	706	2.2	430	16	44
Egypt	646	2.0	280	36	18
Algeria	573	1.8	730	15	38
Pakistan	567	1.7	130	67	8
Kenya *	477	1.5	200	13	37
Peru	468	1.4	740	15	31
Zambia	458	1.4	520	5	92
Subtotal	24473	75.1			
Other (53 countries)	7125	21.9			
Total**	32566	100			

*   Including portions of loans to the East African Community
**   Excluding loans to IFC at $ 512 mln.

Source: *Annual Report* (1977: 128-129); *World Bank Atlas* 1976.

attendant risks were thought to be so great, however, that private capital would be unable to fulfil the demands and expectations without some form of government guarantee. The then Secretary of the US Treasury, Henry Morgenthau Jr, in his address at the closing of the Bretton Woods Conference, stated that 'the chief purpose of the Bank is to guarantee private loans made through the usual investment channels' (UN Monetary and Financial Conference: *Final Act and Related Documents* [US Govt. Printing Office, 1944], 9). Ironically enough, these guarantee powers have not been used. It soon became evident that if the Bank were to establish its own credit, it would be much better for it to issue its own obligations. The first offer of $250 million was issued on the US market in July 1947 and was over-subscribed.

In some ways the Bank operates similarly to an ordinary investment bank. It borrows funds on the international capital markets and lends the proceeds to developing countries. It is therefore hemmed-in between three groups: its major shareholders, i.e. the governments of capitalist member countries; its financiers on the international capital markets; and its present clientele, the developing countries. In whatever the Bank does it has to pacify these three interest groups; they may have different and often conflicting interests, extending within and between the groups. It must do so at present while having been given a charter, in an earlier era, which forces the Bank to be extremely conservative in its policies.

We begin our discussion of the Bank's major financial policies with a summary of its balance sheets given in Table 2.5. A choice of three years has been made: the end of fiscal year 1967, the last full year under the Woods presidency, the end of fiscal 1973, marking the last relatively 'normal' year of Bank operations prior to the increase in petroleum prices in late 1973 and the turnabout in the world economy; and the most recent balance sheet as at June 30, 1978.

The $125 million in loans approved but not yet effective at June 30, 1967 represent 14 per cent of new lending in FY 1967. The lending targets set by McNamara have had the effect that large numbers of loans are presented to the Board during the last quarter of the fiscal year. The $1324 million in 1973 in the category approved but not yet effective is equivalent to 65 per cent of FY 1973 lending, and the $4731 in 1978 was 78 per cent of FY 1978 lending. It often takes a few months before borrowers and guarantors, if any, have signed the loans and related documents which may require them to take certain action and to provide certain documents to the Bank. This 'bunching' of projects in the last quarter causes considerable concern to EDs in that effective scrutiny of proposals is then almost impossible.

It appears from the Annual Report, for instance, that 64 out of 137 Bank loans and 48 out of 99 IDA credits were approved by the Board in 18 sessions during the months April, May and June 1978: an average of 6-7 project proposals per session. Each project is accompanied by a voluminous appraisal

Table 2.5 *Summary balance sheets, IBRD ($ mln)*

	June 30, 1967		June 30, 1973		June 30, 1978	
ASSETS						
Cash and short term investments		1166		3594		8981
Loans, total	7127		15953		37796	
Less – approved but not yet effective	125		1324		4731	
Effective loans held by the Bank		7002		14628		33065
Other assets		832		1273		1645
Total assets		9000		19495		43691
LIABILITIES						
Borrowings		3075		8868		22581
Undisbursed balance of effective loans		2261		4955		13706
Reserves		1023		1750		2483
Capital – authorized	22849		30397		33045	
Less – uncalled portion	20565		27357		29741	
Paid-in capital		2285		3040		3305
Other liabilities		356		882		1616
Total liabilities		9000		19495		43691

Source: Derived from *Annual Reports.*

report, and EDs are at a considerable disadvantage in forming a soundly based opinion on submitted projects – let alone in detecting any irregularities. This is all the more because EDs do not have their own staffs, with the exception of one assistant.

Liquidity policy

As at June 30, 1978 the Bank maintained almost $9 billion in short-term assets, equal to 40 per cent of its funded debt. The Bank's liquidity policy requires it to maintain liquid holdings, at any given time, equal to a minimum of 40% of estimated borrowing for the subsequent three years (*Annual Report* 1977: 89). The reason for this sizable liquid position is that the Bank wants to maintain short-term liquid assets at a level that can adequately meet all its requirements without the need to borrow new funds for prolonged periods of time (Rotberg 1976: 2. Mr Rotberg has been Treasurer of the Bank since 1969). The short-term assets are to meet financial requirements for service on its debt and disbursements on loans. The liquidity position is in excess of current needs to give the Bank the flexibility to decide where, how much, at what cost, and on what maturity terms it will borrow, rather than having its requirements leave no alternative but to borrow under unfavourable conditions. These may be of a general or of a more specific nature. For instance, in all countries the Bank needs Treasury permission to borrow (Articles of Agreement, Article IV, Section I [b]). Moreover, as priority is usually given to government's own borrowing requirements and to the needs of domestic borrowers, the Bank may find itself last in line, even if it is given preferential access compared to other non-resident borrowers.

The short-term assets are fully invested, mostly in the US money market, but they are highly liquid. Consequently, the net cost of holding the liquidity instead of reducing funded debt, is small or may even be negative. For instance, the average return on investment during FY 1978 was 7%. The average cost on the funded debt was about 6.9% (*Annual Report* 1978: 105). Including own capital and reserves, the cost of all funds reduced to 6%. (*Ibidem*: 105).

Paid-in capital amounts to $3.3 billion. Reserves of $2.5 billion could accrue because the Bank has never in its history paid dividends to its shareholders. These funds are thus available at no cost to the Bank which has in all years made a profit, albeit at modest levels. These profits have been much too low to maintain capitalization in an inflationary world, however, especially since the early 1970s.

Borrowing policy

In order to avoid undue dependence on one financial market, the Bank has worked successfully over the years to make its obligations acceptable to investors all over the world. In the early years the only market open to it was that of the United States, where most borrowed funds were raised through the 1950s. During the 1960s the Bank pressed to establish a substantial and widespread market for its securities. Germany was the principal source of funds in the late 1960s, Japan in the early 1970s, certain members of OPEC in 1974 and the United States again since. The Bank estimates that as at June 30, 1978, 26% of the Bank's obligations were held by investors in the USA, 24% in Germany, 13% in Japan, 11% in Switzerland and 6% in Saudi Arabia. The remaining 20% of outstanding borrowings were held by investment institutions, including central banks and government agencies in more than 80 countries; 44% of borrowings is denominated in US dollars, 25% in German marks, 13% in Japanese yen, 12% in Swiss francs, and the remainder in eleven other currencies. (*Annual Report* 1978: 105, 145).

Whether the increasing diversification of the Bank's sources of finance will permit the Bank to pursue other and perhaps more liberal lending policies in the future, without alienating its traditional support, is uncertain. It depends upon whether investors in OPEC countries, for instance, are more progressive than those elsewhere. There is little evidence that this is the case. On the other hand, heavy Bank borrowing in OPEC countries may be made conditional upon changing the pattern of Bank lending by country. It is at least conceivable, for instance, that Arab oil producing countries, when considering the Bank's request to permit it to tap their capital market, will expect the Bank to lend more in Arab non-oil producing countries in future (see also Table 2.3).

The market for the Bank's obligations consists of two main categories. At December 31, 1975 about 40% of total outstanding debt, or $5.4 billion, was held by 'official' investors: governments, their agencies or central banks (Rotberg 1976: 4). Part of this amount, $1.1 billion, was in the form of two-year US dollar bonds which are customarily rolled over by government agencies and central banks, and could be classified as *de facto*, though not *de jure*, long-term investment. The remainder is in intermediate to long-term obligations.

The financial support given by these official institutions has also laid the groundwork for the World Bank's issues in the public market which have absorbed the remaining 60% of Bank bonds.

The Bank is a relatively long-term lender at fixed interest rates, financing that lending with debt of similar maturity. The average life of the Bank's entire outstanding debt was seven years at December 1975. The average life of its public debt outstanding, however, approached ten years, and its sizable capital and reserves have 'infinite maturity'. The maturity structure of the Bank's debt may be compared with the average life of its outstanding loans receivable which, again in December 1975, was about eleven years (Ibidem: 8).

The Bank's financial structure may be seen another way. Of the $6.5 billion of World Bank obligations which fall due in the five years beginning January 1, 1976, over three billion are held by governments or central banks that have consistently demonstrated their commitment to refinance maturing debt. Rotberg points out that 'it would be reasonable to suggest that there are few, if any, Banks which have liquid resources equal to twice their public debt falling due in the next five years' (Ibidem).

The Bank's policy of matching the maturity of its loans and borrowings may be seen as unnecessarily cautious. But if intermediate or longer maturities are not available in amounts compatible with its current lending levels, due to prolonged market instability, the Bank

would not take the easy way out by financing its lending program through short-term or floating-interest-rate debt. Rather it would draw down its liquidity, until the market stabilized. And if the market did not stabilize for, say, several years, the Bank would use the further option of reducing its lending program and thereby its future cash requirements. Alternatively, the Bank would raise the interest rate on new loans to the point where it could prudently borrow intermediate and longer term resources at higher cost (Ibidem: 9).

Capital structure and capacity to lend

The Bank started in 1946 with an *authorized* capital of $10 billion in terms of US dollars of the weight and fineness in effect on July 1, 1944. This initial capital basis has been increased on several occasions; in 1959 authorized capital was increased to $21 billion; in 1963 and 1965 a total of $3 billion was added to accommodate new members; and in 1970 a further modest amount of $3 billion, from $24 to $27 billion in 1944 dollars, was added. The Bank initially considered requesting an $8 billion increase in 1970, in line with the increase in IMF quotas, but decided not to do so because, at the same time, it faced the need to ask for a replenishment of IDA funds. This amounted to $800 mln a year from the same member countries that would have to make the major contribution to the Bank's paid-in capital, and the burden all this would involve was judged to be too heavy (Mason & Asher 1973: 116).

Subscribed capital up to 1976 amounted to $26 billion in 1944 dollars, or equivalent to almost $41 billion in current dollars. Of this sum only 10 percent has been paid in. The remainder is uncalled and can be employed *only* to meet the obligations of the Bank to holders of its securities (Articles of Agreement IV, 8 [c]). It cannot be used for administrative expenses or for lending or disbursements. In short, it is for the protection of Bank bond-holders and cannot be used for the conduct of operations.

Financial analysts (see for instance World Bank: *A Financial Appraisal* prepared by Morgan, Stanley and Co. Inc. and The First Boston Corporation, 1973), in appraising the Bank, sometimes discount the value of this callable margin for as far as the poorer countries are concerned, on the assumption that, though legally bound, they may have difficulty in paying-up if the need should arise. Therefore, analysts sometimes only count the uncalled capital subscription of the so-called Group of Ten (rich countries) comprising about 56% of total IBRD capital, or of the US alone: 23% of the share capital in 1976 (*Annual Report* 1976: 124-25).

As shown above, however, the policies concerning liquidity, diversification of sources of borrowings, maturity mix of debt, accumulation of reserves and lending levels have been designed to ensure that the callable capital need never be called! In Rotberg's words: 'we operate the Bank as if that guarantee of callable capital did not exist' (Rotberg 1976: 9).

Yet it is largely on the strength of the uncalled capital subscription that the Bank's debt obligations are rated Aaa by Moody and AAA by Standard & Poor in the United States. They are currently marketed at yields competitive with government or government-guaranteed obligations in many countries. ensuring that the Bank obtains its funds, the basis for its lending operations, at the lowest possible cost.

An important aspect of the Bank's capital structure is the limitation it imposes on its lending. The total amount of outstanding loans held by the Bank may never exceed the total of its unimpaired subscribed capital, surplus and reserves (Article III, 3). This is an extremely prudent prescription. It ties the Bank's lending operations *not*, as in the case of private institutions, to its capacity to borrow, but directly to its capital base, in a ratio of 'one-to-one'.

The World Bank's traditional debt-equity measurements are of some interest. Paid-in capital, reserves, and net income for the first six months of fiscal 1976 totalled $5.2 billion at December 31, 1975, and the Bank's outstanding debt $13.7 billion, providing a debt-equity ratio of 2.65:1. With the addition of $28 billion of uncalled capital to protect the holders of Bank obligations, equity rises to $33 billion and the debt-equity ratio to 1:2.40. This is extremely low compared to commercial institutions which may have a debt-equity ratio of 20:1 and no limitations on their outstanding loans (Rotberg 1976: 13).

In the course of 1976 major decisions were taken to cope with the effects of world-wide inflation on the Bank's lending and on its capital structure. In May 1976, after deliberations that had lasted two years, the Executive Directors recommended an $8.3 billion, in 1976 dollars, selective increase in subscribed capital. In addition, an increase of $104 million was approved to accommodate new members. If fully taken up, the total subscribed capital of the Bank would rise to $39.2 billion. The required approval of the resolution by Governors exercising three-fourths of the voting power in the Bank was given in May 1977 (*Annual Report* 1977: 90). This increase was a matter of considerable urgency. On June 30, 1976, Bank loans had amounted to $22.7 billion, and unimpaired subscribed capital, reserves and surplus to $32.8 billion (*Annual Report* 1976: 5), giving a loan: equity ratio of 69%, increasing to 79% if loans approved but not yet effective are included. *Outstanding* loans, the relevant items in terms of the Articles of Agreement, stood at only 41% of capital and reserves. Disbursements must eventually catch up with previous commitments, however, and this ratio was bound to increase rapidly in subsequent years. Repayments on old loans, $609 mln in FY 1976 and $708 mln in FY 1977, would provide only minor relief to offset new loans disbursements. A net loan margin of $6.7 billion thus remained which, at the recent rate of increase in net lending, would have been exhausted in less than two years, coinciding roughly with the end of McNamara's second term of office.

The proposed increase of authorized capital was called 'selective' in that allotments were made only to those individual members who accepted increases in their IMF quotas. This selectivity reflects a long-standing policy to the effect that, when members accept increases in IMF quotas, they are also expected to request increases in their subscriptions to the capital of the Bank. A resolution to increase quotas in the IMF, arising from its sixth general review of member countries, was approved by the Fund's Board of Governors in March 1976. They now reflect the new strength of OPEC.

If subscribed in full, the Selective Capital Increase would lower the voting strength of the Bank's five biggest shareholders: USA, UK, Germany, France and Japan, by 2.18% to 42.56%; it would decrease the voting strength of other developed countries by 0.58% to 18.79%; would reduce the voting strength of the non-oil developing countries by 1.38% to 29.43%; and increase the combined voting strength of petroleum exporting developing countries from 4.44% to 9.22% (*Annual Report* 1976: 6). The major OPEC countries appear to favour relatively conservative financial policies, and it would appear that the balance of power within the group of World Bank shareholders is not likely to be upset in accommodating their new economic strength.

Although the proposal to increase IBRD's capital base has been accepted (which was in some doubt as the US was initially reluctant to cooperate), the Bank has only a few years respite before it hits the statutory ceiling on lending again, assuming that the recent rate of Bank expansion is maintained. In May 1976 the Executive Directors also decided, however, that the future lending programme 'would not be based on the assumption that a further increase in capitalization would be approved until members agreed on such an increase.' It was acknowledged that 'the level of lending programs for fiscal 1977 *and beyond* of some $5.8 billion, 16 percent above the FY 1976 level, could be sustained' (*Annual Report* 1976: 6; emphasis added). That decision has subsequently been modified. For 1978 a level of $6.1 bln was approved and $6.8 bln provisionally for fiscal 1979, to be reviewed in mid-year (*Annual Report* 1978: 10).

Under the Articles of Agreement, the EDs had no choice but to propose increase capitalization. Its provisions closely tie future Bank lending to government action on increase of its capital base, and enable the major shareholders to exercise firm and direct control.

An alternative proposal that the EDs might have made in searching for additional room for expanded Bank lending, if they thought this to be desirable or possible, would have been to drop Article III.3 of the Articles of Agreement. The effect would have been twofold. Firstly, it would have increased the importance of the criteria of international financial markets at the expense of those of governments in decisions about the Bank's scope for lending, enabling the Bank to test its borrowing power and credit rating. We have noted earlier that commercial institutions frequently have debt-equity ratios of 20:1 without apparent effect on their borrowing capacity. Allowance has to be made for the fact, of course, that the Bank lends to numerous developing countries whose credit-worthiness is limited. A ratio of say, 10:1, would nevertheless enlarge the scope for bank lending from the present limit of about $31 billion to $50 or over $300 billion respectively, depending upon whether the uncalled portion of present capital subscriptions is excluded or included. The Bank would be forced to investigate which debt-equity ratio would be acceptable to the market, and the implications it would have for the Bank's credit ratings.

Secondly, a decision to drop the provision of Article III.3 would not necessarily diminish the control of shareholders. A few together would still have majority voting power, and could thereby prescribe how far management could go in expansion. National governments would still have to give permission for the Bank, as a non-resident institution, to place a bond issue in the national capital market. What would probably no longer be required is that, in most countries, government would have to obtain parliamentary approval for each increase in capital subscription.

The current system under which the Bank is financed is government-oriented. It implies that parliaments are involved *before* the Bank can make its first loan after reaching the present statutory lending limit. A shift to a more market-oriented institution would mean that parliaments would only become involved in supplying additional capital to safeguard Bank bond holders when all other means at its disposal had been exhausted. These means are: to run down its liquidity, to roll over borrowings, to raise its interest rates on lending, and to readjust its level of lending. Only *after* these instruments have been used to the full will shareholders be called upon to provide additional funds to rescue the Bank's bond holders.

During discussions in fiscal 1976 on the Selective Increases in Capitalization, the Executive Directors acknowledged that further talks would be necessary on a General Capital Increase. In fiscal 1977, EDs agreed that they 'would make their best efforts to reach an agreement by June 30, 1978 for concluding their negotiations regarding a General Capital Increase' (*Annual Report* 1977: 7). Some progress has been achieved during fiscal 1978 through informal discussions. The need for the Bank to have a general capital increase that is sufficiently large to permit its lending to grow in real terms over the next five years was endorsed, but discussions on its future role and on the appropriate size of a general capital increase will continue (*Annual Report* 1978: 10).

It is interesting that the various requests to increase the Bank's resources to which the 1977 Annual Report alludes (pp. 7-8) are couched in general terms, notwithstanding the fact that the bulk of past IBRD lending has benefited relatively few developing countries (see Table 2.3). The forces that favour an increase in IBRD capital apparently attempt to argue a general case, irrespective of the country distribution of the loans to which a general capital increase would give rise and which resulted when the Bank first set specific lending targets in 1968. (See also Chapter V.)

Terms of Bank lending

In November 1946, the Bank decided that all borrowers should be treated alike at any given time with respect to rates of interest. No special treatment was to be accorded to selected countries on the basis of differences in credit-worthiness, size of shareholdings or size of loan (Mason & Asher 1973: 154). This conveniently saves the Bank from having to rate borrowing countries' credit-worthiness on a continuous scale. By not varying its rates between countries, the Bank's decision is reduced to whether or not it is willing to lend, to country A or country B. In a grey world it is convenient but difficult to distinguish black from white.

Although the Bank was free to set its own terms, the need to acquire the bulk of its new funds from capital markets dictated that the terms of its loans be governed largely by the terms of its borrowings.

Lending rate

The Bank established its first policy on loan charges in 1947. A commitment fee of 1.5% on undisbursed amounts was set, and the lending rate to be charged from the day of disbursement fixed at 0.25% above the Bank's cost of borrowing for the same maturity, to which a 1% commission was added. The commitment charge was reduced by one-half to 0.75% in 1960 and to 0.375% in 1964, but in 1967 was restored to 0.75% to compensate the Bank for the cost of holding funds pending disbursement and to encourage faster disbursement of loans. Between 1965-67 some high income borrowing countries were charged up to one percent more than the standard IBRD lending rate. This applied to seven loans in all, to Japan, New Zeland, Italy and South Africa ('IBRD lending to higher income countries' [PRC/M/73.-3], June 18, 1973: 22).

A major review of lending rate policy was undertaken in late 1967, when market rates were at historically high levels. Most EDs agreed that the traditional formula of 1.25% above borrowing cost would lead to excessively high lending rates and was no longer acceptable. It was agreed that 'the rate should be kept as low as compatible with the maintenance of the Bank's ability to raise in the capital markets of its members, or otherwise borrow, the funds it needs' (IBRD: 'Financial Policies', R73-55, March 28, 1973: 11-12; Mason & Asher 1973: 210-213).

Interest rates at which the Bank borrowed continued to rise, but the EDs decided not to increase the lending rate proportionately. This soon produced a 'negative spread' between marginal borrowing and lending rates, the maintenance of which obviously cannot continue indefinitely without seriously reducing net income, and thereby the Bank's capacity to borrow. The negative spread was 'financed' by the difference between average and marginal interest rates on borrowings, the availability of large own capital funds and reserves relative to borrowings and high yields on short term investment.

In 1976 the lending rate policy was again subjected to major review, and a new formula was put into effect on July 1st of that year. The lending rate is now to be reviewed at the end of each quarter and adjusted to the average weighted cost by amount and maturity of funds borrowed by the Bank in the preceding twelve months. To this calculation a positive spread of 0.5% is to be added to arrive at the interest rate that the Bank will charge borrowers on new loans approved in the ensuing quarter.

This formula is to be applied pending consideration by the Executive Directors of a further comprehensive review of the Bank's lending rate policy, including analysis of a proposal calling for 'full-cost average', and consideration, among other possible alternatives, of a policy in which the lending rate would be adjusted periodically during the disbursement period of a loan (*Annual Report* 1976: 6-7). During 1977 and 1978 this review did not yet produce a new policy.

The upshot of the changes already introduced and the tenor of further proposals appears to be that the Bank is under strong pressure to harden its terms. The element of an interest subsidy, implicit in the negative spread which had prevailed since 1968, has been removed. The lending rate which had remained fixed at 7.25% since September 1970, was increased to 8% in August 1974, 8.5% in January 1975, and to 8.85% on June 1, 1976, but declined from 8.9% to 8.2% in fiscal 1977, and to about 7.5% for most of 1978. Although such rates are high, it should be remembered that under present levels of international inflation the real rates of interest are substantially lower, and may even be negative.

Maturities

In the early 1970s, standard terms for Bank loans were seven years grace and 25 years maturity, repayable in annuity form.

During fiscal 1976 it was decided that the method of amortization would be modified for loans approved from July 1, 1976 onwards. This will result in the loan principal being repaid in equal amounts rather than in gradually ascending amounts over the amortization period, as implicit in the annuity formula. Repayment terms of future loans will be such that the average grace period and final maturity do not exceed 3.8 years (down from 7 years) and 19 years (down from 25 years). Countries will be grouped according to income levels for the determination of terms. These modifications are said to have been designed to help ensure that loans outstanding and disbursed would not rise above the statutory limit imposed by the Articles of Agreement (*Annual Report* 1976: 6).

The change in repayment profile, and the shortened grace period and final maturity will indeed cause a further substantial hardening of IBRD loan terms and will bring them much closer to straightforward commercial loans. The implications of this narrowing gap between Bank and commercial terms for Bank leverage in pursuing distributional income goals in its lending will be taken up in Chapter VI.

Third Window

On July 29, 1975 the EDs approved a resolution that established the Intermediate Financing Facility. This was a response to the greater need felt by non-oilproducing developing countries, in particular, for funds at soft terms. This Facility became effective on December 23, 1975 when *pledges* of $100 million in contributions to the Interest Subsidy Fund for the Third Window had been received. Subsidy Fund resources are supplied by some of the Bank's members and by non-member Switzerland on a *voluntary* basis. The Subsidy Fund supplements interest payments due to the Bank from borrowers by making semi-annual payments equalling 4% a year on the outstanding principal of loans made on Third Window terms. The difference between this 4% and the Bank's standard interest is paid by the borrowers.

The Third Window, additional to IBRD and IDA, is a direct descendant of an earlier proposal by David Horowitz, Governor of the Bank of Israel and head of the Israeli delegation to the first UNCTAD conference in 1964. Horowitz had suggested that the difference between the Bank's borrowing rate and the lending rate to developing countries should be subsidized by an interest-equalization fund maintained by annual appropriations from the industrialized countries. This proposal was extensively studied by the Bank but got nowhere at the time in terms of possible implementation (see Mason & Asher 1973: 213-17).

The Third Window could help to considerably increase soft term lending by the Bank at relatively small cost to contributing members, at least in the early years of the programme.

By the end of fiscal 1976, contributions amounting to $124.9 million had been paid into the Fund, sufficient to subsidize approximately $600 million of loans. Third Window loans will continue to be provided on the same terms, and repayment schedules will be along the lines of *older* Bank loans, and not be subject to the hardening of terms discussed earlier. They will thus be of the annuity type – with a standard grace period of seven years, and final maturity of 25 years (*Annual Report* 1976: 7-8). Eligibility criteria for the Third Window are analogous to those for IDA eligibility. Out of the Third Window total of $600 million, $477.8 million was commited in fiscal 1976. In fiscal 1977 a few more contributions enabled the commitment of a further $222.6 mln.

Although the Third Window could fulfil a useful role in providing soft loans to the poorer developing countries, i.e. those with per capita income below $375 (in 1973), industrialized countries have thus far shown only limited interest in funding it. Four countries initially contributed 68% of available funds: Canada, Kuwait and the Netherlands $20 million each, and Saudi Arabia $25 million. The United Kingdom paid $10 million, and Venezuela $10 million, with five others splitting the remaining $19.9 million. France and Belgium affirmed their intention to contribute to the Interest Subsidy Fund, pending parliamentary approval (*Annual Report* 1976: 7), but no contributions were received from the USA, Germany and Japan, among the other rich member countries. The 1977 Annual Report does not mention the Third Window, which appears to be closed.

Summary

This review of the Bank's major financial policies has brought to light some of the elements which its management has to take into account in order to meet the criteria of its financiers and major shareholders.

The financial policies are designed in such a way as to ensure that the funds required to support lending operations are available when needed and at the lowest possible long-term cost to borrowers. The Bank succeeded in establishing a triple A rating in the international bond markets in the mid-1950s largely on a record of lending to developed countries, and has since maintained that rating despite a shift in lending to developing countries. It acquires its funds on terms comparable to those prevailing for government bonds.

In assessing the performance of a financial intermediary three ratios are frequently used: debt-equity, interest coverage, and rate of return on equity. The latter is not applicable to the Bank. The other ratios have worsened since expansion began under the McNamara presidency, but they are still quite favourable compared to commercial banks, and there is no evidence that the Bank's credit rating has been affected as a result of their deterioration.

Maintaining this credit standing may be taken to imply that, in order not to ruffle the feathers of financial analysts, the Bank should only gradually introduce policy changes. Any rash action which might be seen as indicating imprudence in the management of its financial affairs must be avoided. In many respects the Bank is more conservative and has more safeguards available as an agency than do commercial institutions.

A major strength of the financial structure is that the Bank can call on capital that is nine times as great as its paid-in capital. All shareholding governments are individually and legally committed to honour any call on capital to protect   bond holders. No other institutions has such backing by all non-socialist industrialized countries which together hold the majority of shares. Nevertheless, financial policies are such that a call for capital is not expected to arise. The Bank's liquidity is high and its borrowing geographically diversified, and additional lending will be sacrificed to protect its bond holders should the need arise.

Finally, Bank lending is constrained not by its capacity to borrow but by the size of its capital, a limitation of one-to-one. This means that the Bank does not have the opportunity to test its own market standing.

The implications of the recent decisions are that a period of slower growth may be in store for the Bank. Also, terms of lending have hardened considerably and this will negatively affect its capacity to exert leverage on its borrowers in general and for poor-oriented projects a..d policies in particular.

DETERMINANTS OF BANK LENDING BY COUNTRY

The founding fathers of the Bank were strongly influenced by experiences gained with international loans during the 1920s and 'thirties. The views of the

USA and the UK on how to reconstruct the post-war international economic system dominated the discussion leading up to the Bank's establishment (Oliver 1975), and a number of 'ground rules' were laid down which still govern its activities today. Although formulated in the aftermath of a ten-year depression followed by a world war and bearing the imprint of the experiences of that period, these ground rules were said as recently as 1971 to 'have stood the test of time well, forming as they do a code of operations which is as relevant to the Bank's activities in 1971 as it was in 1946' (*Policies and Operations: The World Bank, IDA and IFC* [June 1971], vii). This shows considerable complacency in the extraordinary foresight of the founding fathers in having designed a structure that is apparently still appropriate to serve the needs of a radically changed world. Perhaps some doubts have since begun to form about the suitability of those ground rules: the quoted statement was dropped in the September 1974 edition of the same booklet.

In approaching the lending activities of the Bank two questions need to be asked. First, to what countries does the Bank lend or not lend? Second, if the Bank is willing to lend to a country and assuming that that country is willing to borrow from the Bank, the issue arises of how much the Bank will lend.

Factors influencing the country distribution of Bank loans

The Bank by no means lends to *all* the 129 member countries. It excludes lending to countries which are deemed rich, and also *de facto* lending to a number of very poor countries. In the period 1969-73 loans were made to only 63 countries: 6 in Eastern Africa, 9 in Western Africa, 12 in Asia, 15 in Europe, the Middle East and North Africa, and 21 in Latin America. Four basic factors, taken together, appear to shape the actual pattern of lending.

Capitalist ideology

The most explicit statement on the virtues of the market mechanism espoused by the Bank in its early years may be found in the *Report on Cuba – Findings and Recommendations of an Economic and Technical Mission Organized by the IBRD in Collaboration with the Government of Cuba* (Washington 1951): 'For, to date, none of man's efforts to repeal the law of supply and demand have been successful' (p. 158). The report was intended to reflect the views of the Mission, which were not necessarily identical to those of the Bank; but the letter from the President of the Bank to the President of Cuba which accompanied the report (pp. v/vi) in effect endorsed the Mission's recommendation and came close to identifying the Bank with the Mission's views (cited in Adler 1972a: 34-35, note 14).

The ideological issue of capitalism versus socialism has caused the absence of most Eastern European Socialist countries from the Bank membership list. Yet a clear-cut judgement is difficult to make: Yugoslavia and Romania apparently find Bank membership and active borrowing compatible with their ideological aversion to capitalism. Many African and Asian countries profess to follow their own variety of socialism, yet see no apparent conflict with the Bank's capitalist premise. Very few countries refuse to borrow from the Bank on the strength of the capitalist versus socialist principle.

The major issue on which the ideological nature of the Bank still emerges is that of nationalization. Under its Article of Agreement I (ii) the Bank is directed to encourage international investment and to supplement private capital when the latter is not available on reasonable terms. It thus has a direct interest in establishing and maintaining satisfactory relations between member countries and their *external* creditors. Normal practice is for the Bank to inform governments who are involved in nationalization disputes that it will not assist them unless and until they make appropriate effort to reach fair and equitable settlement (IBRD: 'The World Bank, IDA and IFC: Policies and Operations' [June 1969], 31; Ibidem 1974: 44-45). This formulation still leaves the Board considerable scope for judging what is meant by 'appropriate effort' and what constitutes a 'fair' settlement.

It is an interesting fact that nationalizations in Latin America often create serious problems for international lenders as compared to the relatively smooth nationalizations, perhaps on an increasing scale, in Africa and Asia; to say nothing of OPEC's recent nationalizations of subsidiaries of the major international oil companies. The majority of the latter have been carried out apparently without seriously affecting multilateral financial flows to the nationalizing countries. The difference may be due to several reasons: compensation arrangements may be thought to have been satisfactory to creditors, or other interests – political, economic or strategic – may take on overriding importance.

At this point the decline of Peru as borrower should be noted (Table 2.3). No loan commitments were made in FY 1969-73 with the exception of a $30 mln loan for the reconstruction of roads destroyed by earthquakes. This loan was provided as calamity relief. Non-lending to Peru has coincided with the coming into power of a government which, *inter alia*, has nationalized the International Petroleum Company and has refused to compensate on the grounds of *excessive* past profits. After this issue was resolved, IBRD lending resumed: $75 mln in 1974 and $234 mln in 1975-77, but none in 1978. Similarly, no loans were made to Chile under President Allende, although projects had been prepared and were ready by Bank standards (see *The US and Multilateral Development Banks* 1974: 50-52 for a brief discussion of that episode in the history of the Bank). After the military took over and economic policies were reversed, the Bank resumed lending: $13.6 mln in 1974, $113 mln in 1975-77, but none in 1978. In both Peru and Chile creditworthiness indicators have deteriorated very rapidly in recent years (*Annual Report 1977*: 122-113). Other, generally earlier, instances of non-lending due to unsettled expropriation conflcts are given by Mason & Asher (1973: 338).

It is no longer unacceptable for the Bank to lend to publicly-owned corporations, other than in traditional sectors of transportation and electric power where public ownership, at least outside the USA, has been quite common. For a long time the Bank's management had been convinced that, regardless of the cultural background and the politico-economic structure of the potential borrowing country, industrial enterprises were better managed in the private sector and that governments would have enough to do managing a public sector that did not include industrial enterprises (Ibidem: 466).

The very few publicly controlled industrial projects which the Bank financed in its early years were all designed to be turned-over to private control at a specified stage.

It had been realized as long ago as 1948 that the Bank could not do very much for private enterprise directly as long as it suffered from the disadvantage that it could only lend against a government guarantee, which was neither readily given to a private business, nor willingly sought by the latter, for fear that the government would include its supervision as a condition for giving the guarantee. To overcome this disadvantage the International Finance Corporation was finally established in 1956 (Ibidem: 345-50).

The main channel for the Bank in financing industry has been through its support for Development Finance Corporations. Yet as late as 1968 the Bank accepted that DFCs could be publicly owned, and the DFC Department shifted back from IFC to the Bank! The very slowness of the Bank in changing its collective mind on the issue of ownership is remarkable in view of the absurdity that hitherto it had insisted that money which it supplied against a government guarantee not only *should* but *must* be administered free from direct government control! There is apparently no inconsistency in feeding capital to private industry through a government-owned financial institution and believing at the same time that industrial development is best left to private enterprise (Ibidem: 466, 473).

The Bank's views on the 'proper' role of public and private sector enterprises began to change during the 1960s. This was due to its experience in lending to African countries where private enterprise was all but non-existent, plus the need in Asia for government participation if fertilizer production was to be rapidly expanded. The Bank's concern in industrial enterprise was not so much the locus of ownership as the effectiveness and independence from political pressure of their management (Ibidem: 473).

The Bank's overriding concern with effective management and its insistence on independence from political pressure has, however, led it to adopt practices which can be criticized when seen from a different perspective.

The Bank frequently lends to 'autonomous' governmental agencies, and often makes the establishment of such agencies a prerequisite for lending. When the institutional infrastructure is weak, as is the case in many developing countries, it seems sensible and businesslike to help create institutions that 'work' and get things done. Such institutions become instruments through which the World Bank exerts leverage on policies of developing countries, and enable it to increase areas of certainty and to minimize uncertainties which may hinder the execution of financed projects (Tendler 1975: 103-105). But the effect of such arrangements, if widely adopted, is that an international decision-making process evolves which, at the international level, gives the Bank some of the power of a surrogate government and, at the national level, builds up a powerful segment of the administrative arm of government but bypasses non-technocratic governmental decision-making, including the legislative and judicial branches (Howard 1977: 4). The pursuit of 'effectiveness' strengthens accountability of the executive or of an autonomous agency to the World Bank and weakens the accountability of the government to the people of the country. In pressing for the limitation of undesirable domestic political influences, the Bank weakens the legitimate political foundations of responsible government. It thus reinforces other trends towards executive supremacy within the developing country and, by concentrating power in autonomous agencies managed by 'neutral' technocrats, helps to set the stage for authoritarian government (Ibidem: 6). Thus, one can argue, the Bank meddles in issues concerning the most desirable economic order which countries may wish to decide for themselves, and it may be questioned whether the Bank has a right to do so.

Market eligibility

The Bank may make a loan if prevailing market conditions are such that, in its opinion, the borrower would be unable to obtain the loan elsewhere on terms that the Bank considers to be reasonable (Article III, 4 [ii]).

On the basis of restored market eligibility for international loans, lending to most European countries has been phased-out from the mid-1950s. It has already been noted that the last loan to Japan was made in 1966, after which Japan rapidly evolved into a Bank lender rather than borrower.

There are a number of countries, however, which, although able to borrow on their own credit in capital markets, are considered unable to borrow in sufficient volume or at rates sufficiently close to those prevailing in the market to meet their needs. Since 1967 the Bank has continued to lend in small volume to countries such as Iceland, Ireland, Israel, Finland and New Zealand, which were judged to be in this situation (Mason & Asher 1973: 193).

The Bank was set up as a temporary institution for a supplementary role. Its purpose was

to promote private foreign investment by means of guarantees or participations in loans and other investments made by private investors; and when private capital is not available on reasonable terms, to supplement private investment by providing, on suitable conditions, finance for productive purposes out of its own capital, funds raised by it and its other resources (Articles of Agreement I [ii]).

This recognizes the primacy of foreign private investment, and the role of the Bank was seen as to assist in restoring and possibly speeding-up the time when prospective borrowers would be able to raise funds in the international capital market as and when needed. Once that state of affairs had been reached the Bank was thought in some circles to have fulfilled its role. (In the early 1950s the IBRD, which rented its office space, was offered a plot of land on which it could erect its own building. Although the offer was attractive in many respects it was turned down on the advice of the Bank's New York bankers because, they argued, to build its own headquarters would not be compatible with the public image of a temporary institution! See Adler 1972a: 36, note 17.)

The application of the market eligibility test can therefore be used to screen additional countries in terms of terminating prospective borrowing from the Bank (see Chapter V). The application of this test leaves considerable room for judgement, particularly in respect of determining the 'sufficient volume to meet a country's needs'. Both volume and needs are amenable to a number of possible policy instruments and thus need not be taken as immutable for the calculation of a 'gap' to be financed by foreign loans, or as justification for a continuation of Bank lending to certain countries.

Creditworthiness

Countries which are thought by the Bank not to be creditworthy will not receive a Bank loan, by order of the Bank's Articles of Agreement.

> In making or guaranteeing a loan, the Bank shall pay due regard to the prospects that the borrower, and, if the borrower is not a member, that the guarantor, will be in a position to meet its obligations under the loan; and the Bank shall act prudently in the interests both of the particular member in whose territories the project is located and of the members as a whole (Article III, Section 4 [v]).

This provision in its charter does not encourage the Bank to be bold and adventurous in opening-up pioneering avenues of activities in countries with weak balances of payments, and rightly so, because the Bank works with borrowed money.

Several issues pertaining to creditworthiness are worth pursuing. What are legitimate debts, and how can willingness to repay be assessed? How is capacity to repay measured and assessed? What are the consequences of the Bank's creditworthiness analysis for the pattern of its lending? And finally, what is, or should be seen to be, the role of the Bank in debt rescheduling operations in view of the past record of such activities?

In the early years, the prime preoccupation of the Bank's management was to prove the creditworthiness of the Bank itself in order to build up its standing in the financial community. Bank loans to countries that were already in default on foreign loans might be disquieting to purchasers and potential purchasers of Bank bonds. In addition, the Bank was to help nurse borrowing countries to market eligibility for their capital needs. And clearly: 'existing defaults are the most obvious obstacle to the restoration of credit' (Second Annual Report, cited in Mason & Asher 1973: 180). Clear evidence of a borrower's willingness to settle outstanding debts was thus made a prerequisite for loans.

The willingness to settle old international debts may be weak or even lacking for a variety of reasons. Some countries may argue that foreign public loans to previous governments are like water under the bridge. Bygones should be bygones. They should not, it is sometimes argued, be honoured, particularly if it is known or alleged that such loans may have been obtained under suspect circumstances, influence peddling, collusion or corruption between lender and borrower. A new government which claims to be 'cleaner' than its predecessor will demand the chance for a fresh start, and this will be impossible, or at least hampered, if the new government is stuck with too many old problems. In rare cases such a position may pay off for a debtor. In the context of Realpolitik, other interests may outweigh the claims of past lenders. In recent times only Indonesia has achieved a major success in disposing of the huge debts left by the Sukarno regime. The Indonesian settlement virtually wiped the slate clean! (Ohlin 1976: 212; Klein 1973).

Default on foreign private debts may be considered part of the normal risks of lending. The lender, in the context of a capitalist world, charges a risk premium to the borrower. If the enterprise goes bust creditors have to take their losses and write off the bad debts. Normally, no further claims can be pressed thereafter. International private loans are then treated in an analogous fashion to domestic loans.

Some governments may consider that financial assistance by the rich countries is to be seen as compensation for past colonial exploitation. That it is given mostly in the form of loans rather than grants is seen as unjust. Loan repayment is not seen as morally binding because it would put additional claims on the receiver for what he considers as an obligation by the lender in reparation of past unjustices. After most wars, victors force claims for the settlement of war damages upon the defeated countries. This happened after the First and Second World Wars. Former colonies that fight more or less bloody wars for their independence may claim similar rights of victor's spoils. That retribution has not taken place is due to the fact that as yet they do not have the power to enforce such claims. But the sentiments of revenge are the same. Why has the USA been willing to provide large-scale, mostly *grant*, aid in its Marshall programme to Europe even including former enemies, they argue, knowing full well that the net cost of that aid to the USA economy was quite small. The money was spent mostly on the purchase of American goods, thereby helping the USA economy which was suffering from under-utilization of capacity. Why is it then, that assistance to the present LDCs is mostly through loans? Cancellation of all or part of foreign public debts would enable the developing countries to buy more from the industrialized countries, and thus would not signify a great sacrifice to the rich countries.

In the light of such considerations it is by no means certain what borrowers and lenders will consider as recognized debts.

The assessment of a country's *willingness* to settle foreign debts naturally involves major judgements by the Bank's management. It is extremely difficult to judge commitments to honour foreign debt and, given the possibility of widely differing views about the propriety of portions of outstanding debts, the depth and the sincerity of publicly expressed commitment to do so (see, for instance, Mensah 1973, for a revealing and bitter discussion of debt and development in the context of Ghana's problems).

Shifting the spotlight from psychological to economic aspects of creditworthiness may be more consistent with Article III, section 4 (v) of the Articles of Agreement which requires the Bank to judge repayment prospects before lending. It does not, however, eliminate the need for judgement.

How should creditworthiness, i.e. the *capacity* to repay, be measured? Should it be confined to assessing the prospect that the country will be able to meet only interest charges on a given (and gradually rising) level of foreign debt? The rationale for counting only interest charges is that amortization of existing debts may be automatically refinanced by rolling over. To include amortization schedules assumes that borrowers in due course would reduce their net outstanding debt to zero, and may give rise to gloomy repayment and thus creditworthiness prospects. Few countries are seriously expected to ever repay their national debt in full, it being customarily rolled over. However, there may be doubts whether a country will always be able to borrow enough in the international capital market to cover amortization on existing debt, plus its needs for additional capital. There are limits to the amount of gross borrowing that can be undertaken by any single country, and this limits the external debt service burden that can be incurred without running into balance-of-payments difficulties (Mason & Asher 1973: 180-81). Although such limits may be real, it may still be possible to take less than the full amortization into account.

These may be debating points for economists but to the Bank's management debts are debts, contracts are contracts, and a concept of international lending based on anything other than full repayment is immoral. Creditworthiness, according to the management, should be judged by conservative standards (Ibidem: 181). This position is still held by the Bank today as far as its own lending is concerned. No provisions are made for bad debts as a matter of principle. In that sense, too, the Bank is probably unique in the world!

Its statutory need to judge repayment prospects of loans has involved the Bank from an early date in the study of the foreign debt of developing countries. The Bank maintains an extensive reporting system on debts contracted by LDCs, based on reports from debtor countries, and these are usually a prerequisite for lending. This is in contrast to the DAC, which bases its debt statistics on information from creditor countries. The two systems do not generally tally.

An economic index of creditworthiness that is frequently applied is the so-called debt service ratio, i.e. the proportion of a country's earnings from exports of goods and services which is absorbed by interest and amortization payments on public and publicly guaranteed foreign debt. Similar to gross national product as an index of development, the debt service ratio is a somewhat simplistic measure, but it has nevertheless 'shown strange powers of survival' (Avramović 1964: 38), because no equally useful alternative has been suggested. *Faute de mieux*, international lending institutions have at times leaned upon this ratio, whose value is dubious for several reasons.

Projected debt service ratios are extremely sensitive to alternative growth assumptions for exports. Moreover, Bank loans have a final maturity of 25 years and long-term growth assumptions are consequently relevant for any calculations, but these long-term prospects are extremely difficult to guess or to forecast. Most Bank reporting does not extend beyond a period of five to ten years, and is thus of only limited usefulness in deciding upon future repayment capacity for new loans. Calculating a country's capacity to import by extrapolating exports and terms of trade, and subtracting debt service payments, overlooks the fact that many imports are accompanied by their own financing through suppliers' credits, and are thus independent of import capacity as traditionally calculated. Perhaps the most helpful factor in assessing creditworthiness is to assume that the real burden of payments on past debts will decline under inflationary conditions. But inflation may affect LDCs' import prices more than their export prices, thus diminishing the 'gains' on this account (see UNCTAD 1979).

The fast-growing indebtedness of developing countries has also led to a gradual change in the judgement of when the debt service ratio becomes dangerously high. Countries are apparently able to survive with debt service ratios of up to 30%, much more than was thought possible or desirable 15 to 20 years ago.

Two ratios are thought by the Bank to be of some importance for monitoring the creditworthiness of borrowers: the development of the debt service ratio, and the share of total medium and long-term debt of a country which is held by the Bank. The first is an indicator of the risk that a debt crisis may occur. The second ratio indicates whether the Bank may become a dominant creditor that cannot avoid becoming involved in re-scheduling its own loans if such negotiations are to achieve any significant debt relief. The first condition of creditworthiness discriminates against very poor countries with limited resources and inadequate management capabilities to put available resources to good use. The second condition inhibits the Bank from lending in large volume to countries which are not favoured by other creditors, regardless of their economic and managerial potential. These ratios are seen, however, in the wider context of the capability and soundness of economic policy makers in the borrowing country, as assessed by the Bank's management.

In early 1973 a senior staff meeting was held to decide on an activity plan, including a proposed lending programme for Romania which had become a member of the Bank. A first economic mission to Romania had been unable to extract sufficient data for a detailed economic analysis; nor could a customary creditworthiness analysis be made. Language problems were obviously one factor. But the Romanians also did not see the need to provide data for such an analysis. They merely promised to repay what they wanted to borrow, and felt capable of judging for themselves how far they could go into debt to the Bank. When questions were raised on this break with established Bank practice, which forced the Bank to decide in the absence of relevant data, Mr McNamara stated that he had 'great faith in the financial morality of socialist countries in repaying debts', pointing to Yugoslavia's fine record. When one of the Bank's vice presidents ventured to remark that in this line of reasoning 'Allende's Chile had perhaps not yet become socialist enough', this was received in icy silence.

Nevertheless, the judgment to go ahead with lending was basically correct. If Romania wanted to reorient its economic policies away from exclusive reliance upon the Soviet bloc, it obviously would do all it could to make a success of its first attempts to gain access to Western capital and knowhow. Yet the narrow economic justification for Bank lending is subject to doubt, Romania's trade is overwhelmingly with COMECON countries and thus in inconvertible currency; there is only a trickle of foreign exchange earned from the West, out of which Bank loan repayments have to be made. The Bank's 'exposure' may then be relatively high, unless other western creditor countries follow suit.

The Bank has in the past published several comprehensive studies on indebtness (Avramović 1958; Avramović & Gulhati 1960; and Avramović & Associates 1964). A more recent study is the 'Staff Study of the External Debt of Developing Countries' (August 18, 1971, Sec M71-407; a summary of which was published in the *Annual Report* 1971: 50-56). This study has been extensively discussed by the Executive Directors, but also, and perhaps more significantly for its policy implications, with the governments of major creditor countries prior to publication. It is thus an important publication in that it makes the Bank's policy on the debt issue very explicit.

The Bank has expressed willingness to provide policy advice directed to the avoidance of debt problems. It is prepared to participate, on request, in preparing and securing agreement on the most appropriate measures of relief in cases of serious debt servicing difficulties. All this is gratuitious, standard fare and facile. What really counts is (a) that it is willing to alleviate a country's debt service burden *only* through the provision of new loans on appropriate terms; and (b) that it does *not* plan to participate directly in re-scheduling *its* debts because this could have an adverse effect on the volume and cost of capital available to it, which would, so the Bank argues, penalize countries which have avoided debt difficulties (Staff Debt Study: 6-7). As a general principle, the Bank considers it would be highly undesirable if the 'preferred creditor' position which has been accorded to the Bank were to be undermined (Ibidem: 51). The difficulty with not wishing to get involved is that the Bank cannot be proven wrong or too pessimistic, until it is tried, which so far has not been done.

Debts and debt service payments of developing countries had grown rapidly during the 1950s and 1960s. Yet the 1971 Debt Study concluded that the debt servicing prospects of only four countries which account for about one-fifth of the total debt of developing countries are serious.

A further group of 12 countries, representing about one-third of total debt of developing countries, were thought to be vulnerable to temporary debt servicing difficulties, while the remainder of the countries studied were not expected to face major problems.

There is reason, however, to be somewhat sceptical of the Bank's work on the debt issue.

In the opinion of Mason and Asher, the Bank's 1971 assessment of the prospective debt position of less developed countries in the 1970s has been 'rather optimistic' (1973: 226). More explicit is the statement by Charles Frank in commenting on the debt study:

Given the Bank's prominent role and its need to maintain its own financial health, it is highly unlikely that it would ever become a purveyor of 'gloom and doom' through its financial projections. Any dire projections by the Bank are likely to be self-fulfilling. There is always the danger, however, that the Bank's buoyancy in describing financial prospects could contain an element of self-deception (Frank 1973: 129).

Frank and Cline's study for USAID on *Debt Servicing and Foreign Assistance* (1969) is more pessimistic than the study by the Bank staff. Among its conclusions we read (pp 30-31): 'It [their study] indicates that caution should be exercised with regard to expanded use of institutions which because of their use of borrowed capital must lend on near-commercial terms'.

The published accounts of the Bank's debt analysis appear to down-play fears that a debt crisis is imminent. This is in stark contrast to findings of other UN organs or meetings, notably UNCTAD, which plead for across the board debt relief and whose studies have predicted a debt crisis to have been just around the corner for years. The upshot, then, is that different UN organizations espouse contrary views, thus undermining the effectiveness as well as the credibility of the different organizations.

It should also be added that Mr McNamara committed the Bank to double its lending programme between 1969-73, the effects of which could not be reflected in the debt status at December 1969. If the debt study had taken a pessimistic tone, the expansion plan would have been jeopardized. It should also be noted that between 1969 and 1974, the Bank committed 46% of its stepped-up lending levels to eight of the 12 countries in the category which it had characterized as vulnerable to temporary debt servicing difficulties (Group 2 in the Debt Study). Perhaps the Bank's management believed that by stepping-up its loans with relatively long maturities it could ward off pressures within those countries to contract additional large amounts of suppliers credit with short maturity. In this line of reasoning, the Bank would alleviate balance-of-payments difficulties and contribute to long-term development needs.

It might be asked whether there is a role for the Bank in debt negotiations, and how LDCs should react to Bank initiatives in the light of past debt rescheduling operations.

The term structure of most foreign debt has been of major concern to the Bank. Cairncross observed as long ago as 1959 that the Bank had at times been 'almost excessively vehement in its warnings of the dangers of reliance on medium-term credit' (Cairncross 1959: 29). This theme also runs through the 1971 Debt Study. In the absence of adequate possibilities for long-term foreign financing, however, some countries are often unwilling or unable to face up to the political consequences of foregoing development to save their balance of payments. This is true in rich (e.g. the UK post-war record) as well as poor countries.

Between 1956 and May 1973, 22 multilateral debt renegotiations took place involving nine countries (Klein 1973: 17-20; see also the 1971 IBRD Debt Study; and IMF: *Multilateral Debt Renegotiations: Experience of Fund Members*, August 5, 1971). Seven of those negotiations required more than one debt rescheduling.

Most debt relief agreements have been on terms close to those of the original suppliers' credits on which relief has been requested, i.e. debtor countries have been kept on a short leash. There are a number of reasons for this rescheduling on almost the same terms as those of the original credits on which relief had been requested: commercial contracts such as suppliers' credits are expected to be honoured, and readily available debt relief on highly concessionary terms is thought to threaten the sanctity of other suppliers' credits held by other creditors. Secondly, creditors have been concerned that the government seeking debt relief should pursue policies consistent with rapid restoration of a balance-of-payments equilibrium, including an adequate allowance for debt service. If consolidation were a normal form of development finance and if there were some simple procedure by which debtors could appeal to their creditors for relief, the creditors fear that debtor countries would not follow prudent external debt management policies.

Although many suppliers' credits were initially private debts, debt relief negotiations almost always involve the governments of creditor countries.

Multilateral debt renegotiations may appear to have been organized as a series of *ad hoc* arrangements. In fact, however, an institutional arrangement has been established for considering debt relief questions through what is known as the 'Paris Club'. This has no formal organization but, because of the frequency of debt rescheduling requests, the same representatives of major creditor countries usually meet to deal with such requests. Fundamentally, the group is held together by a mutual desire to negotiate as a group to establish a common response, and to avoid being played off against each other by debtor countries (Klein 1973: 18).

If at least some debt rescheduling operations result from excessive reliance on medium-term suppliers' credit, it would seem reasonable at least to ask how so much suppliers' credit could be given in the first place. The answer is simple.

Most creditor countries have established government-financed export credit insurance corporations, whose objective is to stimulate capital goods exports, to promote domestic growth and employment, and to open up or expand markets abroad for the rich countries through cheap export re-financing facilities. The existence of this insurance facility, however, may entice suppliers to take commercial risks which, in its absence, they would not dare to take. At issue is therefore whether such government-sponsored re-insurance agencies themselves pursue policies which can be described as irresponsible in respect of LDCs. It is too often and too easily assumed by creditor countries that debt crises in LDCs are mainly caused by imprudent management on their part. But insecure and volatile export earnings or, increasingly, protectionist measures in the Western countries, hamper the LDCs in discharging international obligations in a more normal fashion, through increased exports to creditor countries.

It is evident that official creditors simply refuse to assume any part of the real risk on export credit financing. They use a great deal of their political and financial strength to throw the *whole* risk on the debtor, often threatening to curtail official aid. Ohlin observes:

Experience so far has shown that voluntary restraint is hardly to be expected from government agencies which have as their task the promotion of exports. It is nevertheless disgraceful that governments in rich countries are not able to co-ordinate this activity better with their aid policies.

If and when things go badly wrong, the guaranteeing agencies take over the claims. They have collected a fee for the guarantee and generally also manage to collect the debt. It is an anomalous aspect of the relationship between rich and poor countries when they actually report a profit (Ohlin 1976: 219, 221).

The World Bank is not in a position to tell the rich countries that they should be more prudent in granting export credit facilities. This could threaten employment prospects in major capital goods industries in the rich countries, the Bank's major shareholders with controlling voting power. On the other hand, it would deprive developing countries of capital goods needed for growth unless appropriate amounts of alternative long-term finance could be provided to substitute for suppliers' credits. But its built-in optimism on debt issues may have substantially retarded a broad-based move to cancel all or part of outstanding credit to poor countries.

With creditors operating through the Paris Club 'cartel', giving mostly short-term relief and refusing any other discussion about a more comprehensive and longer-term solution to what appears to be a problem of increasing concern, we should perhaps, in the interests of the debtors, search for an alternative strategy that could split the cartel.

As long as a reasonable degree of competition exists between major industrialized countries, export markets will be determined *inter alia* by the attractiveness of credit terms given by selling countries. These pressures will tend to lower interest rates and lengthen credit terms. Market forces would thus help bring about a better term structure of outstanding debt and thereby lessen debt problems. It is then in the interest of debtor countries to exploit conflicting interests between major creditors to the maximum possible extent.

The Bank should not and does not offer long-term consolidation loans for diverse suppliers' credit. This would mean that the Bank would quickly end up as the dominant external creditor of several countries, weakening its portfolio and perhaps its credit rating. Moreover, it would force the Bank to become even more of a hardliner on debt repayments than it already is. Most important, it would limit the bargaining scope for debtor countries in that concentration among creditors would be reinforced.

McNamara's thinking on the Bank's future role in debt issues is as follows: If private lenders are to increase their assistance to developing countries, they need better information. The World Bank could help meet that need. If supported by the international banking community, the Central Banks, and the borrowers, 'we could go further and assist in the preparation and publication of comprehensive debt reports for each borrowing country' (1976: 19).

McNamara thus feels that the Bank might play a useful role in the more effective organization of the creditor cartel! But the interests of developing countries may be better served in a different way. In some cases this might be by obscuring data on borrowing outstanding, and by borrowing from diverse sources, as has been done in recent years. If a 'debt crisis' occurs, debtors should try to negotiate with creditors separately for maximum counter leverage. Debtor countries would need to threaten selective retaliation to non-cooperating creditors. If sufficient creditor interests are at stake, for instance, the size of creditor country assets in the borrowing country of geopolitical interests, creditors would have to agree to roll-over or to consolidate on terms better than obtained hitherto, in order not to lose future markets or assets which can be held as hostages in the debt renegotiations. Chile under Allende achieved a modicum of success in this manner.

Obviously, such a strategy of brinkmanship could only work in the economically more powerful of the LDCs, say Mexico or Brazil, who are major holders of external debts facing possible debt problems. But they may argue that major creditors have so much at stake in their countries that they will be bailed out anyway. This strategy may not work for small countries, and may even backfire. But then small and weak countries do not receive much credit in the first place.

Why was Indonesia treated so generously while Ghana was given such a hard time? 'Probably', as noted by Ohlin

... it was not without importance that in the case of Indonesia no single creditor was as dominant as the British were in Ghana and that the creditors, therefore, asked a prominent banker, Hermann Abs from Deutsche Bank, to draft a proposal for a settlement. Unlike government officials from finance ministries and export credit guarantee agencies, whose task it is to protect the tax payers' money, Mr Abs was used to bad debts and his principal concern was to restore creditworthiness and to enable growth to be resumed along sensible lines (Ohlin 1976: 212).

The message should be getting through to developing countries that if a debt crisis occurs and rescheduling becomes inevitable, the governments of the capitalist countries may give them a worse deal than the enterprises of those countries.

If the Bank were called upon to assist debtor countries in debt renego-tations, it might find that, rather than to administer the exercise for creditors, as is current practice, its 'best' advice could be that debtor countries seek a series of bilateral negotiations to maximize their (limited) bargaining strength. The paradoxical situation would arise that a multilateral agency should advise against multilateralism! It is doubtful, though, whether the Bank could get away with such advice because the members of the Paris Club prefer to use the Bank as enforcer of *their* interests in matters of debts. As a result, it may be in the interests of *debtor* countries *not* to request the Bank to play a visible role in the staffwork for debt negotiations. They should perhaps refuse a role for the Bank. Debtor countries' interests may even be served by collaboration in 'lukewarm' fashion with the Bank's debtor country Debt Reporting System. In view of these considerations there is little reason to be happy with the Bank's important role as sponsor of aid consortia, because it may have speeded up and intensified existing pressures for cartel formation among major donors, and thus also among major creditors. After all, East European countries have borrowed over $40 billion in the Eurodollar market, without creditors having the 'benefit' of World Bank-provided country economic studies and foreign debt status reports.

Recent Developments

The major structural feature of the 1970s is the growth of LDC external debts held by private banks. Between 1969 and 1975 the private banks' share of ex-ternal public and publicly guaranteed debt rose from seven to 23% (*Annual*

Report 1977: 109, and 102-103 for notes on coverage). This means that a widening group of countries has obtained access on an unprecedented scale to sources of external funds. Most of these credits are programme loans, implying increased discretion over their use by LDCs, compared to Bank-provided project loans. Hence, the leverage of the Bank as regards policy issues in countries which have obtained alternative sources of external funds, has been correspondingly diminished. White has shown that the advantages of speed, flexibility and freedom in procurement of Eurocurrency credits may outweigh the relatively more favourable terms of Bank loans, if proper account is taken of the delays inherent in project loans (White 1976a: 233-42).

Between 1969 and 1975 the external public and publicly guaranteed debt outstanding increased from $62.5 to $173.9 billion (*Annual Report* 1977: 109, and 102-103). In the face of this increase, some creditor countries have begun to modify their position by agreeing to cancel all or part of their loans to a selected number of borrowers, despite the Bank's habitual optimism about LDC ability to cope with rising debt.

On the basis of preliminary data it would be difficult to argue that World Bank lending overall has increased to a point whereby the Bank would be vulnerable in case of default in view of it having become a dominant creditor; it is not impossible, however, that for individual countries the exposure of the Bank may have reached levels which require deceleration of future lending.

Nor can it be argued that the growth of the World Bank has been excessive within the context of the *net* flows from multilateral institutions to developing countries, giving rise to fears of World Bank domination in that area (see Table 2.6).

Table 2.6 *Net flow from multilateral institutions to developing countries*
(shares)

	1965	1970	1974
World-wide institutions	80	69	69
– World Bank			
IBRD	28	28	28
IDA	26	9	21
IFC	1	4	3
– UN	24	28	16
Regional institutions*	20	31	31

*   excl. OPEC Multilateral Institutions

Source: OECD-DAC *Review* 1975: 123.

Between 1965 and 1974 regional institutions (IADB, AFDB, AIDB, EEC, EIB) increased relative to world-wide institutions. If we had included multilateral institutions set up by OPEC countries, which are not included in the table but which have grown markedly in recent years, the shift would have been even more pronounced. The IBRD share has remained constant. The low share of IDA in 1970 reflects the protracted delays in the second replenishment of IDA.

Specific project provision, programme lending and local currency financing

The Articles of Agreement specify that the Bank shall lend for 'specific projects' and for 'productive purposes' (Article I [i], III.1 [a], III.4 [vii]). This provision originated in the founders' desire to avoid such ill-considered loans as the balance-of-payments loans of the 1920s, when the use of the proceeds was unspecified. Numerous bonds had been sold for general purpose financing − programme financing as it is now called − mostly by Latin American and European municipalities. Their proceeds were rarely well supplied and no-one attempted to evaluate the performance or even the creditworthiness of the economies concerned (Mason & Asher 1973: 266). Large-scale defaults occurred in the 1930s, which may have been due more to the general depression than to the improper use of individual loans. Only in 'special circumstances' could programme loans be considered by the Bank (Article III.4 [vii]).

In 1971 the EDs decided that such special circumstances may arise, subject to specific demonstration in each case, when: (i) the borrowing country has an acceptable medium-term or long-term development programme, with supporting economic and financial policies, which is judged to provide a satisfactory basis for external assistance in a given amount; (ii) the needed transfer of resources from external lending in support of the development programme cannot be achieved effectively and expeditiously by the financing of investment projects, including justifiable local currency expenditures.

The policy on programme lending was reviewed again in April 1977, when it was generally agreed that the expansion of IMF facilities (the Compensatory Financing Facility, the Extended Fund Facility and the Trust Fund), had considerably increased the need to coordinate action on programme loan requests with the IMF, whereby it might often be useful to arrange a mutually supportive Bank-Fund policy package which would help alleviate short-term or medium-term balance-of-payments problems.

The improved availability of compensatory financing from the Fund should enable countries with short-term payment difficulties, arising mainly from fluctuations in world prices of their traditional exports, to finance their needs from this source.

Some developing countries may benefit from continuing programme lending over a period of years because of the inherent structural features of their economies. Programme lending in such cases should be employed as an instrument in assisting a country to obtain specific development objectives (*Annual Report* 1977: 10-11). In terms of the judgements to grant programme loans in specific cases, the Board has in the past been severely biased.

The early post-war loans to European countries: France, The Netherlands,

Denmark and Luxemburg, totalling $497 mln (Mason & Asher 1973: 178), were negotiated *not* in terms of specific projects but on the basis of the loop-hole left by the 'except in special circumstances' clause (Cairncross 1959: 16; Mason & Asher 1973: 25). In fact, most programme loans of the 1950s were to *developed* countries which successfully resisted Bank efforts to 'projectize' loans and to exercise 'end-use' supervision over the proceeds of the loans (Ibidem: 270, 273).

Developing countries have had much less success in obtaining programme loans from the Bank, even when some have argued that they were capable of spending the money as judiciously, in their own eyes, as the developed coun-tries. The dislike for programme lending to LDCs on the part of a number of Executive Directors has been strongly influenced by IDA experience with industrial import credits to India and Pakistan during the 1960s (Ibidem: 281). Criticisms were voiced to the effect that the Bank had been set up as a project lending institution, and that the links between industrial imports and specific projects were weak, that the loans amounted to balance-of-payments support which was the task of the IMF, that the Bank was expected to finance their imports retroactively, and that the Bank was to accept India's plans, which were judged not to have been very successful (Ibidem: 282-89).

The proportion of programme lending to IBRD/IDA commitments was in the range of 4-7% in the early 1970s; it increased to nearly 9% in 1975, but declined to 6% in 1976 and to 2.3% in 1977 (*Annual Report* 1977: 10). Future programme lending in the range of 7-10% was thought by the EDs to be a not unreasonable expectation of the incidence of 'special circumstances' (Ibidem: 11). In addition to India, $525 mln, and Pakistan, $180 mln, sizable programme loans were given in the period 1972-77 to Bangladesh, $300 mln, Korea, $175 mln and Egypt, $140 mln. These countries received 85% of all programme loans over that period (*Annual Reports*). In 1978, programme loans dropped to 1.8% of total commitments.

A 'project' is a discrete investment programme specified as to character, location and time (Chadenet & King 1972: 4-5). It may, however, comprise a great variety of items. The requirement for the Bank to consider mostly specific and well-prepared projects tends to slow down its rate of resource transfers. More important, however, is that the capacity to prepare projects is itself a function of the level of development of the borrowing country. Poor countries, and also the smaller ones, are usually deficient in institutional capacity to prepare suitable and viable projects for submission to the Bank or, for that matter, to any other external lending organization which is concerned that its funds should be used according to the conditions it states. To some extent the Bank can assist the small and poor countries in project preparation by making available either some of its own staff or by providing funds for the hire of consultants. But given the limitations on its own staff, there are clearly limits to what the Bank can realistically do, at least in the short run.

It may thus be easier for the Bank to become involved in a multi-billion dollar project to modernize the Brazilian steel industry, for example, than in one worth only a few million dollars in Lesotho or Upper Volta. The latter type projects may even require more Bank staff-time than the former in absolute terms.

An aspect of project lending is that the Bank usually restricts itself to the foreign exchange cost of proposed projects, barring 'exceptional circumstances' (Article IV, 3 [b]). This provision was weakened somewhat in the IDA Articles to 'in special cases' (Article V, section 2 [e]). The Bank's charter thus does not particularly encourage the development of local industries, which might benefit through a learning-by-doing process in the build-up of expertise and knowhow. In addition, it is at least conceivable that local industries may operate at different factor proportions than foreign firms. This may give a boost to better labour use, which is highly desirable under prevailing high levels of under-employment of labour in many LDCs. In the light of such considerations, the Bank has modified the conditions specifying the applicability of local currency financing and its procurement procedures. Gradual widening of the criteria has had the effect that local currency financing became the Bank's preferred method, compared to. programme loans, of contributing to the foreign exchange component of development programmes sums over and beyond those required to buy the imports needed on Bank-financed projects. Between 1961 and 1968 IBRD disbursed $3.3 bln on loan commitments, of which 27% were local expenditures. In that period IDA disbursed $1.3 bln of which 14% local expenditures. The rather surprisingly low percentage of IDA local currency lending is in large part accounted for by the fact that India and Pakistan, IDA's largest borrowers, were supplied with sizable import credits for specified industrial imports. A reconsideration by the Executive Directors of the issue of local currency financing in the light of the recommendations of the Pearson Commission, led to the conclusion that no change in the guidelines established in 1968 was necessary (see Operational Policy Memorandum 1.22 [June 1, 1971]; Mason & Asher 1973: 277-81).[2]

The 1968 guidelines stated that, in principle, the Bank was prepared to consider loans for projects involving local expenditure if the following conditions were met:

(a) the borrowing country has a suitable development programme and is making an adequate development effort; *and*
(b) this development programme requires funds in excess of the savings that can be raised locally and the capital, public and private, that can be obtained from other external sources; *and*
(c) these funds cannot reasonably be provided to the country in adequate amounts by financing foreign exchange expenditure on development projects (i.e. there are insufficient investment opportunities of this kind); *or*
(d) although there are sufficient investment opportunities of this kind, the

Bank could have a greater beneficial influence on the country's develop-ment if it diverted its financing toward other projects of key importance requiring some local expenditure financing.

The amount of a loan for foreign expenditure is limited by the estimated amount of such foreign expenditure; sometimes a lesser amount is fixed (e.g. in Venezuela, because the overall requirement of the economy did not justify the amount of lending which would otherwise have been appropriate on narrow project grounds (Mason & Asher 1973: 279 n. 42).

On the other hand, the amount of a loan which also includes (or may in-clude, according to the outcome of bidding) some local expenditure has no such limit and has to be a matter of judgement from case to case in the light of the following considerations:

(a) the economic position of the country and its need for external capital; generally the poorer the country the greater is the proportion of the cost of the project which the Bank is prepared to finance;

(b) the financial needs of the borrowing entity and the desirability of en-couraging an adequate local contribution to the financing of the project and an adequate local stake in its success;

(c) the amount necessary to enable the Bank to influence the organization and execution of the project and the policies relating to the sector concerned;

(d) the size and character of other projects in the country which the Bank might finance, either entirely on the basis of foreign exchange expen-ditures or to include some local expenditure (Operational Policy Memor-andum, 1.22 [June 1, 1971]: 2-3).

The Bank is required by its Articles of Agreement to ensure that the pro-ceeds of loans are used with due attention to economy and efficiency (Article of Agreement III, Section 5 [b]). From this it follows that the Bank should exercise end-use supervision over procurement under Bank loans. The Bank considers that in most cases international competitive bidding is the best method for achieving the economic and efficient procurement of the goods and services required for the development projects it finances. It also ensures that suppliers and contractors from all its member countries have an opportunity to compete in providing goods and services by the Bank.

There may be special circumstances in which international competitive bidding may not be appropriate and the Bank may accept alternative pro-cedures. For example:

(a) where the borrower has convincing reasons for maintaining a reasonable standardization of equipment;

(b) where the number of qualified suppliers is limited, e.g. of spare parts for existing equipment;

(c) where the amount involved in the procurement is so small that foreign firms clearly would not be interested, or that the advantages of international competitive bidding would be outweighed by the administrative burden involved ('Guidelines for Procurement under World Bank Loans and IDA Credits' [April 1972], 2).

Thus, even when local currency financing has been permitted, its actual use could be restricted as a result of the general requirement of international competitive bidding.

Developing countries have therefore pressed for a domestic preference margin for Bank financed projects on the grounds of the infant-industry argument for industrialization. Such a preference would enable newly developed local industries to compete with established foreign firms. From 1961 the Bank gave a 15% preference margin to bids from local manufacturers. This policy assisted a limited group of countries with relatively well-diversified local capabilities — Mexico, Brazil, Argentina, Spain, Portugal and Yugoslavia. But not until 1973 was a domestic preference of 7.5% nominal, accorded to building contractors in civil works in LDCs after protracted and at times acrimonious debate. This was to be granted only to countries with less than $200 per year per capita income as estimated by the 1973 World Bank Atlas, and only for a trial period of one year (Preferences for Domestic Contractors, R73-291 [December 21, 1973]: 1-2). This trial period was extended until January 1979.

As more countries develop their local industrial capacity, with or without foreign assistance, the Bank's insistence on international competitive bidding may lead to its future exclusion from lending in cases where the government adopts protected (reserved) procurement in support of local industry. Such exclusion will make it impossible for the Bank to channel its technical assistance with its lending in such sectors.

The conflict on the Board between proponents and antagonists of granting a domestic preference translated itself into arguments used by Bank staff in trying to sell the idea to grant the preference to the Board. On the one hand, staff argued, preferences will benefit infant construction industries which are beginning to develop in a number of lower middle-income countries in Africa, Asia and Central America and which require some protection at this stage of their development. Many of these countries are among those where Bank-financed construction constitutes a relatively large proportion of total construction activity in the country and where preferences could be important. This holds in particular if civil works contracts are 'sliced' sufficiently to fit them to the capacity of local contractors. On the other hand, so staff argued, if preferences are granted to domestic contractors, there may be more international tendering of civil works contracts to the extent that what is now protected procurement in some countries is opened to international competitive bidding (Domestic Construction Industries, R73-177 [July 12, 1973]: 16). The latter argument caters to the rich countries, in that it offers prospects for future foreign penetration in LDCs in presently 'closed markets', through the Bank as overseer of competitive bidding (Mason & Asher 1973: 187).

Other factors determining Bank lending

The level of lending and the rate of growth which the Bank can maintain are also influenced by many factors which are largely outside its power of influence. Basic to Bank lending is government's attitude to the role of foreign capital. But there are other factors. For instance, in some countries such as Costa Rica and Venezuela, each external loan needs to be approved by parliament. Serious delays may occur which may jeopardize the whole project if its basic premises should change in the meantime. In other countries, Bank projects may be caught in political conflict between central or national government and regional or state governments, as in India and Nigeria for example. From the viewpoint of meeting ambitious lending targets set for the Bank staff by McNamara, it is often easier to do business with authoritarian regimes than with democracies: the decision-making process may work so much faster in the former! Calamities such as war, flood, earthquake or drought obviously affect the Bank's lending operations in that they divert attention from the regular work on hand and disturb normal procedures. In view of all this, it may seem of doubtful use to set lending 'targets' for the Bank, a practice initiated by McNamara.

Summary on determinants of the country distribution of Bank lending

We have discussed a number of factors which are seen as important determinants of the distribution of Bank lending by country. It may be helpful to summarize them briefly. In Chapter V we shall analyze the actual pattern of Bank lending in greater detail from the perspective of whether it can be changed to serve the needs of poorer strata of world society.

The significance of the Bank's capitalist ideology has gradually been eroded. Mixed-economy as well as many socialist countries see no objection to borrowing from the Bank, nor does the Bank see ideological obstacles to lending. The only major remnant, but a crucial one, of its ideological base is that the Bank cannot lend to countries which have nationalized *foreign-owned* private property and are unwilling to make appropriate effort to reach fair and equitable settlement. The 'willingness' to negotiate and the 'fairness' of the settlement can be broadly defined and are subject to an important element of judgement. The Bank does not make lending dependent upon a settlement of nationalization of *domestically*-owned private property. That is considered an internal affair!

Application of the principle that the Bank should be seen as a lender of last resort means that it phases-out its lending to countries which have reached levels of development that make them 'market eligible'. Such countries can obtain international finance in amounts and on terms judged reasonable by the Bank, and continued Bank lending will then no longer be justified.

The application of the creditworthiness criterion as a pre-condition for Bank lending leads, on the other hand, to countries which have weak balance-of-payments prospects being excluded altogether from receiving Bank loans. In view of the Bank's firm position against any re-scheduling of its loans, it will also have to monitor its exposure in another group of relatively small and poor countries. It should not become a dominant creditor which can not avoid becoming involved in the eventuality of a needed debt re-scheduling, even though its own lending is on relatively hard terms and may represent a considerable burden for the borrowing country. This concern for its exposure inhibits the Bank from providing large loans to countries which, for some reason or other, do not also receive large amounts of credit from other creditors. Often these will be relatively small countries which are of little strategic importance because of geopolitical considerations or which do not possess rare and important raw materials, and are consequently more or less 'forgotten' by the international community.

The specific project provision in Bank lending discriminates against relatively small countries in which there are few productive and viable projects. It also discriminates against countries, whether large or small, which have relatively low levels of human resources development. Limited skills in preparing projects suitable for Bank financing may or may not be accompanied by limited institutional capacity in executing projects. In brief, such countries have limited 'absorptive capacity'. The requirement of international competitive bidding gives it a bias that favours established foreign firms over newly-established firms in LDCs. The 'domestic preference' policy mitigates this bias somewhat.

Finally, there are a number of factors which are largely outside the power of the Bank to prevent their occurrence or to remedy their consequences. These factors may be incidental and ad hoc, yet they may considerably slow down the Bank's rate of lending and they cast doubt on the possibility of setting specific lending targets for the Bank.

The cumulative impact of all the above factors is quite formidable, and appears to make it especially difficult for the Bank to lend to small, instable and poor countries.

The country distribution of Bank lending, as shown in Table 2.3, reflects the judgements of successive Bank presidents concerning which countries were eligible for loans, given the numerous factors which management has to take into account. Such judgements can and do change over time. Together they provide the structural context in which the Bank has to operate and which demarcates the latitude for individual judgement of successive Bank presidents. The McNamara era does not and cannot reflect a clear break with the past.

Our discussion of the major determinants of Bank lending shows that the IBRD can lend in large volume to countries with reasonable balance-of-payments prospects, and adequate economic management, i.e. middle and upper-middle income countries, some of which may soon become market-eligible. Some have already obtained access to Eurocurrency credits on an unprecedented scale. This new phenomenon, together with the hardening of terms of Bank loans, means that the Bank's leverage on country policies has diminished and will continue to do so. Lending by the Bank should in any case not be pushed to the point where it becomes a dominant or even major creditor, unable to stay out of debt re-negotiations if these should prove unavoidable. Numerous countries with low incomes, narrow resource bases and structural balance-of-payments problems are, from the Bank's point of view, credit risks and not bankable on country grounds.

NOTES

1. The following disbursement rates applied approximately in the early 1970s for different sectors as a function of the time lapsed (in years) since the signing of the loans.

sectors/years	1	2	3	4	5	6	7	8	9	10 a.o.
Electric power	12	21	19	18	14	7	4	2	1	1
Transportation	6	18	21	19	14	9	5	3	1	4
Agriculture	5	19	18	11	7	4	4	17	13	2
Industry	9	17	23	19	12	8	5	3	1	3

Source: Programming and Budgeting Dept. (May 5, 1972).

2. Reid's statements to the effect that when McNamara became President of the Bank 'only five percent of Bank Group lending was for local costs', and acclaiming as a 'great triumph' for McNamara that 'this percentage has gone up from five to ten percent' are in error (Reid 1973a: 800-801).

III

GROWTH AND EVOLUTION OF THE INTERNATIONAL DEVELOPMENT ASSOCIATION

HISTORICAL BACKGROUND

Introduction

While IBRD borrows in the international capital market, IDA receives most of its funds from the public aid budgets of donor countries. This means that contributions to IDA are decided upon by donors not only under changing perceptions of the rationale and functions of aid, but also under changing perceptions about the effectiveness of alternative channels of dispensing available aid flows. This makes IDA a very vulnerable institution.

The establishment of IDA, almost accidentally as a fund administered by the Bank, has enabled the Bank Group to continue its worldwide activities (Mason & Asher 1973: ch. 12; Weaver 1965). In 1960, the outlook for an agency like IBRD, equipped only to make loans at close-to-commercial rates of interest to countries unable to borrow elsewhere, would have been bleak. With lending to the rich countries being phased out and many newly independent countries in Africa and elsewhere not or no longer credit-worthy, the Bank was restricted to lending to a few countries in the middle incomes range. The IDA, by permitting lending to poor countries, has widened the range of Bank Group activities, both in lending to other countries and as regards sectors.

The founding of IDA represents a victory in the LDCs' unabating campaign for a multilateral source of investment funds at low cost. Although this campaign was waged mainly in the General Assembly of the United Nations, the fund was finally established at the address of the Bank. This in itself was rather peculiar because pressure for establishing an investment fund with soft terms of lending had derived major impetus from criticisms voiced within the United Nations about the harshness of the Bank's project selection criteria and of its lending conditions. Moreover, the Bank had initially denied that there was any need for a soft loan window. At a later stage, the Bank's management feared that affiliation of a soft-term money window with the Bank through amending its existing Articles of Agreement would lower its prestige on the world's

---

Notes to this chapter may be found on pp. 90-91.

capital markets on which it depended for its own funds. Consequently, the Bank and IDA at first published separate annual reports, in order not to give the impression that the Bank was 'contaminated' by the IDA. Not until George Woods succeeded Eugene Black as President of the Bank was a joint annual report brought out to demonstrate the close links, in terms of management, project standards and staff, between the two institutions (Mason & Asher 1973: 390 n 17). The International Finance Corporation, however, continues to publish an individual annual report and to maintain its own separate organizational structure and identity even though IBRD and IDA also provide considerable financing for industry.

Prehistory of IDA 1949-59

The origins of IDA can be traced to the proposal by the Indian economist V.K.R.V. Rao in 1949 that a new international organization should be set up: the United Nations Economic Development Administration (UNEDA). This idea later re-emerged in discussions in the UN Economic and Social Council as the Special United Nations Fund for Economic Development (SUNFED). Between 1950 and 1960 the campaign in the UN for a vehicle to promote the financing of development was led primarily by Chile, India and Yugoslavia. The prehistory of IDA has been narrated elsewhere (e.g. Mason & Asher 1973; Hadwen & Kaufman 1960; Weaver 1965; and Asher 1957), and for our purpose it is only necessary to highlight a few of its aspects. The time involved in such a technically simple matter as setting up a fund should stunt any optimism that international decision making can quickly respond to changing circumstances. Moreover, since its establishment IDA has had a history full of problems and conflict.

The developed countries, led by an increasingly isolated USA, at first resisted attempts to set up an organization with soft conditions of lending. Delaying tactics were adopted and finally the campaign was deflected. The World Bank became the major beneficiary of these diversionary tactics.

The initial position of the USA was to rely primarily on the activities of (American) private business for any assistance required by developing countries. Additionally, the World Bank should be relied upon for the financing of certain types of projects which were recognized to be of great significance for the development process but were considered less suited for financing by private capital.

In 1951, the Bank's management considered that the greatest obstacle to a larger flow of finance to developing countries was the dearth of well-prepared projects which could be financed at normal Bank conditions. It was feared that soft loans might lead to soft, i.e. ill-prepared, projects which would negatively affect the Bank's standing in international capital markets. True, the Bank recognized that capital was needed for projects in education, health and other fields deemed indispensable to the development process. But such projects should preferably be financed by gifts and grants and not through soft loans (Mason & Asher 1973: 385-86).

Since 1954, the USA had accumulated substantial amounts of foreign currencies from the sale of surplus agricultural commodities, made available mainly under Public Law 480. As the volume of these inconvertible currencies increased, confusion within the USA about their economic value and political significance also increased. In February 1958 Senator Monroney therefore proposed that an International Development Association be set up to be linked to the World Bank. The USA would transfer significant portions of its local currency nesteggs to the IDA, for the latter to lend on long terms and at low interest rates. Such loans were to be repayable in local currency. In Monroney's view such an arrangement would supplement World Bank loans at no extra cost to the USA.

The continuing pressure exercised in the UN for the establishment of SUNFED produced some indirect results. The decision taken in 1956 by the Bank's Board of Governors to establish an International Finance Corporation can be attributed in part to a desire of the Bank's principal shareholders to respond in concrete fashion to mounting pressure in the UN for new types of development finance. The establishment of the UN Special Fund in October 1958 to finance preinvestment work was an even clearer response. And Eugene Black had to admit: 'IDA was really an idea to offset the urge for SUNFED' (Weaver 1965: 28). If there had to be a multilateral soft loan window it was better that it be attached to the Bank rather than to the UN Secretariat. The rich countries, which were expected to provide the bulk of the finances for such a facility, apparently had more confidence in the capability of the Bank which they controlled through the weighted voting system. Moreover, the anti-communist witch hunt activities of Senator Joseph McCarthy dating from the height of the cold war in the late 1940s and early 1950s, had hampered the UN in building up a staff as capable as that of the Bank, and this factor also worked in favour of affiliation with the Bank (see on the UN: Hazzard 1973).

Structure of IDA

The structure which the Executive Directors of the Bank gave to IDA under instructions from the Board of Governers, differed in several important respects from the expectations held in various circles. On the issue of voting rights, several countries, notably the Benelux, Britain and South Africa, considered that a formula based on Gross National Product or a similar yardstick of ability to pay would be fair and just. The actual formula for the distribution of voting rights, however, was similar to that adopted for the Bank. IDA membership was to be limited to members of the Bank, thus ensuring that IDA would also be under firm control of the developed countries.

IDA membership was divided into two classes: Part I for the rich; Part II for the poor. The classification was based largely on per capita incomes, with a few exceptions: Japan was to be in Part I despite its relatively low per capita income at that time. Israel, with its much higher per capita income, was put into Part II. Since 1960, Iceland and Ireland from the Third Replenishment and New Zealand from the Fourth have moved from Part II to Part I status.

Not all Bank members elected for IDA membership. As at June 30, 1978 Bank membership stood at 132, and IDA membership at 120. The twelve exceptions were Portugal, Luxemburg, Romania, the Bahamas, Barbados and Jamaica, Bahrain, Qatar and the United Arab Emirates, Singapore, Venezuela and Uruguay.

Membership of IDA is beneficial for poor countries because it provides access to soft money. First, however, they have to contribute to the capital of the Bank from which they derive no benefits through loans unless they are creditworthy or in due course become so.

For the richer Part II countries, IDA membership means that they may be expected to contribute to any replenishment of IDA on a voluntary basis, or graduate to Part I status with its much stronger pressure to contribute. On the other hand, they will not receive benefits from IDA, particularly if and when IDA lending is increasingly focused on the poorest countries (see further Chapter V). Their interest in IDA is thus very limited.

The EDs showed no enthusiasm for the idea expressed by some members of the US Congress, that IDA should be saddled with inconvertible currencies. That politically tricky problem was left to the USA to solve. IDA deals in hard, freely convertible currencies for both lending and repayment. The existence of sizeable holdings of US-owned local currencies unquestionably hastened the creation of IDA but has had no effect on its operations (Mason & Asher 1973: 393). Analogous to the practice of the Bank, IDA prefers project financing rather than programme financing, much to the disappointment of India and other countries. Under pressure from the USA — Congress by then having become allergic to giveaways — the choice was also made for soft loans rather than grants, despite the initial aversion expressed by the Bank's management. The standard terms of IDA credits are quite favourable, however. Credits are repayable in hard currency over 50 years, but payments start only after ten years. Thereafter, one percent of the principal is paid per year during ten years and three percent per year during the remaining 30 years. Credits bear no interest except for a service charge of 0.75% per annum over the credit amount outstanding. This charge contributes to the administrative cost which the Bank, according to some sort of internal management contract, charges to IDA for its work in connection with the credits, their preparation and supervision (IDA: *General Conditions Applicable to Development Agreements* [Washington, 31 January 1969]; Articles of Agreement VI, 6[b]).

The Articles of Agreement made it clear that IDA was to have a 'more benign personality' than the Bank.[1] This was to show in its favourable lending conditions. The IDA could lend to a poor country after it had been established that the latter was not creditworthy for Bank loans. Yet strict project standards were established that were similar to those for Bank loans. Criticisms in respect of tough Bank project conditions, voiced in the General Assembly of the UN, went unheeded. Furthermore, IDA did not need to concentrate to the same extent as the Bank on electric power and transportation: it could also interest itself in projects of a more social character. Its Articles of Agreement specify that financing by IDA shall be for purposes which, in the opinion of the Association, are of 'high developmental priority' in the light of the needs of the area or areas concerned and, except in special circumstances, shall be for specific projects (Article V, 1[b]).

IDA's original charger became effective and binding for member states when a qualified majority of the members, representing 65 percent of total initial subscriptions, had been approved. Amendments to the Articles were to be approved by at least three-fifths of the members, having four-fifths of the total voting power. These provisions gave a veto power to the USA in view of the weight of its vote and the size of its contribution. This veto power has been retained in subsequent replenishments.

The growth and viability of IDA thus depend critically upon one member country, the USA, which has proven a very unreliable partner from the perspective of continuation of IDA activities.

GROWTH OF IDA ACTIVITIES

In Table 3.1 it can be seen that IDA commitments and disbursements have grown rapidly. During 1968 the lending volume dipped because IDA did not have further commitment authority, due to the delay in the Second Replenishment. A similar, though not as large, reduction occurred in 1977. The total amount available for IDA was then substantially less in USA dollar terms than it had been when the Fourth Replenishment Agreement was negotiated in Nairobi in September 1973. Instead of the $4501 million originally visualized, the amount actually available for the three-year period 1975-77 was only $4151 million (*Annual Report* 1977: 5,6). This was due mainly to exchange rate changes that were not compensated by contributors (see below, p. 64).

Table 3.2 summarizes the geographical distribution of IDA credits, the breakdown over the various presidencies being similar to that for IBRD lending made in the previous chapter.

IDA lending to Indonesia, which received a major share in 1969-74, was eliminated in 1975-77, and reinstated to some extent in 1978. Indonesia's share, taken largely from equally poor India and Pakistan, has gone mostly to

Table 3.1 *Growth of IDA lending, fiscal years 1961-78*

Fiscal year ending in	Nr. of operations	Commitments ($ mln)	Disbursements ($ mln)
1961	2	101	–
1962	16	134	12
1963	17	260	56
1964	17	283	124
1965	18	309	222
1966	12	284	267
1967	17	353	342
1968	16	107	319
1969	29	385	256
1970	50	606	143
1971	51	584	235
1972	68	1000	261
1973	75	1357	493
1974	69	1095	711
1975	68	1576	1026
1976	73	1655	1252
1977	67	1308	1298
1978	99	2313	1062

Source: *Annual Reports*

Table 3.2 *Geographical distribution of IDA credits, in percent*

	Black 1961-63	Woods 1964-68	McNamara 1969-74	McNamara 1975-78
India	60.6	44.1	38.2	40.1
Pakistan	5.0	13.8	5.3	5.7
Bangladesh	1.6	3.3	1.8	8.7
Indonesia	–	–	11.2	1.0
Subtotal	67.2	61.2	56.5	55.5
East Africa	5.9	12.3	14.6	17.4
West Africa	–	6.2	8.3	9.0
Other Asia	5.9	8.8	8.1	6.7
EMENA[a]	6.8	7.9	9.4	8.9
LAC[b]	14.2	3.6	3.1	2.5
Subtotal	32.8	38.8	43.5	44.5
Total	100.0	100.0	100.0	100.0

(a) Southern Europe, Middle East and North Africa.
(b) Latin America and Caribbean.

Source: *Annual Reports*

what is now Bangladesh. The share of India, Pakistan and Bangladesh moved from a record high of 67.2% under Black via 61.2% under Woods to only 45.3% in 1968-74, to rise again to 54.5% in 1975-78. There has been a slow but steady increase in IDA lending in both East and West Africa.

SOURCES OF FUNDS, AN OVERVIEW

IDA is dependent upon the governments of the rich countries for periodic replenishments of its funds. This puts the President of IDA, who is *ex officio* the same person as the President of the Bank, in a weak position vis-à-vis the Executive Directors, who represent both IBRD and IDA members. Within statutory limits, the Bank places its own bonds on the capital markets of the world, and the Bank President is therefore in a relatively stronger position to push his plans than he is in his function as President of IDA when he has to ask for funds, cap in hand. As President of IDA he cannot determine the total scope of the lending programme, but can only hope to influence the pattern of expenditure. As Bank President he has a strong influence on the size and pattern of lending activities.

This dichotomy in the role of the President is becoming something of the past. Whenever the Bank approaches its statutory lending limit, it has to ask simultaneously for an increase in its share capital and for a replenishment of IDA funds. Such a situation existed in 1970 and may again occur in the context of the upcoming Sixth Replenishment. The Bank and IDA then become competitive rather than complementary in their search for funding, an increase in IBRD capital being equal to a grant because no dividend is ever paid by the Bank. Contributions to IDA are also grants, but loom larger in view of the fact that only 10 percent of increases of IBRD capitalization needs to be paid in.

Subscriptions to IDA were originally planned at a level of $1 billion with $763 million to be contributed by Part I countries and the rest by Part II countries. The latter were obliged to pay only ten percent of their contribution in gold or freely convertible currency, and even this amount could be spread over five years. The remainder was payable in local currency and could be made in five instalments.

At first, the Executive Directors considered that replenishments of IDA funds should be designed to provide the Association with funds for a five-year period. Starting with the First Replenishment, however, two modifications were made. The replenishment period was reduced from five to three years on the grounds that it would be easier to persuade parliaments to appropriate funds for the shorter period. A five-year period exceeds the tenure of government and parliament in most major donor countries and may be problematic from the viewpoint of parliamentary control over public expenditures. The Pearson Report recommended that IDA funds should again be replenished every five years in order that IDA might improve its medium-term planning (Pearson Report 1969: 230). This suggestion has not been followed through. In any case, it seems rather futile, to discuss the replenishment period irrespective of the level of the replenishment.

The time needed to process a project from its conceptualization to preparation, appraisal and approval may be two to three years. As there is no certainty about commitment authority and the subsequent availability of IDA funds, however, considerable risk is involved in preparing projects for which finance may not be forthcoming. This uncertainty is much reduced for Bank-financed projects because the Bank has more say in borrowing the necessary funds, both in volume and timing.

The second modification in the funding of IDA replenishments was that the total amount should be contributed by Part I countries. This idea had been proposed by Bank staff when IDA was still on the drawing board, but rejected by the USA as being politically unsaleable (Mason & Asher 1973: 406). Negotiations now take place between Part I country deputies in the absence of representatives of Part II countries, and thus in the absence of moral or other suasion which the latter might be able to exercise.

Negotiations about supplementary finance frequently extend over two years before being concluded at the level of government executives. The American Administration, in particular, has not been able to declare itself freely in negotiations over the last ten years because Congress, as legislator, does not wish to be confronted with pre-negotiated and morally binding commitments. In other countries the relations between government and parliament are less antagonistic, yet delays can occur when negotiated agreements have to be approved by parliament. Development aid contributions, which in many countries have low priority, may easily be victimized by internal political conflicts which sometimes are not even related to the issue of development aid *per se*.

As a result, preparations and negotiations regarding replenishments of IDA funds have become almost permanent. Differences of opinion and past conflicts are given insufficient time to blunt their edges before being re-shapened in the next round. The cumulative effects may well be irritation and decreasing willingness to negotiate, particularly if the same countries repeatedly cause major problems.

Except for minor adjustments, IDA replenishments have taken the form of supplements rather than of increases in the original participations. To increase the contributions of Part I countries only would lead to adjustments in voting rights. Over time, the influence of Part II countries would then soon disappear and this, of course, is not acceptable.

The funds actually made available to IDA from initial subscriptions amounted to $796 million for the first five years, permitting an annual commitment level of $160 million during 1960-64. The first replenishment in 1964-66 was at a level of $250 million per year. The American Congress was then only a little late in giving its approval. The first replenishment was negotiated in less than two years, from September 1962 to June 1964, but negotiations for the second lasted from September 1965 to July 1969. George Woods initially proposed an annual level of $1 billion, but ultimately received only $400 million per annum. Resistance to the high figure came mostly from member states of the European Economic Community (EEC), who had earlier negotiated an extension of the treaty with the Associated African States and Madagascar for the period 1964-69 (the Yaoundé Convention, July 1963). The European countries were also annoyed that Woods had first begun negotiations over the size of the US contribution, and did not start discussions with other Part I members until April 1967. In itself this was not altogether illogical since the USA still provides the largest single contribution.

Another major issue in the Second Replenishment negotiations was the pressure exerted by the USA in seeking balance-of-payments safeguards. The balance of payments problems in themselves were not unrelated to the increasing cost of the war in Vietnam.

The USA favoured procurement-tying arrangements for its IDA contribution, but this was strongly objected to by most other countries. Only a few years earlier European nations had been as zealous as the USA in protecting their balance-of-payments, and they continued to tie most of their bilateral aid. A compromise solution was eventually worked out in an *ad hoc* arrangement to accommodate American demands. The USA was given so-called 'end of queue' treatment (Mason & Asher 1973: 410). The United States would not have to contribute on a *pro rata* basis until July 1, 1971, at the earliest. Until then, it would contribute only that portion of its share that represented identifiable IDA procurement in the United States; a postponement period of three years would be granted for the deferred amounts. The majority of Part I members would in the meantime compensate for those deferred amounts, namely, the difference between the American *pro rata* share for each payment period (its absolute ceiling regardless of the amount of procurement in the USA) and the amount put up to cover actual procurement in the USA.

This delay in ratifying the Second Replenishment almost exhausted IDA's power to grant new credits in spite of advance payments by other countries, for which they were not yet legally bound, and of the transfer of a sizeable part of the Bank's profits to IDA (see Table 3.1). Final ratification by the USA occurred in July 1969.[2]

Negotiations for the Third Replenishment, at a level of $800 million per year, began in December 1969. Congress did not give its approval until September 1972, just before the annual meeting of Bank and Fund in Washington. Once again, advance payments by other countries had to bring relief. As an additional pressurizing tactic on the USA, the Board of IDA, influenced by McNamara and pending the availability of funds, had dared to conditionally approve projects totalling $319.5 million or 32 percent of the year's total, without having the authority to sign such credits. This tactic was embarrassing for the USA and not without risk for McNamara, whose appointment for a second term of office was then not yet assured.

Negotiations for the Fourth Replenishment, for a level of $1500 million per year for 1975-77, in line with the Pearson Commission Recommendation except for inflation between 1969-75 (Pearson 1969: 230), were initiated in the Autumn of 1972. An agreement was negotiated in Nairobi on the eve of the Bank/Fund Annual Meeting, during a session that was at times acrimonious, and was announced on September 27, 1973. The draft Bill, however, was defeated by the US House of Representatives in January 1974 by 248 votes to 155. No problems had arisen in the Committee stage, as the Bill was strongly supported by the Administration. The Bill came before the House, however, on the first day after the Christmas recess during which members had been able to sense constituents' feelings about the Watergate affair and about the increases in international petroleum prices announced in December 1973.[3] A determined effort was subsequently made by public and private groups to have this decision reversed, and in July 1974 Congress voted 225 to 140 in favour (Howe 1975: 68). Further delays occurred in the Senate, however, and it was not until January 1975 that the American government officially notified the IDA of its participation. In the meantime IDA had again been tided-over by advance contributions by twelve Part I countries (*Annual Report* 1975: 5).

The acrimony in Nairobi was due to the fact that several regressive features were introduced into the agreement at the behest of the USA. A major element in the negotiations was the *decline* of the relative US contribution from 40 to 34 percent of the total amount, causing a different burden-sharing arrangement with compensation coming from Germany and Japan.

The 'maintenance of value' clause in IDA's Articles of Agreement (Article IV, Section 2), which had been maintained during the first three replenishments as a matter of policy, was dropped during the negotiations for the Fourth. (The clause implied that whenever the par value of a member's currency is reduced or its foreign exchange value has, in the opinion of the Association, depreciated significantly, the member shall pay to the Association within a reasonable time an additional amount of its own currency sufficient to maintain the value, as of the time of the subscription or of the Replenishment agreement. This provision, however, only applies so long as and to the extent that such currency shall not have been initially disbursed or exchanged for the currency of another member. Similarly, the Association shall repay a member whose currency has appreciated).

The 'maintenance of value' clause protects IDA's assets that are available for lending against the effects of the devaluation of several major currencies, and maintains the burden-sharing relationships among members by fixing the relative value of their contributions until disbursement time.

Several countries which have devalued their currencies in the past, for instance Britain in 1967, have had to pay compensation to IDA. The devaluations of the dollar in December 1971 and again in February 1973 have meant that the USA has had to pay large supplements to IDA and to other multilateral agencies.[4] As a consequence, it began to favour abandoning the maintenance of value clause although it had formerly resisted such a move when suggested by other countries whose currencies were weakening.

The abandonment of the clause is perhaps understandable in an age of floating exchange rates, but it has provided a precedent that is perhaps applicable to other international organizations which customarily have the same provision in their charters, and whose assets may be eroded in similar fashion to IDA assets.

A third feature of the Fourth Replenishment agreement refers to the timing of payments. A payment option in four years instead of the customary three years was included ('Report of the Executive Directors to the Board of Governors on Additions to IDA resources; Fourth Replenishment', October 30, 1973), which effectively reduced the amount to be appropriated in each year, thereby enhancing the chances of legislative approval. Moreover, the first instalment could be *delayed* up to one year to enable some countries to avoid having to appropriate the last instalment for the Third Replenishment *and* the first instalment for the Fourth Replenishment in the same fiscal year, i.e. 1975.

Negotiations for the Fifth Replenishment began in November 1975. Almost a year later, McNamara reported that 'progress was painfully slow' (Manila Speech: 33). In Nairobi negotiations had been held on the eve of the annual meeting, but no such tactics were possible this time.

Progress was slow after Manila: the American presidential elections prevented some issues from being solved. Not until March 16, 1977, after a meeting of the Deputies in Vienna, could agreement be reached on $7.6 billion for the three years 1978-80. Of this total $51.66 million was 'unallocated'. The agreement could not become effective in time, i.e. before July 1, 1977, but most contributors expressed their willingness to provide commitment authority to IDA by making funds available in advance of the Fifth Replenishment, on condition that (a) there be a collective undertaking to do so, involving the participation of most donors, and (b) the 'bridging' arrangement would become operative only after governments had given IDA formal notification that contributions equivalent to $1.2 billion had been made (*Annual Report* 1977: 6). In effect, about $1.3 billion was made available.

The Fifth Replenishment became effective in November 1977, when the USA notified IDA that it would pay the first instalment of $800 million of its commitment (*Annual Report* 1978: 11-12). Negotiations had taken place under unusually difficult circumstances, in view of the recession in nearly all developed countries (Vibert 1977), compounded by the fact that some members made use of the different payment options allowed under the Fourth Replenishment. The USA, Canada and Finland chose to pay in four equal instalments while the USA also took up the option of a one-year delay. France postponed payment of its second instalment ('Method of Payment' IDA/RLP/ 76-4, January 1976: 3).

For the Fifth Replenishment it has been agreed that members should be allowed one of the two payment options but not both, although it is hoped that they will not avail themselves of either (IDA: 'Additions to Resources; Fifth Replenishment', March 30, 1977: 8).

The American administration, in particular, has had to face the problem of asking large appropriations with which to clear the backlog, making the fight for Congressional approval of the Fifth Replenishment very difficult indeed. During the negotiations, the USA made a conditional rather than an unconditional pledge, as had been practice on previous occasions. The other countries were then forced to defend themselves, in effect, to avoid being left out on a limb. Thus, even though Congress authorized the full contribution in November 1977, other countries stipulated that their yearly instalments be triggered by actual US payment of each portion of its pledge. With Congressional approval of the second instalment being given in October 1978, on the last day of the session, the second instalment of the Fifth IDA became available for the fiscal year starting July 1, 1978!

The Fifth Replenishment agreement, like the Fourth, allows for payment in national currencies without the maintenance of value obligation.

Replenishments of IDA funds are thus fraught with many problems. Despite its initial resistance, the USA had promoted and sponsored the IDA in the late 1950s, yet it has since been the greatest obstacle to IDA's smooth functioning, being late five out of five times in ratifying replenishments. The constant haggling has occurred under both Democratic and Republican presidents, and is thus apparently not directly related to the composition of the Administration in power. The average US Congress Member is simply inimical to foreign aid.

The IDA also receives funds from sources other than through the replenishments. Some countries have at times made special supplementary contributions, notably Denmark, Norway, Finland, New Zealand and Sweden under the Second Replenishment − $71.4 million. Some Part II members made voluntary contributions to the Third Replenishment: Ireland, Spain, Yugoslavia − $10.5 million, and $19.3 million by Israel, Spain and Yugoslavia to the Fourth. Switzerland, a non-member has made 50-year interest-free loans amounting to $12.1 million to the Second Replenishment and $31.8 million to the Third. In June 1976, however, a referendum defeated a government proposal to provide a loan of Swfr. 200 million ($66 million) which was to have been the Swiss contribution to the Fourth IDA (*International Development Association* 1977: 28). Since then, Australia, Ireland, Kuwait, the Netherlands, Norway and the UK have made additional contributions totalling $45.5 million (*Annual Report* 1978: 12).

In the agreement for the Fifth Replenishment several countries promised to contribute for the first time: Korea $1 million, Saudi Arabia $250 million and the United Arab Emirates $51 million. The UAE is not yet a member of IDA, but has stated that it is considering whether to apply for membership (IDA 1977: 29 n. 4). The contribution of OPEC countries to IDA has fallen substantially short of the anticipated $1.5 billion, apparently because they do not feel that they should compensate for the delinquency of Part I countries in meeting their commitments on Official Development Assistance overall. Kuwait, a Part I country, increased its contribution substantially, from $27 million to the Fourth to $180 million to the Fifth Replenishment. In 1978 Saudi Arabia provided an extra contribution of $100 million (*Annual Report* 1978: 12).

Other Part II countries contributing to the Fifth Replenishment are Spain $21 million, and Yugoslavia $8.1 million.

Of much greater quantitative importance has been the transfer of World Bank net profits: a cumulative total of $1.2 billion between 1964 and 1977 (*Annual Report* 1978: 150). Transfers to IDA represent almost half the Bank's total net earnings since 1964 (*International Development Association* 1978: 28).

Since the early 1960s it had been considered anomalous that the Bank should accumulate profits while at the same time seeking funds for IDA from member governments. Eugene Black had opposed the transfer of Bank surplus to IDA because of a personal commitment made to the financial community when IDA was formed that there would be no financial connection between the Bank and IDA (Mason & Asher 1973: 407). George Woods believed that the Bank could easily survive any adverse repercussions that transfers might cause. Since 1964, IDA's resources have accordingly been increased by a portion of IBRD's net annual income. With two exceptions: in 1964 when the amount was $50 million and in 1967 when it dropped to a token $10 million, the transfers were initially in the amount of $75 to $100 million and have been $100 to $110 million since the early 1970s.

Two points should be made regarding the practice of transferring Bank profits to IDA. In recent years, Bank profits have been far too low to avoid a rapid worsening debt-equity ratio as a result of inflation. But larger profits, also with a view to transferring large amounts to IDA, are objected to by Latin American countries who, under current eligibility criteria, receive only very limited amounts of IDA funds (see Table 3.2); on the other hand, they receive large amounts of Bank loans. As they see it, an increase of Bank profits would require increases in Bank interest rates that would be higher than otherwise necessary. This would mean that they would in fact pay an interest subsidy to an agency from which they derive almost no direct benefit and of which some of them are not members.

The nominal amounts of the IDA replenishments have increased considerably, but increases in real terms have been more modest. As a result of high inflation in the 1970s, the value of the Fourth Replenishment, $1500 million per year, is not significantly larger than that of the Third, $800 million per year. And the real value of the Fifth IDA may be no higher than that of the Fourth.[5]

PROSPECTS FOR ODA AND IDA FINANCING

The motives and the rationale for giving aid may be quite contradictory, not only within countries, but also between countries and over time. The net outcome in terms of trends in the volume of official development assistance (ODA) reflects the combined support base of alternative motives for giving aid.[6] The relative ability of IDA to secure its funds appears to have weakened over time. Firstly, because of ODA's downward trend as percentage of GNP; secondly, because of divergence in the distribution of ODA between bilateral or multilateral channels; and thirdly, because of the increase of multilateral channels. Since the early 1960s, OECD's Development Assistance Committee has urged several targets for development assistance by its member countries, encouraging them to devote one percent of their GNP to net total flows, official and private, to developing countries. This target has been accepted by all members, but in 1973 had been reached by only six countries: Belgium, France, the Netherlands, the UK, Canada and Sweden (*Development Cooperation* 1975: 129). Prior to this target, accepted in 1968 following UNCTAD recommendations in March of that year, the goal of one percent for net flows had been related not to GNP but to national income. The linkage with GNP represented an average increase of 25 percent over the original target (*Development Cooperation* 1968).

A second aid target, more relevant for IDA funding and also pushed by the DAC, concerns the ODA share in the net total flow of resources to developing countries. DAC members were to devote 0.7% of GNP to official development assistance. This target has *not* been accepted by Austria, Italy, Switzerland and the USA. Only four countries: Belgium, the Netherlands, Norway and Sweden, accepted it without reservation. Four others: Australia, Denmark, France and New Zealand, accepted it with a target date *after* 1975; and the remaining countries: Canada, Finland, Germany, Japan and the UK, *without* a target date (*Development Cooperation* 1975: 129).

Sweden was the first and only country to reach the ODA target in 1974 (0.72% of GNP), being joined by the Netherlands in 1975 (0.75%, against Sweden 0.82%) (McNamara, Manila Address 1976: 40).

While the actual trend in net total flows has shown a slow but steady increase, the trend of ODA from DAC members has declined since the mid-1960s if both flows are measured as percentage of GNP. In recent years, the OPEC countries have emerged as major donors, their contributions comparing quite favourably with those of DAC members (see Table 3.3).

Private flows, which are largely beyond direct government influence, have apparently grown much faster than government-controlled public flows of official development assistance. There is considerable variation between countries, however, in trends of total flow and of ODA performance. Australia and New Zealand have channelled most of their flows in the form of ODA, as have

Table 3.3 *DAC members' net flow as percentage of GNP*

	1964-66	1970	1973	1974	1975	1976	Target
Total flows							
− DAC	0.75	0.77	0.79	0.81	1.05	0.97	1.0
− OPEC	–	–	1.88	3.47	4.01	3.28	–
ODA from							
− DAC	0.44	0.34	0.30	0.33	0.35	0.33	0.7
− OPEC	–	–	1.41	2.01	2.70	2.14	–
ODA as % of total flows							
DAC	59	44	38	41	33	34	70

Source: *Development Cooperation* 1975: 131; 1976: 206; 1977: 84, 85, 164.

the Scandinavian countries. On the other hand, Austria and Switzerland have provided very little ODA. Major donors like the UK, USA, Canada, France, Germany and Japan *all* reduced their share of ODA in total flows between the mid-1960s and the first half of the 1970s.

The World Bank's projections of the likely availability of ODA from DAC members up to 1980 show only modest growth when measured in constant prices (see Table 3.4). ODA will thus remain extremely scarce in the foreseeable future. Apparently the various motives for giving aid, however impeccable they may seem to some, are not strong enough to produce sustained growth of ODA commitments up to the long expressed targets.

Table 3.4 *ODA flows from DAC members*

	1960	1965	1970	1975	1976	1977	1978	1979	1980	1985
ODA ($ bln)	4.6	5.9	6.8	13.6	13.7	14.8	18.0	20.3	23.0	41.8
deflator	0.38	0.42	0.47	0.90	0.92	1.00	1.14	1.23	1.32	1.85
as % of GNP	0.52	0.44	0.34	0.36	0.33	0.31	0.33	0.33	0.33	0.35

Source: McNamara, *Annual Address* 1978.

Bilateral ODA versus multilateral ODA and IDA

ODA flows are bilateral or multilateral, according to the individual choice of the different countries. Large countries like the USA can afford a large bilateral aid programme to further their policy aims. Similarly, former colonial powers like France and the UK have traditional interests with their former colonies which lead to bilateral relationships. Small donors without such traditional ties may have greater difficulty in deciding which countries to support. The cost of maintaining bilateral aid programmes may be a factor in their preference for multilateral ODA channels, quite apart from ideological considerations. The Pearson Commission recommended that donors devote a minimum of 20% of ODA to multilateral development aid by 1975. The DAC average for 1972-74 has moved ahead of the Pearson target, reaching 25 percent. The large countries, however, were at the lower end of the scale. France, in particular, allocated only 14% of its ODA to multilateral ODA. The USA and Japan were also below the DAC average. OPEC countries show a strong preference for bilateral ODA and for multilateral regional channels. In terms of geographical distribution most OPEC aid goes to Arab and other Muslim countries (*Development Cooperation* 1975: ch. IX; 1977: 88 ff).

Even after the basic choice has been made between bilateral and multilateral ODA, donors must further choose which channels to support for multilateral ODA.

Major multilateral aid channels are (a) the UN agencies, (b) the EEC, mostly the European Development Fund (FED) and the European Investment Bank (EIB), and (c) the global and regional development banks. The latter include the capital subscription of IBRD, IDA, and the Asian (founded in 1966), African (1964), and Inter-American (1960) Development Banks. (For a comparative analysis of the three banks see White [1970]). Not all countries are members of all agencies, and the choice of which to support is largely a matter of which agency best fits the foreign policy objectives, broadly defined, of the donors. For instance, the EEC comprises only nine of the 17 DAC members (Luxemburg is a member of EEC but not of DAC). Similarly, until recently, and with the exception of the USA and Canada, DAC countries did not belong to the Inter-American Development Bank, although Germany, Norway, Sweden, the UK and the Vatican had established Special Trust Funds under IADB administration (IADB *Annual Report* 1975). Between 1973 and 1976 negotiations led to the Declaration of Madrid, confirming the intention of twelve non-regional members to join IADB (*Internationale Samenwerking*, 10, 2 [1977]: 55-59). All DAC countries are members of the Asian Development Bank, but the USA only very recently joined the African Development Bank; this was in line with the division of spheres of influence recommended by the Clay Report in 1963.

The World Bank, the three main regional banks and the EEC by and large compete with each other for ODA. All three regional banks have recognized the limitations of bank lending on commercial terms and have endeavoured to establish facilities for making grants and grant-like loans. This tends to make them more dependent on DAC member countries which supply most of such aid. True, the conditions leading-up to the establishment of the regional banks were different in each case and different expectations may have been nurtured about the capability of the institutions to better serve the needs of the regions concerned (see White 1970). But to the extent that all three Banks require a 'soft term window' they are directly dependent upon the donors. Neither of them can have much scope in this respect unless it ensures the financial assistance of all or several of the four large donors. The USA, France,

Germany and Japan together supplied almost 70% of total ODA by DAC member countries in 1973-74 (*Development Cooperation* 1975: 130).

In contrast, IDA has a wider membership and thus, in principle, has to serve the needs of a global community of countries. In practice, however, as Table 3.2 shows, IDA is insignificant in Latin America. In all, some 28 developing countries do not qualify for IDA credits because they are not sufficiently poor.

A suitable rationale for a global institution like IDA would be for it to succeed in correcting the inequities which result from adding the various bilateral aid programmes. It is a well-established fact that high aid receipts, whether measured by commitments, gross disbursements, net disbursements or net transfers, are associated not with need in any developmental sense, but with the donors' pursuit of commercial or strategic interests, and with a special relationship between donors and recipients, notably that of colonial dependency.[7] The 'small country effect', which gives countries with small populations higher per capita receipts than countries with large populations, is also well-established.

The Pearson Report recommended 'that IDA formulate explicit principles and criteria for the allocation of concessional development finance and seek in its policies to offset the larger inequities in aid distribution' (Pearson 1969: 227). The Pearson Commissioners apparently believed that IDA was at liberty to devise a correcting mechanism, but this has not been the case. In the words of J. Burke Knapp, Senior Vice-President of the Bank and IDA: 'IDA was to correct the mistakes and misallocations of various aid agencies. The trouble with this suggestion is that precisely these donors are also providing the lion's share of IDA funds, and they would not take it very kindly if IDA wanted to correct the pattern of aid which is given by them bilaterally.'[8]

However, if the IDA allocation pattern cannot differ notably from that of the sum of bilateral aid flows of major donors, it is in a weak competitive position vis-à-vis other multilateral aid agencies which increase in number and diversity. In recent years, for instance, a UN Environmental Agency has been established in Nairobi; a Population Fund (UNFPA) and an International Fund for Agricultural Development have been called for; a UN Capital Development Fund was established in 1966 and revitalized in 1974; a UN Revolving Fund for Natural Resources Exploration has been set up, and also an Information and Research Centre for Transnational Corporations. The 'capital'-oriented agencies, in particular, may require considerable amounts of money compared to the primarily 'technical assistance'-oriented programmes.

Some of these funds have been motivated and established partly by a desire to attract more resources by emphasizing activities in sectors which have recently come to acquire priority at the international level, and partly in order to mobilize a portion of the surplus resources of OPEC countries within institutional frameworks which they may find more acceptable as a basis for extending their cooperation. Beyond these, the initiatives taken by major industrialized countries towards establishing new institutions, represent an attempt to project their own scheme of priorities on the international scene and to avoid that obligations on substantive issues impinge on their domestic policies. One of their objectives is said by Dubey to be to 'weaken the existing UN organizations which, according to them, are suffering from the tyranny of the majority' (Dubey 1977: 89).

In this climate of proliferation of new institutions, whose desirability, provided they are each narrowly focused in terms of the range of their activities, and are made more clearly accountable for them, has been argued forcefully by White (1976b), the IDA has to compete for its sources of finance.

Principles of burden sharing

Once each country has decided on the volume of its aid, its distribution between bilateral and multilateral channels and, within the latter, for IDA versus other multilateral channels, negotiations can begin about burden-sharing arrangements among donors in the IDA replenishment. In principle, two approaches can be followed. On the one hand, individual donors may decide how much they are willing to contribute under a system of voluntary contributions. On the other hand, it may be felt that distribution keys should be developed so that each donor, measured by some standard, does 'its fair share', and whereby donor interaction over standards becomes an instrument with which to influence the outcome of the negotiations.

Reliance on voluntary contributions has certain disadvantages. If certain countries should feel that they are making good the reduced contributions of others, their willingness to be generous again next time may lessen. Contributions may then cumulatively shrink, which seems undesirable as long as the purpose of the effort is worthwhile. UNDP, for instance, which relies on voluntary contributions, was financed in 1977 by $9.50 per Danish citizen, $0.47 per US citizen and $0.02 per Soviet citizen (Andersen, in a commentary on Dubey 1977: 99). It is questionable whether such inequity can long be sustained.

Due to their relative stability, percentage shares of contributions under earlier replenishments were considered as 'just'. Any significant change in the relative contributions of particular member states could lead to pressure for a comprehensive renegotiation of the relative shares of all countries, or might affect the overall size of the replenishment. This possibility, in fact, jeopardized the negotiations for the Fourth Replenishment, and has been a major problem ever since.

One argument in favour of a reconsideration of distribution criteria may be that the relative strength of nations has changed over time, and that distribution keys that reflected the situation when they were initially agreed upon are no longer relevant. During negotiations for the Fifth Replenishment it was decided that a general discussion on the matter should be held prior to the negotiations for the next Replenishment.

This discussion should be seen against the 1979 US Foreign Aid bill which stated that it was the 'sense of the Congress' that American shares of future contributions should not exceed 25% for IDA, implying a further reduction, and revealing a strategy to maintain American veto power at the cheapest possible price.

A number of possible burden-sharing criteria may be put forward. It will be recalled that initial IDA subscriptions were determined in line with participations in the share capital of the Bank. Over time, proportions in the Bank's share capital have changed following periodic revisions of IMF quotas; in particular, the British share in the total for Part I IDA countries declined from 17.2% to 14.6%, and the American share from 42% to 37% between 1960 and 1969.

Apart from historical precedent, always important if any other rationale is impossible to maintain, it could be argued that no strong reasons exist for equity in the shares between IDA and the Bank. Bank shares are linked to the IMF quota. These quota, based on IMF's role in assisting countries to correct *short-run* balance-of-payments disequilibria, gave less weight to national income and more weight to foreign trade, to the relation between exports and national income, and to fluctuations in exports. IDA, however, gives long-term development assistance, and other criteria and weights would be more appropriate. The distribution of Special Drawing Rights, however, is also linked to a country's quota in the IMF (Gold 1970; Habermeier 1973; Haan 1969). An indirect link between IDA and IMF quota thus ties up with the assistance that a country may expect in the event of temporary balance-of-payments problems. The larger that support, the lesser the need to make development aid an instrument of balance-of-payments policy.

Another burden-sharing criterion may be that countries see their contribution in the light of the distribution of IDA funds to countries which are important to their own 'vital interests'. In hearings before Congress for the Third Replenishment, for instance, the argument was voiced that the US share in IDA should be reduced because IDA credits went largely to South Asia and Africa and not to Latin America where the USA has considered itself to play a special role since the unilaterally declared Monroe Doctrine in 1823. Similarly, France and the UK could argue that IDA should do more in their former colonies. Contributions to IDA are then in fact directly linked to IDA lending policies, in particular its allocation over countries.

Members of the US Congress sometimes also argue that development aid should be seen in relation to total foreign assistance. This would reopen the discussion of alternative aid channels and their relative merits and demerits, and would be difficult to tackle as long as ultimate benefits are considered more significant than a particular aid channel. At times, however, total aid includes military assistance, and the opinion held by some is that as the USA makes the greatest contribution to the defence of the so-called 'free world', Western Europe, in compensation, ought to contribute more to the burden of economic aid. A significant share of American military expenditure, whether domestic or foreign, however, does *not* serve the interests of other contributors to IDA and it is unlikely that this argument will gain wide acceptance.

A number of possible indicators of burden sharing are shown in Table 3.5.

If individual shares in total GNP of Part I IDA countries are taken together with per capita income as indicating the capacity to pay, the contribution of the USA appears to be far too small, even when allowance is made for its declining share of total GDP since 1961. Shares of 40% in the Third IDA and 34% in the Fourth and Fifth are still large, of course, as compared to contributions of other countries, and the USA has at times argued that its share should be reduced because it might be embarrassing to be such a dominant partner. At best, a reasoning that seems to reflect selective embarrassment!

Shultz has argued (1973: 1-2) that the shares renegotiated for the Fourth IDA reflect 'equitably the relative economic strengths of industrial nations', but this conflicts with reality. Japan did too little in the Third, but is at par with respect to its contribution to the Fourth if allowance is made for its below average per capita income. Britain's economic power is clearly on the decline and it could justifiably argue for a much greater reduction of its share in IDA than that negotiated for the Fourth Replenishment. At present, Britain pays about twice its share on the basis of GNP. Canada, the Scandinavian countries and the Benelux are the main advocates of IDA and are prepared to do more than their share. Together they provided 17.7% to the Third IDA and 18% to the Fourth, and are thus minor but significant contributors. France should increase rather than decrease its share. France does quite a lot overall, but is not favourably disposed towards IDA, preferring bilateral aid and the FED among multilateral channels. It also feels that IDA is too strongly dominated by the USA. Just as France prefers the FED, Japan prefers the Asian Development Bank.

As could be expected, the figures indicate that the net balance-of-payments effect of IDA is insignificant. An average net deficit for all Part I countries together of about $20 million per year is truly negligible.

If shares in IBRD capital subscriptions are taken as a distribution key for burden sharing — a view currently argued by Japan — in that relative voting power should broadly correspond to total contributions, the USA, the UK and and France are not doing enough. Germany, Japan and traditional IDA supporters have contributed disproportionately large amounts to the Fourth IDA replenishment.

Germany and Britain are relatively large beneficiaries in terms of procure-

Table 3.5 *Indicators for burden sharing*

	GDP 1961 (a)	GDP 1972 (a)	GNP 1973 (b)	GDP/N 1961 (a)	GDP/N 1972 (a)	GDP/N 1973 (b)	Net Bal. of Payment effect 1960-72 $ mln. (c)	IBRD Capital shares 1960 (d)	IBRD Capital shares 1969 (d)	Procurement shares 1967-71 (e)	Total trade with LDCs 1970 (f)	IDA Replenishment 3rd	IDA Replenishment 4th	IDA Replenishment 5th
US	54.2	45.9	43.1	199	157	145	−262	42.0	37.0	20.3	29.3	40.0	34.0	33.0
UK	7.9	6.0	5.7	100	77	72	+122	17.2	14.6	24.3	12.0	13.0	11.3	11.1
Germany	8.5	10.0	10.9	103	116	125	− 7	6.9	7.7	18.3	10.4	9.7	11.7	11.5
France	6.9	7.6	7.8	100	105	106	− 6	6.9	7.2	7.6	9.1	6.2	5.7	5.7
Japan	5.5	11.5	13.0	39	77	85	+148	4.4	5.7	9.7	15.8	6.0	11.2	10.8
Canada	4.1	4.1	4.0	152	135	128	−118	5.0	5.3	4.1	2.7	6.2	6.2	6.1
Scandinavia*	3.3	3.6	3.7	111	117	118	−118	3.9	5.0	3.4	3.5	6.9	7.0	6.9
Italy	4.0	4.6	4.4	53	60	57	− 3	2.4	4.8	5.3	6.2	4.0	4.1	4.0
Benelux	2.6	3.2	3.5	82	99	104	− 16	6.7	6.5	3.7	7.6	4.6	4.8	4.7
Other**	3.0	3.5	4.0	60	55	61	− 25	4.6	6.4	3.3	4.3	3.4	4.0	5.5
Total	100	100	100	100	100	100	−285	100	100	100	100	100	100	100

* Norway, Sweden, Denmark, Finland, Iceland.
** Australia, Austria, Kuwait, South Africa.

Notes:
(a) *National Accounts of OECD Countries 1961-1972* (OECD, Paris 1973): 10-11; UN *Yearbook of National Accounts Statistics* (1974), Vol. III.
(b) 1975 *World Bank Atlas*.
(c) Amount of 4th Replenishment (IDA/RPL/72-2, November 20, 1972, Table 7). The net balance of payments effect is the difference between IDA receipts of subscriptions and contributions, and payments for procurement of goods and administrative expenses.
(d) *Annual Reports*.
(e) IBRD, Programming and Budgeting Dept., 6/29/72.
(f) IMF: *Direction of Trade* (1970).

ment shares out of IDA credits. The small countries, mostly without former colonial empires, have received too few contracts. *Projected* rather than *past* export orders, however, should count in future negotiations. The competitive advantage of Germany vis-à-vis the USA may have diminished following the devaluation of the dollar against the mark. Japan's competitive position on that account should also have deteriorated somewhat, but Japan did not enjoy an extraordinarily large procurement share. The falling value of the pound should make the UK even more competitive despite its already large procurement share. The use of such shares as an indicator thus leads to considerable complications in terms of contributions of major donors.

If total trade with LDCs were used as an indicator, the USA would seem to be doing rather more than its share, but France, Italy, Japan and the Benelux are not doing enough. Canada and the Scandinavian countries, on the other hand, far exceed their share.

Use of these indicators should be selective because they do not all lead to the same conclusions. From IDA's viewpoint, any indicator should lead to an acceptable distribution of contributions between countries, while the level of any replenishment should be maximized. No such composite indicator has been adopted, however, and the announced discussion about burden sharing in general is not necessarily a useful activity in that it may harden conflicting positions.

The various indicators are perhaps more useful in the framework of bilateral consultations about IDA replenishments, but even then the use of the various keys should not be pushed too far.

From the point of view of negotiating IDA replenishments, the trick is to maximize total contributions by a selective use of distribution keys. This is done by inducing favourably disposed countries such as Canada, Sweden and the Netherlands to propose high contributions in absolute amounts, adding the essential clause, 'provided that this amount corresponds to the desired share in the total of the replenishment'.

Multilateral aid and donor control

From the late 1960s onwards, the USA attempted to direct more of its aid to multilateral channels in order to 'depoliticize' it, extract it from the 'polluting' influence of narrow national economic interest groups, and restore some of its humanitarian purity. Advocates of this new line included the Perkins Commission (1968), the National Planning Association (1969), the Committee for Economic Development (1969), Huntington (1970), Brown (1972) and Reid (1973). The Peterson Commission Report, for example, advised that:

The US should redesign its policies so that ... the international lending institutions become the major channel for development assistance and US bilateral assistance is provided largely within a framework set by the international organizations (Peterson 1970:2).

President Nixon followed up on this recommendation (Nixon 1970).

The new emphasis fell primarily on the multilateral development banks: from four percent of total US foreign assistance in 1962 to 23 percent in 1973. Total multilateral foreign assistance from the USA increased from eight to 28 percent during the same period. In terms of dollars, the trend has been to reduce the amounts appropriated for bilateral aid while increasing annual appropriations for multilateral foreign assistance (Library of Congress 1974: 127). The Executive Branch and Congress, however, showed considerable resistance to the idea of channelling more funds through international institutions, not only for reasons of 'control' but because it was felt that the US government had acquired unique expertise in the matter and should use it (US State Department 1976: 30). This resistance is likely to increase in future.

Some proponents of a change in the aid allocation programme believe that multilateral aid administration could bring greater impartiality. In Asher's words:

International agencies can decide not to provide aid for ... certain purposes or unless certain eligibility requirements are met – and those decisions may be the product of bitter political infighting. Once they decide the terms ..., however, international agencies cannot afford to discriminate among members on political, ideological, or military grounds (Asher 1970: 131).

Other observers emphasize the degree of manoeuvring which occurs during the formation and initial policy formulation stage within the organizations, and note that truly non-political activity in this critical development area is impossible, even for the most careful institutions.

For instance, White writes:

Most multilateral agencies ... claim that their operations have the 'advantage' of being free of political considerations. If all that is meant is that institutions do not have foreign policies in quite the same way as national governments, then it is a truism. If anything more is meant, then it is false. Quite apart from the patent absurdity of characterizing the UN system as a non-political system, it is reasonable to ask what kind of frame of reference it is, and whether it is an 'advantageous' one, that can exclude the political content of choices in development policy (White 1970: 15).

With regard to the choice of a specific multilateral channel, we have already seen that IDA was originated in response to the proposal to establish SUNFED under the UN General Assembly in New York.

With the relative growth of aid being channelled through multilateral agencies, notably the Banks, political interest in them has also increased, simply because they have become too big to be ignored. It was the relative unimportance of multilateral aid channels in the 1960s which allowed the banks latitude in their operations and enhanced their supranational aspirations.

Some of the ways in which governments have shown stronger interest are concerned with procedural matters which would facilitate a closer scrutiny of activities by member governments generally. Others relate to substantive policy positions, for instance, as regards the voting behaviour of the American EDs in the multilateral banks when expropriation of foreign properties is under discussion.

Legislation authorizing US contributions to IDA, the IADB and ADB (PL92-245/246/247, March 10, 1972) includes a statutory requirement, known as the 'Gonzalez amendment', that American Executive Directors should vote against any loans or other utilization of funds for the benefit of any country which has:

(1) nationalized or expropriated or seized ownership or property; or
(2) taken steps to repudiate or nullify contracts or agreements; or
(3) imposed or enforced discriminatory taxes or other exactions, or restrictive maintenance or operational conditions against any US citizen or any corporation, partnership, or association not less than 50 percent of which is beneficially owned by US citizens.

The Gonzalez amendment thus extends to the multilateral sphere what the Hickenlooper amendment to the Foreign Assistant Act of 1962, expanded in 1963, had laid down for bilateral aid.

The Hickenlooper amendment was deleted from the 1973 bilateral aid bill, in which a substituted 'waiver' provision gave the President greater flexibility than mandatory sanctions could give. This new waiver provision created a bizarre inconsistency in that it made multilateral policy *legally more stringent than bilateral policy*. Proponents of bilateral revision preferred similar multilateral laws but were unable to re-establish consistency. The 1974 IDA bill encountered such deep trouble that no one who supported its general concept dared to burden it with controversial modifications (see Lipson 1976: 415).

It is not without interest that the shift in World Bank policy towards the poor, introduced in September 1973, followed closely on the changed focus of the 1973 US Foreign Assistance Act. This set the stage for the third phase of American aid policy in focusing on 'the poor majorities'. In the 1950s foreign aid had been justified primarily as a national security measure, needed to strengthen allies and to build up low-income countries so that they would be less vulnerable to communist invasion or take-over. In the 1960s – the second phase – the trend was more towards strengthening a number of countries against internal subversion, but there was also a trend towards development as a goal in itself (US State Department 1976: 27).

Some governments are attempting to force greater accountability upon the Bank Group and other multilateral agencies, and to reinforce guidelines and instructions for policy. The establishment of an Operations Evaluation Department in the World Bank owes much to US pressure in trying to implement the Selden Amendment (1967 and 1973), exerted through the National Advisory Council on International Monetary Affairs (Library of Congress 1974), and the General Accounting Office (GAO 1973).

Under President Carter, efforts are being made to introduce 'human rights' considerations into the operations of multilateral institutions. In the language of the 1979 US Foreign Aid Bill, the President should propose and seek adoption of an amendment to the Articles of Agreement of IBRD to establish human rights standards to be considered in connection with each application for assistance.

Regardless of what one thinks of the validity of the argument, it is clear that attempts by one country to expand the range of concerns, may invite other countries to follow through in suggesting issues that are of concern to them. A situation will then quickly develop in which the Bank is so constrained that it can no longer function effectively. On the other hand, if such moves stem from deep-felt concern in the political constituency that supports aid allocations, neglect to take them into account may further erode support for future budget allocations.

LENDING POLICIES: DISTRIBUTION BY COUNTRIES

IDA funds are offered on very concessionary terms and are therefore more valuable than IBRD loans to recipient countries. Due to the scarcity of IDA funds, the Bank has become very deeply involved in the problem of IDA allocations.

IDA wanted to set its money to work quickly, and countries which joined the organization betimes had a head start. This partly explains why IDA commitments were initially concentrated in South Asia and Latin America, and why relatively few credits were given to Africa, which was in the midst of political colonization.

IDA funds are allocated on the following criteria: poverty, measured by income per head of population; limited creditworthiness for conventional loans; 'economic performance'; and the availability of well-prepared projects. Only the lack of creditworthiness for conventional loans is mentioned in IDA Articles of Agreement (V, 1[c]). On this ground, IDA lending is now excluded to Indonesia (except for an amount in 1978) and Nigeria, two major oil exporting countries which, though poor, are judged creditworthy for Bank loans.

In 1968 it was decided that an income per head of $300 was to be the point above which there would be a 'strong presumption against' IDA credits. A new method of calculation — GNP at market prices as against factor cost, and currency conversion factors extending over longer periods — made this figure equivalent to $408 in 1973. A new upper limit of $375 was then decided upon, but it did not exclude any country that had previously qualified for IDA (see the 1972 *World Bank Atlas* for a description of the new calculation procedure). This limit was increased to $520 per capita in 1975 dollars.

In 1968 another specific policy decision was taken regarding the rationing of IDA to larger developing countries: India 40%, Indonesia 11% but only between 1969-74, Bangladesh 6% and Pakistan 5%, together were to receive 62% of IDA funds, corresponding roughly to what they would receive on the basis of equal amounts per head of population. That realizations do not quite match these allocations is due to incidental factors mentioned in Chapter II (p. 52).

Lending to countries in Africa, particularly Sub-Sahara Africa, has expanded rapidly since they become independent. In 1963 there were only three IDA recipients in East and West Africa. This increased to 18 in 1964-68 and to 31 in 1969-73 and 26 in 1975-78 (*Annual Reports*).

In terms of allocation per head of population, IDA shows a 'small country bias', though not as severe as in most bilateral aid programmes. If the 47 countries with per capita incomes of less than $250 which received IDA in the period 1969-74, are classified by population size, one finds that twelve countries with less than five million inhabitants each received $7.7 per capita, against $6.9 for the seven countries with populations between 5-10 million, and $4.3 for the eight countries between 10-20 million inhabitants. In comparison, India received $3.6, Pakistan $5.5 and Indonesia $4.9 per capita in that period (*Annual Reports*).

The preference for small countries, particularly those in Africa, can only be understood in terms of the changing political interests of major donors. The allocation reflects, *inter alia*, the USA's decreasing interest in neutralist India after the late 1950s, and the gradual 'erosion of the relationship' (Lipton & Firn 1976) between the UK and the Indian sub-continent, whose population was more than 13 times that of Britain. On the other hand, many former colonies of France and Britain in Africa have considerable amounts of raw materials that are of value to donors. Most of these countries qualify for IDA on the poverty criterion, the use of which virtually excludes Latin America, where most countries have higher average per capita incomes. Small country politics in the UN leads to support for special measures for certain groups of countries such as the 'land-locked' and the 'least-developed', groupings which are defined in such a way as to exclude the large, populous and poor countries.

In actual fact, a redistribution of funds over the larger developing countries would mean little to the latter and would deprive the smaller countries of a substantial part of their capital inflow. For instance, if per capita amounts for countries with less than five million inhabitants were to be reduced to the IDA average of $0.80 in 1972-74, the resources that would thus be freed would add an average of six cents per head to allocations to countries with more than 20 million inhabitants ('IDA Lending Policies' 1973: 13).

As a worldwide institution, IDA has to spread its activities over as many of its clients as possible. The proliferation of nation states, a good many of whom are eligible for IDA credits, entails that funds have to be spread more thinly. This obviously reduces the impact on each country but at the same time, consolidates the pattern of geographical allocation. It is inconceivable that IDA could base its activities on criteria that excluded any large group of countries (see further Chapter V). If this were ever to be the case, IDA would lose the political support of those countries and would also cease to be 'world-wide'.

The 'economic performance' criterion is also a complicated factor: 'Despite difficulties in judging "performance", borrowing from IDA necessitates a more thorough investigation of "performance" than borrowing from the Bank' (Mason & Asher 1973: 404 n. 41, and 420-56). Poor countries have to 'deserve' IDA assistance. Moreover, IDA does not lend to countries which are debarred from receiving Bank loans due to poor international financial behaviour, particularly default on debt and compensation claims ('IDA Lending Policy' 1963: 4). In this respect, too, IDA is twin to the IBRD. An early authoritative pronouncement on economic performance as a test of eligibility was made by Eugene Black at the 1961 Annual Meeting: 'A necessary condition in all cases is evidence that the borrowing government is making a real effort to mobilize its own resources and to gear its financial policies to development.'[9]

The development indicators which are usually taken into account and are analyzed in country economic reports are: various rates of growth of national product, or incomes per head of population; rates of growth of factors of production, especially domestic and government savings; and balance-of-payments prospects. In line with the Bank's new concern about income distribution trends, increasing attention is now given to policy measures that affect the poor, although in the absence of hard facts, very impressionistic evidence is sometimes used.

How should changes in growth indicators be judged? If there has been a good harvest or export prices have risen, most growth indicators look quite 'good'. But by what standards should they be judged? What is the welfare function: growth, distributional objectives, any trade-offs between the two, and any other element: balance-of-payments equilibrium, price stability, employment growth? Should *results* or *effort* of economic management be evaluated, and how can the two be separated? How does one arrive at common standards on which to judge inter-country comparisons? How does one allow for differences in managerial capacity between countries, differences that may themselves be related to the level of development, particularly of human resources?

The issue of limited creditworthiness has already been dealt with, and we need now only point out the apparent paradox of the twin tests of performance and creditworthiness.

On the one hand, a country that does well on the economic front rates high on the performance scale, to the point of being penalized by having to graduate to hard Bank loans. Good performance is frequently equated with 'good' economic management and contributes to creditworthiness. On the other hand, a country that does poorly qualifies for IDA on lack of creditworthiness grounds, and is rewarded with soft IDA credits rather than hard Bank loans. A country with a surplus on its external accounts may have achieved this by resisting short and medium-term borrowing; it then has low debt service ratios and builds up its creditworthiness, e.g. for Bank loans. A country which has borrowed at short-maturity has poorer creditworthiness prospects and *thus* receives IDA credits. The former country is therefore penalized for its prudent financial management, even though that may have been at the cost of development.

BANK GROUP LENDING POLICY: DISTRIBUTION BY SECTOR

Tables 3.6 and 3.7 show the sectoral distribution of Bank Group lending, and of Bank and IDA lending separately. Despite difficulties involved in the classification, it is clear that since the early 1960s the Bank Group has lent over a much wider range of activities. Loans and credits tend increasingly to incorporate subcomponents from other sectors. Other agencies may co-finance parts of more comprehensive development schemes, together covering a series of related activities which extend beyond even broadly defined sectoral classifications. For instance, a good deal of recent lending for 'agriculture' is in fact for 'agro-industry' and not for new programmes of rural development or farmers' projects (US Library of Congress 1974: 47). Lending for agriculture and education began under Woods and has been aggressively pursued by McNamara. Loans for population and nutrition projects, for urbanization and tourism, are recent undertakings. New dimensions have thus been added to the World Bank's activities over time, which have changed both the character and the image of the Bank Group.

This diversification was started by the creation of IDA.

At the same time that the Bank has exercised a restraining influence on IDA, IDA has been a liberating influence on the Bank. The Bank's unwillingness during the 1950s to lend for certain types of projects – education, water supply, housing and similar non-self-liquidating ventures – helped to build up the pressure for an IDA. But after IDA came into being, the illogic of a policy whereby a less creditworthy country would have access to Bank Group assistance for a wider range of projects than would a fully creditworthy country was finally recognized. The Bank then found it possible to make loans for the same types of projects as IDA (Mason & Asher 1973: 415).

It is by no means obvious why sectoral patterns of IDA and IBRD lending should differ. The range of permissive activities is the same, and only the balance-of-payments impact differs. Although IDA goes to poorer countries, it does not follow that their needs in the agricultural sector are relatively greater. In fact, the opposite could be argued. Richer countries tend to have a more developed infrastructure, and lending should focus on directly productive activities. In the poorer countries a lack of basic infrastructure may be a major

Table 3.6 *Sectoral distribution of Bank/IDA lending (in %)*

	Through 1963	1964 -68	1969 -74	1965 -78
Agriculture	8.6	12.3	20.7	32.4
Education	0.1	3.1	5.1	4.2
Development Finance				
Corporations	3.9	9.6	9.1	10.5
Energy	–	–	–	0.7
Industry	10.3	2.3	5.9	8.5
Programme loans	3.3	9.0	5.5	4.7
Population and Nutrition	–	–	0.5	0.6
Power	34.5	29.0	17.6	12.7
Telecommunications	0.9	3.0	4.7	2.2
Tourism	–	–	0.7	0.8
Transportation	38.3	29.1	24.6	15.9
Urbanization	–	–	1.0	2.5
Water supply and Sewerage	0.2	2.4	4.4	4.1
Technical Assistance	–	–	0.2	0.2
	100	100	100	100

Source: *Annual Reports.*

impediment to the productivity of lending for agriculture. In other words, an antithetical allocation emphasis would be more appropriate.

The diversification of Bank Group lending may be viewed from different agencies. Firstly, in the context of the evolution from a 'bank' to a 'development agency'. In the vague words of Mason & Asher:

The essence of the difference between a bank and a development agency, is the greater concern of the latter with development goals, strategy, and performance, with meeting the most pressing developmental needs as well as with financing good projects, and with rationing its resources to take all claims upon them properly into account' (Mason & Asher 1973: 381).

Secondly, a less charitable view is that, in retrospect, the diversification of Bank Group activities contributed to the disintegration of the UN system. This system, of which the Bank is part, evolved along broadly functional lines with separate organizations dealing with specialized areas: IBRD for economic infra-structure, FAO for agriculture, UNIDO for industry, WHO for health, UNESCO for education, etc. Then why did they not apply their expertise to the pursuit of large-scale investment projects within their area of competence? Why did, instead, the World Bank branch out and engage in activities which seem to fall within the area of competence of other specialized agencies? Other specialized agencies have always stressed research and technical assistance, and presumably have greater knowledge of the problems in their functional areas due to their long involvement. Despite this advantage, the advice given by other specialized agencies has been ineffective relative to that of the Bank. Regard-

Table 3.7 *Bank and IDA lending by major sectors (in %)*

| | FY 1961-68 | | FY 1969-74 | | FY 1975-78 | |
	IBRD	IDA	IBRD	IDA	IBRD	IDA
Agriculture	13	25	16	32	28	44
Infrastructure*	68	53	59	38	41	30
Others	20	22	25	30	31	26
Total	100	100	100	100	100	100

* Telecommunications, Electric Power, Transportation, Urban Development, Water Supply and Sewerage

Source: 'IDA Lending Policies' (IDA/R73-7, Febr. 7, 1973) Table 7, and *Annual Reports*.

less of whether that advice has been good or bad, Bank advice has tended to be more effective because only the Bank is in a position to offer the prospect of a foreign loan. The influence of other UN agencies is thus eroded.

THE PRE-INVESTMENT FUNCTION IN THE UN SYSTEM

The pressure which developing countries had brought to bear in the 1950s for a multilateral capital assistance channel in the form of SUNFED, led instead to the creation of IDA. A significant but indirect benefit of that pressure was the establishment of the UN Special Fund in 1958 under the chairmanship of Paul Hoffman, who had played a major role in its creation (Mason & Asher 1973: 568 n. 10). The functions of the Special Fund were clearly distinguished from technical assistance (on the insistence of the developed countries). Its basic objective was to fill the functional gap in the existing spectrum of international institutions with an organization devoted to 'pre-investment' or, in the words of General Assembly resolution 1240 (XIII) 'to facilitate new capital investments of all types by creating conditions which would make such investment either feasible or more effective.' If the UN could not have its own capital fund, it could at least try to stimulate a larger flow of capital investment to the developing countries through 'pre-investment projects'. The Special Fund was combined in 1966 with the UN Expanded Programme of Technical Assistance to become the United Nations Development Programme (UNDP). In the hope of obviating the build-up of a big bureaucracy of its own, UNDP decided to work through 'existing agencies', i.e. through the specialized agencies of the UN.

At the end of the first decade (1959-69) of Special Fund/UNDP operations, total allocations by UNDP and recipient governments for pre-investment purposes amounted to $2.5 billion, but 'follow-up investment' resulting directly from these activities totalled only $2.1 billion.

Many Special Fund projects were not pre-investment projects in the strict sense of the term, i.e. projects whose objective was to identify and prepare proposals for capital investment. Approximately one-third of the total allocations were utilized to establish or strengthen training institutions, and another third for research and other projects, most of which were not likely to directly generate capital investment. But the remaining third, consisting mainly of basic infrastructure, agriculture and natural resource surveys, should have contributed directly to the identification and preparation of projects for capital investment. On the basis of this assumption, the ratio of follow-up investment to the cost of UNDP pre-investment activities would be approximately 5 to 2. This may understate the performance of the programme to the extent that there is a time lag between UNDP studies and any follow-up.

About 75% of follow-up investment resulted from a small group of large-scale public utility projects for the development of power, transportation, telecommunications and water supply facilities. The other sector in which significant follow-up investment has occurred is that of agriculture – about 20%. The balance is made up of small investments in mining and industrial sectors (Reports to UNDP Governing Council, DP/L.73 and DP/L.130; Taylor 1970).

Up to 1969, more than two-thirds of the total $2.1 billion follow-up investment had been financed or stimulated by the World Bank Group through loans or credits, 'joint financing' organized by the Bank from other multilateral sources, and local currency financing supplied by governments.

The Jackson Capacity Study calculated as reasonable a ratio of 'follow-up' investment to 'seed-money' of 48:1 (Jackson 1969: Part II, 58 and Table 3.11). In an earlier study, the Netherlands Economic Institute (NEI 1961) arrived at the following ratios:

40:1 for industry, transport and power;
20:1 for mining, and
30:1 for agricultural investment projects.

Compared to these rough and ready figures the actual performance of UNDP, with a ratio of 5:2, has been grossly disappointing.

The specialized agencies of the UN have not only executed but have also initiated pre-investment projects, and the role of UNDP has therefore been largely confined to that of a funding agency. The resulting reports have regrettably been more technical than investment-oriented, i.e. were almost totally devoid of the financial data and analyses necessary for investment decisions. The considerable technical competence of the specialized agencies is reflected, but UNDP has *not* added the missing element to transform the reports into 'bankable' projects leading to investments, as laid down in its mandate. These investments would have been sponsored by the specialized agencies in collaboration with all other interested parties.

The World Bank sought to overcome its lack of expertise by entering into a number of cooperative agreements with FAO and UNESCO in 1964, with

WHO in 1972, and with UNIDO in 1974. *Ad hoc* co-operation with ILO is also extensive (*Annual Report* 1977: 182). One possible approach which the Bank could have pursued would have been to use the cooperative programmes as instruments to make the specialized agencies more investment-oriented, in line with the mandate given to UNDP. The UN might then have evolved into a set of specialized agencies which combined technical assistance and follow-up investment programmes in their functional area. Instead, particularly under McNamara, the Bank has hired its own staff in those functional areas, thereby increasing its distance from the other agencies.

The Bank sees the cooperative agreements in such a way that the Specialized Agencies are providing 'services to the Bank'. In the words of Warren Baum, the Bank's Vice President Projects Staff: 'there is a large separate staff in the FAO *working full time for the Bank* on the identification and preparation of projects .... UNESCO *performs similar services for the Bank* in the field of education' (Baum 1970: 4, emphasis added). This attitude of superiority is enhanced by the fact that the Bank finances 75% and the specialized agency 25% of the cost of staff of the cooperative agreement (Mason & Asher 1973: 571-73).

To take the example of the FAO: after reviewing the preliminary findings of selected UNDP pre-investment projects, the Cooperative Programme sends a reconnaissance mission to the field to work with the project team, to assemble additional data and to identify an investment project for consideration by the World Bank. Upon the latter's approval, the Cooperative Programme prepares a final-stage feasibility study in a form suitable for final loan appraisal by the Bank. The joint FAO/IBRD missions can be relatively short-term and low in cost, due largely to the substantial data and assistance made available to them by the UNDP/FAO pre-investment project staff in the field.

These arrangements are satisfactory to the Bank, because they enable it to programme its pre-investment activities for the ambitious lending targets set by McNamara. The financial benefits have also been substantial. A UNDP survey cost about $1 million to UNDP and $1.5 million to the recipient government in the late 1960s. A bankable report could then be produced at an estimated average cost of $50,000 outside the UNDP system (Taylor 1970: 5, 6).

The IBRD has thus taken over the specific task of UNDP, namely, the organization of the pre-investment function within the UN system. The UNDP had been 'delegated to picking up the pre-investment tab for the World Bank' (Ibidem: 4).

At issue is not the efficiency of the arrangement, but the policy implications of a process by which the cream of the investment potential of more and more UNDP pre-investment projects, for which large sums of money have been contributed on a multilateral basis, is skimmed-off for the exclusive use of one source of financing: the Bank.

Some consequences of the failure of UNDP

The failing role of UNDP during the 1960s had several important consequences for the position of the Bank and of the UN system, and also for the international situation as regards aid flows.

Within the United Nations, the Bank — under firm control of the developed countries — has taken over leadership in the field of development because it is the only agency with a *de facto* investment function. As it diversifies its activities and pirates staff from other agencies, its reliance on other agencies decreases. Contradictory views about the appropriateness of different policies, such as may exist among different agencies, are introduced into the Bank but are not necessarily resolved. In inter-agency conflicts the view held by the Bank tends to carry more weight because *its* views determine whether or not to lend, regardless of the merits of alternative views. The Bank is also the only UN agency under direct Western control and in which the Western countries continue to have a major financial stake.

In other UN agencies, however, resolutions taken by the majority of member countries sometimes prove unpalatable to the West and particularly to the USA. The response is then to suspend payment, as happened in UNESCO, or even to withdraw altogether —witness the action of the USA in withdrawing from ILO in November 1977. The adverse effects of such petulance are extremely difficult to counteract.

Continuation of the technical assistance function of the specialized agencies is also likely to be threatened and the supremacy of the Bank reinforced by such actions, thus further eroding the role of the agencies. UNDP allocations to the specialized agencies have made it possible for them to undertake studies in addition to those covered by their normal budget. The need for such studies is difficult to assess objectively, and they are consequently vulnerable in times of curtailed budgets. Because UNDP studies resulted in very limited follow-up investment, they created little goodwill for the agencies.

The UNDP was intended to lead to 'capital investment of all types', a global spectrum in which the Bank Group is only a minor participant. If UNDP functioned according to its mandate, it would help to fill the project pipeline of other multilateral development banks, bilateral investors and domestic investors, and in doing so, would build up greater goodwill and understanding for its own role. It would justify its own existence and thereby generate more goodwill and support for at least some activities of the various UN specialized agencies.

Under the prevailing pattern of UNDP activities, other potential investors are forced to turn elsewhere and to seek additional resources for pre-investment work from major contributors to UNDP, to the detriment of the latter. Taylor ascribes the unsatisfactory work of UNDP to a 'functional and professional failure to carry the required pre-investment work to the final stage, that is, to produce fully bankable reports and feasibility studies in a form suitable for an investment decision' (Taylor 1970: 8-9).

The World Bank cannot be blamed for this failure of UNDP to follow through on initial general surveys. But it can be blamed for lack of self-restraint. It has diversified in all directions without concern for the impact of its actions on the maintenance of a viable UN system in which specialized agencies can play a major role. The specialized agencies should become more investment-oriented, and should be aided by UNDP. As most of the Bank Group's resources are obtained in such a form that they can be lent only to 'credit-worthy' countries, the Bank also becomes instrumental in tapping UN know-how and efforts to channel funds to a relatively few, large and predominantly middle-income countries, which are quite able to pay for their own studies if these are thought necessary.

As a mechanism for transferring funds for investment purposes, the UN system may easily become paralyzed if the World Bank continues to be its only major investment agency. It is in the interest of specialized agencies, therefore, that they diversify their activities and develop other channels than the World Bank to promote investments.

UNDP should at least follow the changes in aid trends observed over the last decade, with the rapidly increasing role of regional development banks, and cater to their pre-investment needs more substantially than it did during the 1960s.[10] In doing so, it faces continued competition, however, from the World Bank.

During the early 1970s the Bank became very active in linking up with public and private lending institutions in an attempt to maintain and strengthen its leadership role in international development. Against IBRD/IDA commitments in fiscal 1973-76 of $20.2 billion, co-financing was obtained of $6.0 billion in 27% of Bank Group operations; 54% of additional finance came from official sources, 39% from export credits and 7% from private foreign sources (World Bank: 'Co-financing' 1976: 17-18; *Annual Reports*).

The Bank asserts that 'in general, experience has shown that co-lenders of all types have been significantly influenced by the depth and thoroughly of the Bank's analysis of countries' economies, its appraisal of particular projects, and its supervision of project execution.' Moreover, it is said, the Bank's efforts have 'promoted more efficient and economic use of the total external resources available' ('Co-financing': 5, 14). These judgements are somewhat surprising. The Bank is a relative newcomer in major sectors of its lending and in a number of countries. Moreover, 1973-76 marked the beginning of a major reorientation of Bank lending based on a direct approach to target groups of the poor and a general endeavour to improve the income distributional effects of its lending. These new concerns have been described as major and innovative and were to require much trial-and-error. To judge, at least prematurely, new projects as being successful, conflicts with trial-and-error approaches. If projects fail, co-financiers share the mistakes; if they are successful they will share the praise. But if the Bank's early experience of lagging disbursement is shared by other financiers through jointly financed projects, the new experiments will slow the flow of resources to developing countries, at a time when most of them have to cope with sudden and severe balance-of-payments difficulties. Joining up with other donors in risky and experimental ventures increases the vulnerability of recipient countries on external account. In effect, the Bank thus plans for uniformity of judgement, style and practice, rather than for diversity, and it may be questioned whether this is compatible with more efficient use of external resources.

Co-financing 'probably does not induce an *absolute* increase in official funds available to a particular country, but newer agencies may find that co-financing speeds up their spending capacity' (Ibidem: 14-15). The effects of Bank-led co-financing arrangements are that the Bank projects its new priorities on established agencies and conditions newer agencies to follow its own operational style and practices. An agency must be deeply convinced of the appropriateness of its judgements and the outcomes of experiments which it induces to be undertaken to assume such a vulnerable position.

The Bank's role with respect to export credit agencies and private sources is equally ambivalent. Its generally optimistic assessments of the debt-carrying capacity of most developing countries may induce credit agencies and commercial banks to adjust their credit-rating and increase their lending quota through co-financing. They cover themselves by 'relying on the Bank's judgements' (Ibidem: 10), and the Bank reciprocates by including 'cross-effectiveness' and 'cross-default clauses' in its loan agreements (Ibidem: 10). Such practices will accelerate the indebtedness of developing countries and strengthen the cohesion among creditors, forcing debtors to take the interests of the latter into account when framing national policies and setting national priorities. It is unlikely, however, that the priorities of external commercial creditors will normally coincide with priorities favouring the poorer segments of society.

CONCLUSION

It is increasingly difficult for IDA to obtain the funds which it needs for its continued existence. That the political constituency in favour of aid is weakening in many countries is shown by the persistent shortfall on ODA targets. In addition, competition among alternative ODA channels is increasing and burdensharing disputes further hamper replenishment procedures.

On the other hand, the number of IDA eligible countries has increased dramatically. Together with the scarcity of ODA, this leads to increasingly rigid country allocation patterns.

The diversification of Bank lending has weakened other UN agencies and fostered Bank pre-eminence in the international development effort. While it is doubtful whether this has caused total aid flows to LDCs to increase, it has fostered an aid network through consortia in which Bank views are substituted for those of other donors and LDCs alike.

The reappraisal of past development efforts and the need to find new and more appropriate development strategies is likely to lead to increased uncertainty and to demands for a more diverse pattern of relationships between donor and recipient countries. A diminished rather than an enhanced leadership role for the Bank would seem more appropriate.

NOTES

1. Geoffrey Wilson, Vice-President of the Bank and IDA, Address before the Institute of Banking and Financial Studies (Paris, 4 June 1964); cited by Mason & Asher 1973: 397.

2. See Barbara Eschenbach: 'History of the Second Replenishment' (Third Replenishment Working Paper No. 23, 26 August 1969, World Bank, Programming and Budgeting Department; internal memorandum).

3. See Congressional Record, House, 23 January 1974, H. 135-151; Statement by the Honorable George P. Shultz, Secretary of the Treasury, before the Subcommittee on International Finance of the Banking and Currency Committee of the House of Representatives, 14 November 1973.

4. The maximum amounts required to be appropriated by the US for each multilateral institution are as follows:

in $ mln	1971[a]		1973[b]	
	Callable	Paid-in	Callable	Paid-in
IBRD	509	51	703	71
IDA	0	122	0	161
IADB	146	224	277	233
ASDB	9	9	12	12
Total	664	406	992	477

(a) Appropriated in HR 14582, PL92-306, enacted May 1972
(b) Appropriated PL93-142, approved October 26, 1973

As callable capital is not expected to be drawn upon, however, only the supplements on paid-in capital will be paid; these can be spread over 10-11 years each until drawn upon (The US and Multilateral Development Banks 1974: 151).

5. The volume of Bank Group lending in real terms is difficult to assess. Procurement stretches over ten years. Projects may have different compositions between domestic and imported goods and services between sectors, and the sector mix of Bank lending will change. Imports have to be weighted by likely sources of future procurement. Competitive strength may differ between countries as well as between different categories of products. In most of the country-specific five-year action programmes of Bank activities – which form the basis for Bank lending projections – many 'projects' listed for the period 3-5 years ahead are strictly notional, as the projects are often not even identified by sector, leave alone by content.

6. The concept of 'aid' can be defined, briefly and statistically, as all non-military transfers of resources to developing countries on concessional terms, i.e. on terms more favourable than market terms. Official Development Assistance is used here in the DAC definition (see DAC: *Development Assistance* [1969]: 239-245). It comprises all flows of resources to less-developed countries and multilateral institutions provided by official agencies, including state and local governments, or by their executive agencies, which meet the following tests:

(a) they are administered with the promotion of the economic development and welfare of developing countries as their main objective; *and*

(b) their financial terms are intended to be concessional in character, with a grant element of at least 25 percent. Excluded from ODA are two important categories of flows, namely, export credit transactions and the purchases by central banks and governments of bonds issued by multilateral development banks at market rates (Ibidem, 242).

7. See OECD 1967: Ch. VII; DAC 1968 *Review*: Ch. VII; DAC 1969 *Review*: Ch. V; Little & Clifford 1965; Henderson 1971; Mikesell 1968: Ch. 9; Wall 1973: Ch. 8; White 1974: Ch. II.

8. Knapp, in Lewis & Kapur 1973: 49-50; see also 'Memorandum to the Executive Directors on Pearson Recommendation, No. 32, concerning criteria for the allocation of IDA credits' (17 June 1970), 4-5.

9. There is an extensive literature, mostly unhelpful, on aspects of economic performance. For a 99-item bibliography see DAC: *Performance Compendium* (Paris, OECD 1973). For studies relating to the Bank see Kamarck (1970, 1972), Mason & Asher (1973, chapter 13), Williams (1968), Cline & Sargan (1975).

10. There is some evidence that UNDP has indeed become somewhat more 'output'-conscious. Reported investment commitments in 1972-76 amounted to $19 billion, of which $13 billion resulted directly from recommendations of UNDP-assisted pre-investment surveys and feasibility studies. The balance was due to pre-investment undertakings closely associated with UNDP-assisted projects. This compares to project expenditure of $1.6 billion. Investment performance thus appears to have improved, although no breakdown is available by types of projects, training, surveys and pre-investment projects proper. Local contributions to UNDP studies are also not specified.

Financing sources show more variation as compared to the 1960s. Domestic investment accounted for 53 percent, and multilateral sources for 30 percent (of which IBRD/IDA 82 percent), and bilateral financing 16 percent. These figures and those for the 1960s should be treated with caution because of timelag between studies and follow-up investment (UNDP: *Report of the Administrator for 1976*, DP/255/Annex I, Tables 5, 13 and 14).

IV

BANK STAFF

INTRODUCTION

A primary problem which faces any new international organization is how to organize its staff. What should be its guidelines for staff recruitment and promotion? Personnel policies are important, especially during the formative years. Patterns then become established which, once entrenched, tend to be very difficult to change. Interests will establish themselves which play a role in how initially set personnel policies will evolve.

Personnel policies become more complex if the countries which wish to set up an international agency have dissimilar backgrounds, cultures or levels of development. Complexities increase even further if the agency is subject to major changes over time through accommodations when new members join the organization, or when the main thrust of its activities is redirected.

On November 5th, 1947, the World Bank officially became part of the UN system. The legal agreement which confirmed its status as a specialized agency was, in the words of Mason and Asher, 'more nearly a declaration of independence from the global organization than of cooperation with it' (Mason & Asher 1973: 559). The 1969 Jackson Report showed that inter-agency conflicts play a very important role in the UN, and negatively affect its capacity to function effectively.

One aspect of the independence of the World Bank vis-à-vis ECOSOC and other specialized UN agencies has been its greater freedom to hire personnel without reference to their country of origin. The Articles of Agreement of the institutions of the Bank Group specify in Article V, Section 5, that the 'staff owe their duty to the Bank Group and to no other authority'. Also, 'in appointing the officers and staff the President [of the Bank] shall, subject to the paramount importance of securing the highest standards of efficiency and of technical competence, pay due regard to the importance of recruiting personnel on as wide a geographical basis as possible.'

UN personnel policies have always received wide attention within the General Assembly. Since 1962 the Secretary-General has been required to

---

Notes to this chapter may be found on pp. 107-108.

report annually on the application of recruitment guidelines laid down over the years. These have become gradually more complex, partly due to pressure stemming from the addition of new members, and partly to the introduction of new tasks as the concept of the UN's role expanded.

Nowadays, the recruitment of staff for professional and higher-level UN posts, other than those requiring special language qualifications, must aim at the following objectives: (a) equitable geographical distribution of staff in the secretariat between regions and within each region; (b) a regional balance of staff in senior posts; (c) predominance of staff from the region in each of the regional economic commissions; (d) an increase in the number of women in the Secretariat in general and in senior posts in particular; (e) an improvement in the age distribution of staff through the recruitment of more young men and women; (f) a better linguistic balance within the Secretariat measured by the number of staff able to work in the various languages of the organization; and (g) a large proportion of staff on permanent or long-term appointment as a means of ensuring the stability and efficient operation of the Secretariat (see, for instance, UN General Assembly, 28th Session, A/9120, 21 September 1973).

The Bank, in contrast, does not have an elaborate set of regulations on hiring policy such as are applicable to the UN, nor is the composition of its staff subject to the same close annual scrutiny. It is difficult to obtain recent and detailed data on the composition of the World Bank's staff and, in the absence of a direct and close public scrutiny of its hiring and promotion practices, it may be useful to analyse that staff in some detail.

GROWTH OF BANK STAFF

The growth and the distribution by country of origin of professional World Bank staff is given in Table 4.1, which shows that the share from Part I countries has been slowly reduced. In 1977, however, the USA and the UK together still accounted for almost 39 percent of total Bank professional staff.

As of 1977 only 7 countries accounted for 62 percent of total professional staff: the US (610), UK (296), India (134), France (129), Germany (118), Canada (76) and the Netherlands (72). A further seven countries accounted for another nine percent: Australia (62), Pakistan (47), Chile (43), Belgium (40), Japan (33), Philippines (31) and Sweden (29). Large countries which are very poorly represented include Bangladesh with eight, Indonesia with only three staff members, Mexico with five, and Brazil with five professional staff members. In all, 96 nationalities were represented on the Bank staff in 1977, albeit many only minimally. Ten countries had one representative, fifteen countries had two each, and 18 countries had 3-5 staff members each (*Administrative Budget* FY 1978).

Table 4.1 *Growth and composition of IBRD/IDA staff 1950-1977*

Nationality	June 30, 1950 %	May 31, 1960 %	April 30, 1965 %	April 30, 1968 %	April 30, 1973 %	April 30, 1977 %
United States	63.9	45.2	36.1	31.3	25.7	26.2
United Kingdom	12.8	14.1	16.4	17.9	13.1	12.7
Other Part I	16.7	26.5	31.4	29.0	31.0	29.1
Total Part I	93.3	85.9	84.0	78.2	69.8	68.0
Europe (other)	2.3	2.8	3.1	3.3	4.6	3.5
Africa (other)	–	0.7	1.0	2.5	3.7	4.4
Asia (other)	2.2	6.7	8.8	12.2	14.8	16.2
LAC (other)	1.7	3.2	3.1	3.7	7.1	7.8
Stateless	–	0.7	–	0.1	0.1	0.1
Total Part II	6.7	14.1	16.0	21.8	30.2	32.0
Numbers	180	283	487	806	1750	2326

Source: World Bank, Personnel Department; and *Administrative Budget* (FY 1978).

REPRESENTATION

We may ask to what extent the Bank staff is representative of its membership.[1] First, we may compare the staffing situation with that of the UN Secreatriat. The UN has perfected a system of desirable ranges of numbers of posts per country, taking into account the percentage contribution to the UN budget, a minimum number of posts for each member state on the basis of membership, and a 'population reserve' to allow for such differences in population as do not receive sufficient weight in the other two factors. Table 4.2 indicates the degree of over or under-representation of the various regions.

Africa is over-represented in the UN but is grossly under-represented in the World Bank staff. Western Europe is very much over-represented in the Bank, while Latin America and the Middle East are both under-represented, using UN norms.

The UN and the World Bank may not be comparable if a dichotomy is construed between the presumably more 'general' nature of the work of the UN Secretariat and the 'specialized' nature of the World Bank in common with FAO, UNESCO, ILO and UNIDO. It could also be argued, however, that the 'specialized generalist' of the UN Secretariat does not differ materially from the 'generalized specialist' into which many special agency staff have evolved, with the result that 'specialized specialist' work is often farmed-out to outside consultants, even in the 'specialized agencies'.

The geographical composition of Bank staff may also be compared with the distribution of voting power within the World Bank. This is shown in Table 4.3.

Although the weighted voting strength of IBRD favours Part I countries, the rich countries still seem to be over-represented, largely due to the heavy

Table 4.2 *Relative representation of UN and Bank staff in 1973**

	(1) UN actual strength over UN norm	(2) WB prof. actual strength over UN norm
Africa	1.08	0.38
Asia and Far East	0.89	0.84
Western Europe	1.15	1.53
Latin America	1.15	0.77
Middle East	1.03	0.71
North America & Caribbean	0.88	1.06
No. of posts (actual)	1996	1504
Others, not included	316	140
Total of posts	2312	1644

Source: Calculated from UN, A/9120, 21 Sept. 1973, Table A, and Annex Table 8; World
Bank: *Administrative Budget* FY 1974, and *Annual Reports*.

*   The UN classification has been used. Eastern European countries which are not members of the World Bank, and the category 'others' have been excluded. Of UN staff
only the posts subject to geographical distribution requirements are included. In addition, the UN employed in 1973 819 staff members in positions which required
special language knowledge.

Table 4.3 *Relative representation of World Bank staff, compared to IBRD*
voting power in 1973

	Professional staff	Non-professional staff
US	1.14	1.03
UK	1.45	1.03
France	1.32	0.70
Germany	1.11	0.15
Japan	0.48	0.44
Other Part I	0.90	0.69
Total Part I	1.09	0.80
Europe (non-Part I)	1.05	0.68
Africa	0.44	0.54
India	1.62	1.70
Pakistan	2.15	1.67
Other Asia	0.74	1.68
LAC	0.84	1.81
Total Part II	0.84	1.35
Stateless (No.)	1	4
Total staff (No.)	1644	1742

Sources: As for Table 4.2.

ORGANIZATION CHART

International Bank for Reconstruction and Development

International Development Association

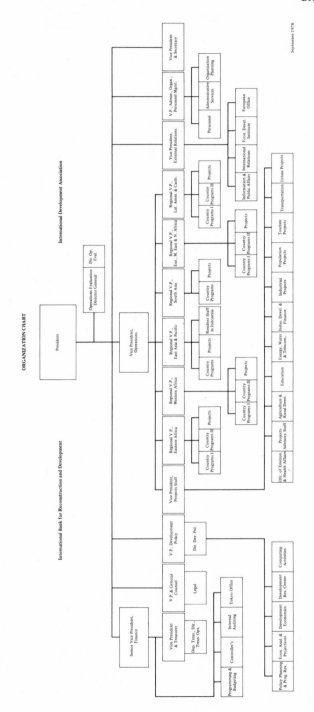

September 1978

r:lative over-representation of the UK and France. Africa remains under-represented, but India and Pakistan are over-represented in the professional staff category. Japan, of the major shareholders, is heavily under-represented.

Part II countries are on the whole over-represented for non-professional staff. English is the working language of the Bank, and this helps to explain the poor showing, for instance, of Germany and Sweden. In addition to India and Pakistan, the major sources of over-representation are to be found in 'other Asia' and in Latin America. Major contrasts in terms of staff in the two categories are shown in Table 4.4, from which it will be seen that the Philippines provides a major contingent of non-professional staff. In fact, it ranked second in 1973 together with the UK, after the USA with 410 non-professional staff.

Table 4.4 *Bank staff: selected countries*

| | WB Staff | | | WB Staff | |
	Prof.	Non-Prof.		Prof.	Non-Prof.
France	100	56	Philippines	17	166
Germany	90	13	Australia	32	70
Netherlands	57	10	Jamaica	3	39
Sweden	27	1	Trinidad & Tobago	3	26
Total	274	80	Total	55	301

SENIOR BANK STAFF

Thus far we have focused on broad comparisons of overall staff numbers by region. The geographical allotment of staff within the Bank may be measured by examining their distribution by rank and by income class. Table 4.5 shows the ratios of staff by country and region in three salary categories, compared to the Bank-wide average distribution of staff over the income categories. In addition, we list the distribution of 113 'management' functions as classified by the Bank's Personnel Department: comprising Vice-Presidents, Directors, Chief Economists and other senior staff.

It will be seen that in 1973 the UK, even more than the USA had a disproportionate share of its staff in the high income category. If percentages of 'management' staff are computed over staff in the high income bracket for the major countries, however, the USA and Germany prove to have been relatively well-represented in management with 24.3% and 24.1% respectively. France rated average (19.4%) with all Part I countries (19.8%), but the UK was quite low in the management category in 1973 with only 13.6% of its staff enjoying incomes of over $21,000. A higher than average proportion of British staff were in the high income bracket, and yet they did not occupy many 'management' positions, a good many staying at the senior project specialist level

Table 4.5 *Ratios of staff distribution by income class compared to overall staff income distribution, per April 30, 1973*

	Under $14000	$14000 –20999	$21000 and over	Management
USA	0.99	0.87	1.20	44
UK	0.64	0.80	1.42	15
France	0.87	1.01	1.03	7
Germany	1.05	1.04	0.92	7
Japan	1.36	1.19	0.59	2
Other Part I	0.75	1.08	0.98	16
Total Part I	0.87	0.94	1.14	91
Europe (non Part I)	0.66	1.24	0.76	6
Africa	1.07	1.39	0.39	–
India	1.63	0.90	0.91	2
Pakistan	0.28	1.23	0.92	4
Other Asia	1.46	1.19	0.55	4
LAC	1.61	1.05	0.70	6
Total Part II	1.31	1.14	0.68	22
Total staff (No.)*	208	860	575	113

* Total staff 1644, of whom the tabulation excludes one stateless person.

Source: Calculated from *Administrative Budget FY 1974*, Section III.

without advancing further. Whether this was then by choice, or because they were not judged of 'management caliber' is an open question. In 1972 the salary range of specialist staff was extended to prevent their having to move into managerial positions for which they had neither the inclination nor capacity.

Japan, India, Africa, 'other Asia' and Latin America still have large proportions of staff in the lower salary bracket.

Part I countries filled 81 percent of all management functions, with the USA, UK, France and Germany together accounting for 65 percent of all management functions in 1973.

The major reorganization of 1972 has not been used by management to materially change the representation of Part II countries. Escott Reid considers it one of McNamara's main failures as Bank president that he did not increase that representation in the senior ranks, for which the reorganization presented a splendid opportunity. In this judgement he is supported by Mason & Asher (1973: 737). The trend has even been to the contrary, according to Reid. On the basis of the Annual Reports, Reid observed that George Woods had sharply reduced the proportion of principal officers of the Bank and IDA who were citizens of the USA, from 55 to 40 percent. During McNamara's first five years of office, this 'desirable trend was reversed' (Reid 1973a: 809; 1973b: 186-87). During McNamara's second term of office no major changes have occurred although changes in individual countries are of interest: rising num-

Table 4.6 *Composition of management by nationality (1972* and 1978**)*

Citizens of	April 30, 1972	April 30, 1978
USA	41	36
UK	21	14
Germany	8	10
France	5	10
Netherlands	8	3
Other Part I	10	18
Total Part I	93	91
Argentina	–	3
India	1	6
Pakistan	4	5
Other Part II	14	10
Total Part II	19	24
Total Management	112	115
As % of total professional staff	7.5%	4.7%

* Includes Directors, Deputies, Chief Economists and other senior staff
** Includes Vice-Presidents, Directors, Assistant and Deputy-Directors

Source: Administrative Budgets, 1973 and 1979.

bers in 'management' for France and India, and sharp declines for the UK and the Netherlands. Several US nationals were brought in at high levels, often lateral transfers from US AID, which has faced severe budget cuts and thus staff reduction.

After more than 30 years, the World Bank is thus still predominantly staffed by nationals from Part I countries, with a heavy relative over-representation of nationals from former major colonial powers in the professional cadres. In comparison with the UN, the Bank has made very limited progress towards internationalizing the composition of its staff, particularly at higher staff levels.

FACTORS IN THE RECRUITMENT OF BANK AND UN STAFF

During the Bank's first year the recruitment process was necessarily on a catch-as-catch-can basis. Some staff were borrowed from the US government; persons of other nationalities who had been in the western hemisphere on wartime and early post-war assignments, including participation in the Bretton Woods and Savannah Conferences, were picked up as those assignments ended.

As the Bank shifted its main activities from reconstruction to development, staff recruitment became closely tied to the process of decolonization. Former colonial service officers saw their career perspectives changed as a result of accelerated localization or indigenization of top cadres in the newly indepen-dent countries.

The Bank provided an attractive alternative in that it offered a career perspective, albeit initially only for a narrow range of occupations that were most relevant to its main lending activities: transportation and electric power. On the other hand, the UN came under strong political pressure to have its membership reflected in the composition of its staff, and consequently had to find substitutes for officers from former colonial powers. The UN could not yet do without the experience and capabilities of such officers, however, and they were retained on short-term contracts.

It was decided fairly early on that the Bank should try to build a staff of *career* employees who would have no competing loyalties, and who could gradually acquire expertise in the problems of international finance and development.

Others, staff members from Part I countries without a colonial past, acquired their initial development expertise during the 1960s through a succession of short-term contracts in countries where 'high level manpower' shortages were greatest, and where new governments tried to diversify recruitment away from the former colonial master (see Madison 1965, for a discussion of the situation in the early 1960s).

The relative under-representation of Japan and Latin America, however, cannot be explained in terms of the decolonization process. Socio-cultural explanations are applicable here, particularly with respect to the Japanese; other countries had plentiful career opportunities due to rapid economic growth, e.g. Brazil and Mexico. Latin Americans who wished to live in Washington also had the option of working for the IADB, where Latin American influence is much greater than in the World Bank.

Decolonization has resulted in tremendously increased career opportunities for nationals in the newly independent countries, particularly in Africa where decolonization was often accomplished within a very short time period.

Those who happened to enter the high level job market at that time had enormous opportunities, colonization having been of relatively shorter duration than in Asia and indigenous cadres at independence being very thin. In view of the opportunities that were available at home, it is somewhat surprising that, by 1973, Africa was already over-represented in the UN (see Table 4.2).

Another complex of factors which influences the supply and the characteristics of experienced technical assistance personnel, has to do with the lifecycle phase of their families. Job mobility can be high when children are either very young or grown-up. In other words, when considerable first-hand field experience has been built up, mobility may be greatly reduced, so that expertise can be used only in restricted areas and functions.

A personnel recruitment policy which stresses competence, which is frequently assumed to be based on academic credentials from a university of good reputation, and which stresses experience in developing countries, must almost inevitably result in a staff composition such as the Bank has acquired.

Nationals from many developing countries were late starters, their countries not having joined the Bank until the early 1960s; moreover, their educational backgrounds and their past experience were far less favourable.

An added advantage of a recruitment policy that is oriented towards field experience is that it brought to the Bank a number of people who were personally acquainted with key officials in the countries concerned. This was considerably advantageous for subsequent Bank-country relations. Transfers of staff cause this specific advantage to be lost, but some gains are still likely due to an increasing comparative perspective.

THE YOUNG PROFESSIONALS' PROGRAMME

Given recruitment standards which stress professional competence and considerable field experience, the cards seemed stacked in favour of an overwhelming recruitment of staff from a limited number of countries. To overcome the apparent dilemma that this posed, the Bank in 1963 inaugurated a staff recruitment programme that was specifically aimed at young, promising, but inexperienced graduates who could be trained inside the Bank and would make their career in the Bank.[2] The programme may thus be viewed as a means by which the Bank could help redress any imbalances in the composition of its staff.

From the start of the programme until June 1977, a total of 581 young professionals (YPs) were recruited from 81 countries, as detailed in Table 4.7.[3]

Table 4.7 *Recruitment of YPs by region*

Percentage recruits from	*Woods 1963-68*	*McNamara 1969-74*	*1975-77*	*Total*	*YPs voting power*
Part I					
USA	8.2	14.2	17.1	13.9	0.61
UK	9.0	7.3	9.0	8.3	0.95
France	8.2	7.7	9.0	8.3	1.91
Germany	7.4	4.6	3.0	4.6	1.00
Other	30.3	25.4	19.6	24.4	1.02
Total	63.1	59.2	57.8	59.6	0.92
Part II					
Europe	4.9	3.1	3.5	3.6	1.13
Africa	4.9	10.8	9.0	9.0	1.14
Asia	18.9	17.7	18.1	18.1	1.16
LAC	8.2	9.2	11.6	9.8	1.17
Total	36.9	40.8	42.2	40.4	1.15
Nos.	122	260	199	581	

On the whole, recruitment from Part I countries relative to IBRD voting power has declined in favour of recruitment from Part II countries. The share of US nationals is increasing strongly, though it is still below voting strength. Recruiting from France is excessive, but probably results from the Bank's need to have staff who are able to work in francophone Africa. Recruitment from Germany has fallen off to normal levels while that from Africa has substantially increased under McNamara. Recruitment from individual countries is shown in Table 4.8.

Table 4.8 *Recruitment from selected countries*

Recruits from	1963-68	1969-74	1975-77	total	$\dfrac{YPs}{voting\ power}$
Sweden	2	14	–	16	2.10
Canada	2	8	3	13	0.59
Ghana	1	2	8	11	5.73
India	11	18	10	39	2.17

By September 1978, 151 YPs (26% of those appointed) had left the service of the Bank, having stayed on average for four years. Analysis of those who left between 1974 and 1978 shows that they had stayed about one year longer than those who had left before 1974 (Van de Laar 1975). It may be that the tightening jobmarket since the early 1970s played a role in reducing staff mobility. On average, turnover has been somewhat greater for YPs from Part II countries.

It is not possible to indicate those who left the Bank because of dissatisfaction or because attractive job offers were made as a result of their success. Eleven of the 74 leavers who have been analysed elsewhere (Van de Laar 1975), had stayed over six years in the Bank; five of them had risen to division chief rank, which would put them into management lines. Some of the latter, mostly British YPs, had joined the European Economic Community after its expansion when new members were admitted. Of the 77 YPs who left between 1974 and 1978, only two had risen to the rank of Division Chief in their final posts.

YPs from less developed countries may experience a sharp conflict between the career orientation of the YP programme and manpower shortages in their home countries. YPs may be highly sought after because of the contacts they established within the Bank, their familiarity with Bank thinking and its procedures. In fact, they may become quite useful at home through their ability to formulate funding proposals in such a way as to make them look 'attractive' to international lenders. Thus, their leaving the Bank after a relatively short period may not necessarily be a 'loss' for the YP programme and the Bank, although such 'leakages' will inevitably retard the advancement of YPs from developing countries within the Bank's management structure.

In Table 4.9 we analyse the status of YPs as at September 1978.

Table 4.9 *Young Professionals by status at September 1978*

Year of appointment	Appointed	Departed	Senior staff
1963	11	5	6
1964	19	8	9
1965	19	13	1
1966	33	16	9
1967	21	10	7
1968	19	11	3
1969	31	13	3
1970	52	17	3
1971	55	18	4
1972	47	11	1
1973	47	13	–
1974-77	227	16	–
Total	581	151	46

Of the 46 senior staff members, 34 were from Part I countries; of the twelve from Part II countries, five came from India. The advancement pattern reflects the former recruitment bias, early recruits having benefitted from the expansion under McNamara by being promoted at a relatively young age. At the level of Director and Assistant Directors we find eleven former YPs from Part I countries, and only one from a Part II country. With job mobility perhaps being reduced in future and the prospect of consolidation and slower growth of Bank activities, more recent recruits may be expected to progress more slowly into senior ranks within the Bank than their predecessors. It would seem, therefore, that the relative over-representation of Europeans, including managerial ranks, will perpetuate itself. A broader representation of LDCs at those ranks is likely only in the very long run. Past recruitment practices in combination with career service will ensure that the Bank remains predominantly staffed by donor countries.

THE FUTURE

While the UN may have internationalized its staff too quickly, at the cost of staff morale and of job security, it is not inconceivable on the other hand, that the Bank has been too slow in this respect. As long as the present situation continues the Bank will retain its image of being essentially a Western bank which attempts to tell the LDCs how to organize their economic order. Many Bank staff may believe that they do this in the best interests of the LDCs, but it is hardly surprising that others interpret such efforts as arrogant impositions, all the more so since growing awareness of institutional and cultural factors in the operation of Bank-supported projects raises doubts about whether westerners can handle such issues without showing paternalism.

Various suggestions have at times been made regarding future staffing of the Bank. In all cases major judgements are involved about possible effects. The timing of major personnel policy changes is also important. Until the late 1960s heavy recruitment from developing countries would have competed strongly if not unduly with the shortages of high level manpower that prevailed in many developing countries. Heavy recruitment from LDCs in the 1970s and 1980s in order to replace nationals from over-represented countries, including the higher ranks, is likely to be strongly resisted by incumbent staff. Not only would it affect their career prospects within the Bank, but dwindling career opportunities elsewhere may be scarce under present-day conditions. To increase the internationalization of Bank staff would be easier to accomplish under conditions of continued organizational growth than of consolidation and slow or no growth.

An issue that should be considered in further rapid internationalization of Bank Group staff is how it would affect the support given to the organization. Would the Bank be able to borrow in the international capital markets if a major proportion of its senior managerial staff were recruited from LDCs? Almost all attempts to establish international capital funds under international control have failed. True, a few developing countries have acquired access to the Eurodollar market, although on less favourable terms than those that the Bank can obtain on the loans which it normally floats. Such access may be less readily granted, however, to an internationalized Bank with major representation from and lending to countries whose creditworthiness is more limited, unless it operates on standards that are even more strict than those of the World Bank. The Asian Development Bank, for example, models its operations closely on those of the World Bank, i.e. it discriminates in its lending to those countries which the World Bank does not judge creditworthy. The African Development Bank may have other aspirations, but it remains a weak organization.

Strong pressure exercised by LDCs to internationalize the World Bank[4] may be evaded by the Europeans, who might choose to build the European Development Fund into a more effective organization at the expense of the IDA. The USA could perhaps return to bilateralism, or to the IADB, unless persuaded that American personnel representation in IBRD/IDA would continue to be adequate. Whether or not adequacy should be interpreted as maintaining the current heavy over-representation of European countries and of the USA remains to be seen. It would obviously not be in the interests of the LDCs to internationalize senior staff only to find out that funds dry up. It is equally clear, however, that the Bank's personnel policies, if not drastically changed, are not likely to lead to major changes in the composition of its staff in the foreseeable future. But who is to initiate any change? The EDs are not likely to do so because their interests are served by the present weighted voting system. The management of the Bank is not likely to be eager because staff would be antagonized. We have already noted that management did not use the 1972 reorganization to promote LDC staff, although it did have the effect of replacing older, less flexible staff by younger people who were more dynamic, or, which is not necessarily the same, by staff more in tune with McNamara's very personal management style.

Westerners, particularly former colonial masters, almost inevitably step on sensitive toes of officials in newly independent states. Morris, writing in the early 1960s, stated

Few observers would deny that an unhappy air of superiority often issues from the place [i.e. the Bank's Washington headquarters]. I have sensed it all too strongly myself, from staff members who have been kind enough to read this manuscript and left me feeling as though I have just failed the entrance examination to a course of creative writing. It is amusing to see what diverse response this sparks. I once attended the signing ceremony of a loan to some small member nation of the Bank .... Lofty indeed was the condescension with which the Bank, whose purpose is the making of loans, agreed to make this one, and fawning to a degree was the deference with which the money was accepted, the borrowers' representative assuring the management that he was positively grateful for the difficulties the Bank had placed in their way, which had made them feel not only richer, but happier and more civilized too, and had convinced them, he seemed to suggest, that such obstructive and delaying tactics ought properly to be applied to the governing of all human affairs. On the other hand, an Indian delegate once reminded fulsomely that the Bank had lent his country a total of $600 million, turned with a sweet but abrasive smile upon the management and offered them his hearty congratulations (Morris 1963: 62-63).

Mason and Asher note that 'the Bank's record in selecting staff for foreign assignment is not one of uniform success' (1973: 743), and more generally that 'to the less developed world, the Bank often seems arrogant, remote, and demanding' (Ibidem: 71).

Mensah complains about 'some of the apprentice economists who come to write pontifical judgements about Ghana' (Mensah 1973: 10), while Nsekela notes that

the World Bank cannot claim freedom from the overwhelming arrogance of many North Americans and Europeans and of most North Atlantic or European-centred so-called global institutions. Its 'experts' have always 'known better', even when their first need was for the most elementary data, which an impartial observer might have supposed to be a precondition for forming any views on what was correct. One observed, rather grandly to some of my colleagues: 'I know what we should do in Tanzania. Of course, I have not been there yet, but I shall be out soon and stay long enough to learn all the facts I need to know. Probably two weeks' (1977: 76).

Faster and broader internationalization of staff may not in itself lead to greater sensitivity to the needs of Third World countries, and several causes for tension may continue to arise. Reid notes that the art of development diplomacy is more difficult to master than the art of most other types of diplomacy. The main reason is the strain arising from a relationship between the representative of a giver and the representative of a receiver. A young, inexperienced officer from the Bank may be assigned to a project appraisal mission where he will be discussing the project with an experienced senior official of the borrowing country. The senior official can find this extremely irritating, particularly if he belongs to a society very conscious of status, as are the societies in most of the developing two-thirds of the world. The opposite situation can be equally irritating. The Bank Group officer may find himself discussing a project with relatively junior local officials on the spot, who may believe that part of their job is to minimize difficulties in the way of the success of the project. This usually becomes clear very soon to an experienced officer, and can make him short-tempered (Reid 1973b: 92-93).

To improve developing country representation does not mean that all officers from developing countries will better comprehend the problems of LDCs than all officers from the rich; it implies, according to Reid, that

normally their chances of having a better understanding are better. Some, especially if they come from the upper classes of a highly stratified society, will have an inferior comprehension to that of most officers from rich countries. The experience of the Bank Group has demonstrated that many officers from developing countries are as insensitive to social aspirations or political problems as colonial guards – indeed, sometimes more so. Much of the present ruling classes of Latin America, for instance, or of parts of Asia and Africa, are not particularly sensitive to new aspirations. Yet it is from these ruling classes that the Bank normally recruits, thus satisfying its conscience about greater diversity without necessarily introducing greater sensitivity (Ibidem: 186).

The educational background of YPs shows that over 95 percent of those from Part II countries have done part or all of their academic studies overseas (Van de Laar 1975). In fact, the majority are recruited from a narrow range of predominantly American institutions. Ten of these account for 45% of all institutions listed for graduate studies. They are: Harvard; Oxford; Princeton; Stanford; Columbia; the University of California at Berkeley; Massachusetts Institute of Technology; the University of Pennsylvania, in particular the Wharton School; the London School of Economics; and the University of Paris. Next in line is a group led by Cornell University and the Fletcher School of Law and Diplomacy, followed by a group of universities that include Cambridge, Chicago, Wisconsin, Yale, Johns Hopkins, particularly its School of Advanced International Studies, and, perhaps somewhat surprisingly, the Universities of Louvain in Belgium and of British Columbia in Canada.

Internationalization of staff does not by itself change the character and operational policies of the Bank. It remains a Bank, and conflicts between LDCs and the Bank may remain, regardless of who is the specific representative of the Bank. The Bank has to contend with other pressure groups as well and bank staff is often caught between conflicting intergovernmental struggles.

Representatives from LDCs may not be very effective spokesmen for changing Bank policies and practices. If they want to survive in the Bank and to make a career there, which is financially and professionally probably more rewarding than other alternatives available to them, many will quickly learn to conform to majority thinking, to avoid taking controversial positions or otherwise to make themselves 'odd man out'. The pressure of bureaucratic survival generally does not allow an exceptional person to last for long. A representative from a rich country, on the other hand, may occasionally take a more radical position because, if need be, he may obtain work in his home country.

While rapid internationalization of staff might weaken the support of financiers of the Bank, a conscious effort to rapidly increase LDC staff may stimulate an undesirable brain drain from those countries and will not improve their relationship with the Bank. Moreover, Bank staff rotates frequently between assignments, and there is little reason to assume that the Bank will acquire more detailed knowledge of the intricacies of the functioning of LDCs, deeper understanding of which is absolutely necessary to enable the design of suitable projects, and to judge the chances for their successful implementation to reach the poor in these countries.

NOTES

1. The data in this section are taken from the FY 74 Administrative Budget. These data differ from at least some of the data as provided in the FY 78 Administrative Budget as is shown below. These differences are unexplained in the sources. It is however felt that for the broad analysis in this section the picture is not materially altered as far as the generalizations are concerned.

Professional staff by nationality	Per 4/30/68		Per 4/30/73	
	FY 74	FY 78	FY 74	FY 78
UK	134	144	221	229
USA	225	252	431	450
Other Part I	224	248	520	567
Part II	135	162	472	504
Total	718	806	1644	1750

2. Data are derived from Bank brochures published to date on the Young Professionals programme. Those who took up appointment through 1973 have been classified by the month of their reporting for duty. Of the earlier group, 25, presumably the whole October 1973 selection, reported for duty during the first half of 1974, although exact details are not available. No information is available about the employment dates of more recent YP groups, who are therefore listed by the publication date of their selection. The length of delay between selection and actual reporting for duty is unknown but may be up to six months, in view of the need to re-locate to Washington.
3. A total of 18 (including one woman) Dutch YPs have been recruited, making the Dutch the sixth largest nationality grouping within the Bank. They include two engineers (TH Twente, TH Eindhoven), one non-Western sociologist, one agricultural economist (LH Wageningen) and one who has completed two 'doctoral' studies, in economics and sociology (Free University). The remaining eleven are economists: four from Groningen, three from Tilburg, and two each from Erasmus University and the University of Amsterdam. One YP did not obtain a degree in the Netherlands but in the USA; another obtained degrees from Cambridge and from the London School of Economics. The others have also been peripatetic. Two did some undergraduate work in the USA and three others some graduate work: for a Master's degree in Business Administration at the University of California in Berkeley, for a Ph.D. in economics at the same institution, and for a Ph.D. in international studies at the School of Advanced International Studies of Johns Hopkins

University. Three more list graduate studies in Switzerland: at the Graduate Institute of International Studies in Geneva, and the Lausanne School of Business Administration. Finally, one YP also studied economics at the University of Kiel. In addition to study items, other things catch the eye of World Bank recruiters: internships or trainee periods, often arranged through the AIESEC organization, and experience as UN associate expert in Mexico, Swaziland and West Samoa; as trainee in South Africa; OECD Planning Fellow in Turkey; trainee in Germany, USA and Indonesia; trainee at the European Economic Community; Acting Head, Research Division in Surinam; Research Assistant in the World Bank; Foundation Fellow in Frankfurt; trainee in the USA and Australia. Two Dutch YPs did not list any prior overseas experience. The two engineers had enjoyed additional business studies abroad, a combination which is to be found among many foreign YPs.

The backgrounds of the Dutch YPs are not typical of the average Dutch university graduate. This may help to explain the stringency of the selection procedure for those who wish to join the Bank in order to see the world.

The recruitment of Dutch YPs has been irregular. None were selected in the early years 1963-65, though it may have been that Dutch nationals were then heavily over-represented in Bank staff. They were also not selected in 1969 and in 1976, which might have been in compensation for the fact that four were admitted in 1968 and 1975. Two Dutch YPs were recruited in 1970, 1973 and 1977 and one in each of the other years.

Of the 18 Dutch YPs, seven had left the Bank as at September 1978, having stayed for an average of almost six years. One of them rose to division chief in 1978.

Three other nationals in the YP programme had enjoyed part of their formal education at Dutch institutions: one in Rotterdam, and two at the Institute of Social Studies in The Hague. Of the latter, one became Assistant Director in the Bank in 1974, and Director in 1978, and the other left the Bank in 1978.

4. Nsekela (1977), suggests that LDCs should have at least 50% of the voting power, as an intermediate target.

V

ECONOMIC GROWTH AND POVERTY, AND PROSPECTS FOR A REALLOCATION OF WORLD BANK GROUP RESOURCES

INTRODUCTION

The issue of international redistribution is of considerable interest and has been neglected in the recent discussion. When McNamara announced his plans for the Bank during his second term of office, for instance, he stressed *overall* expansion. Moreover, he said: 'We plan to place far greater emphasis on policies and projects which will begin to attack the problems of absolute poverty, and far greater emphasis on assistance designed to increase the productivity of that approximately 40% of the population of our developing member countries who have neither been able to contribute significantly to national economic growth, nor to share equitably in economic progress' (McNamara 1973: 9, 10). This is rather vague when compared to the formulation of the targets for Bank Group lending during McNamara's first term of office. In September 1968 the Bank Group announced that it would double its lending in the next five years: lending to Latin America would be doubled and to Africa tripled. With respect to sectoral lending targets at least a threefold increase of lending for education was foreseen, and a fourfold increase for agriculture (McNamara 1968: 5-10).

The absence of specific regional and sectoral targets for McNamara's second term of office might lead one to infer that the country allocation of Bank Group lending as it had evolved in the period 1969-73, was satisfactory or at least not contrary to the new focus on problems of absolute poverty. On the other hand, there was a new Bank target for lending to agriculture: an increase of 40% in real terms for the next five years (McNamara 1973: 25), in line with and not exceeding, the overall rate of growth of Bank lending. In his closing remarks, McNamara referred to the record of the meeting which, in his view, showed 'strong support from Governors of developing and developed countries alike for my proposal to launch a sustained attack on the problems of what I have called absolute poverty. I sense wide agreement with my judgement that the heart of a strategy for this attack must be the development of policies and project techniques that will raise the productivity of small-scale, subsistence

---

Notes to this chapter may be found on p. 140.

farms' (*Summary Proceedings* 1973: 202). He added, however, that the 'battle against rural poverty can only be fought and won in conjunction with a continued drive toward general economic development. The World Bank, therefore, will continue to sponsor industry, power, transport and other projects outside the agricultural sector as we initiate the new programs to help the rural poor' (Ibidem: 202).

Similarly, the Bank-sponsored publication *Redistribution with Growth* (Chenery et al 1974) gives considerable attention to the development of a target group approach for various categories of the poor, and to policy packages which may benefit them. Leys (1975) doubts whether such policies could be implemented. It is remarkable that 'strident calls are made for *national* redistribution', but that there is relative silence on issues of 'international redistribution' (Lal 1976: 732).[1] As we have noted earlier, the Bank is the only UN agency with fairly substantial funds at its disposal to back up redistribution policies. The omission of any discussion in *Redistribution with Growth* of what international redistribution would mean for the allocation of the Bank's funds is therefore regrettable, to say the least.

While it is only logical that the Bank continues to work in sectors in which it has for long been involved and has obtained a comparative advantage, from the perspective of a concerted attack on the poverty problem supporting activities should be undertaken predominantly in those countries which face the gravest problems of absolute poverty. Allowance should be made for the fact that the search for effective means with which to reach the poor is, and will probably continue to be inconclusive until more experience and knowledge is gained.

Direct Bank Group lending for the poor may, for various reasons, be inappropriate or impossible under present Bank policies. Efforts should nevertheless be made in those areas where lending under current policies is possible, in order that resources may be freed for a country and its government to do the things that the Bank cannot do directly. Hence, in a poverty-focused strategy, the first question to ask is about a reallocation of Bank Group resources by countries. The second question is how the poor can be effectively reached in those countries, and this will be discussed in Chapter VI.

POST-WAR ECONOMIC GROWTH RECORDS

Aggregate performance of developed and developing countries

The UN, the World Bank and the OECD have produced figures on comparative growth performance of LDCs but the various estimates differ substantially. Discrepancies between agency estimates are particularly striking for Africa: growth rates of per capita product based on UN estimates are about a third higher than those of the World Bank, and two-thirds higher than those of the OECD. Even for Latin America, UN growth rates tend to be higher than those based on OECD and World Bank estimates. Kuznets finds such large differentials disturbing: 'one would wish that the estimating work behind these results could be unified in some way to produce a single set of acceptable measures' (Kuznets 1972: 191).

Table 5.1 *Growth rates for less developed regions. UN, OECD and World Bank estimates 1950s and 1960s*

	Real GDP			Real GDP per capita		
	1950s	1960s	1950-67 or 1950-68	1950s	1960s	1950-67 or 1950-68
East and Southeast Asia						
UN	4.0	4.4	4.2	1.9	1.9	1.9
WB	4.0	4.7	4.3	1.9	2.1	2.0
Latin America						
UN	5.5	4.9	5.3	2.6	1.9	2.4
OECD	4.9	4.7	4.8	2.0	1.7	1.9
WB	5.0	4.5	4.8	2.1	1.6	1.8
Africa (excl. S. Africa)						
UN	4.9	4.2	4.6	2.7	1.7	2.3
OECD	4.0	3.3	3.8	1.8	0.8	1.4
WB	4.0	4.0	4.0	1.7	1.6	1.7
Middle East (incl. Israel)						
UN	6.9	6.5	6.5	4.1	4.0	3.8
WB	6.0	7.2	6.5	2.9	4.2	3.4

Source: Kuznetz 1972: 192.

Widely differing figures for the mid and late 1960s were again published in 1975, as shown in Table 5.2. Since then, major changes in the classification of country groupings have made comparisons less easy.

Table 5.2 *Growth rates for developed and less developed regions, 1961-72*

	Real GDP				Real GDP per country			
	1961-65		1966-72		1961-65		1966-72	
	UN	WB	UN	WB	UN	WB	UN	WB
Developed Countries	5.4	5.2	4.3	4.7	4.1	3.9	3.2	3.6
Developing Countries	5.1	5.4	6.3	5.8	2.5	2.9	3.6	3.3
Africa	5.7	4.8	6.3	5.0	3.0	2.3	3.4	2.3
Middle East	7.2	8.2	8.1	7.6	4.0	5.1	5.3	4.5
East Asia	4.4	5.5	5.4	7.2	1.8	2.9	2.8	4.7
South Asia		3.8		4.4		1.3		2.0
Latin America and Caribbean	5.1	5.3	6.6	5.8	2.2	2.4	3.8	2.9

Source: World Bank, *Annual Report* 1975: 86-87. UN *Yearbook of National Accounts* (1975), Vol. III, Table 4A.

More recently attempts have been made to integrate and reconstruct Bank and UN published data. While this is obviously commendable, enabling *ex post* analysis of the historical growth record from a more authoritative set of figures, it must be asked whether past policy advice, based on such apparently diverging data bases, has not led to 'wrong', i.e. ill-founded economic policy recommendations.

The most recently available data, published by the World Bank, trace developments through the first half of the 1970s. These are shown in Table 5.3.

Table 5.3 *GNP per capita annual growth rates, 1951-1975*

	1951-60	1961-70	1971-75	1951-75
South Asia	2.7	1.5	0.5	1.8
East Asia	3.3	4.0	4.8	3.9
Sub-Saharan Africa	2.4	1.6	2.1	2.0
Middle East	5.0	4.4	6.4	5.0
Latin America	2.1	2.5	3.7	2.6
All developing countries	2.8	3.2	3.0	3.1
OECD countries*	3.0	3.7	1.9	3.2

* Excluding Greece, Iceland, Portugal, Spain and Turkey.

Source: World Bank: *Prospects for Developing Countries 1978-85* (November 1977), 5.

These various sets of published figures show roughly the same broad historical picture. In terms of per capita income growth DCs and LDCs showed about comparable growth rates over the period 1951-75. Since LDCs show higher average population growth, their economic growth rates have been higher than those of the DCs.

In East Asia and Latin America growth has accelerated during the period. The Middle East has shown the fastest growth but this declined during the 1960s. Economic growth in Sub-Sahara Africa also declined in the 1960s, but recovered in the first half of the 1970s. Only South Asia has shown a steady decline in GNP per capita growth rates from the 1950s through the first half of the 1970s. Both South Asia and Sub-Sahara Africa experienced below average growth rates over the period as a whole.

Some adjustments

The aggregate agency-produced growth data have been subjected to considerable methodological criticism by Kuznets (1972), who made a variety of adjustments to the UN published estimates for East and Southeast Asia and for Latin America, for the period 1954-58 to 1964-68. Residual growth estimates for Africa and the Middle East are omitted by Kuznets as being subject to too much error to be credible (Kuznets 1972: 187-92). Kuznets's adjustments are of considerable importance, particularly as international comparisons so often use only the published 'raw' data, even disregarding the discrepancies between figures from the various agencies.[2] We are interested only in the outcome of the calculations in order to show rough orders of magnitudes of the impact of adjustments needed to make the statistics more comparable.

Kuznets makes the following suggestions.

(i) Indexes of the combined totals for GDP are usually derived by compiling indexes for subregions or individual countries, multiplying them by a set of fixed weights (in the UN calculations, GDP at a factor cost in 1963 dollars), summing the results, and dividing by the sum of weights. In this procedure the growth rates of per capita product of the regions (and of the countries) are weighted by the shares of the regions (or countries) in total *product*, modified by the differential movement of the populations of the regions or countries covered, relative to the movement of the total population.

Kuznets proposes an *alternative* procedure which uses only population shares as weights, and leaves out the effects of different levels of per capita product in the subregions. This alternative calculation does not permit the greater growth rate of the subregion with the highest per capital product, as measured by its *total* product, to inflate the growth rate of the product of the whole region or group (Ibidem: 193-94).[3]

Use of the alternative procedure is justified as follows. When GDP totals for regions or countries are combined under the conventional procedure, the rise in the product of one is treated as if it directly benefited the others. The alternative procedure denies the relevance of this *pooling of product* and suggests that *population numbers* be pooled as the proper base for weighting the growth of per capita product of populations of different size (Ibidem: 194).

Aggregate growth rates of per capita product derived by the conventional method will be higher than those weighted by total population alone if (a) the higher per capita product subregions have the highest growth rate; or if (b) the population of the higher per capita product subregions increases more rapidly than that of the lower per capita product subregions, or if any combination of the two yields a positive excess.

A similar reasoning can be extended to countries within a region (Ibidem: 194, 198). The result of these adjustments for subregions and countries are shown in Table 5.5, lines 3 and 4.

(ii) The alternative calculation procedure can similarly be extended to population groups within a country. This refinement has received considerable attention since it was adopted in *Redistribution with Growth*. Chenery et al (1974), proposed (p. 39) that development performance should be monitored not simply in terms of GNP with its implied income weights for population groups, but in terms of the distributional growth pattern whereby the weights for each income class reflect the social premium on generating growth at each income level.

Under conditions of considerable internal inequality, the growth of GNP measures the progress of population groups which appropriate that income *as if* benefits accrue to other income groups as well. The Kuznets procedure weights the income growth of individual population groups. It is then also possible to assign greater weights to the progress of lower income groups, i.e. poverty weights, as suggested in *Redistribution with Growth*. There are thus three ways to measure an increase in welfare, whereby such an increase is defined as the weighted sum of income growth of all groups. Thus, if the welfare functions are defined in terms of the size distribution of income, we obtain the following equations:

$$G = w_1 g_1 + w_2 g_2 + w_3 g_3 + w_4 g_4 + w_5 g_5$$

(a) Actual income weights LDCs (average) 0.53   0.22   0.13   0.07   0.05
(b) Population weights (Kuznets)   0.20   0.20   0.20   0.20   0.20
(c) Poverty weights (Chenery et al)   0.10   0.15   0.15   0.30   0.30

Chenery et al have calculated increases in welfare with the use of the above welfare function, and some of their results are given in Table 5.4. As may be seen from the sample cases, short-term effects on welfare may be sizeable.

Table 5.4 *Income distribution and growth*

| Country | Period | Income growth | | | Annual increase in welfare | | |
		upper 20%	middle 40%	lowest 40%	(A) GNP weights	(B) Equal weights	(C) Poverty weights
Taiwan	1953-60	4.5	9.1	12.1	6.8	9.4	10.4
Sri Lanka	1963-70	3.1	6.2	8.3	5.0	6.4	7.2
Korea	1964-70	10.6	7.8	9.3	9.3	9.0	9.0
Brazil	1960-70	8.4	4.8	5.2	6.9	5.7	5.4
Venezuela	1962-70	7.9	4.1	3.7	6.4	4.7	4.2
India	1954-64	5.1	3.9	3.9	4.5	4.1	4.0

Source: Chenery et al 1974: 42.

The authors limit the use of population weights to monitoring progress in welfare as measured by GNP to population groups *within* countries. Kuznets is of the opinion, however, that the use of population weights *within* countries is less appropriate than *between* countries. The rise in income of one domestic group can and does redound to the benefit of others *if* the additional income is invested in capital that would raise the productivity of every inhabitant of the country. Thus if the spread effects of such investments are greater nationally than internationally, the conventional procedure would be preferable. Dependency theorists, like Frank and Laclau, may tend to argue that linkages between enclaves in the LDCs and the metropolis are stronger than those between the enclaves and the rest of the LDC economy. Modernization theorists may argue that the development process enhances national integration and that these national linkages become more important than international linkages. The weight of the evidence is probably with the latter view, even though international linkages of investment and income flows may be quite substantial in some cases. Application of the population-weighted growth index internationally is thus to be preferred over the Chenery proposal to do so only within a national context.[4]

Beckerman (1977) has criticized the method used in *Redistribution with Growth* to adjust GNP growth rates for changes in income distribution, on the grounds that (1) no clear interpretation can be given to weights attributed to the income growth of individual income groups, and (2) no precise meaning can be attached to the adjusted growth rates obtained. Hence, it is as yet impossible to use the *Redistribution with Growth* methodology for monitoring the growth of LDC incomes, all the more so because data on the size distribution of income represent only statistical categories and do not help to identify the socio-economic characteristics of those who receive the lowest shares. Not until these population groups can be identified in their structural characteristics will it be of use to consider them as target groups whose progress can or should be monitored.

(iii) The growth rate of total product of a country or region can be viewed as a weighted average of the growth rates of output in the various sectors. Kuznets questions whether the weights used in combining sectoral outputs and growth rates for LDCs and DCs are comparable, because the ratios of prices of industrial products to those of agricultural products are generally much higher in the former than in the developed countries. The industrial sector and perhaps also the services sector consequently have greater weight in current price estimates for LDCs than they would have in those for DCs. To obtain better comparability Kuznets proposes some 'rough but realistic' corrections (Kuznets 1972: 203) by putting the ratio of industrial (I) prices to agricultural (A) prices in LDCs at 1.5, compared with 1.0 in DCs, and by putting the ratio of services (S) prices to agricultural (A) prices at 1.25 to 1.0. The results are given in Table 5.5, line 5.

(iv) The growth of the services sector in LDCs is generally higher than that of GDP. Some of these services may not be in the nature of final product and reflect merely the cost of urbanization and modernization. The sector has been omitted for East and Southeast Asia, implying that the growth rate of output of the services sector is assumed the same as that of the combined agricultural and industrial sectors. A rapid urbanization process is noted for Latin America, which means that the proportion of total final consumption at the higher relative prices of urban communities introduces an element of inflation even into the constant price estimates. Allowances of a two-to-one differential in per capita final consumption in rural and urban communities, at the same prices, and of a price differential of 1.5 to 1.0, have been introduced (Ibidem: 206). The effect of this modification is given in Table 5.5, line 6.

The cumulation of the various adjustments leads to rather substantive changes in the UN published data, as is shown in Table 5.5.

Table 5.5 *Annual growth rates of per capita product, 1954-58 to 1964-68,*
LDCs and DCs, successive adjustments

	East and Southeast Asia	Latin America	LDCs*	DCs incl. Japan	excl. Japan
1. Total as reported in UN sources (conventional weighting)	1.71	2.16	2.21	3.38	nc
2. Omitting some countries (for better definition and greater reliability)	1.71	2.16	2.00	3.31	2.96
3. Weighting regions by constant population	1.71	2.16	1.80	4.07	3.10
4. Adjusting for individual country weights	1.46	2.34	1.64	4.11	3.14
5. Adjusting for changed weights of I and S sectors relative to A sector (LDCs only)	1.22	2.20	1.42	4.11	3.14
6. Other adjustments**	0.89	1.74	1.06	ne	ne

Note: nc = not calculated, ne = not estimated.
*   Excluding Africa and the Middle East, data for which have been deleted because of unreliability. See also Table 5.2 above.
** Those under point (iv) in the text.

Source: Kuznets 1972: Table 9.

These figures show a much gloomier picture of the growth of performance of LDCs as compared to that of DCs than the raw data presented earlier, but may be assumed to be more comparable than the official data. If it is accepted that the growth record of Africa and the Middle East is no better than that of ESEA and LA, which seems at least plausible in view of Africa's slow growth, and if the trend is extrapolated backwards to the early 1950s, then the relative disparity between average per capita incomes in rich and poor countries apparently did not increase from a multiple of 10.7 in the early 1950s to 12.0 in the late 1960s, but to sixteen. Moreover, Kuznets based his calculations on the most optimistic data, those of the UN, and not on the lower estimates of World Bank and OECD (see Table 5.2). Incomes in rich and poor countries and between groups of poor countries thus seem to grow away from each other much more quickly than is often asserted, and tensions between the two groups are likely to increase if these trends continue over the next 25 years. If any broad-based attempt to halt these diverging income trends is to be launched, attention will need to be directed towards those regions which have experienced slow growth even from very low average per capita income levels, i.e. towards South Asia and Sub-Sahara Africa.

The extent of poverty

Several attempts have been made in recent years to estimate the numbers of people living in conditions of poverty. The World Bank and the ILO have arbitrarily defined poverty lines, taking per capita incomes at 85% of GNP per capita at factor cost. Data from national accounts have been combined with information about the size distribution of incomes of individual countries. The population below any poverty line can then be read off the Lorenz curve at the point where the slope of the curve equals the ratio of the poverty income level to per capita income (Chenery et al 1974: 10).

Data on the size distribution of incomes are limited and of generally dubious quality. Early compilations may be found in Kuznets (1963), since when a major contribution has been made by Adelman & Morris (1971), who produced data on income distribution for 44 developing countries. In working with the Adelman-Morris data, however, Paukert noted that they contained mistakes and inconsistencies (Paukert 1973: 124), and his own data, pertaining to the situation around 1965, are to be preferred. The World Bank has also been heavily involved in compiling data on the size distribution of incomes. These were reported on firstly by Ahluwalia (in Chenery et al 1974: Ch. 1); secondly in the Bank's Sector Policy Paper on Rural Development (1975); and thirdly by Ahluwalia (1976). The most recent data (Jain 1975) are for as many as 81 countries, six of which are communist (Bulgaria, Czechoslovakia, Germany DR, Hungary, Poland and Yugoslavia), with about two-thirds of the remainder among the LDCs. Jain does not claim responsibility for quality, but Kuznets considers that the extension of coverage to more countries with inadequate data bases than those for which he published data in 1963, calls for greater discretion. The inclusion of communist countries obviously requires some thought concerning the institutional conditions of income distribution and their comparability with market economies. More relevant is the probability that estimates for many LDCs rest on 'extremely flimsy foundations'. The likelihood of securing a defensible estimate for a country such as Sudan, Libya or Benin is small. And what should one think of size distribution of income for countries which have never had a population census? (Kuznets 1976: 4). One might add that population censuses are sometimes deliberately tampered with if the outcome is to serve as a yardstick for political representation or for the distribution of central government finances to regional governments.[5]

The Bank uses 'poverty lines' of $50 and $75 of annual per capita income (in 1971 prices). The ILO (1976) uses somewhat different standards based, for its definition of 'seriously poor', on the average earnings of unskilled labour in

large-scale manufacturing enterprises in India, and on the equivalent of one
rupee per person per day in Indian terms for its category 'destitute'. These
figures have been converted into a crude 'purchasing power parity' index, on
the assumption that a typical basket of goods consumed by the poor and
costing US$1 in Western Europe could be obtained for 20 cents in Asia, 23
cents in Africa and 36 cents in Latin America. This avoids the distortion associated with conversion based on official exchange rates, and reflects more
accurately the fact that many items consumed by the poor do not enter into
international commerce (see Richards 1976, for details).

On this basis, the poverty line of the 'seriously poor' is equivalent to per
capita income of US$500 in Western Europe, $180 in Latin America, $115 in
Africa and $100 in Asia. Similarly, the 'destitute' comprise those with an in-
come equivalent to US$250 in Western Europe, $90 in Latin America, $58 in
Africa and $50 in Asia. The last number coincides with the lower World Bank
standard.

Table 5.6 shows percentages of populations below the poverty lines, as
calculated by the World Bank and the ILO.

Table 5.6 *People in poverty, around 1970*

	Asia	*Africa*	*Latin America*	*Total*
World Bank				
below $50	415	115	30	560
below $75	620	165	50	835
Total population (1969)	1080	360	260	1700
ILO				
destitute	499	134	73	706
seriously poor	853	239	118	1210
Total population (1972)	1196	345	274	1815
% of population				
World Bank				
below $50	38	32	12	33
below $75	57	46	19	49
ILO				
destitute	42	39	27	39
seriously poor	71	69	43	67

Source: IBRD, *Rural Development* (1975), 79 (this calculation has a wider country coverage than the presentation in Chenery et al 1974);
ILO, *Employment, Growth and Basic Needs* (1976), 22.

Country coverage by the two agencies is apparently not the same. For Asia
and Africa, ILO estimates for 'destitutes' fall somewhere between the two
poverty lines used by the Bank, while for Latin America ILO finds many more
'destitutes' than the Bank, which follows from ILO's higher valued consumer
goods basket for the poor. In all, some 40 percent of total population in all
developing market economies may be said to live in a state of absolute poverty,

i.e. 'destitute'; 70 percent of these live in Asia, some 19 percent in Africa and 10 percent in Latin America.

The growth of poverty

In addition to global calculations of the extent of poverty, several attempts have been made to calculate the growth (or decline) of poverty over time.

The ILO applied the methodology shown in the previous section to 1963 and to 1972 in order to calculate changes in poverty over time, and using the same income distribution data. The calculations show that poverty increased, by ILO standards, between 1963 and 1972. This is shown in Table 5.7. Whereas the proportion of population in each poverty category declined slightly in each region, this was offset by demographic expansion, so that the group in poverty increased in absolute numbers. Of the 32 individual countries for which data are available, the number of 'destitute' increased in 17 countries and those who suffered from 'serious poverty' increased in fourteen.

Table 5.7 *Increase in poverty, 1963-1972 (mln. of persons)*

Region	Total population	Seriously poor	Destitute
Asia	195	92	34
Africa	68	26	5
Latin America	62	1	4
Total	325	119	43

Source: ILO (1976), 23.

The most recent data that document the spread of poverty are to be found in the study by the ILO World Employment Programme (ILO 1977). This shows that in most Asian countries the incomes of the very poor have fallen absolutely, that the proportion of the rural population living below a designated 'poverty line' has increased, or both. Statistical investigations were restricted to Asia and to one sector of economic activity, the rural sector, because this contains the biggest concentration of mass poverty in the world. The empirical studies cover four populous states in India (Uttar Pradesh, Bihar, Tamil Nadu and the Punjab), Pakistan, Bangladesh, Sri Lanka, Malaysia, Indonesia (with special reference to Java) and the Philippines, and the People's Republic of China by way of contrast. The only major market economies of South and Southeast Asia to be excluded are Thailand, Burma, Nepal and Taiwan. In the first three of the latter the distribution of rural income and the incidence of rural poverty are unlikely to be very different from the rest of the region. In one sense, circumstances in these countries were less favourable in that, over the decade ending in the mid-1970s, per capita food production in Nepal and Burma actually declined while that in Thailand remained unchanged.

Most of the other countries studied, in contrast, showed some increase in per capita food output over the same period (Ibidem, Ch. 1). The situation in Taiwan is different but Taiwan is a very special case (Griffin 1976: Ch. 7). Socialist countries in the region, other than China, have all been affected by war in recent years, or have turned socialist only in the current decade. Their experiences are therefore both less useful and more difficult to analyse.

The ILO-sponsored study attempts to determine the trends in absolute and relative incomes of the rural poor, whereby the scope and method of analysis had to be adapted to available information, making inter-country comparability difficult. The authors have covered the longest time period possible, and have brought the story as close to the present as possible, covering a period that varies from a decade to a quarter-century. In each case, however, the analysis includes the period during which the new 'green revolution' technology was adopted. This is of particular interest for our present study because, according to the Bank, the proposed strategy for rural development should be based in part on these technologies (see further Chapter VI).

What, then, were the findings? First, a level of real income was defined below which all households were classified as poor. In most studies the 'poverty line' was derived from an estimate of the income necessary to ensure a minimum diet, although they differed widely as to the contents of a minimum diet. In each case, however, it was found that the proportion of population below the 'poverty line' has increased over time. Second, the real income of decile or quintile groups at different points of time were calculated and here it was found that the real income of the lowest groups has declined over time. The range over which this has occurred differs: in the Philippines, for example, the bottom 20 percent of the population experienced a decline in real income, but over 80 percent of the population in Bangladesh.

The other major empirical finding concerned the trend in real wages of agricultural labourers. In most of the countries for which measurements could be obtained real wages remained constant or there was a significant downward trend. In a few cases the trend was ambiguous, although even then there was always clear evidence that living standards had not improved. Within the group of agricultural labourers the importance of skilled labour and of operators of mechanical equipment —concomitants of the green revolution – has increased considerably. Given the initial shortage of skills, the rise in demand for such workers has undoubtedly caused a relatively rapid increase in their wages. On the other hand, the balance between the supply and demand for more traditional types of labour became increasingly unfavourable over time, and wages consequently failed to rise (ILO 1977, Ch. 1).

In contrast, the statistical evidence for the People's Republic of China, although less complete than that from other countries, demonstrates convincingly that rural inequality and poverty have been reduced enormously.

One of the principal underlying causes for this was apparently an effective initial land reform (Ibidem, Ch. 12).

Finally, there is the collection of studies on income distribution and poverty in India (Srinivasan & Bardhan 1974). The official Agricultural Labour Consumer Price Index for deflating the consumption of the rural poor, and the official Working Class Consumer Price Index for deflating that of the urban poor, are combined with the National Sample Survey expenditure distribution. It appeared that in 1968-69 as much as 54 percent of the rural population of India were below the poverty line of Rupees 15 per capita per month, and that 41 percent of the urban population were below the poverty line of Rs 18 per capita per month, all at 1960-61 prices.[6]

Using the same data, the percentage of rural people below the poverty line apparently increased from 38 percent in 1960-61, to 45 percent in 1964-65, 53 percent in 1967-68, and to 54 percent in 1968-69. Urban population below the poverty line increased from 32 percent in 1960-61, to 35 percent in 1964-65 and 41 percent in 1968-69. The direction of change remains the same under all the various alternative minimum standards for the poverty line suggested in the literature (Bardhan 1974: 124, 130, 131).

After reworking and updating the National Sample Survey data through 1973-74 Johri and Pandey conclude:

the year 1970-71 now appears to be the great historical dividing line in the post-Independence India that separates the previous period of relative stability in the population of the poor, from the one that followed, and is marked by great acceleration. The cataclysmic jump in the rate of poverty proliferation occurred from 4.24 % per year in the decade preceding 1970-71 to the highly abnormal rate of over 19 % (Johri & Pandey 1978: 4).

PROSPECTS FOR REALLOCATION OF BANK GROUP RESOURCES
TOWARDS POORER COUNTRIES

If these data on the post-war growth record are to be believed, there has indeed been a growing divergence of per capita income trends between rich and poor across and between countries. The absolute differences in real income are probably not as great as figures on GNP per capita would indicate (Kravis et al 1975, 1978), yet differentials have widened. A major long-term target for development assistance should be those who lag behind and the absolutely poor, and this is what the Bank aims to do (McNamara 1973: 9). Because poverty is concentrated heavily in Asia, a focus on (South) Asia, and to a lesser extent on Africa, would mean relative decline of external assistance to Latin America. This might have considerable implications for the Bank's future role there, and for its character as a World Bank which should help as wide a clientele as possible.

The Bank's Sector Policy Paper on Rural Development shows politically-adjusted thinking (1975: 20-21). In the mid-1970s, on the basis of a $50 annual income, some 550 million people suffer absolute poverty in the rural areas of the developing world. Three-quarters of these are to be found in Asia, and almost two-thirds of that subtotal in India, Pakistan, Bangladesh and Indonesia. In contrast, the developing countries of Latin America and the Caribbean account for only 4 percent of the population in absolute poverty. Significantly, 53 countries whose annual per capita incomes are more than $150, taken together account for only 8 percent of the absolute poverty in rural areas.[7]

In addition, the Rural Development paper introduces the notion of 'relative poverty' comprising those who receive less than one-third of the national average per capita income. This concept relates to the wellknown proposition that welfare can be seen as a function of absolute as well as of relative incomes. National governments often begin to initiate welfare measures for those below one-third of average GNP. This group of relatively poor has a 'better' geographical distribution than the absolute poor: 48% in Asia, 25% in Africa, and 27% in Latin America. Together they make up 18% of the total population of developing countries, in contrast to 34% under the absolute $50 poverty standard.

The absolute poor are then added to the number of those whose per capita incomes exceed $50 but are less than one-third of the national average. With explicit reference to the 40% figure which has gained currency since McNamara's 1973 Nairobi speech, the group of the poor is constructed from the absolute and relative poor.

Such a mixed target group is analytically rather confusing though politically perhaps understandable. Given the extreme income dualism in many Latin American countries, the introduction of the relative poverty concept puts Latin America back into the picture from which it could almost disappear using only the Bank's absolute poverty criterion. The mixing of the two groups, however, has the undesirable effect that people whose income level is less than $50 are lumped together with people with much higher incomes in other parts of the world: up to $540 in Argentina, $335 in Yugoslavia, $295 in Mexico, $290 in Iran and $250 in Brazil, on the basis of national average incomes for 1973 (*World Bank Atlas* 1975).

In adjusting for purchasing power differences between continents, the ILO managed, on more defensible grounds, to incorporate more Latin Americans in its geographical distribution of poverty. The World Bank on the other hand, took recourse to an amalgamation of quite different population groups. No such amalgamation was carried out in *Redistribution of Growth*, perhaps because that book did not reflect Bank policy as did the Sector Policy Paper on Rural Development. Only the latter had the benefit of prior management and Board discussion and approval.

While the use of size distribution of incomes provides a yardstick by which the poor may be identified statistically, average per capita incomes provide a more practical measure by which to delineate the broad focus of Bank lending for the poor, giving some rank order to the countries, which is of greater significance than absolute per capita income levels. Moreover, a low per capita income figure usually indicates that a country also scores low on many other development indicators and therefore, despite its shortcomings, may serve as a proxy for 'poverty'. We shall use this as a yardstick in our discussion of a reallocation of Bank Group resources by country.

Reallocation of IBRD lending

Customarily, the world is divided into rich and poor countries, and the Bank phased-out lending to the former at the close of its reconstruction phase. Since the early 1950s it has concentrated its lending on the developing countries, and it could perhaps be argued that it is already focusing on the poor of the world, and that no change in the future country allocation of Bank funds is called for. Such reasoning would be trite, however.

To underpin a major long-term change in direction of future Bank lending, it seems necessary that, at any given level of lending 'overall', it should be focused on a narrower range of countries. A number of countries need to be declared 'developed', allowing the Bank to gradually phase-out its lending to them and enabling resources, money and staff to be concentrated on the others.

To avoid having to make difficult choices of priorities between countries, it may be argued that lending to higher income countries may be continued provided it is directed to their poorer regions. Structural bottlenecks and regional parities can always be cited to justify the continuance of past lending patterns. No-one will deny that the UK and Italy face serious balance-of-payments, structural and regional problems. Yet Bank lending to them has been phased-out in the past, and the Bank should take a similar decision now for another group of its members.

At issue is where to draw the line for inter-country priorities. Are regional income disparities in higher income countries judged more intractable than national development problems in those with lower average incomes which may also face regional and sectoral problems? Countries with higher average incomes have attained a broader resource base which enables them to pursue policies directed towards redistribution with or from growth, than have countries whose lower average incomes give them much less to distribute. To the extent that Bank Group assistance is usually marginal, it can probably better be used to help increase the national pie in poorer countries than to back up redistributive policies in richer countries. Countries with population pockets in absolute or relative poverty, say the Northeast of Brazil or the southern states of Yugoslavia, often display strong political, social and cultural cleavages which may cause minority groups to be excluded from the political process which decides on resource allocation. The notion that international donors should step in in cases where the national body politic is either unable or unwilling to do much for its own poor, assumes that international solidarity should be greater than national solidarity. This is likely to run into very serious political opposition in at least some donor countries.[8] The experience of such minority groups with continuous confrontation with the prevailing power structure may have caused them to withdraw to regions and activities where such confrontation can be evaded. It is then difficult to imagine that external official assistance, which has to operate through national governments and the existing power structure can be a lever for improving the terms of their incorporation into the wider national society.

Moreover, many higher income countries have by now ample access to alternative sources of external finance. The leverage associated with Bank lending will then be much less than in lower income countries which do not have such access to the same degree. A reduced future role for the Bank in those countries fits its purpose as a lender of last resort. On balance it therefore seems that reallocation of lending by country would be preferable and more promising than a reallocation to poorer regions within relatively more developed countries. This is not to say that Bank studies and policy advices in higher income countries should also cease. It may still be worthwhile to study whether the nature of new technologies reduces the chance that lagging population groups will ever be able to catch up in a modernization process which benefits them. But it would then no longer be possible for the Bank to link advice to loans, and thus to add a stick to the carrot.

A second argument for avoiding the issue of establishing priorities between countries is that poorer countries may not have sufficient bankable projects to permit a rapid expansion of Bank lending. In the past, the dearth of well-prepared projects has been said to be the main constraint on the volume of bank lending (Baum 1970). George Woods held this view, while McNamara tested this assumption by setting ambitious lending targets which were subsequently surpassed. Over time, capacity to prepare projects undoubtedly has increased in most countries, and there is no obvious reason why a shift in lending to lower income countries should mean that quantitative lending targets could not be met, particularly now that the Board's discussions, in the context of the General Capital Increase, centre on a future growth of lending of 5% per year in real terms, compared to 8% in the early 1970s. The pressure to spend money, however, may lead to a preference for different types of projects. If meeting quantitative lending targets is seen to be important, it is very tempting to spend money in juicy chunks for purposes that otherwise would not be considered. When the Bank became involved in a multibillion dollar programme for modernizing the Brazilian steel industry it could easily have committed more than the $242 million actually invested in the projects in fiscal 1972.

This amount may have been no more than 10-20% of total programme cost, yet it represented 8% of total IBRD lending in that year. Similarly, other sectors can absorb vast amounts of funds, e.g. hydropower stations, electrification schemes, chemical industries, petroleum investments, and so on. Thus it would seem that a shift to poorer countries need not conflict with quantitative lending targets.

It may well be possible, however, that excessive concern with quantitative lending targets may hamper the search for small and difficult projects that will directly benefit the poor. A predilection for large capital-intensive projects may still be defended on the grounds that such Bank intervention would free national resources for the poor. Whether such compensating action would really occur might be difficult to prove, however, certainly if one way to measure a shift in Bank resources is to study what the Bank *itself* will finance in future projects in implementing its new strategy. Justification for lending for traditional projects and sectors in which the Bank has a comparative advantage, would then have to be found in demonstrating that a country has shifted its national policies in such a way as to increase chances for improving the conditions of lagging population groups. This is a tall order in the absence of sufficient knowledge and understanding about the nature of the growth process and of the effects of policies on different population groups.

A third argument against refocusing Bank Group lending may be that lending to poorer countries may run into creditworthiness problems. Perhaps so, but such risks are not confined to poorer countries. Some rich countries also have limited external creditworthiness. Moreover, the assumption would then be that Bank lending in 1969-1974 was not risky and did not meet with constraints stemming from limited creditworthiness of the recipient countries. To the contrary, however, the Bank made nearly half its new loans in that period to countries which the 1971 Bank External Debt study judged to be vulnerable in that respect. Nevertheless, as lack of creditworthiness of recipients is perhaps the most serious constraint on Bank lending, the issue will be taken up again in some detail below (p. 136).

A final argument frequently heard against a major reallocation of resources towards the poorer nations is that the very poor are beyond being helped, that to assist them will merely prolong their misery without providing any hope that their conditions will be improved in the long run. Such harsh condemnation of the 'Fourth World' may be 'sweetened' somewhat by ascribing the misery to 'unjust' ruling structures, and it is sometimes rationalized by saying that any support given to those structures will perpetuate human misery. In contrast, so the argument goes, external aid should be focused on those who have a real chance to develop on their own strength; aid should not be dissipated to those beyond relief and, in any case there is insufficient aid to help everybody.

Apart from the reprehensible arrogance of those who wallow in relative affluence in condemning those who can barely keep their heads above water, several other factors should be considered. A withdrawal of aid may indeed hasten the downfall of an 'unjust' regime, but there is no guarantee that it will be succeeded by one that will prove less 'unjust' and oppressive. Confronted with the same stubborn problems of hunger and poverty, new regimes are likely to forget their campaign promises once they gain power or, in the many instances where changes in government merely reflect intra-elite exchanges, election promises for broad-based reforms are not even made *ex-ante*, let alone implemented *ex-post*.

Neglect of the Fourth World by aid donors does not mean that that world will cease to exist, and arguments that the rich cannot afford more aid are untenable when confronted, for instance, with the resources that they waste on useless armaments: total world military expenditure in 1976 was more than the GNPs of Africa and South America combined! (Barnaby 1977: 21).

Losers

What possibilities are open to the IBRD to do *relatively* more for poorer countries? Several options may be pursued seriatim.

As of June 1978, loans amounting to $967 million, or 2.9 percent of its total portfolio, were owed to the Bank by Part I countries: some $399 million by Japan, and the remainder by ten other Part I countries, with Australia ($120 mln.), Finland ($82 mln.) and Ireland ($137 mln.) accounting for the bulk. Advance repayments of those debts, particularly by 'past borrowers', would provide the Bank with an extra margin of lending capacity. Such advance repayments can only be requested, however, and may be objected to if pressure is exerted because 'contracts are contracts'. Japan's current balance-of-payments surplus could no doubt be used to repay debts to the Bank, but it may be that Japan would consider early repayment in conjunction with a refusal to permit the Bank new access to the Japanese capital market for the immediate future for new bank borrowings. The net gains for the Bank, though not insignificant, are thus not likely to be very great, and only a few countries could be called upon to give the Bank extra lending space.

An easy way for the Bank to narrow its list of future clients would be to harmonize the various definitions of LDCs that are in current use. Prior to its new orientation on the poor, the Bank still lent to member countries which, according to the UN classification, should not be on the list of developing countries. This is summarized in Table 5.8, which shows that lending to these countries is now negligible to all but Greece. A further reduction would not give the Bank much scope for a major reorientation of its lending to poorer countries. Lending to Greece may perhaps cease when that country joins the European Economic Community in the near future.

Table 5.8 *IBRD lending to high income countries*

Country	Per capita GNP in 1975	1969-74	1975	1976	1977	1978	1985-78
Iceland	5620*	11	–	–	–	–	–
Finland	4710	75	20	–	–	–	20
New Zealand	4680*	24	–	–	–	–	–
Israel	3469	140	35	–	–	–	35
Spain	2750	240	33	–	18	–	51
Ireland	2390	123	–	30	–	–	30
Greece	2340	152	70	70	71	90	301
Total		765	158	100	89	90	437
annual average		127					109
as % of new commitments		6.3					2.1

* *World Bank Atlas* 1976, Annex.

Source: *Annual Reports*. The per capita income figures in this and the following tables are taken mostly from the 1977 *Annual Report*. A shift in the base period from 1973-75 to 1974-76 means that the estimates differ from those shown in the Annex of the *World Bank Atlas* 1976.

A major concentration of effort and funds on the poorer countries would seem to call for a more drastic curtailment of countries that are eligible for Bank lending in the future. Let us consider the implications of a lowering of the upper limit to, say, about twice the upper eligibility limit for IDA lending, or above $1000 GNP per capita in 1975 dollars. To take a broader range, say, up to three times the IDA limit, or about $1600, would not yield enough in terms of lending volume and numbers of countries, for which a discussion might be initiated about possible stabilization and longer-term phasing-out of Bank lending. The 20 countries thus obtained are listed in Table 5.9. The group is of interest for several reasons: geographically, ideologically and politically. It includes nine countries in Latin America, several OPEC countries, the two large Eastern European socialist countries which are members of the Bank, and Portugal, a member of long-standing which became an active borrower in 1976. The group also includes six major customers of the Bank — Iran, Argentina, Yugoslavia, Romania, Mexico and Brazil, which together accounted for 29% of the Bank's portfolio as at June 1978 (Table 2.4).

IBRD lending to the OPEC countries in this group has ceased since 1974, whether temporarily or permanently is not clear. For the medium term they enjoy a resource surplus and, if they should need additional resources, could attract funds from the international capital market. To the extent that they would want to avail themselves of technical assistance, the Bank could provide this on a reimbursable basis. While Iran and Venezuela can continue to borrow from the Bank, this is expected to be offset by a reverse flow of funds (World

Table 5.9   *IBRD lending to countries with per capita GNP over $1600 and $1000 (1975) respectively (in $mln)*

Country	GNP p.c. 1975 ($)	Population 1975 (mln)	New IBRD commitments** 1969-74	New IBRD commitments** 1975-78
Bahamas	3110	0.2	–	10
Gabon	2540	0.5	16	5
Singapore	2450	2.3	84	25
Venezuela	2220*	12.0	136	–
Oman	2100	0.8	8	17
Trinidad & Tobago	2000	1.1	56	12
Iran	1660	33.4	823	53
Total		50.3	1123	122
annual average			187	41
as % of new commitments			9.3	0.6
Portugal	1570	9.6	–	241
Argentina	1550	25.4	319	485
Yugoslavia	1550	21.4	548	1073
Uruguay	1300	2.8	53	62
Panama	1290	1.7	100	106
Iraq	1280*	11.1	120	–
Cyprus	1240	0.6	53	35
Romania	1240	21.2	60	823
Jamaica	1110	2.0	54	131
Fiji	1090	0.6	18	17
Lebanon	1070***	3.2	40	50
Mexico	1050	60.0	1073	1302
Brazil	1030	107.0	1307	2055
Total		266.6	3745	6380
annual average			624	1595
as % of new commitments			30.9	30.2

*   1976 *World Bank Atlas*, Annex.
**   totals may not add up due to rounding.
***   1974.

Bank: *Questions and Answers*, March 1976: 12); the two countries have not made use of this option to date, however. The last loans to Iran were in August and September 1974, i.e. for projects which were well-advanced before the new policy took effect. Similarly, lending to Iraq has ceased and lending to Gabon has been very limited.

Lending to the seven countries whose per capita incomes are over $1600 declined from 8.3% of total in 1969-74 to 0.6% in 1975-78, a very sizable reduction indeed, which may be sustained in future, i.e. these countries may be able to fend for themselves. The decrease is largely due to the fact that Iran no longer borrowed from the Bank.

Thirteen countries had a per capita GNP of between $1000 and $1570 in 1975.

Lending to Argentina is clearly controversial. Between 1972 and 1976 it received no loans at all, but lending of no less than $320 mln was approved in FY 1977: for highways $105 mln; electric power for Buenos Aires $115 mln; and Development Finance Companies $100 mln. The $165 mln approved in FY 1978 was for grain storage and agricultural credit. The power loan includes arrangements to extend electricity to 250,000 people living in about 110 shanty towns (*Annual Report* 1977: 70). Although the military regime took measures in 1976 to restore external creditworthiness in order to make lending possible, few would rate the regime as deeply concerned with improving the lot of the poor. On country grounds it is thus difficult to justify lending to Argentina, particularly if heavy weight is given to national policies to benefit the poor. On project grounds, however, the power and agricultural projects seem to be defensible. The US abstained from voting twice in 1977 (IBRD and IFC) and voted against three loans to Argentina proposed by the IADB, on human rights considerations, thereby stressing its view that the mere restoration of creditworthiness was insufficient justification for a resumption of lending by international financial institutions (Long Hearings: 565).

Heavy Bank lending will obviously tend to legitimize the military regime. Many outsiders will find it difficult to avoid the conclusion that the Bank and its management is hypocritical; this will harm the image of the Bank and destroy much of the goodwill that McNamara has tried to create in reorienting policies towards the poor. These policies can only be successful if there is also national commitment to the same effect, and it is difficult to argue that that is the characterizing label of the regime presently in power in Argentina.

Lending to Portugal is quite different: an unpopular military dictatorship was overthrown and Bank lending may be seen as assisting the country to develop along more democratic lines.

Lending to Mexico has barely kept up with inflation. The future availability of oil revenues for that country makes it seem likely that Bank lending can gradually be reduced in relative terms.

Lending to Yugoslavia and Romania has a clearly political significance, in that both countries are trying to change from their strong Soviet Russian orientation. It therefore seems unlikely that the Bank will pressure them to reduce their borrowings. In fact, annual lending to Yugoslavia rose from annual levels of $91 mln in 1969-74 to $268 mln in 1975-78. Lending to Romania has also developed remarkably quickly, given the very short duration of its relationship with the Bank.

The outlook for future lending to this group of 13 countries remains rather vague. Portugal might be inclined to seek assistance from the EEC. Lending to Yugoslavia and Romania may continue at high levels for political reasons, and Mexico and Brazil are both at the lower end of the per capita income scale. The scope for 'savings' in this group to be diverted to poorer countries is thus fairly limited.

While lending to the 13 may continue at high absolute levels, the leverage which the Bank can exercise on them in pursuit of better income distributional policy goals is obviously diminished, although it may be questioned whether it has ever been very great in view of their size and sophistication in setting their own priorities. Brazil, Mexico, Yugoslavia and Argentina have been among the largest borrowers in the Eurodollar market,[9] and this has reduced the significance of the World Bank in their external financial flows in recent years, and thereby its leverage in pressing for new distributional objectives.

If pressure on the Bank increases to phase-out lending to higher income countries in order to do more for those with lower average per capita incomes, the process of Bank withdrawal from large parts of Latin America will be accelerated. The Bank, on its own saying, will need considerable time to develop projects and policies that will benefit the poorer strata of society, and it may well be that by, say, the mid- to late-1980s, that expertise will no longer be relevant as many LA countries will have become independent of Bank tutelage. From this perspective, it seems strange to have introduced the concept of relative poverty which, as we have noted, had as its objective the inclusion of Latin America in an improved geographical map of poverty. Though the need for a poverty orientation may continue in large parts of Latin America, the Bank will then no longer be in a position to assist implementation through direct lending activities.

One argument sometimes used for caution in 'declaring' countries to be 'developed' rather than 'developing' is that past borrowers may evolve into contributors to IDA: an argument that may not have much appeal for Latin America. Several countries in the region are not even members of IDA whose credits to Latin America are very limited, given IDA eligibility criteria. Cultural and social affinity may be important forces in instigating aid programmes, however, and it is difficult to believe that Latin American countries would be willing to contribute through IDA to African and Asian nations. They are more likely to give preference to bilateral programmes and to the FSO of IADB in a regional context than to IDA, whose American domination they resent even more than the US role in the IADB. Venezuela, for instance, has not contributed to the Fifth IDA replenishment.

'Winners': the poorest?

First, let us look at IBRD lending to the group of 'poorest countries' as classified by the Bank (IDA 1977: 40-41). Poor countries may receive considerable IDA credits in addition to (limited) amounts of Bank loans. Two countries, Indonesia and Nigeria, though at present enjoying somewhat higher average per capita incomes, are in a special category because they are major oil exporters.

Of the Least Developed Countries (LLDCs), according to the UN classification, 17 receive no IBRD loans at all. Tanzania is the largest current recipient (see Table 5.10). Altogether, the LLDCs received 2.8% of IBRD loans in 1969-74 and only 1.4% in 1975-78. The latter figure is even over-stated in that it includes some Third Window loans whose subtraction would reduce straight Bank loans to 0.9%.

Table 5.10 *IBRD lending to poorest countries ($ mln)*

Least Developed	Population 1975 (mln)	GNP p.c. 1975	IBRD new commitments 1969-74	1975-78	of which Third Window 1976-77
Bangladesh	78.6	90	18	–	–
Ethiopia	28.0	100	38	–	–
Guinea	5.5	130	74	–	–
Malawi	5.0	130	–	26	17
Tanzania	14.7	170	115	184	42
Uganda	11.6	250	52	–	–
Sudan	15.6	270	5	32	32
Botswana	0.7	350	42	51	4
17 others*	79.6	–	–	–	–
Total	239.3		343	293	94
annual average			57	73	47
as % of new loans			2.8	1.4	13.4
Other Poorest					
Burma	30.2	110	–	–	–
India	608.0	140	263	1018	159
Zaire	24.7	140	–	100	–
Sri Lanka	13.6	150	48	–	–
Pakistan	69,2	160	215	235	60
Madagascar	8.8	200	21	7	–
Sierra Leone	3.0	200	8	7	–
Kenya	13.4	220	182	364	32
Total	770.9		737	1731	251
annual average			123	433	126
as % of new loans			6.1	8.2	35.9
Petroleum exporters					
Indonesia	132.1	220	48	1724	–
Nigeria	75.0	340	402	325	–
Total	207.1		450	2049	–
annual average			75	512	–
as % of new loans			3.7	9.7	

*   Rwanda, Upper Volta, Mali, Burundi, Somalia, Nepal, Chad, Afghanistan, Niger, Benin, Haïti, Lesotho, The Gambia, Yemen, A.R. Central African Empire, Yemen PDR, West Samoa.

Source: *Annual Reports.*

The group of LLDCs includes Bangladesh. The $18.4 mln loan, however, was made in 1969, i.e. to Pakistan before the war of secession. Those pre-war loans to Pakistan have subsequently been split on the basis of geographical impact.

IBRD non-lending to Ethiopia and Uganda in recent years is understandable in view of political developments in those countries. Guinea is a special case: of the $73.5 mln lending total for 1969-74 $64.5 mln was lent in September 1968 for the construction of an 85-mile railway and related port developments for the exploitation of valuable bauxite resources for export (*Annual Report* 1969: 13). That project was described then as 'one of the largest the Bank has ever made in Africa' (Ibidem). It is thus a classic case of an enclave project whereby the debt service is directly linked to bauxite exports, and thus isolated from what happens in the country at large. Lending to Botswana similarly includes a $32 mln loan approved in June 1971 in connection with a large copper and nickel mining venture (*Annual Report* 1971: 25). This is again an enclave-type project. Botswana's mineral wealth gives the country favourable development prospects, while its proximity to South Africa also helps to make it a special case politically.

In sum, prospects for IBRD lending in this group are bleak, with the exception of countries which have valuable minerals, reasonable balance of payments, and hence creditworthiness prospects.

The group of 'Other Poorest' countries are on average much more populous than the LLDCs. IBRD lending to this group rose from 6.1% of total commitments in 1969-74 to 8.2% in 1975-78. Excluding loans from the Third Window, the increase was only to 7% of total new loans.

Lending to India includes $150 mln in 1977 for petroleum and natural gas production facilities (*Annual Report* 1977: 72), and $120 mln for telecommunications in FY 1978. Zaire received a $100 mln loan in January 1975 to increase copper and cobalt production, the first Bank loan to that country since its independence in 1960 (*Annual Report* 1975: 61). Again, this is a loan with an enclave character securing the debt service on the loan.[10] Most recent lending to Pakistan has been for traditional sectors: railways, power, pipelines, and a fertilizer factory.

Lending to Kenya is increasing quickly and is well-diversified over economic sectors; no loans for major mineral extraction ventures are included.

IBRD lending to 33 countries, with combined populations of one billion people in 1975, and all belonging to the group with the lowest average per capita incomes, increased from 8.9% of total new lending in 1969-74 to 9.6% in 1975-78, but this drops to 7.9% if loans on Third Window terms are excluded. We have seen that a sizable share of IBRD lending to these countries is directly linked to projects of an enclave-type character, which tends to accentuate dualism in their development.

Lending to Indonesia and Nigeria has been stepped-up from 3.7% of total in 1969-74 to 9.7% in 1975-78. Both are major petroleum exporters, and thus have much improved creditworthiness prospects. Lending to Indonesia in 1975-78 increased to such an extent as to make it one of the Bank's largest lending programmes, second only to Brazil. Prior to the oil price increase, Indonesia had been a major recipient of IDA (see Table 3.2). Lending to Nigeria is rather erratic. Problems with project preparation may be one factor; on the other hand, housing costs in Lagos are now so exorbitant that most of the staff of the resident mission, established only a few years ago, are being withdrawn.

Bank involvement in mineral and energy development was reappraised early in FY 1978. Lending for power has been a traditional mainstay of the Bank. Following the changes in relative prices since 1973-74, emphasis is now given to non-oil sources of power generation. Studies carried out by the Bank show that some 50 to 60 oil-importing less-developed countries have a potential for producing petroleum, oil and/or gas, but that only 14 are producers at present (Friedman 1978: 2). While decisions to exploit endogenous fuel resources may reduce import costs for LDCs, such exploitation will also tend to weaken the power of the OPEC group in respect of price fixing and will not displease major oil-importing Western countries. It is not at all clear, however, whether energy-saving technologies will be sought and stimulated, although this seems desirable in view of the fact that oil and gas are exhaustible natural resources. Until recently the Bank had not financed petroleum production for two main reasons: relative prices did not justify it, and where the economic justification was not in doubt, finance was available from other sources. As we have seen, these restrictions have now been waived.

The Bank's increased interest in the exploitation of non-fuel mineral resources is due largely to the fact that the industrialized countries have become critically dependent on imported minerals for their own production while, at the same time, conflicts have sharpened between LDCs and the traditional international (Western) mining concerns. The Bank believes that it can act as 'active catalyst' in bringing the various parties together (*Annual Report* 1978: 21). It is not at all clear, however, what policy lines the Bank should or can pursue. Should it conserve mineral resources for the future use of LDCs, thus advocating higher import prices for industrialized countries, or should it help to accelerate exploitation, leading to lower import prices for the developed countries, at the risk that future availability for LDCs will be reduced?

'Gainers': the not-so-poor

Next we examine IBRD lending to a group of countries whose per capita GNP in 1975 was between $250 and $520, the level above which there is a 'presumption against' IDA lending. This group includes 17 countries with total populations in 1975 of 175 million. IBRD lending to the group is detailed in Table 5.11.

Together, they received 10.9% of new Bank loans in 1969-74 and 17.4% in 1975-78, or 16.3% excluding loans on Third Window terms. Four countries in the group: Egypt, Thailand, the Philippines and Morocco, account for 79% of its total population; they received 77% of new Bank commitments in 1969-74 to the group and 78% in 1975-78.

Table 5.11 *IBRD lending to low income countries ($mln) (GNP p.c. between $250-520 in 1975)*

Country	GNP p.c. 1975 ($)	Population 1975 (mln)	IBRD new commitments 1969-74	IBRD new commitments 1975-78	of which Third Window 1976-77
Togo	250	2.2	–	60	–
Egypt	260	37.2	–	675	62
Cameroon	290	7.3	83	118	24
Mauritania	320	1.3	–	–	–
Eq. Guinea	320	0.3	–	–	–
Thailand	350	41.9	347	534	26
Bolivia	360	5.6	23	226	10
Honduras	360	2.9	46	96	12
Senegal	360	5.0	23	63	21
Philippines	380	42.2	291	1204	35
Liberia	410	1.5	23	82	4
Swaziland	440	0.5	–	24	–
El Salvador	460	4.0	59	80	9
Papua N.G.	470	2.8	49	16	–
Morocco	470	16.7	375	450	25
Jordan	380	2.7	–	–	–
Congo PR	510	1.3	–	46	–
Total		175.4	1319	3674	228
Annual average			220	919	114
as % of new loans			10.9	17.4	32.6

Several developments are of interest. The whole relative increase was due to three countries: Egypt, the Philippines and Bolivia. Egypt, which had not received a Bank loan since 1959, received $675 mln in 1975-78, a very remarkable change in the Bank's creditworthiness judgement of the country. Egypt's exports of petroleum or petroleum products are about equal to its imports, so its net earnings from oil may not have been greatly affected by the oil price increase (*Annual Report* 1974: 30). Egypt, of course, has benefitted from financial assistance by Arab OPEC countries until 1979, while the new pro-American policy orientation of the government no doubt also plays a role. Yet the level of new lending is surprisingly high. Egypt's heavy debts to the Soviet Union, its extreme population pressure, and the risk of the continuing Middle East conflict, make it implausible that a straightforward conventional creditworthiness analysis has been the deciding factor in this lending. It is thus doubtful whether the Bank has followed its own rules for lending.

Lending to the Philippines accelerated sharply from an annual level of $48 mln in 1969-74 to $301 mln in 1975-78. The country has been hard hit by economic events in recent years. Its balance-of-payments current account moved from a surplus of $520 mln in 1973 to a deficit of $210 mln in 1974 and $860 mln in 1975. Its term of trade had improved by 12% in 1974, but deteriorated by 33% a year later, and continued to decline in 1976 (*Annual Report* 1976: 43; *Annual Report* 1977: 42). Apparently, the Bank feels that longer-term growth prospects for the Philippines are sufficiently optimistic to justify a major effort to maintain the recent growth momentum. Moreover, it should not be forgotten that the 1976 Bank-Fund Annual Meeting was held in Manilla, and the provision of extra loans may well have been a goodwill gesture on the part of the Bank.

Lending to Bolivia has also been stepped-up considerably in recent years. $226 mln provided in 1975-78 was for no less than twelve different operations. In July 1969, a single loan of $23.3 mln was made for a gas pipeline. Bolivia is a net exporter of petroleum and this has a considerable impact on the country's creditworthiness prospects (*Annual Report* 1975: 47). It is also rich in minerals.

Political events in Thailand interrupted IBRD/IDA lending in fiscal year 1975. Thereafter it was resumed, at the rate of $228 mln in 1976, $108 mln in 1977 and $198 mln in 1978.

The $60 mln lent to Togo in FY 1976 was for a regional industrial complex jointly owned by that country, the Ivory Coast and Ghana. This will supply high-quality clinker for cement production in the three countries, and brings together no less than eight co-financiers (*Annual Report* 1976: 66). Togo had not previously received an IBRD loan, and it is likely that the project hinges on the creditworthiness of both or one of the other partners. Similarly, Congo received $38 mln in FY 1976; this is in fact the 1974-78 investment plan of the Agence Transcongolaise des Communications which services a large area in central Africa, including Congo, CAE, and the southern parts of Cameroon, Gabon and, to a lesser extent, Chad (*Annual Report* 1976: 33).

In sum, although lending to the group of what has been termed low-income countries has increased in relative terms if we compare the period 1975-78 with 1969-74, several rather special circumstances apparently played a role in changing the lending pattern. The Bank judges country prospects individually, and since variations in circumstances may be large and may change abruptly over time, it is doubtful whether groupings of countries are very meaningful. Yet, because IDA credits to low-income countries are diminishing, they may have to rely heavily on IBRD and other public financing until their economic structures are diversified and strengthened to attract external funds from a broader spectrum of financiers. Higher income countries can obtain funds from the international capital market and, from the perspective of increasing concern with poorer countries, IBRD loans should preferably be channelled towards those which do not have alternative options to the same extent. It is sometimes argued that public external finance is less volatile than private external finance. As shown, World Bank finance can also be quite volatile, and is thus not always a stabilizing factor in development finance. It would help this group of countries if the Bank could provide greater continuity in its own lending.

The major determinant of IBRD lending is the creditworthiness of member countries. The 1971 Debt Study considered the debt-servicing prospects of only four countries to be serious: Sri Lanka, Ghana, India and Pakistan. As Table 5.10 shows, lending in real terms to Pakistan has not changed very much, and IBRD lending to Sri Lanka ceased in early 1970. Only the prospects for Ghana are now judged to be more favourable: that country received $6 mln in all of 1969-74, but $134 mln in 1975-78 though the quality of its public management seems to be gradually deteriorating. The Bank's judgement of India's creditworthiness has also taken a turn for the better.

The 1971 Debt Study judged twelve countries to be vulnerable to temporary debt-servicing difficulties resulting from unexpected fluctuations in foreign exchange availability. Ten of these are among the 24 largest Bank clients (Table 2.4); only Chile and the Ivory Coast are excluded. A shift in Bank lending to lower income countries thus does not automatically weaken the Bank's portfolio.

Among the countries thought vulnerable in 1971, only the Philippines ($180 income p.c.), Ivory Coast ($540) and Korea ($560) have income levels that fall within the IDA eligibility range. Most of the others that are thought vulnerable have relatively higher income levels.

IBRD new lending to these twelve countries is detailed in Table 5.12. Overall, it declined from 49.3% of total new commitments in 1969-74 to 44.3% in 1975-77, but this was due mostly to the sharp reduction of lending to Iran. Within the group there has been a shift towards lending to countries at relatively lower income levels, notably Korea and the Philippines. If it may be assumed that such countries have greater need of financial assistance than those at higher levels, it could be argued that the Bank would be justified in pushing its loans towards the former even though this would increase Bank exposure in those countries.

Between 1973 and 1976 the total external debt of developing countries has almost doubled. The indebtedness of some prominent countries, including Brazil and Mexico, increased even more, and so did the proportion of borrowing from private sources. Brazil, Yugoslavia, Argentina, Korea, Chile, Turkey, Colombia, the Philippines and Peru have been the principal debtors in the middle income group of countries.

On the whole, the Bank's 1977 External Debt study is optimistic that the international financial community can 'handle' the much increased debt levels in non-disruptive fashion. The stability of the large private debts of many of the largest borrowers is now of primary concern (*Debt Study* 1977: 107).

The Study argues that

the presence of the multilateral financial institutions which can *carefully and impartially* evaluate a borrowing country's short- and long-term situation vis-à-vis total borrowing has thus become an essential component of the maintenance of current levels of private capital flows to developing countries and of their soundly based expansion in the future (Ibidem: 103; emphasis added).

Table 5.12 *IBRD lending to countries thought vulnerable in the 1971 External Debt study*

	GNP p.c. 1975	1969-74	1975-78
Iran	1660	823	53
Yugoslavia	1550	548	1073
Argentina	1550	319	485
Mexico	1050	1073	1302
Brazil	1030	1307	2055
subtotal		4069	4968
as % new commitments		33.6	23.5
annual average		678	1242
Chile	990	45	113
Turkey	900	678	744
Peru	760	105	234
Tunisia	730	169	277
Korea	560	498	1505
Ivory Coast	540	117	322
Philippines	380	291	1204
subtotal		1901	4399
annual average		317	1100
as % new commitments		15.7	20.8
Total		5970	9367
annual average		995	2342
as % new commitments		49.3	44.3

Source: *Annual Reports.*

While a careful analysis of growth prospects and of economic management is obviously better than haphazard and casual analysis, it should be realized that the 'impartiality' of Bank analysis may at least be tempered by its own very high stakes in the debt field, as shown in Table 5.12. The Bank needs to be optimistic in order not to damage its own financial health. This was true in 1971 and again in 1977.

From the perspective of the 'weather vane' function of Bank creditworthiness ratings and lending, a future reduction may be interpreted as a loss of faith in countries' creditworthiness. On the other hand, the Bank may well overrate its own influence. The major private foreign banks have now so much outstanding to these higher income countries that they can do their own sums.

The future allocation of IBRD resources

The Bank states that its current regional distribution of lending is not the direct result of any overall regional policy considerations, but that it emerges from lending programmes to individual countries. The question is whether such totting up of individual programmes can lead to acceptable results.

We have seen that the rapid expansion of Bank lending in the early 1970s was absorbed by a few countries (see Table 2.3). Were these results in accordance with *ex ante* expectation? (see Reid 1973). Similarly, since the Bank became concerned with the poor, no major change has so far occurred in lending towards the poorer countries. An evaluation of the World Bank and of the Inter American Development Bank noted that the 'World Bank was not successful in increasing its share of total lending to the poorest countries' (Weaver 1978: 26). This conclusion is largely confirmed by our own analysis, and undermines the Bank's claim that its focus on the poor should be taken as seriously as it was intended to be. Now that the Board is taking greater direct interest in the scope of Bank activities, it would seem logical that it should not only review the overall volume of IBRD lending, but also the distribution by country and income levels. Strenuous efforts should be made to redirect the pattern of IBRD lending towards the poorer countries. In as far as limited creditworthiness is an issue, Bank lending in the early 1970s has been risky. Questions of limited absorptive capacity can be solved, given time.

Reallocation of IDA resources

The geographical distribution and allocation by income levels of IDA resources has received much more attention in the past than the specific allocation problems of IBRD resources. This IDA distribution has already been dealt with in part, and is shown in Table 5.13 according to income class. It will be seen that, during the last few years in particular, a considerable shift in lending has occurred towards the least developed countries. The groups 'marginal' and 'other poorest' have had to give way. Lending to 'marginal' countries in 1975-78 was confined to four only.

Lending to the group of countries whose per capita incomes were between $266-520 in 1975-78 amounted to only 11.3% of the total, and went to 18 countries. A further reduction of lending to this group by lowering the upper eligibility limit for IDA is thus likely to meet with considerable resistance by the Board, and would not free any large amount of funds for redistribution to poorer countries.

If IDA allocations were to be re-oriented according to population weight, the following results would be obtained, based on countries with more than 20 mln inhabitants. Ethiopia, Egypt, Bangladesh, Burma, India and Pakistan accounted in mid-1975 for 77% of the populations of all countries which received IDA credits under the Fourth Replenishment period. In 1975-78 they received 61.4% of total IDA commitments. From this perspective it could be argued that further concentration on those countries would be justified, even if the relatively higher per capita income of Egypt is discounted somewhat. A slight 'improvement' in the IDA allocation pattern could be achieved in this way, although attempts by the Board to reduce India's share should be resisted.

Table 5.13 *Distribution of IDA credits by country and income classes 1961-78*

No. of countries		1961-68	69-74 ($ mln.)	75-78	1961-68	69-74 in %	75-78
25	Least Developed Countries	382.5	1041.9	1516.5	20.9	20.7	32.9
10	Other Poorest	1079.0	3021.5	2515.2	58.9	60.1	55.2
21	Intermediate ($266-520 p.c.)	139.6	594.0	476.0	7.6	11.8	11.3
14	Marginal (above $520 p.c.)	230.7	369.6	31.3	12.6	7.4	0.6
70	Total	1831.8	5027.0	4539.0	100.0	100.0	100.0

Source: IDA, 1978, and *Annual Report* 1978.

If the poor countries are to be helped materially, the overall bilateral allocation of Official Development Assistance should be considered. This is shown in Table 5.14 for the period 1969-72. It appears that 57% of total DAC ODA went to countries whose per capita incomes were over $200 (in 1971).

Table 5.14 *ODA: Bilateral disbursements, 1969-72 average*

1969-72 average	LLDCs	Others under $200	$200 -375	$375 -700	$700 -1000	$1000 and over	Total
$ mln	446	2181	2221	472	509	280	6109
$ per capita	3.2	2.2	6.3	2.3	5.2	3.2	
% of imports	20.1	25.2	12.3	2.9	3.7	1.2	
% of GNP	3.4	2.0	2.2	0.5	0.7	0.3	

Source: Development Cooperation, 1974: 164.

Compared to the bilateral ODA flows, IDA's current allocation is much more focussed on the poorer countries. If the DAC countries would be willing to focus their ODA on the poor countries, a substantially increased flow of resources would result.

Within the framework of a basic needs strategy, Streeten and Ul Haq (1977) of the World Bank have argued for a $2 bln annual increase (in constant prices) over the period 1980-2000, to be allocated 80% to the poorest countries and 20% to those in the middle-income group; i.e. a dramatic reversal of the current 40:60 relationship.

The implementation of such a shift would encounter considerable difficulty. As we have seen in Chapter III, the giving of aid is often focussed on specific countries with which 'special' relationships exist, often dating back to colonial times.

The DAC finds that 39 of the 42 largest aid recipients could be considered to have a special relationship with a DAC member. In 1969-72, they received per capita commitments of $37.6 against $2.6 for other countries. These 39 units accounted for only 3% of the population of LDCs, but received 28% of recorded bilateral ODA commitments. Even more striking, they accounted for 34% of the *increase* in bilateral commitments between 1969 and 1972, and 50% of the increase in bilateral disbursements (Development Cooperation 1974: 167). They include six countries with per capita incomes of more than $1000 and 13 with per capita incomes of more than $700 (in 1971).

The use of an average per capita income limit effectively discriminates against most of Latin America and many countries in North Africa and the Middle East. Many countries would thus object strenuously to a more widespread and effective use of this yardstick for future allocations of ODA. Many would like to maintain the privileges and benefits under prevailing 'special relationships'. Others would want to allow for poor-oriented project criteria and for the use of the *relative* poverty concept (see page 122 above) in order to continue to receive ODA. The decision taken in 1976 by twelve European countries to join the Interamerican Development Bank, whereby they are also expected to contribute to its Fund for Special Operations, is regrettable from the perspective of redistribution of scarce future ODA to the poorest countries.

NOTES

1. *Redistribution with Growth* is a joint publication by the World Bank's Development Research Center and the Institute of Development Studies at the University of Sussex, and does not represent official World Bank policy. Hollis Chenery, one of its main authors, however, is the Vice President Development Policy of the Bank, and as such the most senior Bank official with direct responsibility for broad development policy issues.

2. Kuznets's article should be consulted for details of the methods used. Further study and the use of more recent information, e.g. Kravis et al (1975 and 1978) should enable considerable improvements.

3. See Annex I for the algebraïc exposition of the two methods for calculating growth rates. Kuznets's alternative proposal has since been used in the Bank's publication 'Prospects for Developing Countries' and in the 'World Development Report, 1978'.

4. It is remarkable and regrettable that Kuznets's pathbreaking article, with its quite pertinent implications for major data publishing organizations as well as for the appraisal of the acceptability of published data, is not even mentioned in the bibliography in *Redistribution with Growth*, which appeared two and a half years later.

5. For an interesting case history of manipulated censuses see Aluko (1965) and Eke (1966) on Nigeria.

6. Poverty lines at less than Rs 20 per capita per month at 1960-61 prices were recommended by the Indian Planning Commission in 1962 in a pathbreaking perspective study, by Pitambar Pant et al, on the implications of planning for a minimum level of living 1961-76 (Srinivasan & Bardhan 1974: 9-38).

7. These figures, taken from the text of the Rural Development Sector Policy paper, are a rough update of the data presented in the Annex to that paper, reproduced in Table 5.6.

8. See the 'Long' Hearings 1978. Part I: 811.

9. The External Debt of Developing Countries, World Bank (November 1977).

10. Zaire needed a bilateral debt rescheduling with the US in 1977 and also from the Paris Club (NAC: *Annual Report* 1977: 98-99).

ANNEX

Alternative procedures for calculating combined GDP growth rates for several subregions or for countries within subregions.

Let Y_1, Y_2, Y = products of subregions 1 and 2, and total, respectively (for simplicity the illustration is limited to two regions so that $Y_1 + Y_2 = Y$);

P_1, P_2, P = populations of subregions 1 and 2, and total, with $P_1 + P_2 = P$;

I_1, I_2, I = per capita products for subregions 1 and 2, and total, with $I_1 = Y_1/P_1, I_2 = Y_2/P_2, I = Y/P$;

r_1, r_2, r = growth rates of products in subregions 1 and 2, and total;

g_1, g_2, g = growth rates of populations in subregions 1 and 2, and total;

k_1, k_2, k = growth rates of per capita products in subregions 1 and 2, and total, with $1 + k_1 = (1 + r_1)/(1 + g_1)$, $1 + k_2 = (1 + r_2)/(1 + g_2)$, $1 + k = (1 + r)/(1 + g)$

The conventional calculation for combined total is as follows:

$$(1 + k) . Y/P = \left[Y_1(1 + r_1) + Y_2(1 + r_2) \right] : \left[P_1(1 + g_1) + P_1(1 + g_2) \right] \quad (1)$$

By simplifying, we derive

$$1 + k = \left(\frac{1 + r_1}{1 + g} \cdot \frac{Y_1}{Y} \right) + \left(\frac{1 + r_2}{1 + g} \cdot \frac{Y_2}{Y} \right) \quad (2)$$

If we set $a_1 = (1 + g_1)/(1 + g)$, and $a_2 = (1 + g_2)/(1 + g)$ equation (2) can be rewritten as:

$$1 + k = \left(\frac{1 + r_1}{1 + g_1} \cdot \frac{Y_1}{Y} \cdot a_1 \right) + \left(\frac{1 + r_2}{1 + g_2} \cdot \frac{Y_2}{Y} \cdot a_2 \right) \quad (3)$$

and this in turn can be simplified:

$$1 + k = \left[(1 + k_1) \cdot (P_1/P) \cdot (I_1/I) \cdot a_1\right] + \left[(1 + k_2) \cdot (P_2/P) \cdot (I_2/I) \cdot a_2\right] \quad (4)$$

The suggested alternative calculation, using superscripts to distinguish it from (1) is as follows:

$$1 + k' = (1 + k_1)(P_1/P) + (1 + k_2)(P_2/P) \tag{5}$$

Using this weighted mean, and retaining the same population growth rates over the period, we derive:

$$
\begin{aligned}
1 + r' &= (1 + k')(1 + g) \\
&= (1 + k_1)(1 + g_1)(P_1/P) + (1 + k_2)(1 + g_2)(P_2/P) \\
&= (1 + r_1)(P_1/P) + (1 + r_2)(P_2/P)
\end{aligned}
\tag{6}
$$

Source: Kuznets 1972: 193-94.

VI

ISSUES IN SMALL-FARMER PROJECTS

INTRODUCTION

When the Bank began to shift its lending focus towards the poor, it chose the small farmers as its main target group. McNamara suggested that the goal should be 'to increase production on small farms so that by 1985 their output will be growing at the rate of 5% per year.' A number of essential elements were identified:

— acceleration in the rate of land and tenancy reform;
— better access to credit;
— assured availability of water;
— expanded extension facilities backed by intensified agricultural research;
— greater access to public services;
— and most critical of all: new forms of rural institutions and organizations
    that would give as much attention to promoting the inherent potential and
    productivity of the poor as is generally given to protecting the power of the
    privileged (McNamara 1973: 16-17).

To assist in implementing this target with the aid of its lending policy, the Bank needs to identify and clarify policy positions on a number of issues relevant to the rural strategy that it advocates. Two factors make this necessary. Project preparation is primarily the responsibility of governments and/or agencies in the developing countries. If they wish to involve the Bank in project implementation, it will obviously be to their advantage to know the conditions that the Bank will require them to meet, additional to the promise that they will promptly repay the requested loan. Such advance knowledge may influence the decision whether to submit the request for financial assistance to the Bank or to some other financier, whether foreign or domestic.

But in the numerous cases in which the Bank is itself actively involved in shaping projects, Bank staff also needs guidance on issues that may arise in the process of project identification, preparation and evaluation, to ensure a reasonable degree of consistency in Bank practice between countries, and to simplify project preparation procedures.

Notes to this chapter may be found on pp. 207-208.

The formulation of guidelines for agricultural projects 'new style' obviously involves generalization, preferably based on comparative empirical research of past approaches to reach the small farmers. There is then a considerable risk of overstepping the bounds at which such generalizations are sufficiently specific to provide relevant guidance. In reality, almost all projects have to be tailor-made to take account of local conditions and circumstances in their endless variety. If suitable guidance is not forthcoming, however, changes in policy direction envisaged for the Bank or for any other agency, will be difficult to actualize.

Most aid agencies have been reluctant to formulate project policy guidelines in detail: it is a difficult task and it lays the agency open to professional critique of its position, thus making it more vulnerable.

It is therefore highly commendable that, since the early 1970s, the Bank has made serious attempts to formulate its policy positions in respect of sectoral objectives in its series of Sector Policy or Working Papers. Guidelines for project staff were usually found in the *Operational Manual*, Project Director's Memoranda, and occasionally in Staff Papers, but most of these documents were not readily accessible and it was quite difficult to review and evaluate evolving Bank practice. The first Sector Papers were produced between September 1971 and June 1972.[1] A second series published in 1974-76 gave much more attention to the design of policy guidelines for projects in various sectors to benefit the poor.[2] These papers have been approved by the Bank's Executive Directors, and can thus be said to represent official Bank policy. They must therefore form the basis for a preliminary assessment of the Bank's chosen rural strategy.

The Bank is a relative newcomer in the field of lending for agriculture and rural development, having been involved by and large since the early 1960s (Yudelman 1977: 16). By 1973, the Bank had several hundred agricultural projects under way. How did they fare? Interesting data have been provided by Yudelman who joined the Bank in 1972 and in 1973 became Director of the Department of Agriculture and Rural Development (Yudelman 1976a: 25-28). According to Yudelman, 'implementation' refers to the problems encountered in the life of a project which has been conceived and designed, in conjunction with the host government, to attain some given objectives. It does not refer to the evaluation of the impact of a project on incomes or output, but rather to the fulfilment of the requirements of the project. For example, completion of the setting-up of a credit bank and disbursement of loans, implementing the requirements of the production, introduction and dissemination of new varieties of seeds, fulfilling the needs for construction of roads and storage, meeting specifications with establishment of livestock ranches and the steps taken to implement the schemes that are agreed upon. Yudelman notes that

despite the care taken by the Bank staff and by governments in the conception and design of projects, by the Bank's own standards only 23 percent of the several hundred agricultural projects underway in 1973 were judged to be trouble-free. At the other end of the spectrum 38 percent were deemed to be plagued by major problems.[3] The major problems, when they do appear, usually emerge in the third year of implementation. The region with most of the major problems is Africa.

The most widespread problem is that of management. Forty-seven percent of all projects under way in 1973 had managerial problems, flowing from cumbersome bureaucratic procedures or from the politics of decision-making. Delays in staffing projects are frequent (Ibidem: 25). In fact, it is not inconceivable that major problems arise in the third year due to turnover of the initial, often expatriate, project staff. If a country lacks trained personnel, it is common practice to create a 'special authority' in conjunction with the government in order to expedite matters. Yudelman notes: 'Frequently, Bank projects are not part of the national bureaucracy but are special units requiring special facilities. Project implementation proceeds at a slower pace than under the national bureaucracy – and in many cases that is very slow for a start' (Ibidem: 17).

About a quarter of the Bank's agricultural projects also encounter technical problems: material shortages, lack of necessary inputs, problems of acquiring them. In general, the majority of technical problems are not connected with the development of new technology.

Financial problems, such as cash shortages, cost over-runs, poor accounting and slow release of counterpart funds, impeded the implementation of one-fifth of all Bank projects under supervision in 1973.

Exogenous problems such as political issues or country economic difficulties delayed the implementation of only 14 percent of all projects. Under this heading we find upheavals, general political breakdowns, and disputes over whether some of the conditions for implementing a Bank project infringe national sovereignty. Country economic difficulties include devaluations, abrupt import price increases and the like, and influence the implementation of only three percent of projects.

Finally, there is the category of 'other problems', which encompasses 12 percent of the projects. These refer mostly to difficulties beyond the control of either the Bank or the local government: natural hazards such as the weather, or abrupt price changes in the world market.

Whether one assesses this implementation record of 'old style' projects as good or bad depends largely on what one expected in the first place. But because the World Bank 'insists on very high standards and picks only the best ventures available' (Hirschman 1967: 1), there is little reason to be overly optimistic regarding the performance of all agricultural development projects undertaken by governments or other donor agencies.

When McNamara announced the Bank's rural strategy, he was aware of the implementation status of existing agricultural projects and of the risky course

which he was setting. Projects 'new style' were acknowledged to be more difficult to prepare, and were therefore judged to be more problem-prone (Yudelman 1976a: 26).

McNamara forewarned:

Neither we at the Bank, nor anyone else, have any clear answers on how to bring the improved technology and other inputs to over 100 million small farmers, especially to those
in dry lands. Nor can we be truly precise about the costs. But we do understand enough to
get started. Admittedly, we will have to take some risks. We will have to improve and
experiment. And if some of the experiments fail, we will have to learn from them and start
anew (McNamara 1973: 17).

Our review of key project-related issues relevant to small-farmer projects is
necessarily closely related to Bank documents. In as far as these are intended
to stimulate international discussion about poor-oriented strategies, it is
regrettable that no explicit reference is made to the ongoing academic discussion about a number of these issues, or to the rising flow of comparative
empirical studies which attempt to evaluate past experiences with projects and
programmes aimed at promoting the welfare of small farmers, and some of
which are quite relevant. Such references would enable policy judgements to be
made on the basis of something more substantial than tentative judgements or
casual empiricism. I shall therefore supplement the Bank's analysis with additional references, the search for which has taken substantial amounts of
energy.[4] The search has been rewarded by the occasional finding that the Bank
seems to have drawn somewhat different conclusions to those which some
authors drew from their empirical material. On the whole, Bank papers tend to
show qualified optimism in respect of the Bank's contribution to 'improved'
small-farmer projects in future. It should be realized, of course, that it is difficult if not impossible for Bank staff to show pessimism once management has
gone on public record that the core of a rural strategy should aim at raising
the productivity of small farmers through targetted approaches. This peculiar
institutional difficulty is another reason why it seems useful to place the Bank
policy papers in a wider documentary context.

THE TECHNOLOGICAL PACKAGE AND AGRICULTURAL RESEARCH

In the late 1960s, major technological breakthroughs in food production were
believed to have lifted the spectre of famine in the immediate future and to
have postponed the prospects of Malthusian population disaster. For this
reason the new high yielding varieties (HYVs) of wheat and rice, popularly
known as the 'Green Revolution', have attracted considerable attention. Although these new varieties have been adopted widely and rapidly (Dalrymple

1976), the aggregate average food availability in developing countries has not substantially improved (see Table 6.1). The spread of HYVs over less suitable areas, an international fertilizer shortage in 1973-75 (Dalrymple 1976: 116), and other factors, dissipated much of the earlier euphoria (UNRISD 1974; Palmer 1976; Dasgupta 1977). Several institutions have again projected a gap of between 25 and 40 mln tons of foodgrain for Asia by 1985 (Herdt, Te & Barker 1978).

Table 6.1 *Trends in per capita food production (1961 - 65 average = 100)*

	Latin America	Far East*	Near East**	Africa***
1968	99	100	104	100
1969	101	102	104	102
1970	102	104	102	102
1971	101	102	103	100
1972	99	97	109	97
1973	98	103	100	91
1974	101	98	106	93
1975	100	103	109	91

*   excl. Japan
**   excl. Israel
***   excl. S. Africa

Source: FAO: *The State of Food and Agriculture*

In the past, increases in agricultural production particularly of food crops, has resulted more from expansion of arable land than from increased yields as a result of technological change. Growing population numbers, a limitation on the availability of suitable arable land, and urbanization, make it imperative that future production increases should come more from yield than from areal expansion.

Despite the impeccable logic of this, past international lending for agriculture has had quite different priorities. It has been implicitly assumed that LDCs should avoid the costly and time-consuming process of developing their own agricultural research capacity because sufficient research findings were available in the developed countries that could be transferred to them. As recently as 1975 Johnston and Kilby stated:

The most fundamental factor conditioning structural transformation in contemporary underdeveloped countries is the existence of a large stock of proven technical innovations in the more developed countries. The existence of this technology backlog, much of which is transferable, creates the possibility for late-developing countries to bypass the vast investment of time and resources that the accumulation of this knowledge involved. This opens the way for far more rapid rates of economic growth than those, say, prior to World War I (Johnston & Kilby 1975: 76).

This diagnosis was also reflected in bilateral donor practice. During the

1950s extension and not research was the core of most US rural development strategies (Rice 1974: 23-24). Only since the late 1960s has agricultural research assumed significant importance in US AID programmes (AID 1978: 36).

Moreover, the limited agricultural research that did take place in LDCs was biased in respect of types of products. Before World War II, primary attention was given to major export crops — rubber in Malaysia, sugar in the Philippines, coffee in Kenya, palm oil in Nigeria, coffee in Brazil, bananas in Honduras, etc. Staple food crops were largely ignored. According to figures compiled by OECD, 81% of agricultural research expenditures in Africa went to export crops and only 14% to food crops in 1961. By 1971 the proportion had become approximately equal (cited in Lele 1975: 28).

Interest in international agricultural research in support of increased food production has increased during the 1970s. In May 1971 the Consultative Group on International Agricultural Research (CGIAR) was established, sponsored by the Bank, FAO and UNDP, with the Bank acting as chairman. Between 1972 and 1978 contributions totalled $351 mln including a modest $28 mln, or 8% of the total, contributed by the Bank from its profits (*Annual Reports*). Much of the CGIAR-sponsored research is in support of foodcrops, it having been belatedly recognized that a great deal of adaptive research is needed in the LDCs before superior production packages can be developed under a variety of ecological and institutional conditions.

The superiority of proposed packages must not only be demonstrated, but must also be perceived as such by prospective users. An analysis usually stops after assessing superiority in terms of yield per hectare, while many (African) farmers view profitability primarily in terms of return per labour day worked. The impact of risks due to changes in relative prices between crops, and per crop relative to inputs and outputs, also needs to be fully assessed. Adoption is sometimes hampered because it leads to increased external control over farmers' decision making or to changes in role patterns of men and women. The actual use of fertilizers, even though below optimal, may still be profitable under a whole range of possible inputs (Lipton 1979: 121). But the use of less amounts than those prescribed may well lead to progressive soil degradation in ecologically vulnerable zones, when viewed in a somewhat longer-term perspective. Maintenance of the carrying capacity of the land should be of prime concern in order to avoid the occurrence of what now has become manifest in the Sahel and in Central Java, for instance.

In a recent review of 18 Bank-supported rural development projects in Africa (which all antedate the new Bank orientation), the Operations Evaluation Department found that the recommended technological package sometimes did not meet one or several of the tests. In only four out of 18 cases were production targets achieved or surpassed.[5] The past neglect of adaptive agricultural research may well prove a major constraint in implementing a rural strategy aimed at increasing future productivity of small farmers.

It will obviously take a long time to build up national and international research networks that are capable of generating a continuous stream of new and improved varieties that are not only technically and economically superior, but which also fit socio-cultural and ecological constraints. The increased pressure on the Bank and other agencies that have adopted similar strategies to implement small farmer-oriented projects incurs the grave hazard that insufficiently-tested packages will be recommended and imposed which will expose the farmer population to unacceptable risk.

The Bank's role in plant research will be limited, its main interest being in the assessment of conditions for effective use of new technological packages.

LAND REFORM AND BANK POLICY

A conditioning factor for the livelihood of people in rural areas is the relationship between them and agricultural land. In particular, the distribution of and control over operational arable land in relation to the size of the rural population is a structural characteristic of the agrarian situation in the developing world.

The issue then presents itself of the dynamic relationship between the size distribution of landholdings, tenancy relationships, population growth, and a rural development strategy based on increasing the production of small farmers, in relation to the role of external aid agencies. To what extent is land reform and/or tenancy reform a precondition for successful, broadly-based agrarian progress, and what is or should be the position of the Bank in those cases where land reform is a necessary precondition for such progress?

Land reform (agrarian reform, *reforma agraria*) comprises, in Lipton's definition (1974: 270), (1) compulsory take-over of land, usually (a) by the State, (b) from the biggest land owners, and (c) with partial compensation; and (2) the farming of that land in such a way as to spread the benefits of the changed man-land relationship more widely than before the take-over. The State may give, sell or rent such land for private cultivation in smaller units than hitherto (distributist reform); or the land may be jointly farmed and its usufruct shared, through co-operatives, collective or state farming (collectivist reform). We shall not deal here with collectivist reform. Little is known about its impact on equity and efficiency because those countries which have practiced it so far do not permit research by foreigners. In the USSR, China and Eastern Europe, collective farmers appear to prefer to put their effort into their own smallholdings and often, if they are able to choose, seem to prefer the status of wage-labourers on State farms. Collective farm management also appears to prefer mechanization over the difficult process of labour organization and labour relations when the choice is available (Ibidem: 287, 295).

Land reform without compensation is also difficult to deal with. If land is confiscated as part of a revolutionary process, limited if any public expenditure is involved. Refusal to compensate at all, however, will maximize resistance to land reform at any level of land ceilings on permitted holdings. Full compensation, on the other hand, may make it prohibitively expensive.

Land reform is by definition an equalizing policy, at least in intent. It may accelerate growth, but its primary motivation is to reduce poverty by reducing inequality, though not necessarily through helping the very poorest, or all the poor.

There are several constraints on achieving equality in distributist reform. Viability sets a lower limit to farm size. The Bank's Rural Development paper, referring to unnamed studies, notes that most of the smallholdings in Asia, Africa and Latin America of less than two hectares of arable land and used for traditional low-yielding subsistence production, generate income above the poverty line (1975: 23). A viable 'livelihood holding' should permit an average farm family to enjoy a decent minimum level of income; for a family of five, paying no rent and providing its own labour, ILO's Ceylon Employment Mission (ILO 1971) estimated that such a holding averaged 0.8 ha. of rice land, varying in accordance with soil fertility. Obviously, it would be preferable to be able to measure land in terms of 'efficiency units', varying with crops, soil and water availability.

From the political point of view, it is impossible to fix maximum permissible holdings at the same level as livelihood holdings. Decisive action against the top 5% of landowners should be much 'easier' than against the top 10% and may not yield very much in terms of extra land for redistribution, depending upon the shape of the size distribution. In general, the lower the permissible ceiling, the more landowners are affected and the stronger the likely political opposition against land reform.

The generation of sufficient political support for land reform is probably also a function of the expected or promised pattern of land distribution among the claimants. 'Easiest' would seem the situation whereby action against a small group of landowners would free sufficient land to bring all marginal holdings up to viable size, and also provide all landless workers with enough land for a viable holding at given technological levels. This may reflect the situation in Northeast Brazil, but land reform there is said to be extremely difficult (Barraclough 1973: chapter on Brazil). Most difficult would be a situation whereby even the most egalitarian reform fails to provide viable holdings to all rural families. Resistance by landlords would then be maximal, and the support base of the land reform movement would erode if confiscated land were distributed in non-viable crumbs.

For 'in between' cases a difficult trade-off will need to be made between the permissible ceiling and the allocation of 'spare land'. If the latter is allocated to landless families, relatively few can be provided with viable holdings. To give the landless non-viable holdings is an ineffective method of improving their situation. To use the confiscated land to 'top up' submarginal holdings to viability level would widen the group of beneficiaries enormously and may enhance popular support for land reform.

The choice of beneficiaries may also be influenced by managerial consider-ations in the post-reform era. For minifarmers to move up to viable farms means an enlargement of scale which minifarmers with given agricultural skills may be able to exploit successfully without much outside advice. Former tenants or agricultural labourers may adjust with some advice, but landless families who take up farming for the first time will generally require extensive external support, particularly in the early post-reform period. It may be very difficult, however, to set-up an effective post-reform support organization fast enough to minimize disruption in production. But land reform will directly affect landless labourers who are often dependent on the larger landowners for their income. To tie them over they should be given preferred employment on public works, although this may also be difficult to organize quickly (Lipton 1974).

In parts of South Asia, including Bangladesh and Java (Lipton 1974: 283-84), land reform is perhaps insoluble (see Nurul Islam 1978), but these areas are among those with the largest incidence of absolute poverty (*Rural Devel-opment* 1975: 19). In other parts of Asia, in Africa and Latin America, land-to-man ratios are more favourable and the difficult issue of land reform, it is sometimes argued, can be evaded because arable land is plentiful. This is false on at least two counts. Firstly, the distribution of landholdings has to be seen in relation to the quality of the land, and it may be that in practice control over the best lands is concentrated in a few hands. Secondly, it is not the aggregate national size distribution of holdings which is important, but the regional size distribution.

Another issue is who supplies the urban consumption needs for agricultural produce: large or small farms, each of which has its own resource use pattern. The coexistence of large and small farms in potentially dynamic areas may cause considerable problems of land politics, as has been evident in Kenya (Leys 1975b). It may also have profound effects on the future growth pros-pects of different areas, and a focus on large farms may pre-empt the growth prospects of small farmers.

Effective land reform is very difficult to achieve due to the vested interests of the landowners and to the enormous difficulties of organizing an effective political force that is capable of forcing a change in property rights. Attention is therefore more often focused on other issues affecting land use.

Tenancy reform aims at one or more of the following: limiting rents, typically from the prevailing 50-75% of gross output to one-third; conversion at the tenant's discretion, from crop-share to fixed rental; security against eviction; first option to purchase should the owner sell. Such reforms are usually of limited scope, and in many 'soft states' of the Third World, they break upon the rock of landlord power. The effects of evasion can include insecurity, which worsens both rural income distribution and the standards of capital and land acquisition and maintenance on tenant farms (Lipton 1974: 277).

In most poor countries, the landlords' strength rests upon the scarcity of land, so that tenancy legislation has to fight both market forces where larger population numbers compete for scarce land *and* political power in as far as landlords are powerful in governments which are expected to introduce tenancy reform measures. These considerations lead to Lipton's conclusion: 'if you can do a land reform you do not need tenancy reform. If you can't, tenancy reform will not work' (Ibidem: 277).

A progressive land tax as a device for indirectly changing tenancy relationships is usually also ineffective. Land valuation problems are compounded by the progressivity of the tax. Even more seriously, it evokes the same determined and powerful opposition from big landlords as does land reform, but cannot rely on the active popular support that could be mobilized by a land reform. The beneficiaries of a land tax are the government bureaucrats, against whom the big landlord can easily mobilize disgruntled tenants by saddling them with the land tax.

The introduction of new agricultural techniques which may be expected to result in higher incomes will increase the economic value of the land. Thus, one would expect institutional changes in relationships between the people and the land, difficult enough beforehand, to be even harder to accomplish *after* the process of modernization and intensification has set in. The argument voiced by many practitioners and by the Bank that one should not wait for land reform, but that one should try to modernize agriculture whenever the opportunity arises, may have considerable appeal but runs the risk of accentuating difficulties later on. On this ground, the strategy 'Redistribution *before* Growth', advocated by Adelman (1979), is attractive.

Changes in Bank policy on land reform

In its Sector Policy Paper on Land Reform (May 1975: 11) the Bank concludes that 'land reform is consistent with the development objectives of increasing output, improving income distribution and expanding employment, and that the World Bank should support reforms that are consistent with these goals. However, it is recognized that the Bank cannot force structural change; it can only support appropriate efforts within existing structures.'

A number of policy guidelines include the following. The Bank will make it known that it is ready to finance special projects and programmes that may be a necessary concomitant of land reform, including credit, technical services and infrastructural projects designed to meet the special needs of land reform beneficiaries. The Bank will not support projects where land rights are such that a major share of the benefits will accrue to high income groups unless increases in output and improvements in the balance of payments are over-riding considerations; in such cases, it will carefully consider whether the fiscal arrangements are appropriate to ensure that a reasonable share of the benefits accrues to the government (Ibidem: 11-14). In addition, the Bank will intensify its efforts to study all sorts of issues relative to land reform.

It is, of course, not up to the Bank to decide what it wants to study. Tech-nically, an invitation from the country concerned is required, and elaborate clearing procedures are necessary before studies can be published. Moreover, the Bank does not yet possess the specialist manpower necessary for such studies. To the extent that it acquires that manpower, duplication is likely of studies already undertaken by FAO and others, e.g. USAID, and the Land Tenure Center at Wisconsin. Such studies may have some impact on govern-ments to change their policies, but pressure exerted by foreign bodies may also antagonise reformers within the countries, particularly if the reform movement is nationalistic and suspicious of foreign influence. In countries where land reform is not perceived as a serious issue, such studies may be permitted but will not be heeded. Where land reform is a politically sensitive issue, permission to study it will probably not be granted. International agency staff must follow formal rules of international diplomacy, without having diplomatic status.[6]

This new and positive attitude towards land reform has brought the Bank on a line which has been pushed by others for over 25 years, including FAO (*vide* its publications on land reform).

In the past a number of arguments have been advanced by economists to justify a negative attitude towards land reform programmes. It has repeatedly been asserted that land reform is synonymous with decreases in production (Diebold 1966; Berlin 1967; and Yudelman 1966: 66-67). Three types of argu-ments regularly surface in support of that assertion (Adams 1969; 1970): (1) historical evidence based on the experience of countries such as Bolivia, Italy and Mexico, where land reform has occurred; (2) *a priori* assumptions about farm operating efficiencies following land reform; and (3) predictions that parcellization will block the future modernization of agriculture.

In interpreting historical evidence a distinction must be made between short-term and long-term reform effects on agricultural output. It may well be that political disturbances, bottlenecks in the provision of support systems, and disruption of marketing and transportation facilities, may accompany agrarian reform in the early phases of implementation. Many studies, however, do *not* support a view that land reform leads to a reduction of agricultural output.[7] The 1970 USAID *Review of Land Reform* (June 1970) covering approximately 30 countries, reached a broad consensus: land reform almost never decreases production; occasionally it has a neutral effect, most often it has a positive impact (Adams 1973: 134).

Those who argue on *a priori* grounds that land reform will decrease output often extend their arguments to the following: that land reform substitutes a lower quality management factor; that it may reduce farmer access to credit markets and transportation; and may reduce participants' access to new inputs.

In the Latin American context, up to three-quarters of the best agricultural lands used to be operated by absentee owners (Barraclough & Domike 1966). Majordomos acted as caretakers and production was adapted to yield some net return under this system of weak management. Share-tenant arrangements can cause some improvement in land utilization, but the inefficiencies of the system are apparent: disincentives regarding long-term investments in land stemming from insecurity and economic blocks to the use of inputs. Land reform, *coupled with* advice, input and marketing services would do away with weak management, could readjust production patterns, and would provide incentives to former share tenants.

More recently, however, the availability of modern technology and programmes which provide physical and institutional infrastructure in rural areas at public expense, may help to reduce the private cost to landlords of developing previously under-utilized lands, and revitalize interest in more active management on the part of absentee owners. Insecurity for tenants and squatters may be increased if capital-intensive technologies in large-scale operations are introduced, as appears to be the case in parts of Latin America at the present time.

A review of available empirical studies on specific parcelization projects in Latin America does not yield a single case in which a change in management through land reform has led to an actual decrease in production (Barraclough 1973). It is also stated that, even if parcelization does not decrease near-term output, it will hinder future agricultural modernization in that no use can be made of economies of scale. A number of agricultural technologies and inputs are perfectly divisible, however, such that small farmers can make use of new developments to counter demographic expansion with higher yields.

Those who argue against land reform assert that it will have a negative effect on rural capital formation and hence will affect the ability to increase long-term output. Little evidence on this point is available. Raup (1967), drawing upon fragmentary country studies and economic logic, concludes that land reform will have a positive impact on farm level as well as non-farm rural capital formation. Adams (1973: 134) reports similar impressions after visiting rural areas affected by land reform in Japan, Taiwan, Colombia, Venezuela, Ecuador and Brazil. Similarly, Lipton (1974), after a careful theoretical analysis, comes to rather optimistic conclusions regarding the positive effects of land reform on farm capital formation.

Few studies are available on the employment effects of land reform. Aside from a few secondary employment effects due to more income being spent in rural areas, there is probably little employment impact from making tenants into landowners. Redistributive land reform which benefits the landless is likely to have strong initial employment effects. Secondary effects may be expected if, after the reform, production techniques become more labour-intensive because former large landowners no longer have the option between organizing production with the help of machines on large tracts of land, and organizing production with possibly vocal, articulate, and hence unpredictable labour on small plots.

Research on the validity of economic arguments often employed against land reform is scanty, fragmentary and not always conclusive, but it seems that the majority of economic arguments advanced against the wisdom or necessity of land reform are not strongly based on evidence. The Bank has now realized this, and has accordingly declared land reform compatible with the broader objectives of development.

Prospects for increased Bank lending for land reform

If economic arguments – and the Bank tries to evaluate its investments in terms of economic considerations – against land reform can no longer be considered valid, can we expect increased lending by the Bank or other donors? Will they exercise direct leverage and provide incentives for reform through their lending activities? Three questions spring to mind. Why would countries be interested in requesting assistance from the Bank? Will the Bank finance compensation? Thirdly, can increased Bank lending be expected for follow-up activities to help deliver the gains to the intended beneficiaries of the land reform and to shorten the possible disruption and hardship in the immediate aftermath of the reform?

In the past, external aid agencies have loaned very little for land reform. From the late 1950s to mid-1968 USAID and its predecessor agencies granted or loaned approximately $100 mln in the very general area of colonization and land reform in Latin America: roughly 30% for penetration roads into colonization areas; 20% directly for colonization; another 30% for agricultural credit which has at least partially supported colonization or parcelization activities; and 20% for mapping, land tilling and land tenure research. In the 1970s some funds were spent on assistance for cadastral surveys, land classification, legal advice, etc. (AID: *Agricultural Development Policy Paper*, 1978: 25, 28). Through 1968 the IADB also loaned only some $30 mln in this general area, almost entirely for colonization (Adams 1969: 4).

Yet in the early 1960s the Alliance for Progress had recognized and stressed the importance of land reform in that region. There is thus a sharp discrepancy between rhetoric and action as far as international lending is concerned.

In two cases in the past the Bank has been directly involved in land reform projects: Tunisia and Kenya. In both cases the occasion for Bank involvement arose from compensation to former landowners, citizens of the colonial power, as part of the settlement of political independence. The World Bank loaned

$18 mln to Tunisia, intended to back a major agrarian reform relating to former French-owned estates which occupied the most fertile land in the country. The reform programme collapsed and the Bank cancelled half the loan (*Land Reform* 1975: 40, 42).

The Bank's Policy Paper on Land Reform fails to mention or comment on loans to Kenya for settlement schemes which were in fact *part transfer payments* (Wasserman 1976: 158; Lele 1975: 8) in connection with the taking-over of formerly British-owned private farms in the 'white highlands' as part of Kenya's independence settlement.[8]

The World Bank and the Commonwealth Development Corporation had been involved from the beginning of the 1960 transfer schemes. The British Government had sought this involvement, especially of the World Bank, not only to ease the financial burden on Her Majesty's Government, but also to help make the schemes less 'political' and to tie the World Bank into Kenya's future economic policies. Settlement planners frequently spoke of the high standards of World Bank schemes and of the 'loan discipline' imposed on the new government. This 'socialization' aspect of World Bank involvement – political and economic learning through supervision and ties – was often considered more important than the actual funds by the planners. British Governments held a similar view. By the time the Kenyan representatives began discussions with the Bank, support had in fact already been garnered by British officials based in Washington. As one Kenyan participant, Carey-Jones, wrote to Wasserman: by the time the Kenyan people began their negotiations, the World Bank was already mentally committed to the schemes. Throughout they continued to have this commitment, no doubt on political grounds (Wasserman 1976: 158). In addition to British Government pressure, the World Bank may also have responded to less formal links with Kenya. Wasserman mentions the close personal relationship between key officials in the Bank and in the Kenyan Government (Ibidem: 158). In view of the Bank's recruitment policy and standards this is not at all surprising.[9]

Although the evidence on past Bank involvement in land reform is at best limited, it nevertheless shows the distinct possibility that foreign governments, to protect the private property rights of their citizens, may wish to take the initiative of involving the Bank in such negotiations. The Kenyan land schemes were the pre-independence government's major method of 'letting steam out of the boiling kettle' (Ibidem: 146) in the Kikuyu Central Region, where pressure had been building up for some considerable time. The Bank was called upon to help stabilize the potentially explosive situation, and to use its influence to prevent development options which would have enabled a much broader redistribution of land over the rapidly growing number of landless Kenyans. The need for a broader-based land redistribution has increased under the impact of very high population growth rates in the post-independence period.

The Bank may also be called upon by its major shareholders to participate in Rhodesia. White settlers of British extraction may need to be given the option of being bought out to facilitate the political solution of Zimbabwe's independence. If such pressure should come from the Bank's major shareholders, notably the USA and the UK, it may not be able to resist. The Bank might then be used as a cover to protect broader political and foreign economic interests in Southern Africa. Such a situation is not unlikely in view of the fact that the USA put considerable pressure on the Bank in 1972 to take an active and leading role in the reconstruction of Vietnam (Kolko 1975). Strong intervention by Sweden and other donors forced the Bank's management to backtrack on internal preparations to accede to these direct political pressures.

The main argument used by aid agencies against the direct finance of reform is that compensation of former landowners is a transfer payment from the public sector to the landholding groups. As the Bank argues (*Land Reform* 1975: 41): 'compensation can have serious implications for income distribution, consumption and investment. It does not of itself create any new productive capabilities in the country.' Our analysis has shown, though, that it is likely that land reform may lead to better resource use, and hence could be considered directly productive.

In the past, there have been few cases in which foreign governments have attempted to involve the Bank in land reform conflicts which are almost always very delicate and politically very sensitive. When land reform affects only domestically-owned properties, foreign governments may not be pressurized by property-holding interests. When it is a burning issue the government is likely to be divided internally, which does not create a favourable environment in which to ask the Bank for arbitration. Adams notes that American support of land reform in Japan and Taiwan appears to have been unique. In neither case was US-owned land involved.[10]

In future, foreign property may well be involved in land reforms. A number of governments or land interests have sought or are seeking to develop under-utilized lands by offering large tracts for sale to international firms. Lack of domestic resources with which to develop the land may be a factor in this decision, but it may also represent a defensive tactic on the part of landholding interests to drum up international support against domestic social pressure for land reform. An appeal to foreign interests on the grounds that their properties, too, may be threatened by reform may increase counter-reformist pressure and thereby the social and economic cost of reform proposals.[11]

Compensation involves the valuation of the lands to be bought and redistributed, a very difficult matter, be it use value, market value, or speculation value in view of future urbanization. Land usage after the reform may be different and this may affect its value. The subsequent introduction of improved agricultural technologies may rapidly increase the income-earning capacity of the land. Uncertainty may also act as a destabilizing force on land values. Land betterment investments in buildings and infrastructure may not be of much value if parcelization is envisaged, for which the present infrastructure is dysfunctional.

As we have seen earlier, the Bank is not willing to lend to countries which nationalize foreign property without fair compensation. In practice, this means that the terms of involuntary land sale, part of land reform, must satisfy the unwilling sellers. If not, they will seek redress, exercising pressure through their governments for the Bank to discontinue all lending. The Bank cannot ignore such pressure, particularly if it comes from major shareholders, and this concern may force it to seek more favourable terms for the seller. Otherwise it might have to stop all lending despite its new policy stand that land reform is an essential condition for achieving the Bank's development objectives. In any conflict between private foreign property rights and social justice, the former is likely to prevail. A number of white settlers in Kenya probably got a very good bargain out of the partially Bank-financed land transfer deal, and valuation procedures were not tightened up until 1966. 'Whatever the scale of cheating, most of it occurred in the early years of settlement' (Holtham & Hazlewood 1976: 127). Several farmers reportedly bought other farms with their compensation money, only to resell them later to the authorities.

Adams, arguing for a change of policy for USAID in respect of land reform, has reopened the discussion of the participation of aid agencies in the financing of land purchases or expropriation (Adams 1969; 1970).

Compensation to landowners often takes the form of issuing bonds.[12] No foreign exchange is involved unless foreign land-bond holders are permitted to take their money out. In view of the fact that its contribution is by and large confined to the foreign exchange cost of projects, the Bank may then be unable to avoid being accused of favouring foreign over domestic landowners in a land reform programme. The Bank's policy would then be inconsistent between classes of land-bond holders.

There has been a great deal of discussion about providing guarantees for bonds issued as compensation for expropriated or purchased land. This might include a system of value-linking to protect the purchasing power of the bond's principal against inflation, or guarantees against default by the issuing country, all of which could make bonds more palatable to large landowners (Prosterman 1966; Please & Christoffersen 1969). The counter-argument in the Bank's Policy Paper is that international maintenance-of-value guarantee of bonds and for compensation would have the paradoxical effect of giving land bonds greater stability than that enjoyed by the currencies of issuing countries (*Land Reform*, 1975: 41). The Bank would then discriminate between land-bond holders and other asset holders, and new sources of privilege would be created.

It is thus difficult to see how the Bank can play a developmental role through direct lending for land reform. The conditions under which it may be brought into the picture may actually restrain a drive towards land reform and/or force the Bank to side with the landowners, thereby exercising its pressure to increase compensation payments.

The third issue, prospects for Bank involvement in post-reform activities, may provide greater promise for Bank involvement. As we have seen, land reform may be accompanied by short-term disruption. These undesirable effects could be mitigated if a delivery system of inputs, transportation and marketing services could be organized quickly enough to substitute for the services previously provided by the landlords. Manpower constraints may be more severe than financial constraints in organizing such a support system, and only the latter can be alleviated by the Bank by financing equipment, facilities and the like. But Bank lending is preconditioned by whether it believes that the reform implementing organization is effective. In general this can be judged only on the basis of a proven track record, which takes time to establish. Time, however, is of crucial importance in such cases. Because the Bank cannot deal directly with the beneficiaries of land reform, it must deal with their organizations whose expected effectiveness will need to be assessed prior to lending. Such lending may be risky, and the Bank sometimes finds itself in considerable difficulties when it tries to assist in institutional arrangements (see Willoughby 1977).

Barraclough points out that governments might support a half-hearted land reform programme in order to accommodate or contain social pressures, but only on the tacit understanding that no effective follow-up will be promoted (Barraclough 1973, part I). Bank initiatives to try to make a success of such reforms by being more than usually adventurous, will not be appreciated unless they can be subverted from within to serve counter-reformist objectives, or land reform can be deflected to peripheral areas.

Lele, discussing some of these problems in the Ethiopian context, noted in 1975 that, despite frequent government policy statements concerning the need for tenancy reform, the former landowner-dominated Parliament had been able to forestall effective remedial legislation (Lele 1975: 42, 43). Increasing attention had been given to settling smallholders on unoccupied government land. Powerful interest groups, however, constrained this alternative: between 1942 and 1970 some 5 mln hectares were handed out, but 80 percent of this land went to civil servants, military and police officials, and other elite, and only about 20 percent to landless peasants or unemployed persons. A number of experiments were made to establish settlements on unoccupied government land, but many of these were in relatively marg⁞ al areas. Only since the mid-1970s has a potentially major and more thorough land reform been undertaken, accompanied as is often the case by considerable violence. The lack of clarity in the political and thus economic outlook makes it difficult for the Bank to lend much to Ethiopia in view of its lack of creditworthiness, and latent nationalization disputes.

In many countries the best lands have probably already been pre-empted;

settlements on remaining lands then start at a considerable disadvantage, which may adversely affect their degree of success. The Bank may perhaps be permitted to experiment in such areas.

AGRICULTURAL CREDIT AND BANK POLICY

In contrast to their small volume of lending for land reform-related activities, the principal external donors have actively provided resources for agricultural credit to developing countries. Credit is often a key element in the modernization of agriculture, in removing financial constraints, in accelerating the adoption of new technologies, and in stimulating the commercialization of the rural economy.

Between 1960 and 1969 some $915 mln external assistance for agricultural credit was provided to Latin America by USAID, IADB, and IBRD. Over half of AID's total direct assistance to agriculture in Latin America has gone into credit activities. In addition, AID has helped channel to agricultural credit institutions several hundred million dollars-worth of 'counterpart funds', and 'local currencies' resulting from programme loans and PL480 sales. About three-quarters of IBRD loans also went to Latin America over that period (Adams 1971: 163).

Until the late 1960s, however, little attention had been focussed on the economics of these activities, and very little careful evaluation of the programmes has been made.

According to Adams, several agricultural credit programmes show the same common assumptions (Ibidem: 163-64). Credit shortage is a major bottleneck, causing low land and labour productivity in traditional agriculture. The future transformation of less-developed agriculture will also require major credit infusions.

Concessional lending arrangements for farm credit are justified because (a) farmers have been exploited by lenders who charge exorbitant rates of interest; (b) most traditional farmers need special inducement to use highly productive inputs for which credit is necessary; (c) low interest rates are further justified as an income transfer mechanism and/or to offset fiscal or pricing policy that adversely affects farmers.

Rural areas are said to have little ability to save and the marginal propensity to do so is low. Almost all funds for credit, therefore, must come from elsewhere.

Those who argue that there is an agricultural credit shortage posit that external funds have largely been absorbed by agricultural credit systems, that credit/product ratios in LDCs are much lower than in DCs, that high interest rates in the informal credit markets indicate a shortage of credit, that demand at the farm level appears insatiable, and that new agricultural technologies have a high credit propensity for external inputs of seeds, fertilizer and pesticides.

On the other hand, a number of empirical studies and observations indicate that there is no such shortage. USAID states that 'scarcity of credit may not at present be an important constraint on production using traditional methods', drawing on a 20-volume, multicountry study.[13] Earlier studies in Africa and Latin America reached the even stronger conclusion that scarcity of credit seldom constrained farm growth, at least in national aggregate (Lipton 1976: 545). Adams studied the credit situation for 18 countries in Latin America, during the 1960s, and found that credit-product ratios were relatively high, about two-thirds of that found in the USA. Agricultural credit also grew rapidly, at 12% per year, but was *uncorrelated* with farm output growth. In the mid-1960s a credit constraint on farm growth was diagnosed in Pakistan; later, however, new seeds and associated costly fertilizers have spread to most wheat farmers across the Punjab, including even the small ones (0-5 acres), despite the lack of really drastic credit expansion or reform (Ibidem: 545).

Most of these studies, however, look at the supply side of institutional agricultural credit and in aggregate terms, and give the impression that the situation is fairly satisfactory. Other studies look at the demand side for agricultural credit and ask about the availability and price of credit to various *groups* of borrowers. From that perspective the situation for small farmers seems quite unfavourable.

Agricultural credit should be seen in the context of farmers' total needs, i.e. both production and consumption needs. A farmer may be able to satisfy part or all of the necessary inputs from his own income, or may retain seeds from the previous harvest. The *residual* part of his needs must be 'financed' by loans: from relatives and friends, sellers' credit, formal financial institutions, advance buyers of crop and money lenders, usually at increasing interest rates and risk of default. To focus only on institutional credit is therefore far too narrow in that it disregards the complexity of the credit structure in rural communities. Institutionally limited and aggregate studies are thus of little use in policy planning on behalf of small farmers.

Only fragmentary information is available on the structure of credit in terms of sources, recipients, rates, uses, mechanisms and impact. The Bank estimates outstanding *institutional* loans to agriculture in LDCs to be about $15 billion. Total agricultural credit outstanding is not known, but the bulk originates in the informal sector and is probably at least five times the estimated outstanding institutional credit. On a continental basis, institutional loans show a high percentage in Latin America, while non-institutional lending predominates in Africa and Asia. Within the institutional sector, public institutions are of much greater importance in Asia and Africa, while in Latin America a substantial fraction of loans pass through the commercial banks. Within the continents there is also considerable inter-country variation.

The percentage of farmers who receive institutional loans is limited. On a continental basis, again with substantial inter-country variation, about five percent of farmers in Africa receive institutional credit, while coverage in Latin America and Asia (excluding Taiwan) is about 15 percent. Almost all these funds are channeled towards the larger farmers (*Agricultural Credit*, 1975: 23). Though institutional credit is growing rapidly, non-institutional sources are still the major suppliers of credit to farmers in most LDCs outside Latin America (Ibidem: 22-23).

The goals of government-sponsored agricultural credit programmes have changed over the last two decades. Their principal objective has historically been to reduce dependence, especially of small farmers, on village money-lenders. Institutional credit was supposed to replace the more expensive loans that farmers had to contract to cover their needs. As emphasis on economic growth has increased, however, the use of credit programmes has been stressed for achieving greater output. In a few of the more prosperous developing countries credit institutions are now used to mobilize rural savings as well to reduce the dependence of agriculture on external funds (see Adams 1978).

Programmes supported by the World Bank and other international agencies are primarily interested in increasing production. Many combine this with concern for the welfare of the small farmer, primarily through raising his out-put as well as by reducing his dependence on the moneylender (*Agricultural Credit* 1975: 21).

Against this background it is necessary to examine how institutional credit channels can give effective assistance to multitudes of farmers, especially the smaller ones. More precisely, the issue is how Bank leverage may influence the entire credit market, both for agriculture and for the economy as a whole, to benefit the small farmers. The Bank's lending record for agriculture will be re-viewed below and a number of current policy positions analyzed. Later, some conclusions will be drawn as regards lending prospects to small farmers.

Past lending record and current Bank policy

Evolution of past lending

Within Bank lending for agriculture, which, as we have seen, has expanded rapidly since the early 1960s, that for agricultural *credit* has grown from less than 20% of total lending to agriculture in 1948-63 to 56% of the total in 1969-73.[14] Over time lending has shifted towards countries with low per capita incomes, but Asia approached Latin America only in 1969-73 in terms of volume of lending and number of projects. The Bank Group contributes on average about 45% to total project cost. In 1969-73 the Bank share increased to nearly 60% for countries with less than $150 per capita income in 1970 (*Agricultural Credit* 1975: 78).

Information on types of Bank-supported credit projects shows that almost a third of the total were livestock loans, and that over 70% of those were made in Latin America, mostly for the development of large-scale commercial ranches. More recently, the trend has been toward smaller-scale livestock operations:

In 1970 the Bank made loans to two Latin American countries for livestock development. In both cases an objection was raised in the board of directors that these loans were made to comparatively affluent farmers, while the vast majority of cultivators in those countries, who were certainly not affluent, were neglected (Mason & Asher 1973: 477).

This experience stimulated the Bank in trying to find small livestock farmers, despite opposition from some of the Latin American executive directors.

The second largest number of loans has been in support of general agriculture, including mixed farming, general on-farm improvements and the purchase of non-mechanized implements, such as ploughs.

In fiscal 1969-73, agro-industrial credits were third in importance. These are intended for processing plants, storage and marketing facilities, and for the aerial spraying of crops. Next in importance are loans for minor irrigation projects, mostly wells and low-lift pumps, usually necessary for the water control that is essential in growing new varieties of wheat and rice.

Lending for crop development — mostly export crops such as tea, palm or cocoa — and integrated agricultural development both emerged as important credit activities during 1969-73.

Loans for farm machinery were among the earliest to feature in the Bank's agricultural credit activities, frequently involving the financing of imports of machinery and using counterpart funds for on-lending to farmers. This is now concentrated in Asia rather than in Latin America (*Agricultural Credit* 1975: 25-26). Some of these loans have been shown to be unmitigated disasters. Between 1966 and 1970 the Bank financed part of the cost of introducing tractor technology to farms in Pakistan with the aid of three credits. The estimated social rate of return, *ex post*, turned out to have been 24% which would seem quite satisfactory for mechanizing farmers in the area. The following 'side effects', however, were noted by evaluators in respect of labour: labour use per cultivated acre decreased by some 40%; this was exacerbated by tenant displacements totalling 4.2 tenant families per farm. Using different assumptions as to the amount of labour provided by tenant families, it was estimated that fulltime jobs replaced by each tractor totalled 11.8, 9.7 or 7.5 respectively. Some of these jobs were compensated by casual labour used on seasonal tasks at a rate which implies an overall *net* destruction of jobs of about five per tractor. 'There is little indication that the labour displaced from agriculture had any significant employment opportunities or productive value elsewhere in the Pakistan economy' (McInerney & Donaldson 1975: ii, 73). The Bank refused further funding when these results became known, but the country borrowed elsewhere and continued the project without Bank support (Weaver 1978: 69). Prior Bank support helped to create vested interests which are now able to fend for themselves!

Table 6.2 Bank Group agricultural credit and total Bank Group commitments for Agriculture, FY 1948-1973

Per capita GNP in 1970 of borrowing countries*	FY 1948-63			FY 1964-68			FY 1969-73		
	Total Agriculture	Credit	Credit in % of total Agriculture	Total Agriculture	Credit	Credit in % of total Agriculture	Total Agriculture	Credit	Credit in % of total Agriculture
	($mln)	($mln)		($mln)	($mln)		($mln)	($mln)	
Less than $150	272.3	10.2	3.7	152.3	63.9	42.9	1045.0	535.5	51.2
$151–$375	85.6	41.9	48.9	165.3	54.8	33.2	831.4	289.6	34.8
$376–$700	82.2	24.2	29.4	251.2	107.7	42.9	532.2	469.9	88.3
Over $700	28.0	13.1	46.8	52.0	52.0	100.0	180.3	127.2	70.5
Total	468.1	89.4	19.1	620.8	278.4	44.8	2588.9	1422.2	54.9

* World Bank Atlas 1972

Source: Agricultural Credit (Sector Policy Paper, May 1975, Annex Table 4).

Figures on the various dimensions of Bank lending for agriculture are given in Tables 6.2-6.5.

The World Bank's initial agricultural credit activities were guided largely by three concerns: (1) the funds loaned should lead to increased agricultural production and productivity; (2) the investments financed should constitute an economic use of resources for both the farmer and the nation; and (3) the support provided should help develop agricultural credit institutions. In practice, these guidelines meant a concentration on commercially viable farms and agriculture-related enterprises. 'Credit was not regarded as a practical means for dealing with the problems of subsistence farmers and agricultural labourers' (*Agricultural Credit* 1975: 24). But the paper adds: the technological improvements of recent years have changed the economics of small-scale farming, making it possible for once marginal farms to become viable and creditworthy enterprises. We shall see to what extent small farmers may be assisted through credit, given the Bank's policy positions which will now be discussed.

Table 6.3 *Lending to farmers and total beneficiaries, by size of farm.*
FY 1969-FY 1973* ($mln)

All regions	On-lending to farmers		Beneficiaries	
	$	%	(10^3)	%
0–5 ha	241.6	24.1	916**	62.6
5.1–10 ha	54.2	5.4	109	7.4
10.1–100 ha	372.1	37.1	402	27.5
over 100 ha	335.7	33.4	36	2.5
Total	1003.6	100.0	1463	100.0

* Based on anticipated results as noted in Appraisal Reports.
** Included in the 900,000 intended small farmer beneficiaries (0-5 ha) are 296,000 in India, and 400,000 under the Ethiopia Agricultural Minimum Package Project (approved in June 1973). The latter project is likely to be in trouble because of prevailing conditions and small farmer beneficiaries may be much less than envisaged.

Source: *Agricultural Credit* 1975, Annex Table 6.

Table 6.4 *World Bank agricultural credit operations, by major end use*
FY 1948-73 ($mln)

	FY 1948-63	1964-68	1969-73	1948-73	%
General agricultural credit	6.9	39.6	240.1	268.6	16.0
Livestock	9.4	145.8	506.6	661.8	37.0
Crop development	–	3.4	105.1	108.5	6.1
Irrigation	20.0	8.2	141.0	169.2	9.5
Farm machinery	48.5	42.0	108.8	199.3	11.1
Fisheries	–	13.7	27.2	40.9	2.3
Agrobusiness	–	–	184.9	184.9	10.3
Integrated agricultural development	4.6	25.7	88.5	118.8	6.6
Forestry	–	–	20.0	20.0	1.1
Total	89.4	278.4	1422.2	1790.0	100.0

Source: *Agricultural Credit* 1975, Annex Table 10.

Table 6.5 *Bank Group agricultural credit operations, by lending channel to*
ultimate borrower (FY 1948-73). Amounts and number of
operations

	FY 1948-63		FY 1964-68		FY 1969-73	
	No.	$ mln	No.	$ mln	No.	$ mln
Commercial channels	4	14.7	6	101.0	27	546.5
Agricultural Banks	9	53.0	15	129.4	33	354.9
Cooperatives	–	–	–	–	11	266.9
Development Banks	3	12.1	5	39.1	17	117.4
Project Authority, Ministry	4	9.6	2	8.9	14	136.5
Total	20	89.4	28	278.4	102	1422.2

Source: Ibidem: Annex Table 14.

Agricultural credit policies

In designing agricultural credit programmes 'new style' the Bank has defined
policy positions as guidelines for its future work. In this section we shall review
some of these, their rationale and their limitations, particularly from the point
of view of small farmers. Credit policy discussions centre on three main issues:

(1) eligibility criteria and security requirements;
(2) the level of interest rates and merits of interest subsidies;
(3) repayment performance.

In brief, the Bank favours an assessment of the productive capacity of small
farmers to substitute for land title as collateral in securing loans. The Bank will
work toward the long-run objective of an interest rate that reflects the cost of
capital, and of providing the capital. An intermediate objective might be to
cover at least the opportunity cost of capital. It favours close supervision,
financial discipline, and a strict policy of repayments of loans backed up by
sanctions when necessary (*Agricultural Credit* 1975: 8, 18-20).

Eligibility criteria and security requirements

Traditionally, institutional credit agencies have required that borrowers pledge some
collateral, usually land, as loan security. This practice, and the low valuation frequently
placed on lands, excludes tenants as well as small farmers who often lack certified titles to
their land. Obtaining and processing documents substantially increases the cost of loans,
delays their disbursement and discourages borrowing by small farmers. Lenders, in turn,
are discouraged because foreclosure is extremely difficult to implement and often politically unacceptable. ... Small farmers and tenants are usually penalized by the cumbersome
and time-consuming procedures involved in applying for loans. Many lending agencies have
rigid procedures for processing loans, whether large or small. These include the completion
of complex forms and a pre-audit of the borrower who, if he is small, is often illiterate.
Before the loan is issued, an official has to visit the farmer's holding, and when the loan is
eventually made, the funds and documents have to be collected at the lending institution
(which may be far from the holding). The repayment terms will often lack the flexibility
needed to accommodate the natural hazards of farming....
  [In contrast,] the Bank has consistently emphasized that the repayment capacity of a

borrower should be determined by appraising the productive capacity of his holding and that this should substitute as the essential criterion for security in loan decisions. For long-term credit and large farmers insistence on land as collateral is quite in order, [according to the Bank. But long-term credit to small farmers will involve an assessment of long-term earnings capacity of small farmers which is highly uncertain in view of the natural hazards of farming. These factors militate against long-term credit for small farmers without land title.]

For short- and medium-term credit, chattel mortgages and liens or mortgages on crop production are appropriate. ... Yet they are not widely used because legal procedures are cumbersome and the security they offer is generally considered to be poor compared with land mortgages. One way to make crop liens more acceptable [as an alternative to the use of land as collateral] is to coordinate repayment with crop marketing. It is being used successfully with those crops which are subject to monopoly situations and are centrally processed, e.g. tobacco, cotton, cocoa, tea, coffee, and sugar cane (*Agricultural Credit* 1975: 8-9).

The proposition to tie loans and repayments to crop marketing rarely works well for food crops which provide ample opportunity for private, uncontrollable sales and lack any technologically-necessary tie-in with processing facilities. Loan repayments can then readily be circumvented and evasion of repayment obligations may be tempting; in other words financial discipline is much more difficult to establish and enforce. For this reason the Bank has been reluctant to become directly involved in farmer credit operations based on foodcrops.

Governments have frequently sponsored the organization of farmers who produce food crops in order to oust the traditional middleman, who was thought to be exploitive. Initiatives to establish competing institutions initially met with considerable popular support, particularly where collection and/or distributive trade channels were controlled by alien minority groups. In many cases, however, the sponsored organizations have been unable to deliver competitively priced services. They also tend to be cumbersome and inefficient bureaucracies, operating at higher cost than the traditional middlemen they were intended to replace. If the free market price is higher than that offered by the crop authority, outside or private sales may boost the farmer's income. The viability of the organization will then be undermined by shortfalls in the volume of crops handled and by asymmetric behaviour of farmers who, on the one hand, make use of subsidized inputs provided by the authorities, but on the other hand do not sell their produce to the scheduled organizations. If such organizations are also used as a taxing device to provide investment funds for the state, as is often the case, it will be even more difficult to compete with the middleman. Evasion then becomes very attractive to the farmer!

Attempts to oust the traditional middleman may improve the financial viability of the crop or marketing authority, but they also eliminate the only instrument whose competition can force the marketing board, cooperative or crop authority to maintain minimum standards of efficiency. Initiatives to enforce a fully captive market are rarely popular with the farmers, whose interests the organizations are supposed to serve! (See, for instance, Beckman 1976 on Ghana).

To an economist, the Bank's advocacy of substituting as collateral an economic base for the customary legalistic basis seems reasonable. Though Bank lending for agricultural credit is not insignificant, however, it is not clear whether the Bank can have much impact on institutional policy changes which may imply the amendment of laws applicable to credit institutions. These changes may also be difficult to adopt if credit institutions work with borrowed funds and repayment is expected as a matter of course. The simplication and decentralization of loan application procedures may present similar problems.

Application of the repayment capacity criterion involves a considerable shift towards decentralized decision making: only the 'man on the spot' can make a valid assessment of individual repayment capacity, taking proper account of all relevant variables. Considerable faith must then be placed on the economic and social expertise of local office staff and on their integrity under pressure from local interest groups, particularly if the local credit representative is expected to slant his lending to small farmers and thus to discriminate somewhat against the larger ones, who are often powerful and influential in local rural communities.

The administration of loans to small farmers will be manpower-intensive and thus costly. Retaining the legal basis or land title for collateral enables decisions to be made at some distance from direct local pressure and by staff who are generally better qualified. Both systems might enable an objective assessment of credit requests. In Africa, in particular, the educational background of village level officials is generally very poor indeed, and is likely to remain so for some considerable time.

Interest rates. Agricultural credit, especially to small farmers, has usually been provided at concessional rates due to social reasons. This practice has tended to inflate demand for agricultural credit, perhaps in excess of real needs. When corrections for inflation are made, real interest rates in many instances are much lower than nominal rates or even negative. Together with the allowance of a risk premium on short-term unsecured loans, this has led to reappraisal of the traditional image of moneylenders in the informal credit market who charge, in nominal terms, what seem to be usorious interest rates.

But why should lending to agriculture be concessional? If there are productive opportunities and capital is scarce, low rates of interest should not be necessary to stimulate investment. On the other hand, if farmers can only afford to pay low rates because investments open to them have low yields, then it is questionable whether such investments constitute the best use of scarce resources.

Low interest rates tend to influence the choice of factor proportions in agriculture in that it may stimulate certain forms of mechanization which are introduced with the help of cheap credit. This may be inappropriate where labour is abundant. Cheap credit may also be used by larger farmers to buy more land, thus worsening the situation of small farmers, tenants, and the landless.

Efforts to mobilize agricultural savings will be frustrated if low deposit rates are offered in line with low lending rates. Similarly, if farmers are required to buy equity in a credit agency, this will be seen as compensating balances and will be burdensome because of low or zero dividends, resulting from a too low lending rate (see Adams 1978).

In addition to these resource mobilization and allocation effects of cheap credit, there are intersectoral effects. When those who have access to rural credit have other interests, credit intended for the agricultural sector may leak into other sectors. Adams's findings of no correlation between growth of agricultural credit in Latin America and agricultural output is hardly surprising in view of the fact that those with access to credit are the larger, usually absentee, landowners.

Anyone with agricultural *and* non-agricultural interests, and access to various sources of credit at differential rates, can cover his total financial needs from the cheapest source of supply, which is likely to be credit intended for agriculture. To label credit as being for agriculture, industry, housing, investment or consumption and to charge differential rates may influence the methods by which financing is obtained but does not control its use because of its fungibility.

Low interest rates to agriculture are sometimes justified as a correction for terms of trade losses between agriculture and other sectors. Low food prices (wage goods) may contribute to urban stability and help industrialization by keeping wage costs down. Industries, which may stay perennially infant (see Little, Scitovsky & Scott 1970), usually succeed in passing on inefficiency losses to consumers, including those in agriculture. Agricultural producers will be twice handicapped: receiving artificially low prices for their products, and paying high prices for industrial products. Therefore, it is alleged, they should be compensated by subsidized credit. Such arguments should be considered very critically, however, particularly when, as is often the case, they are made by representatives of the large farmers who receive the bulk of the credit. Small farmers who have little or no access to institutional credit will not be helped by such a policy.

In view of all this, the Bank has reappraised its policy of low interest rates in agricultural lending. It should work 'towards a long run objective of positive interest rates reflecting cost of lending; an intermediate objective may be to cover at least the opportunity cost of capital' (*Agricultural Credit* 1975: 19). A positive real rate of interest should avoid or at least help to correct, factor proportions which do not reflect relative resource endowments.

This new policy may be difficult to implement because in many instances it will involve two processes; firstly, the elimination of intersectoral distortions and thus leakages of funds; and secondly, a change from a negative to a positive interest rate, including administration charges, which may be substantial when supervising credit to small farmers.

The cost of capital may be built-up as follows. The opportunity cost of using capital for other programmes is seldom less than eight percent in real terms. The costs of administrating credit may be put at three percent of total portfolio. These costs rise as the size of loans falls, as the duration of loans shortens, and as accounting services need to be expanded to cope with large numbers of small-scale borrowers. An efficient small-farm credit institution can operate with administrative costs of between seven and ten percent of its total portfolio, excluding the provision of extension and other public advisory functions normally made available as non-profit public service. The costs of risks and defaults may be put at four percent under normal conditions.

In sum, according to the Bank, total real costs for an efficient institution could be between 15 and 22 percent, depending on the nature of the operation and the size of the loans. Costs of lending to small farmers would be at the upper end of the range and may well be even higher.

Information available to the Bank suggests that most nominal institutional rates for agriculture range from six to 30 percent, averaging about ten percent. After adjustment for price changes, these translate into real interest rates of between -16 and +16 percent, with a mean of about three percent, which barely covers administrative costs and seldom permits payment of an interest rate on deposits that would attract savings.

Commercial lenders anywhere charge from three to 20 times as much as institutional lenders. Payment of such high interest rates seems to indicate, according to the Bank, that borrowers would be prepared to accept an institutional rate of interest of between 15 and 22 percent — which would be much lower than the commercial rate, but still high enough to reflect the real cost of lending to small farmers.[15]

Implementation of the new Bank policy will encounter many and diverse obstacles. The Bank recognizes that many external lenders have accepted the principle that borrowing institutions should on-lend at subsidized interest rates (Ibidem: 13). As long as this state of affairs persists and past policies are not deemed to need change, borrowing entities will have the option of redirecting new funding requests away from the Bank to other donors, probably reducing the Bank's future lending role.

Domestic opposition to a drastic change in policy guidelines for interest rates may be quite formidable. Large farmers who use most of the credit will obviously object while small farmers, if they have previously received credit at lower rates, may be discouraged if they have to pay more. Similarly, industry which needs cheap credit to promote the sale of its products (e.g. tractors for farm mechanization) will object to attempts at restructuring interest rates to approach what are said to be more appropriate relative factor proportions in LDCs. Former policies, including those favouring low interest rates, have brought into being powerful interest groups which are likely to be hurt if those policies are changed.

Small farmers and tenants, even though they do not now receive much institutional credit, may also suffer indirectly. This will happen when, as is fairly common in South Asia, the larger farmer is also the local moneylender. To tighten-up the terms on which the large farmer has access to institutional credit will cause the moneylender to tighten-up his lending activities in the informal credit market, activities which in part at least, have been facilitated by his access to extra liquidity which freed own cash resources. This will reinforce his hold on borrowers who have no other sources of credit: small farmers who cannot get credit may be forced to sell their land to the large farmer *cum* moneylender as a result.

All this makes it difficult to envisage who will exercise the pressure to enforce a change in policy on interest rates, the positive effects of which are doubtful and may be felt only in the long run.

Repayment performance. The repayment of institutional rural credit is generally poor. Nevertheless, despite considerable arrears, most loans are eventually repaid (Ibidem: 13). Non-repayment or slow repayment may be due to many factors. As we have noted, the initial rationale for institutional rural credit was to reduce farmers' dependence on the onerous moneylender. It is thus likely that credit institutions for small farmers will not favour a tough collection policy, which may seem to put it in a position similar to that of the moneylender it was supposed to replace.

In other cases, recipients perceive institutional credits as welfare grants rather than as loans to be repaid (Lipton 1976: 548). When production campaigns use subsidized packages to gain the cooperation of the farmers, the difference may be slight between intended incentives and perceived hand-outs, and those who pushed the programme may not be willing to collect on loans.

In some cases collection of debts is made difficult because of the poverty of the borrower, particularly when he is a small farmer with limited resources. Hoped-for increases in income may not materialize due to natural hazards, and debt refinancing may be necessary if the farmer's livelihood is not to be wiped out. If large areas and many farmers are affected by natural hazard, the enforced collection of existing debts will be a political hazard! If poor repayment is due to general calamitous conditions: floods, severe drought, or suchlike, a solid case can be made for declaring an emergency and for writing-off part of outstanding loans on the ground that farmers will otherwise be over-burdened for years to come by excessive repayment obligations. Rescheduling would then not be appropriate. In extension thereof it could be argued that the Bank should write-off part of its loan to the credit agency. This is not likely to be entertained by the Bank, however, on the grounds that the credit institution would then be reimbursed by the government in order not to undermine the financial viability of the borrowing institutions. The Bank would then have to face the prospect that its own loan might not be repaid.

Contrary to what might be expected, payment arrears are not connected with size of borrowers; in fact, larger farmers seem to have poorer repayment records (*Agricultural Credit* 1975: 42; Lipton 1976: 548). Small farmers, if they cannot get loans, fear that foreclosure may deprive them of their livelihood. Inability to pay is frequently at the root of the problem. Large farmers are important men in rural areas and are often also politically well-connected. They sometimes dare the credit agency to go to court for settlement of outstanding debts, indicating unwillingness to pay. Institutional rural credit may be seen by the traditional local moneylender as a threat to a source of income. In defence of his interests he will try to neutralize the institution through infiltration or undermine its viability through non-repayment of loans.

A tough policy on defaults, particularly as regards taking unwilling larger farmers to court, as advocated by the Bank (*Agricultural Credit* 1975: 40-43), will protect the viability of the credit agency and attack the inequity inherent in giving handouts to the better-off who are strong enough to escape repayment (Lipton 1976: 548). Moreover, if some default, others lose the incentive to repay.

Losses resulting from default have seldom exceeded five percent of loans outstanding on Bank-assisted projects. In the early 1970s, however, such projects experienced serious collection problems in Colombia, Pakistan, Senegal, Tanzania and in certain Indian states (*Agricultural Credit* 1975: 41). In this respect, it should be remembered that much of the Bank-provided credit was for products with a marketing monopoly, which makes collection relatively more simple.

The onus attached to attempts by public credit agencies to take court action would be greatly reduced if they were confined to deliberate defaulters. This becomes largely a matter of attitude and political will. According to the Bank, if external leaders were to withhold funding where that will is lacking, the government's hand might be strengthened (Ibidem: 43). This may be doubted, in that it implies that government is the benign caretaker of the public good. To call upon government to correct social ills is to assume that it is part of the solution and not part of the problem. It fits the 'rational actor' view of government in economic policy and planning, so prevalent in much of the economic planning literature (see Killick 1976). Where government officials and members of parliament have used their influence to obtain benefits for themselves, an appeal to them for corrective action is unlikely to be heeded.

For instance, Kenya, where influential people in government and politics, with the aid of the Bank, bought larger plots (so-called Z-plots) under the land settlement schemes, is perhaps typical:

By mid-1969 no cases of chronic loan defaulters from Z-plot holders had yet been referred to the Attorney General, although by the end of 1969, 158 recommendations for eviction of other settlers had gone to the Sifting Committee in Parliament with 84 evictions resulting (Wasserman 1976: 155, 156).

The 'hard line' on defaulters advocated by the Bank in order to maintain the liquidity and solvency of credit institutions may thus be very difficult to implement.

The Bank cannot deal directly with individual small farmers, the bulk of its agricultural credit having been lent through various intermediaries, as shown in Table 6.5. This policy has proved satisfactory from the management and control point of view, and has been effective in reaching the clientele of large borrowers. In dealing with small farmers, however, the record has been less satisfactory due to high administrative costs, lack of collateral and locational limitations which restrict access. Government efforts to prescribe quotas for lending to agriculture, or partially guaranteeing loans to small farmers, have not encouraged the commercial banks to move substantially in this direction, although some serious attempts have been made. Agricultural Banks and Development Banks are bound by similar kind of limitations, though they lend almost as much to agriculture as the commercial banks (*Agricultural Credit* 1975: 15).

It is not clear how the Bank can influence *existing* channels to shift their lending more towards smaller farmers. If the World Bank were to bypass these channels, unsatisfactory as they often are in terms of bringing credit to small farmers, it would have to create institutions which would insist on prompt repayment of loans and would charge positive real interest rates. This, together with the need for proper loan administration, a firm attitude on default, and considerable internal discipline, hardly seems an attractive alternative from the perspective of intended clients in developing countries.

In order to increase the probability that funds intended for small farmers actually reach them, the Bank thinks it advisable to support *separate* credit programmes for large and small farmers in areas where landholdings differ markedly in size (*Agricultural Credit* 1975: 36-37). It is not always economical, however, to have completely separate and parallel lending organizations for the two categories. In such cases different programmes should be created within a single institution, using the same facilities and personnel, but with separate financial accounts.

Credit is only one of the inputs for improving productivity. In the past the Bank has financed credit programmes for lending to farmers for investments in *fixed* capital. Many longer-term investments in fixed capital, however, are not suitable for small farmers because of size 'indivisibilities', disregarding the issue of collateral (Ibidem: 36-37).

At present, many investment requirements of smaller farmers are *seasonal*, to take advantage of new agricultural technologies. In addition to credit small farmers will need auxiliary inputs, for the delivery of which the Bank prefers the 'package approach'. This combines knowledge of technology, inputs such as fertilizer and seed, and sometimes marketing facilities. Such inputs may be provided by different organizations, with the risk that all the inputs and information do not reach the farmer at the right time; or through a single organization which, in theory, can better coordinate the timing of deliveries.

The Bank has stressed the creation of new institutions to aid the poor, but a number of attempts and movements have already been made to establish institutions with the expressed aim of benefiting the poor. Some of these will be discussed later in this chapter.

Conclusion

This review of factors that influence the distribution of institutional rural credit has shown some of the difficulties in designing, implementing and maintaining rural credit to the poor; both on account of the realities of rural life and on account of the new project lending conditions which the Bank seeks to impose in future, particularly in respect of interest rates and default. The cumulative impact of eligibility criteria, interest rate revision and repayment performance make it likely that the bulk of future institutional credit will continue to go to the relatively better off farmers, traders and middlemen. It is tempting to conclude this section with Lipton's phrase: 'the mainstream institutional approach to rural credit has in most cases achieved little, at high cost' (Lipton 1976: 550). The analysis tends to vindicate the earlier Bank-held position that 'credit was not regarded as a practical means for dealing with the problems of subsistence farmers and agricultural labourers' (see p. 165 above).

INTEGRATED RURAL DEVELOPMENT PROGRAMMES

There is considerable terminological confusion about what is meant by integrated rural development, but as our concern is with the approach taken by the World Bank, we shall follow its terminology.

Rural development is defined as a

process through which rural poverty is alleviated by sustained increases in the productivity and incomes of low-income rural workers and households. The emphasis is on raising output and incomes rather than simply redistributing current income and existing assets, although the latter may be desirable or even essential in an overall rural development strategy which links production with distributive or equity objectives (*Rural Development*, 1975: 17).

Other aid agencies use somewhat different approaches. Rondinelli and Ruddle contrast the following three (1976: 29):

(1) 'Functional coordination strategy, adopted by the Bank, seeks to increase the quality and number of facilities, services, technical inputs and institutions essential to expand agricultural productivity and raise rural income levels.'

(2) 'The rural modernization strategy', pursued by UNDP, seeks to 'transform rural areas from traditional to more modern communities, increase food production, change human attitudes, and create a diversified economic base capable of promoting higher standards of living.'

(3) The 'integrated development strategy', employed by USAID, attempts to 'change the structure of developing nations by focusing aid on agriculture, nutrition, health, population control, education and human resources.'

They also note that 'UN documents are vague about implementing the integrated rural development strategy' (p. 39), while the USAID Working Group for the Rural Poor 'raises a number of operational issues, but leaves them unsettled' (p. 45). In comparison, the authors see the Bank as having gone somewhat further because 'the Bank's rural sector policy papers discuss the problems of rural development in fine detail, [though] its proposals for strategy implementation are less conclusive.'

Ruttan asks (1975: 10), 'Why is it possible to identify a number of relatively successful small-scale or pilot rural development projects, but so difficult to find examples of successful rural development programs?' Various approaches to integrated rural development have been attempted in the last 25 years, some of which will be reviewed here in their strengths and weaknesses. We shall also consider the reasons for Bank involvement. In addition, we shall try to explore the conditions under which successful pilot programmes can be replicated. This is of particular importance for the Bank because of the desirability of building-up a cumulative store of knowledge that can be made available in a variety of conditions in different countries. Developing countries should also view pilot projects from the perspective of replicability elsewhere in the country, to justify perhaps high initial costs, to thwart accusations of favouring specific areas or population groups, and to accumulate their own capability for designing viable strategies.

Colonization and settlement schemes

Colonization, transmigration and settlement schemes seem to be convenient methods by which to provide many small farmers and landless people with better earning opportunities, and have been advocated when spare land is available. In Latin America, before World War II, government policies regarding settlement were spasmodic, often taking the form of legislation rather than practice, and generally motivated by a desire to establish territorial sovereignty. Since 1960 more attention has been directed to the humid tropics in order to offset the external dependency of the region and to create sources of employment through new growth poles in the interior (Nelson 1973: 35). In Latin America, in particular, such schemes have been seen as a way to evade the thorny issue of land reform, and USAID and the Inter-American Development Bank have actively supported colonization schemes through loans (Adams 1970: 431-32).

In Africa, the background to settlement schemes has been either political or humanitarian: political, in order to establish European settlement and to separate tribes into different areas; humanitarian, to evacuate areas infected with sleeping sickness. Interest in settlement schemes also arose out of alarm about soil conservation, especially in the late 1930s and early 1940s. Lack of money prevented implementation on any wide scale until after the Second World War. Settlement schemes were seen as a way of attacking the combined problems of erosion and overpopulation. In the post-war period they were associated with the group or co-operative farming movement, and were encouraged by supposed experience outside Africa, by ideology, and by what were believed to be technical considerations. The third stream of settlement schemes sprang from what Chambers has described (1969: 27) as a 'complex mixture of vision, interests, faith and capital, *all of which were metropolitan in origin*' (emphasis added). The pre-independence decline in initiating settlement schemes was only temporary:

Political leaders were often unaware of the lessons of the failures of many colonial schemes, and were anxious to move away from the piecemeal approaches to agricultural development which had become orthodox policy in the twilight of colonialism. Bold plans and fresh approaches were welcomed, with the greater diversity reflecting heterogeneous foreign influences and different national styles and ideologies (Ibidem: 31-32).

Settlements have been studied by many people of numerous disciplines, yet little systematic comparative evaluation of the settlement experience is available. Evidence is massive, unmanageable and disparate. Current generalized wisdom appears to have largely been derived from two volumes: one by Nelson, in respect of Latin America, and the other by Chambers in respect of (Anglophone) Africa. The recent World Bank Issues Paper: *The Settlement of Agricultural Lands* (January 1978) draws heavily on these sources, as well as on limited experience in Bank-assisted settlement projects.

Between 1962-75 the Bank loaned $429 mln for 28 settlement projects. This averaged about five percent of total agricultural lending, the range being from zero in some years to a high of 14 percent in FY 1974. The 28 projects are expected to benefit some 134,000 families, or 4800 intended beneficiaries per project. About 53 percent of the lending has been for wholly rainfed settlements and the balance for projects with an irrigation component. Malaysia accounts for about 57 percent of all Bank lending for rainfed settlement, but only 18 percent of total direct beneficiaries.

Common problems in World Bank-assisted settlement projects are: management and staff inadequacies; organizational problems, principally the lack of coordination or cooperation among participating agencies, and a failure to decentralize authority; over-ambitious physical targets; incorrect estimates of settler labour needs; low estimates of development costs and difficulties in cost recovery (Settlement of Agricultural Lands, 1978: 8, 45-46).

Most bank-assisted settlement projects have not reached full production, and evaluation is tentative. The economic rate of return of Papua New Guinea's Agricultural Development I project (approved in January 1969) is estimated at 19 percent compared to an appraisal estimate of nine percent. For the Trinidad and Tobago Crownlands project (approved in October 1967) the estimated return is approximately zero, against an appraisal estimate of ten percent. But mid-term estimates of economic returns on projects in Colombia, Malaysia and Senegal do not differ greatly from the 13 percent to 16 percent range at time of appraisal. One large loan of $73 mln for an irrigated settlement in Syria was approved in April 1974, but a sharp escalation of project costs has raised serious doubts about the viability of the project as now constituted (Ibidem: 14, and Annex Table 1. This last statement can be found in the internal Bank paper of June 1977: 14).

Nelson studied 24 projects in the humid tropics of Latin America. These were selected as representative of the principal procedures applied in new-land development since 1950, of a range of ecological and locational situations, and of a variety of institutional conditions. The primary focus is the exploitation of new land in order to generate production, employment, and to shift population toward tropical frontier areas, and all projects involve forest resources in terms of either systematic harvesting or 'disorganized destruction' (Nelson 1973: 71). Nelson's sample included only one Bank-assisted project (Caquetá in Colombia), unless projects go by different names.

Chambers studied one project in Kenya in detail, and widened his analysis on the basis of experience in many other settlements in Africa: in all some 40 schemes in eight anglophone countries, with a heavy emphasis on East Africa, have been examined.

The broad conclusions drawn from these surveys are not very encouraging. Nelson's enquiry restricts measures of success to the following: economic return, employment generation, and self-sustaining regional growth. The question of income distribution has been treated indirectly in terms of the economic status of beneficiaries of the various programmes (Nelson 1973: 261-74).

Nine of the 24 projects are classified as dynamic, having a major impact on employment and apparently with good prospects of economic viability. Seven projects are classed as acceptable, employment generation being less than in the dynamic group and the expected economic performance highly variable. Nine projects with poor performance are characterized as stagnant or slow growing in relation to the massive doses of public or private capital applied to the respective regions.

Nelson emphasizes that his sample of projects is biased, since no real failures are included. No data could be obtained on failed projects as no settlers remained to provide information, and government agencies connected with a fiasco are understandably reluctant to divulge information.

Nelson notes further that

few spheres of economic development have a history of, or a reputation for, failure to match that of government-sponsored colonization in humid tropical zones [in L.A.]. Horror stories abound about expensive ventures that resulted in colonies where few if any settlers remained after several years. The evidence is irrefutable, and failure can be attrributed only to the institutions responsible for selecting the area and the colonists, planning and executing the development program, and subsequently maintaining or abandoning the infrastructure and services in the region (Ibidem: 265).

And further: 'The case studies suggest that failure is directly related to the degree of government involvement in a project, transport costs and the degree of pioneer colonization involved relative to consolidation with peripheral expansion into new areas.'

Within the general context of the level of state direction in colonization, the stage of development at the time the programmes were launched, and natural resource endowments, two factors appear to be crucial to success: markets with associated highway access, and organization for settlement. A universal assumption in land settlement ventures has been that markets exist and that the cost of producing and transporting commodities to these markets will be low enough to yield a competitive price. This assumption has proved the *bête noire* of many projects. Markets are principal bottlenecks in new-land development, and the situation frequently is aggravated by an inefficient or monopolistic marketing structure and high-cost transport stemming from poorly constructed and maintained roads (Ibidem: 266).

Directed colonization is based on the premise that unless the settler is provided with the full range of facilities and services — access, roads, infrastructure, cleared land, housing, resettlement expenses, education, health services, production credits, and extension — the political, social, or economic objectives of land development will not be fully realized.

Practically all recorded colonization failures have been state-directed projects, and there is little doubt that directed colonization has been highly uncertain and risky. It is more susceptible than most state programmes to the vagaries of political manoeuvering, discontinuity of effort, and poor administration.

Whereas directed colonization is usually characterized by considerable government control over colonists which, in Nelson's view, directly contributes to their failure, the three semi-directed projects which he analyzed were notable for their relatively smooth operation. Colonization of the semi-directed type involves specific government investments and programmes of assistance to spontaneous colonists in a region that is in the consolidation stage of development, the specific objective being to upgrade production and to promote spontaneous colonization in peripheral areas (Ibidem: 74, 97, 267).

In an earlier study of literature on Latin America, Adams concludes:

Despite some bright spots the research done paints a picture of frustration in resettlement projects. Health conditions, for example, are generally very bad. Transportation is usually a bottleneck for a number of years after the start of the project. Soils, climate and diseases often sharply limit agro-economic possibilities. ... Many frontier lands are found to be largely settled or the land is of too poor quality to be put into crops (Adams 1970: 432).

Basic infrastructure such as schools, marketing systems etc., is almost always seriously lacking. Settlers usually find that clearing land is time-consuming as well as expensive, and many colonists abandon their parcels. It is very difficult to get technicians to work in such areas and projects are often abandoned by the administrators. All this means that settlers can increase their production and income only very slowly and it is next to impossible for them to repay credit or to obtain additional funds and technical help in order to expand production.

Chambers reached conclusions that were fairly similar to those of Nelson and Adams when he evaluated African settlement schemes. He employed three principal criteria: effectiveness of settlement, the achievement of political aims, and economic developments.[16] His typology of settlements is as follows. Using two sets of factors (physical-territorial, and economic-organizational) and regarding controls as the key indicator, settlement schemes can be separated out into four more or less distinct groups along a rising scale of control over individual activities by the management or community: starting with land tenure only, and then adding successively marketing, scheduled services, and a commercial economy.

Controls increase cumulatively in moving from the simplest (individual holding) to the most complex (scheduled production and communal economy) schemes. Each type of scheme has a dominant imperative. In individual holding schemes it is the layout of the land. In compulsory marketing schemes the imperative is primarily financial, to repay credits and loans, or to supply a processing factory with a crop. Mandatory marketing and controls may extend to a regulation that a crop be grown. In scheduled production schemes the imperative is technical and derives from demands of efficient use of a centrally-operated service, either mechanical or irrigational or both. Controls over settlers include requirements that they should carry out operations according to a co-ordinated time-table. In communal schemes the imperatives are either technical or ideological or both.

Resettlement involving considerable self-help and limited official assistance has generally succeeded in linking people and land in stable relationships that do not give rise to further problems.

Table 6.6 *Extent and forms of control by scheme types*

Types of schemes	Land boundaries planned and controlled	Central Marketing Required	Time settler production activities determined	Labour and rewards shared
Individual holding	yes	no	no	no
Compulsory marketing	yes	yes	no	no
Scheduled production	yes	yes	yes	no
Communal economy	yes	yes	yes	yes

Source: Chambers 1969: 230-31.

Compulsory marketing schemes have been somewhat less effective. Limitations on the effectiveness of settlement have been greater with scheduled production and communal economy schemes. More directly, failure has resulted from regimentation and control and use of sanctions, especially eviction, which are found in most scheduled production schemes, and the associated difficulty experienced by settlers in developing a sense of land ownership. Settlement stability seems highest on individual holding schemes and lowest on scheduled production schemes which depend on mechanization without irrigation.

From the political viewpoint, the simpler schemes appear preferable to the more complex (scheduled production and communal economy). Insofar as displaced populations present political problems, these are effectively removed by settlement schemes and in practice these are usually individual holding schemes. In contrast, complex schemes create rather than solve political problems. Where the distribution of schemes is a form of political patronage, instrument or reward, a demand for more schemes may be aroused, particularly for areas or constituencies which have not yet benefited. Potential settlers may ask why others and not they have been privileged as settlers. The dependent attitudes that often develop among the settlers may also create continuing problems for governments. The collection of population into larger residential units which is a common feature of complex schemes encourages the articulation and aggregation of demands which may be politically embarrassing, whereas the scattering of population on individual holding or compulsory marketing schemes is politically stabilizing through dispersion.

Some post-independence settlement schemes, however, can be regarded as investments in stability and legitimacy. Governments need to be able to show that they are able to act and that they are taking steps to improve life for their people. The Kenya Million-Acre Scheme, which settled Africans on formerly European lands, may be appreciated in this light.

In respect of economic evaluations of settlement schemes, Chambers notes that they have frequently been adverse. Few pre-independence schemes were subjected to rigorous economic scrutiny and criteria of 'success' were loose and unspecified. With the exception of Gezira (Sudan) evaluations of more complex schemes were unfavourable. And even Gezira has come under severe attack as an illusion of development (Barnett 1977). Since independence, projects have been subjected to more searching economic appraisal during and after implementation, usually unfavourably. Critics have qualified their strictures by conceding that most of the schemes considered had not reached maturity, and this is of course a general problem in evaluating projects with long to very long gestation periods.

Not only are evaluations of settlement schemes usually adverse in themselves, there are other issues to consider which tend to affect negatively the settlement approach to small farmers. Land, settlers and staff can have opportunity costs in the sense that these scarce resources could have been put to other productive activities. High staffing ratios on settlement schemes are costly, not only in terms of directly paid salaries, but also in terms of production that might have been achieved if they had been employed elsewhere.

Settlement schemes, especially the more complex, are also high-risk undertakings. Actual risks of inadequate data on natural resources, marketing, and the expected behaviour of settlers, are compounded by the extent to which commitment to maintain the project or programme is irreversible. As more studies are undertaken to fill gaps in indispensable data the larger will be the 'sunk cost' of the project and the stronger the reluctance to withdraw. If the indications provided by some studies are unfavourable, there may be pressure for additional studies in the hope of attaining different conclusions. As potential problems and issues increase there will be more temptation to build additional components into the project and to devise safeguards against possible mishap. And if restrictions on settlers increase as a consequence, their initiative and self-help efforts may be thwarted, the organizational balance will tend to swing towards greater government influence and control, and the risk of failure will increase, as both Nelson and Chambers have made clear.

If planned or directed new settlement schemes have a discouraging record, it is equally difficult to react effectively to spontaneous or indirect settlement; there will then be strong pressure for quick action to avoid being confronted with a *fait accompli*, which will often be irreversible. This may inhibit a careful selection of projects and measures and may well compound rather than alleviate the problems of spontaneous settlement. Inefficient institutions are part of the very definition of underdevelopment.

Although there is growing appreciation of their shortcomings, the Bank notes (*Settlement* 1978: 18) that 'support for settlements continues, in part because of their political appeal, in part to pursue the search for economically sound programmes and, occasionally, to avoid the adverse social and ecological effects of spontaneous development.'[17] The Bank expects that 'measures to improve agriculture in already settled areas will continue to be the major means to achieve rural development objectives' (Ibidem: 8).

As regards operational consequences of future Bank involvement, the Settlement paper notes that the Bank has to be 'highly selective about the type of settlement projects that it finances', and also that 'rapid increases in output frequently are achieved most efficiently by measures that intensify production in already-settled areas.' It would seem, therefore, that the colonization and settlement approach can no longer be used as a stratagem to evade the thorny issue of land reform.

It seems reasonable to suppose that settlement on virgin land would be a more costly method of achieving broadly-based income and employment growth than either land reform or parcellization. Under a land reform scheme the movement of people will be limited, the basic economic and social infrastructure is already available in part, and more is known *ex ante* about soil and crop conditions and marketing prospects.

High unit costs in settlement limit the prospects that successful pilot projects will be replicable. Costs per beneficiary-family and per hectare developed vary widely among Bank-assisted projects. For small-farm rainfed settlement projects, costs per beneficiary-family vary between $850 and $20,000; costs are highest in Zambia ($68,000) where some 300 farm families are being assisted on farms of between 70 and 700 hectares, and work made for about 4,000 permanent labourers. Costs per hectare in settlements with irrigation components are almost quadruple those in rainfed settlements, while costs per family are more than double. Tree crop projects are generally much more costly than annual crop projects, while costs in forest areas are higher than in the savannah (Ibidem: 42-43).

The Bank argues that 'its future contribution should be measured less by the volume of lending than by the type and quality of the settlement activities supported' (Ibidem: 4). It may not have a comparative advantage in handling the social and behavioural consequences of the settlement approach, dimensions which it has all too often neglected in the past. The Bank's advocacy in its economic report on Tanganyika (1961) of the 'transformation approach' (i.e. bringing people together in villages to facilitate economy in the provision of services) as distinct from the 'improvement appraoch' (i.e. trying to improve conditions for farmers whereever they may be) has been an important instance of ill-conceived Bank-provided technical assistance. Against the target of over 60 Pilot Village Settlements, each with about 250 farmers, set in Tanzania in 1964 for achievement by 1969, only eight, most of them only partially settled, had been created by April 1966 when the programme was suspended by the government. The Bank's 1967 economic mission reluctantly admitted that this was the right decision although it meant that earlier Bank advice to the contrary was revoked. In the meantime, considerable amounts of capital had been wasted.

Nelson argues that the essential conclusion to be drawn from theories arguing for or against settlement on virgin lands is that new land development should be postponed pending improved knowledge and institutional structures. Since the positive theory [on settlements] is largely speculative and requires wholly new approaches, an examination of past experience throws little light on the probability of overcoming current institutional and technological bottlenecks through such approaches. On the other hand experience does bear out much of the negative theory which argues against development (Nelson 1973: 281-82).

Outgrowers' schemes and product choice

One particular variant of settlement schemes which has received much attention from planners is that of outgrowers' schemes, which involve the production of tree crops on smallholdings rather than on large-scale plantations. Smallholdings are established around the central nucleus either of a processing plant or of a plantation. The central unit provides technical assistance, inputs and marketing services for the outgrowers. This is a construction that allows some of the marketing and institutional problems encountered in settlements to be more readily overcome.

The Bank Group has participated in nine such projects – a total cost of $125 million to which the Bank has contributed $68 million – affecting some 120,000 families at an average cost of about $100 per family: tea projects in Kenya, Uganda, Mauritius and Indonesia, rubber in Malaysia and Indonesia, cocoa in the Ivory Coast and oil palm in Nigeria (*Land Reform* 1975: 44).

Outgrowers' schemes and the organizations that promote them are mostly successful for crops whose processing for technical reasons must pass through a central processing unit, ensuring in effect a captive market. The crop authority deducts charges for services rendered directly from deliveries of the crop to the processing plants, and thus has an in-built mechanism for recouping its cost. Such arrangements provide safeguards for sponsoring institutions and make the schemes attractive as lending propositions.

The initiative for outgrower projects sometimes comes from (often expatriate) plantation owners or managers, who may be induced to help outgrowers for a variety of reasons, including humanitarian ones. They may make their expertise available at zero or marginal financial cost and derive benefits from the outgrowers by buying their crops, thus assisting their own plantations by improving the capacity utilization of the central processing unit. Outgrowers' produce is often bought at a substantial discount in order to reflect real or alleged quality differences. This makes it desirable for agencies that promote outgrowers' interests to have an independent valuation at the buying point or at the point of delivery as a matter of first priority. One possible drawback of such outgrowers' schemes may be that capacity projections for the processing unit are linked to the plantation at full maturity. If so, the outgrowers' crops may become a temporary balancing item in the processing flow. The consequences of fluctuations in yields of plantation or outgrower crops will then fully be shifted on to the outgrowers, with a destabilizing effect on their income position.

As long as the importance of the outgrowers' crop is small in relation to the plantation crop, the nucleus plantation may not object to calculating the services it provides at marginal cost. But if outgrowers' schemes increase greatly relative to the plantation, the full cost of inputs and extension services will have to be borne by the schemes or by the government. Whether such schemes will then become management-intensive and thus costly will depend on a number of factors. The crops may have a high value added, sufficient to absorb the full costs of inputs, extension and marketing services, and yet leave the farmers a reasonable return. Other factors include the learning ability of illiterate farmers and the time perspective within which such schemes are viewed. It is conceivable that initial management-intensity can be diluted over time. Smallholders should become more capable and experienced, thus lessening the need for a high extension density, particularly after trees or bushes are fully grown. External factors, e.g. lower world market prices, may then cause reappraisal of extension standards to protect farmers' incomes. But whether such a reappraisal will in fact occur is doubtful since it has obvious implications for the employment and career perspectives of the extension bureaucracy involved in the project.

If outgrowers' schemes become large and successful, they may begin to compete with the plantation and perhaps reduce the latter's willingness to support it. A struggle may develop regarding control of the central processing unit and of subsequent stages in the marketing channel. Such conflicts have occurred in the lives of the Kenyan and Ugandan smallholder tea projects. From the early 1970s on, KTDA has developed its own tea factories, whereas previously foreign-owned and managed companies processed its tea on a contract basis.[18]

The struggle between outgrowers' organizations and plantations over control of the processing plant may be influenced by the long-run competitive position between plantation and smallholders production. For instance, trade union pressure to improve the wages of plantation workers may negatively affect the long-term competitive position of plantations vis-à-vis outgrower schemes which do not, in principle at least, have to contend with such pressure. There have been examples, for instance relating to sisal in Tanzania and Kenya from the mid-1960s, whereby plantations were closed and/or converted to smallholder units which were thought better able to absorb necessary cost *reductions* in the face of unfavourable international prices. Moreover, the trade unions did not wish to abrogate the so-called Guillebaud Agreement on sisal which foresaw a substantial phased increase in the wages of plantation workers. But if the plantation side of the production process is no longer profitable the company that owns and/or manages the processing factory will doubtless have to intensify its struggle to maintain control over the plant and subsequent marketing stages in order to safeguard its investments.

The dynamics of outgrowers' schemes, particularly if successful, may have several consequences which can fundamentally change their initial conception. It may be useful to spell these out in some detail for the smallholder tea projects in Kenya and Uganda in which the Bank is involved and which account for a very sizeable share of the 120,000 beneficiaries in Bank-assisted outgrower projects: 66,500 tea farmers in Kenya (1972) and about 10,000 in Uganda (1971).[19]

These projects were designed on the basis of several premises, which all changed considerably during implementation.

Tea was originally seen as a cash crop with which to supplement a subsistence income from foodcrops. The size of the teaplot was fixed on the basis of estimated excess labour of the subsistence farm so that hired outside labour would not be necessary. Seeds were to be provided exclusively by the Kenya Tea Development Authority (KTDA) to guard the quality of the green tea. Earlier (pre-war) attempts to develop smallholder tea on Java and Sri Lanka were judged to have been unsuccessful, and KTDA has therefore from the beginning operated an authoritarian extension system to enforce correct management practices. It even has legal authority to prosecute negligent growers! (Lele 1975: 64, 73).

In the early 1960s agricultural extension officers in the tea areas were put into a considerably higher salary scale than other extension workers.[20] The Department of Agriculture in Kenya thus lost many of its most competent staff to KTDA, which affected the development of the national administrative structure (Lele 1971: 72, note 22). KTDA also had an extension agent/farmer ratio of 1:120 compared to 1:500 in Kenya as a whole. These measures were taken to ensure the success of the project and that KTDA could attract future foreign funding on its own strength. Interest in teagrowing was strong but staff build-up and processing capacity had to be phased, and KTDA initially had to severely ration its seeds. This led to considerable politicking and tension, mitigated somewhat by the fact that more senior posts were filled by expatriates.

By the early 1970s, however, tea-growing technology had changed. New stumps were no longer grown from seeds, but from selected mother bushes. Successful established farmers were able to produce new bushes on their own plots and KTDA lost its exclusive control over the rate of planting. Instead of carefully planning acreage and output in view of weakening world market prices, it had to accommodate the effects of dynamics on the part of the farmers.

The average size of holdings increased to 2.7 ha (Lele 1975: 9) against a designed plotsize of 0.4 ha, an enlargement of scale that was difficult for KTDA to control.[21] The increased holding size led to labour demands that were far in excess of what the subsistence family could provide: hired labour became a necessity, and farmers became overseers. A second consequence has been a further encroachment, far beyond initial expectations, upon the foodgrowing capacity in tea areas to feed farmers and newly hired labour alike. This has led to growing food demands which have to be supplied from other regions in Kenya. The specialization weakens the flexibility and increases the ecological vulnerability of the tea-growing areas. A switch back to food crops would be difficult in view of the considerable investment that has been sunk into tea growing, but attempts to promote the growing of foodcrops are now being made.

These developments need not cause concern if food production and an increase in marketable surplus foodcrops elsewhere keeps up with the rapidly growing specialization. Several problems, however, should be noted.

Tea's relatively high value added as compared to the value added in foodcrop production, at least during the 1960s makes it difficult to increase the extension density substantially in foodcrop areas, on account of associated costs. KTDA's extension effort has cost more than $18 per farmer per year, including the cost of the executive and field staff and of the input package. If this investment were to be made on a nation-wide basis, it would total approximately $35 million, or more than the central government's annual expenditure on agriculture in the late 1960s (Ibidem: 69). Thus, if extension services are taken as indispensable to the increase of food production, shortages in foodcrops may well accompany specialization in export crops, leading to intersectoral and interregional distortions.

The incomes of tea farmers are also very vulnerable. In 1967, the British devaluation of sterling, in which currency international tea prices are quoted, was passed on immediately and in full to the tea farmers, in the form of reduced prices for their deliveries to the tea factories. No attempts were made to reduce factory costs or KTDA operational costs. At that time the maintenance of high supervision density could be justified by pointing out that many new tea farmers were inexperienced; in the 1970s, however, such reasoning is refutable as many farmers have from five to ten years of experience and many tea bushes are fully grown. To lower supervision density in old areas in order to protect farmers' incomes in the face of adverse international prices will diminish career prospects unless plantings can be expanded into new areas. This may be undesirable as it would eventually increase supply and might further weaken export prices. Re-employment of staff in foodcrop areas, in the case of KTDA staff, may have serious implications for upward adjustment of salary scales and costs of supervision.

Farmers' incomes from tea have declined considerably. The appraisal report for the first Kenya tea project (1964) calculated a net return to farmers of KShs 1760 per standard plot at full maturity while farmers were paying off their capital levies, and KShs 2080 thereafter. In 1973, actual incomes per 0.4 ha. were re-estimated at only KShs 1390 in the late 1960s, to decline to perhaps KShs 1250 in the late 1970s.[22] Allowance should also be made for cash outlays for foodcrops which were previously home-grown.

These estimates, however, are still substantially above alternative income opportunities from other agricultural crops. Further conversion into tea crop areas may thus be expected during the 1970s, with any additional cost reduction likely to be borne by the hired labour for plucking. Families may try to compensate lower unit income by increasing the size of their holdings.

After having examined the rationale, the inner dynamics and some of the side effects of outgrowers' projects as practiced during the 1960s, we should also look at some of the broader international aspects of the Bank's support for export crops of the outgrower type.

The Bank's financial involvement in outgrowers' schemes and organizations with captive market characteristics, has tended to sharpen competition between developing countries and to lower the real costs of some products for consuming countries, mostly the rich. For several products the danger of substitution may be remote or minor (see, for instance Avramovic 1978, Section III B and Annex D). It might thus have been possible to obtain higher total incomes for developing countries from exports of these products had investment decisions been evaluated in a world market framework. But until recently this has generally not been the case, and during the 1960s investment evaluations were made by the Bank mostly in a national planning context.

The World Bank has a worldwide responsibility and ought earlier to have realized the repercussions that its lending would have on the competitive positions of different developing countries. This would have avoided playing a zero-sum game or worse.

Within the total, almost stationary value of tea exports, some individual producers have been able to profit. Countries that have gained include those in East Africa, where six of the IDA projects for smallholders tea have been located, totalling $26.1 million,[23] mostly at the cost of India and Sri Lanka. Output from the projects started in the 1960s started to become available from the early-1970s. Africa's share in world tea exports increased from 6 percent in 1955-57 to 17 percent in 1969-71. The share of IDA-supported smallholder tea areas in the total tea area in Kenya, for instance, rose from 4.4 percent in 1959 to 47 percent in 1974. Smallholders have increased to over 70,000 and now hold considerable political and economic power in Kenya.[24]

Prospects for *future* Bank lending in this field of outgrowing crops may be assessed with the aid of a Board Paper on 'Development Policy for Countries Highly Dependent on Exports of Primary Products', dated January 4, 1973 (R73-3), which basically concludes that a 'selective policy will have to be followed in respect of Bank lending for products facing inelastic demand.' Periodic reviews of the market outlook for such commodities will be made to view whether changes in this policy are called for.

An initial outcome of this more selective approach was the Bank's decision taken in August 1973 to undertake *no* further financing of projects involving the production of tea. Any exception to this general policy was to be strictly limited to financing for increases in output in countries with no investment alternatives yielding an acceptable rate of return, and financing of rehabilitation involving no increase in output ('Financing of Tea': 2).[25] It cost the Bank a great deal of whatever limited leverage it had on Kenya in respect of tea.[26] The Bank's management decision taken in mid-1973 to stop lending for new tea plantings did not stop the Kenyan expansion programme; there was merely a substitution among external financiers. Between 1964-74 CDC had concentrated on financing the tea factory sector. It switched its support to financing the planting programme, and the Bank financed the factories necessary to process the tea from earlier planting programmes. All in all, the programme's implementation was delayed one year. On May 14, 1974 the Board approved a loan of $10.4 mln for the tea factory programme which, strictly speaking, it was not justified in financing. The record showed that sufficient private capital could be expected to continue to finance the necessary factories, i.e. Bank financing competed with private external capital, and this it is not supposed to do.

The temptation to initiate crop production for export is great if expected revenues look impressive by national standards. Moreover, project appraisals will be flattered as a result of a high premium in the shadow rate of exchange on the value of exports and by neglect of the price effect of additional output on world market prices. If and when a series of small projects evolve into a large programme and eventually become spectacularly successful, as appears to be the case of East African tea, it is no longer justifiable to neglect the price effects on the incomes of other producers. To charge income losses in India and Sri Lanka to production in the most recently established tea areas in East Africa would affect the cost benefit analysis dramatically, and lead to a rejection of new products. But the real difficulty is how the Bank can withdraw from such programmes which have been promoted in the past and which, if successful, have established considerable economic and political vested interests.

World demand for several products that are suitable for outgrowers' schemes is restricted and a sizeable increase in the number of such projects is not feasible. Moreover, in the design of new projects care should be taken to avoid the imbalance in domestic resource allocation which has prevailed in the past, and which has been briefly illustrated in connection with tea in East Africa. Whereas pressure from traditional tea producers such as India and Sri Lanka has sensitized the Bank to the wider repercussions of its support for new tea producers in East Africa, in recent years pressure has come from other quarters on issues of commodity competition. In October 1977 the USA passed legislation which required the US Executive Directors in the international development banks to oppose loans for exports of palm oil, sugar and citrus if they caused injury to American producers. The impact of such legislation on the behaviour of the Bank is difficult to assess but it is not unlikely that it will tend to respond by framing project justifications primarily in terms of production for the domestic market and rehabilitation of existing production facilities. The USA closely monitors lending proposals through the NAC,[27] which is required to report to Congress in respect of adherence to American legislation, and the Bank would antagonize Congress if it did otherwise.

Other institutional approaches to small-farmer projects

If rural development is to be sustained, inputs should not be examined in isolation, e.g. credit, technology or land. *All* inputs and services must be available at the right time at the right place and in the right amounts. The two approaches discussed above try to take this into account. Colonization schemes on virgin lands attempt to start from scratch, but in doing so, they require considerable institutional expertise to provide all the services that are necessary for success. These services exist at least in part in areas that are already populated and developed but their significance is often not appreciated until truly virgin lands are colonized and settled. Outgrowers' schemes are more easily managed because of an enforceable marketing monopoly, but their spread is limited by the marketing prospects for the products concerned.

A rural development programme depends on all these inputs in their proper sequence and interaction, and its success depends on the strength of the weakest link in the chain of interlocking factors. In practice, responsibility for each input and service is often divided among numerous institutions which are functionally and vertically organized and rarely coordinate their activities at the lowest level where it is really essential.

Consequently, approaches have been attempted which will cut across the many lines of independent and often conflicting autonomy or authority, and coordinate activities in order to make available at the farm level all necessary inputs at the right time. Institution building is an important element in such approaches, and the Bank has stressed the need for new institutions to help deliver inputs to the poor.

Activities may range along a scale, at one extreme of which some countries seek to provide a package of minimum requirements to as large a group as resources permit. This may be called the 'minimum package approach' to rural development. At the other extreme are the more comprehensive programmes which include social as well as directly productive elements. Such programmes require heavy financial and human resources, however, and experience relates mainly to specific area or regional schemes rather than to nation-wide programmes.

The great advantage of minimum package approaches is the promise of low-cost, extensive coverage with comparatively simple objectives and operating procedures. An initial emphasis on a broad-based increase in productivity, through a minimum level of institutional development, may be the most effective way to ensure mass participation in a subsequent more complex type of programme (*Rural Development* 1975: 41). The Ethiopia minimum package approach disucssed earlier may be seen more or less as a 'model' of this method.

In the Bank's limited experience to date, and according to the studies within the context of its African Rural Development Study, published by Lele (1975), important conditions for the success of such programmes are:

a first class technical package much superior to existing practice and neutral scale, an intact social structure in rural areas, a lendtenure system which does not discourage production above subsistence level, and a loose system of credit supervision, with satisfactory repayment rate enforced through firm and visible discipline in the case of government credit (*Rural Development*: 42).

These imply a formidable list of requirements both in respect of the capabilities of the institutions charged with spreading the minimum package over large numbers of farmers (in Ethiopia, blocks of 10,000 farm family units), and in respect of the homogeneity of the recipient social structure both before and during the introduction of the minimum package. Moreover, such institutions are unlikely to have much influence on the many structural and environmental factors that are crucial to their effectiveness, where preconditions for success are less than optimal.

The conditions relating to intact social structures and non-oppressive land tenure systems seem to restrict applicability of this model largely to parts of Africa, though even there land concentration and economic differentiation is progressing rapidly in a number of areas.

The Bank paper notes that 'social and economic stratification [by access to land, farm type, level of skill, and occupation] in many South Asian countries would seem to preclude widespread application of the minimum package approach' (*Rural Development* 1975: 42). Its applicability to large parts of Latin America would seem to be restricted for the same reason.

Comprehensive area development schemes are said to have the special advantage that they can focus directly on the needs of the rural poor through diversified crop and integrated farming systems. They may comprise 'single product projects' (tea, tobacco, cotton, coffee) or they may branch out into a variety of other activities of an economic or social nature (Chilalo in Ethiopia, Gezira in Sudan, Comilla in Bangladesh, Puebla in Mexico and Lilongwe in Malawi, are fairly typical examples of different comprehensive projects).

Such schemes typically operate through a well-funded and well-staffed special authority outside the local civil service structure, and with little community or other direct local participation. They incur the following potential dangers, however:

(a) they may concentrate a disproportionate share of resources on providing benefits to a group that is small in relation to the overall size of the national target group;

(b) they tend to suffer from a programme design that is too ambitious and complex, calling for exceptional leadership that cannot always be made available on a sustained basis;

(c) they may distort priorities in the allocation of resources among sectors (*Rural Development* 1975: 47).

The need for quality staff and management in such schemes is often met through foreign technical and financial assistance. Donor agencies and the World Bank tend to provide large numbers of highly qualified experts (some local, but often foreign), and often require new institutional arrangements as a condition for launching such projects. For instance, all but one of the African rural development projects analyzed by Lele (1975) had these characteristics. Similarly, the Comilla and Puebla projects were extensively assisted by foreign aid and staff. Direct foreign financial assistance hinges on the donor's assessment of the quality of management. When the foreign staff withdraws, whether or not under pressure to 'localize' the top jobs, foreign financing not infrequently also dries up, with a corresponding negative impact on the chances that successful projects will be replicated on a large scale.

The comparative affluence in terms of management and finance in the early phases rarely survives the transfer of functions to the local administrative system. On the other hand, a reluctance to transfer functions may increase pressure stemming from envy of the relatively well-off enclave and/or of showcase projects.

There may be solid reasons why the management of a comprehensive pilot project is reluctant to transfer functions:

(a) indigenous regional and local administration may not have the capability to carry out the necessary policy and coordinatory functions itself;

(b) institutions to handle the commercial aspects, such as agricultural credit and input and output marketing, either do not exist — since the programmes have handled these functions — or do not yet have the administrative capacity to handle them on a large scale;

(c) local organizations and local administrative units developed under the programmes may not correspond to existing local governmental institutions, raising difficult questions related to the maintenance and expansion of the various local services (*Rural Development*: 48).

A partial transfer of functions may recreate the danger of lacking or ineffective coordination between organizations which the programme unit sought to solve by taking the necessary functions in its own hands. Comprehensive area development programmes thus involve *two* rounds of institution building: firstly, the shortcut 'solution' to rural development through setting-up a special programme authority; secondly, the build-up of local structures to which programme functions can be transferred.

The activities of the Academy of Rural Development at Comilla have stood model for a variety of so-called integrated rural development projects (see

Adams & Coward 1972). Contrary to most of its imitations it has existed long enough (Raper 1970) to permit some evaluation of its results. While Stevens (1974) stresses its success in terms of the spread of BARD activities, cooperative credits, technology, farmers' income, training, etc., Rahim, BARD's research director (1972), has shown that progress in Comilla, while good (if costly), was not much better than that in a neighbouring area that was little affected by the scheme. Comilla's founder has subjected the project to severe criticism, centering on its replicability, cost, and dependence on either charismatic leadership or mass commitment, neither sustainable for long in the absence of equality and shared goals (Khan 1972, 1974; see also Bose 1974). Other projects have existed for too short a period, and information on them tends to be limited to the memoires of the first project director.[28]

Many integrated rural development projects of the late 1950s and 1960s were able to attract foreign funding, at least in the early stages, because of the availability of foreign expertise in their management. These factors enabled them to be set up as separate entities, cutting across and in many instances implying a condemnation of existing institutions. The deficiencies of the latter were then assumed to be so severe that it was more attractive to start from scratch rather than to change them into more efficient, viable and effective institutions.

Many schemes, at least in Africa, were staffed in large part by former colonial officers who had seen their career perspective disappear in the wake of political independence and the subsequent acceleration of 'staff localization drives'. They possessed considerable experience in the countries concerned, often spoke the local language and were well-connected with the nationals who had taken their previous jobs. National officials were more attracted to jobs in the capital city and did not greatly object to such institutional innovations in rural areas. Local and regional organizations were weak. If a donor-supported integrated rural development project happened to require a separate institutional set-up this did not meet with great resistance.

But the generation of former colonial officers is rapidly aging. Post-colonial technical assistance typically has been short term, and new officials have generally not learnt the local language, a precondition for effective work in rural areas. They also lack detailed local knowhow, even though in attitude and motivation they may have been 'better' than their predecessors, at least when they started their work.

In present-day conditions in Africa as elsewhere, however, it seems that national officials will encounter much greater difficulties in setting-up an organization that cuts across regional functional competences. Indigenization of the bureaucracy at the national level is well advanced, and local educational institutions are providing increasing numbers of educated people. This leads to spillover effects of increases in locally- and regionally-posted staff. Resistance to the new establishment of an alien body of national officials that cuts across local lines of authority, reference, and power, may well be severe. In fact, the attempt to transplant the CDC and IDA-supported organizational model to Uganda in the mid 1960s, to establish the Uganda Tea Growers Corporation, ran into considerable problems of this sort: Uganda felt that it did not need the foreign managers on whom the Bank insisted.[29] Now, ten to fifteen years later, opposition to alien implants may be more frequent and more determined, restricting the chances to initiate intensive regionally-based integrated rural development projects along the lines of the earlier schemes. New projects will increasingly have to be implemented through the existing regional and local administrative machinery. As in the case of settlements, inefficient administrative systems are part of underdevelopment.

A promising delivery system for spreading the 'new packages' would seem to be the cooperative movement. This has the advantage, in principle, of achieving economies of scale which are also important for fixed and indivisible capital projects; it has a local organization available as channel or instrument for government development efforts; it claims to be able to develop less exploitive relationships with outside forces as compared to traditional middleman systems; while the ultimate aim of its pioneers was to establish a new social order characterized by what they called 'equity' in the distribution of wealth and income (International Co-operative Alliance 1967: 20). The potential of farmers' cooperatives as channels for spreading more productive packages of inputs and marketing increased outputs, is clearly worth pursuing.

The actual workings of a number of cooperatives at local levels have been studied by the United Nations Research Institute for Social Development: *Rural Cooperatives and Related Institutions as Agents of Planned Change*, eight volumes being published between 1969 and 1975 (Geneva). The field research, conducted in 1968-70, included some 40 case studies of individual cooperatives and related institutions in Asia, Africa and Latin America. In addition, three analytical overviews drew upon *other* information on the cooperative movement in the countries concerned.

A major conclusion of this UNRISD study is that rural cooperatives in developing areas today bring little benefit to the masses of poorer inhabitants of those areas and cannot generally be regarded as agents of change and development. The cooperative services and facilities such as government-supported credit and technical assistance channeled through the cooperatives, are usually taken advantage of by the better-off rural inhabitants.

In some places, most poor inhabitants have in effect been excluded from membership of the cooperative. They have neither the resources to join nor the relevant property basis; the services provided have not met their particular needs (i.e. production loans or marketing services which are not utilized by farm labourers), or they could not qualify for the services even if they did join; or they have been excluded by one means or another for ethnic or caste reasons. Cooperatives with restricted membership may be economically quite successful; but while they benefit their limited membership they also tend to increase income differentials within the community, since the poorer inhabitants gain little or no advantage (UNRISD 1975, Vol. VIII: ix, 6-7).

Cooperatives whose membership is community-wide, tend themselves to reproduce the structure of that community. People who are better off control the committees and management and influence the nature and distribution of the benefits. Tenants, share-croppers or farm labourers, for example, do not have and cannot expect to have a voice in cooperative affairs that equals that of their landlords and patrons on whom they depend in daily affairs, however democratic the cooperative may be in principle (Ibidem: ix).

In some cases, the cooperatives were found to be organizations of the *poor* peasants in the community and dedicated to their interests, but these often proved ineffective. Where, on occasion, they threatened to compete seriously with established interests, there was a tendency to undermine them by removing or co-opting their leaders or by forcing them into bankruptcy, a ruse that frequently succeeded (Ibidem: x).

The conclusion that rural cooperatives in developing countries do not generally provide much benefit to the masses of poor people is supported by evidence from quite diverse regions. Representatives of the International Cooperative Alliance have criticized both the representativeness of the sample studies and the generality of many of the conclusions. The analytical overviews, however, also drew upon other evidence. The USAID delegate said that 'an assessment of cooperatives in Latin America made under AID auspices had reached quite similar conclusions' (Ibidem, Vol. VIII: 25, 34). The 1073-page official report of the All-India Rural Credit Review Committee (1969) emphasizes 'the comparative neglect of the small cultivator by the cooperatives, the much larger share of cooperative credit going to the bigger cultivator, and the dangers of a situation in which the funds of development continue to be denied to large sections of the rural community' (Ibidem: xi, 113-115). It is also of interest to note that the early cooperative movement in England 'never succeeded in reaching down to the lower level of working class income', and mainly appealed to the 'better-off sections of the working class, until there was a substantial rise in wages for the main body of industrial workers after the middle of the 19th century' (Ibidem, Vol. VII: x, 70-71; Cole 1944).

The joint statement by UNRISD regional project directors notes that 'rural cooperatives have seldom achieved the development goals set for them by economic and social planners. This has been most clearly evident when the goals have included structural changes' (Ibidem, Vol. VIII: 10).

An extensive quotation from Myrdal's *Asian Drama* would seem to be appropriate:

Unfortunately, the notion that cooperatives will have an equalizing effect is bound to turn out to be an illusion. While land reform and tenancy legislation are, at least in their intent, devices for producing fundamental alterations in property rights and economic obligations, the 'cooperative' approach fails to incorporate a frontal attack on the existing inegalitarian power structure. Indeed, it aims at improving conditions without disturbing that structure and represents, in fact, an evasion of the inequality issue. If, as is ordinarily the case, only the higher strata in the villages can avail themselves of the advantages offered by cooperative institutions — and profit from the government subsidies given for their development — the net effect is to create more, not less inequality. This will hold true even when the announced purpose is to aid the disadvantaged strata (Myrdal 1968, Vol. II: 1335).

While it is not difficult to find critical studies of the functioning of cooperatives, it might be worthwhile to study under what conditions they would appear to have more probability of success. On this question the UNRISD studies are uneven, but Inayatullah's analytical overview of Asian experience is relatively better. He suggests (Vol. VII: 266-70) that productivity gains and economic growth were found to be greatest in agricultural cooperatives where solidarity was high, which were homogeneous in occupation and class, where discipline was good, where cooperatives were seen as instruments for capital accumulation and where efforts were effectively made to improve the supply of water, and provide new seeds within a network of supporting services. As the Bank's rural strategy operates on similar premises, this may indicate the likelihood of success for such an approach, even through such channels as cooperatives. *De facto* exclusive membership on account of class, race, or caste, however, is likely to be a serious problem in Asia, with corresponding negative effects on non-members, the more so as high impact cooperatives have taken a firm stand on the expulsion of defaulters (UNRISD, Vol. VII: 267).

REPLICABILITY, THE BUREAUCRATIC BOTTLENECK, AND THE BANK

The shape of 'integrated rural development' projects will need to be determined in each case according to local circumstances. For the moment we will assume, however, that pilot projects and, if they prove successful, replications will consist of three components: a technological package to increase farmers' productivity, a social service package, and delivery systems or organizations capable of bringing the packages to the rural areas and of assisting in the marketing of increased agricultural output.

Agricultural extension services

The process of modernizing farm practices through the introduction of modern technology often ascribes a major role to agricultural extension services, as intermediaries in the diffusion of innovation. The more extension workers, the greater the possibilities for them to reach the farmers and to assist and/or persuade them to adopt new methods of cultivation.

Standard manpower planning practice for agriculture is to derive targets for agricultural field staff on the basis of desired ratios between extension workers and farmers, which may vary between different types of cultivation. The FAO, in its Indicative Plan for World Agriculture, uses this methodology.

But before subscribing to a strategy to rapidly expand extension services it may be reasonable to ask about their effectiveness in the process of inducing agricultural innovation. The answer will obviously have consequences for donor agency policies in the future, and thus for the World Bank.

Research on the impact of extension is limited because it is very difficult to relate it to economic change, and much of that which is available focuses on one specific indicator only. To measure the number of farmer contacts is inadequate because it assumes that these are productive and can be used as a proxy for resulting change. If extension workers are rated for effectiveness and promotion on the basis of the number of their contacts, they will tend to inflate those numbers and to count anyone within eyesight as a 'participant'. Other approaches to research on extension focus on farmers, who are asked whether they have learned something useful from extension workers. Answers can be compared with information from other sources; for instance, whether the information disseminated accords with the recommendations of agricultural research stations (Cliffe et al 1968, for instance, show that much of it is not); farmers are then ranked on a scale of adoption of modern methods, after correcting for differences in initial conditions.

Evaluations may be attempted by measuring the increase in productivity in a certain area in relation to inputs, e.g. extension, credit, fertilizer, pesticides. Such statistical analysis is carried out at an aggregate level and may hide very important inter-farm variations.

It would seem that a serious evaluation of the impact of extension activities should combine elements of the three approaches outlined above, if it is to reach valid and meaningful conclusions about its contribution to the diffusion of innovation.

A classic study of extension is that by Rogers, Ashcroft and Röling: *Diffusion of Innovations in Brazil, Nigeria and India* (1970), where it is found that contact is a necessary condition for diffusion in less developed countries. But Rice (1974: 390-92) has criticized their study design, arguing that the conclusions overreach the data base and that their findings are probably attributable to unresolved problems of collinearity. The villages and farmers visited by the team enjoyed the simultaneous infusion of other inputs and favourable environmental conditions. Moreover, villages were only included in the analysis which change agencies had identified as those to which they had assigned people to work. Thus, if there were progressive villages with very little contact with change agencies, Michigan State University's research team did not find them.

Rice studied the result of thirty years of American efforts to help build agricultural extension institutions in Latin America. Twelve countries in the

Andes range were sampled, in eleven of which extension services had not pre-viously existed. His study thus offers a good example of 'cross cultural' trans-fer. During the 1950s extension was the centrepiece of most American rural development country strategies; and at the time of Rice's study ten years had passed since the Americans started phasing-out the extension programme, a period thought long enough to allow permanent results to be sought (Rice 1974: 23-24). The analysis was based on a number of elements: interviews with American and local technicians involved, as well as scrutiny of available records and office files of and on the organizations concerned; a review of the literature, analysis of an especially designed impact study comprising nine districts in six countries, and 27 case studies covering five approaches or types of programmes, and a comparison with agencies which had not been supported by the US aid programme. In brief, it encompassed nearly all the elements which a serious study of the extension phenomenon should include.

On two of the criteria to evaluate the US programme: effectiveness (whether the US built viable institutions), and significance (whether the institutions in-creased agricultural productivity), it rates rather low. Some of the most im-portant findings of the study were the following:

(a) the services developed as separate entities, but were not prepared for trans-fer to the bureaucratic environment of the host government; in some cases they were met with unconcealed hostility;

(b) a certain arrogance had already developed among extensionists and the tendency to underrate the importance of functional links with other in-stitutions helped keep extensionists isolated after transfer;

(c) the proposed extension operation is expensive;

(d) no solution was found for low budget allocations;

(e) the image of extension, that is, what people think about extension, is remarkably better than the estimated impact on production suggests it ought to be;

(f) extension played a marginal role in most of the improvements in pro-ductivity that occurred in the study area; the extension services have been neither necessary nor sufficient as an instrument of development;

(g) extension services appear to perform the essential extension function *only* when the services have linked, spontaneously or by design, to research, supplies, credit and marketing authorities in profitable production pro-grammes;

(h) it is already questionable whether the extension organizations as presently constituted will survive;

(i) the mistakes may have been made at the very beginning of the institution-building programmes; the extension operation should not have been in-stitutionalized as an independent entity;

(j) the US technical assistance agencies must accept responsibility for the way the programme has developed; the US got into it for the wrong reasons and got out of it for the wrong reasons (Rice 1974: 417-20).

If American efforts at institution building in Latin America — by exporting its own model of extension services — have not been a startling success according to USAID's own evaluation, what about the effectiveness of the legacies of former colonial masters in Africa and Asia?

Ahmed notes (1975: 86), 'It is an open question to what extent the extension service contributed to the impressive achievement of India's Green Revolution in the late 1960s. The weight of informed opinion seems to be on the negative side of the balance.' It has already been pointed out that the spread of BARD activities in Comilla produced results that were little better than in a neighbouring area not affected by the scheme.

De Wilde notes, in respect of Africa, that

until rather recently agricultural extension work was largely conceived in terms of telling the farmer what to do. In fact, this limited conception has been responsible for much of the frustration of efforts to improve agriculture. Pre-independence governments always relied too much on direction and even compulsion; and even today African governments in their impatience to get things done tend sometimes to fall into the same error. Owing to the shortage of trained personnel and the time required to convince farmers there has always been a natural tendency to favour regulation and direction rather than persuasion. By and large the use of compulsion has done much to set back the cause of agricultural progress. In many areas the extension service is still in bad repute because of its past association with the enforcement of soil erosion control, livestock limitations and the like (De Wilde 1967, Vol. 1: 162).

Attempts are being made in various countries to change the *modus operandi* of extension workers, to induce them to work more through persuasion, and this sometimes requires considerable retraining and improvement in the quality of their jobs. Two incentives are then usually considered crucial to staff performance: salaries and promotion prospects (Lele 1975: 71 ff). But in as far as upgrading and salary improvements go hand-in-hand due to the linkage of government pay-scales to formal qualifications, such a strategy will tend to make the existing extension service more costly. At any level of the available budget a difficult trade-off will have to be made between upgrading and higher pay of existing extension workers versus the expansion of their number. While better-trained workers might be more willing to try persuasion instead of compulsion, given the reality of the training and educational environment in Africa it is not inconceivable that more education for extension workers will merely enhance their sense of superiority, arrogance and social distance from the farmers. A better trained extension worker will not necessarily reach more farmers than one who is less trained. Even if, in de Wilde's words (Ibidem: 163), it has been 'hammered home to them the importance of understanding the farmer and his point of view', it is doubtful whether this will enable them to resist government commands and the compulsion so characteristic of the past. The continued practice of frequent staff transfers makes it impossible for workers to get to know the farmers: much of their time is spent on office-bound activities rather than in the field (see, for instance Cliffe et al 1968).

High-density extension may not only be costly in terms of government resources but also of value added as a result of their activities. In the case of KTDA, both the higher pay scale and the higher density as compared to the rest of Kenya could only be absorbed because of the relatively high value added in tea-growing. Low value added in foodcrops cannot 'carry' the cost of a high-density extension service.

More research on ways and means to make extension services more effective is obviously necessary. How can systems be designed which will provide quality service to farmers at low cost, and how can the incentive of extensionists be put to work other than in the present reality where reward means promotion to a more desirable location and to a work situation which is hierarchically further removed from the drudgery of rural life? A mere expansion along existing lines does not seem a very promising course of action.

The Bank and institution building

In view of the experimental nature of the theory and practice of many new-style projects, the countries concerned and the Bank are interested in gathering and synthesizing experience from ongoing projects, and in applying it to new operations as *quickly as possible*. This 'gathering of experience' is becoming an increasingly important aspect of the Bank's work (Israel 1978: 28, emphasis added), and institution-building activities are likely to be given even more emphasis in future.

There is, however, reason to doubt the specificity of recommendations to be derived from synthesizing experience in rural development projects. Bunting, after reviewing some 60 approaches to rural development, has concluded that 'our experience of attempts to change agriculture during the last 25 years has shown not only that it is dangerous to transplant ideas about institutions, but also that effective results may be achieved in what appear to be similar circumstances by widely differing institutional and administrative arrangements' (Bunting 1970: 726).

A theory of induced agricultural innovation must come to grips with the problem of institutions that are capable of delivering the intended benefits. At present, however, no institutional models are available as to how this could be done.

The literature on institutional change is of little use as a guide to the design of innovations, but some literature on 'institution building' has evolved out of an effort in the field of public administration to provide technical assistance agencies with methodologies for external intervention which would induce more effective institutional performance (Siffin 1972).

A major inference to be drawn from the literature is that it is easier to institutionalize an organization whose operations are primarily concerned with the use of a well-developed technology. Where relatively 'closed system' technologies are available, the behaviour they require for successful introduction and management are particular to their operations – and not to the socio-cultural 'system at large' (Ruttan 1975: 14). This partly explains the success of schemes such as Gezira (irrigation and cotton), of many of the outgrowers' schemes supported by the Bank, and of cooperatives that are built around such technologies.

Where a closed system is not available, effective institutionalization will be exceedingly difficult to achieve.

It is increasingly realized that programmes set up to accomplish certain ill-defined welfare objectives often fall short of reaching them. The major beneficiaries are then not the intended target groups but the bureaucracy that administers the programme (Downs 1966: 3-35; Niskanen 1968).

Ill-specified objectives may well have been a major element in the economic failures of earlier rural development efforts. Foreign aid-supported community development efforts, initiated in many countries in the early 1950s (India, Pakistan and the Philippines, for example), were in serious trouble by the mid-1960s.[30]

Another inference about institutionalization efforts, whether or not effective in themselves, is that many such institutions tend to become 'rising cost industries', because of high unit costs and limited economies of scale. In discussing variety of issues in this chapter we have seen that suggested improvements for the functioning of institutions go hand-in-hand with the upgrading of services which, as long as government salary scales are linked to educational attainment, will increase unit costs. In many African countries the government is the predominant employer. With para-statal organizations expanding in number and scope, there is a tendency to spread the bureaucratic salary system. A constant struggle wages between those who argue for expansion of existing facilities, versus those who favour upgrading them which, for any given budget, limits their scope for expanded coverage.[31] In practice, those who defend their own economic interests often overrule pleas for the interests of the unorganized. This is confirmed in a more general context by Turner & Jackson who found, in a global analysis covering the period 1956 to 1965 and broadened by loosening data requirements to 1950-70, that there had been an extraordinary similarity between the experience of advanced countries and of the modern sector in less advanced countries: labour short and labour abundant. In both groups of countries real wages have risen at similar rates, i.e. about 3.4 percent per annum (Turner & Jackson 1970: 83). Their data fit a simple 'wage-leadership/cost-inflation' model for the world as a whole. This derives from three fairly well-annotated phenomena: firstly, that where productivity is rising, it is easier to concede demands for wage increases than to reduce prices; secondly, wage increases in one sector tend to stimulate pressures for similar increases in other branches; thirdly, wage increases in excess of productivity increases are passed on by employers to prices or, in case of governments, by raising taxes.

In poor countries, workers may appear to have little bargaining power in orthodox trade-union terms (lack of efficient collective organization, strikes, funds, and so on), but urban employees often represent a concentrated political force whose ability to embarrass governments in various ways is much greater than that of the rest of the population. Governments are commonly the major employers of labour, even in the industrial sector; and where other large employers are foreign, they are also often vulnerable.

It appears therefore, that workers in the modern sector are able to capture a significant part of the benefits they help to produce despite increasing open unemployment and the existence of a labour surplus in the traditional sector. Further growth of delivery systems for induced technical change, part of the 'modern sector', may well further strengthen their capability to extract a disproportionate share of the surplus, unless and until the intended beneficiaries of the induced technical change can develop an effective countervailing power to provide incentives for efficient bureaucratic performance.

A major impediment to effective organization of the intended beneficiaries, however, is that each bureaucrat acts partly at least in his own self-interest, and for some officials this is their sole motivation. There is not necessarily any congruence between the bureaucrat's behaviour in pursuing his own interest, and the promotion of public policy objectives (Downs 1966: 79-112).

Even though a 'theory of institution building' is non-existent or rudimentary, one may still believe that institutions that benefit from foreign expertise and resources are likely to be 'better' than those which are less fortunate. In this respect the findings of a major comparative study financed by USAID are sobering. Morss et al studied 26 projects aimed at small farmers in Africa and Latin America. One of their analyses was a comparison of performances of projects that had had a large dose of foreign government (national or international) funding in their early years of operation. Projects were ranked on three measures and each composite score consisted of several indices: overall success, overall local action, and prospects of becoming self-sufficient. Their conclusion was that *for all three measures*, the average scores of projects that received large amounts of foreign funding in early years were significantly *lower* than those of other projects (Morss et al 1976: 217-18). The Bank group has been involved in several of the projects studied.

With regard to the Bank's role in 'institution building', Willoughby, the first director of the Bank's Operations Evaluation Department, had to admit that 'among the Bank's relative weaknesses, one might mention its frequent difficulties in participating effectively at the level of borrower's institutional arrangements, training, and staffing issues' (Willoughby 1977: 30). But these issues are often at the core of the success (or lack of success) of development projects. They formed the main problem area for agricultural projects old-style, and are recognized as a major problem for rural development projects 'new-style' (*Rural Development* 1975: 74-75).

In his study of American efforts to set up agricultural extension services in Latin America, Rice wryly mentions the 'theory of institution building that says that the process of institution building by outsiders will consist in the building of some sort of a structure, its apparent collapse when the foreigners leave, and the emergence of something indigenous out of the ruins and experience' (Rice 1974: 421).

LENDING FOR RURAL DEVELOPMENT: EARLY EXPERIENCES

Notwithstanding the difficulties and problems involved, it is necessary to assess what has so far been achieved in the small farmer-oriented lending strategy. It is not sufficient to merely say that 'the World Bank has been rhetorically active in this area, as its top management officials have repeatedly spoken out on the need for aid to go to the millions of people who live in what they call absolute poverty' (Sanford 1977: 15).

An evaluation of new style projects is impossible; the policy change dates from 1973 and most of the relevant sector policy papers were published in 1974 and 1975. A project takes on average two-and-a-half years to advance from early identification to Board approval, and many of those classified under agriculture and rural development that were approved in the early years may have been too far advanced in preparation to incorporate many novel design features. Most of the approved projects are now in the early stages of execution. Difficulties are apparently already manifesting themselves in slower rates of disbursement than were to be expected on the basis of historical experience (*Annual Report* 1978: 9). But the impact of projects cannot be assessed until a few years after disbursements have been completed in order to see the type of process that has been set in motion, i.e. not until the 1980s. While this timespan for valid evaluation can easily be defended, it is doubtful whether critics of the Bank and of its policies will have the patience to wait that long. Pending evaluation, they would then be expected to give the Bank a mandate to go ahead for the time being and to try to make good on its public rhetoric.

The third *Annual Review of Project Performance Audit Results*, the first to be published, reports on a sample of 70 projects, none of which were new rural development projects (1978: i). Similarly, the latest report of the Operation Evaluation Department on rural development projects[32] covers 18 projects in East and West Africa that were approved between 1967 and 1973. Within the Bank, considerable criticism has been voiced of this report, owing to the inadequate yardsticks, measurements and elements of evaluation that were employed.

A review of changes in lending must therefore be confined for the time being to project intentions, to be inferred from project appraisal reports. More recent reports attempt to measure the numbers of direct beneficiaries of projects. This was not done formerly, and it is not clear what such data imply. In as far as new-style rural projects have become the test for measuring rhetoric against new praxis, there may be a tendency to exaggerate the intended beneficiaries, and thereby also the growth in numbers of beneficiaries.

Table 6.7 shows considerable absolute and relative growth in rural development projects. Evidence is available which corroborates the changing emphasis in Bank lending in *all* sectors towards the poor. The collaborators in a study carried out by the Congressional Research Service (CRS) on the World Bank and the IADB (1978) were given access to all appraisal reports for 1972 and 1977, from which they attempted to determine the intended beneficiaries of projects in all sectors, while recognizing that for some sectors it is difficult to measure specific beneficiaries in any meaningful way.

Table 6.7 *Agriculture and rural development lending FY 1969-78*

	1969-73	*1974-78*
Rural development*		
No. of projects	48	206
Loan amounts ($ mln)	540	5206
Other agriculture		
No. of projects	128	152
Loan amounts ($ mln)	2035	4814
Totals for agriculture and rural development		
No. of projects	176	358
Loan amounts ($ mln)	2575	10020
As % of World Bank totals		
No. of projects	27	34
Loan amounts (£ mln)	20	31

* Projects for which it is expected that 50% or more of direct benefits will accrue to rural poor.

Source: World Bank: Agriculture and Rural Development Dept. (October 1978).

Table 6.8 *Distribution of World Bank commitments by sector and intended beneficiaries, 1972 and 1977, in %*

		A	*B*	*C*
Agriculture	1972	27	46	28
	1977	21	17	63
Other	1972	88	12	–
	1977	78	20	3
Total	1972	79	17	4
	1977	59	19	23

A : intended beneficiaries not specified
B : some project benefits intended to benefit the poor
C : majority of project benefits intended to benefit the poor.

Source: Congressional Research Service (1978): calculated from Table I-18, p. 87.

To put their data into perspective, the CRS study made a similar analysis of lending activities of the Inter-American Development Bank, shown in Table 6.9.

Table 6.9 *Inter-American Development Bank, allocations by sector and beneficiaries among the poor, 1972, and 1977 (in %)*

		A	B	C	D
Agriculture	1972	0	0	39	61
	1977	0	23	29	48
Other	1972	54	25	14	7
	1977	34	31	30	5
Total	1972	45	21	18	16
	1977	27	30	30	14

A : negligible or no specified direct benefit
B : marginal direct benefits peripheral to the main focus of the loan
C : significant direct benefits, at least 25% of project funds were specifically directed towards individuals earning less than one-half of the average GNP per capita of the country
D : predominant direct benefits, projects directed primarily at the poorest sectors of the population.

Source: CRS (1978), calculated from Tables II-19 and II-20, pp. 179 and 165-66.

In interpreting their results, the authors of the CRS study note that IADB poor-oriented loans have increased less than those of the World Bank, but this can partly be explained by the fact that in 1972 a much higher portion of IADB projects were already directed towards the poor (CRS 1978: 1).

The rationale for the establishment of the IADB in 1959 was that it could lend in the 'innovative' social sectors which the World Bank then considered beyond its scope (CRS 1978: 208; on the IADB generally, see White 1970, and CRS 1974). In that perspective the World Bank is now catching up with an institution that was established in reaction to its own narrow and rigid views of its development role.

Another feature of many new Bank loans is that they include monitoring and evaluation units, which is not unreasonable in view of the experimental character of the new lending for rural development. The growth of these units is detailed in Table 6.10. A number of problems have already been encountered, ranging from initial resistance to their inclusion, to lack of interest and of competent evaluating staff, and to data processing bottlenecks. Some M & E units appear to collect base line data of relevance for the project area, but such data should have been an input in the design and not in the execution of a project. Pressure to launch new projects may have been a reason for insufficient preparation and thus for lowering of quality. In as far as usable results are obtained, they can be applied as inputs for possible follow-up projects at a later stage. In an early review of M & E units, the OED has warned about their cost implications. Within the Bank there appears to emerge a feeling that the

Bank does not get its money's worth from such units, as became clear at a Bank-sponsored seminar in Amsterdam in May 1979.

Table 6.10 *Monitoring and Evaluation (M & E) in Bank agriculture and rural developments projects FY 1973-77*

FY	73	74	75	76	77	Total
1. No. of Agricultural and Rural Development Projects	46	51	69	65	84	315
2. No. of projects *with* an M & E component	22	27	41	56	66	212
3. (2) as percentage of (1)	48%	53%	59%	86%	79%	67%

Source: Deboeck 1978: 6

A more serious and structural problem arises when the findings of M & E units indicate the need for major adaptation in ongoing projects. The implication is then that loan agreements may have to be changed drastically, perhaps in terms of amount as well as of content. The logic of experimental projects is that it is only possible to know what is needed once something has been started. This undermines the possibility of *ex ante* project preparation and appraisal as currently practiced. In analyzing the impact of projects, the 'discovery and study of unexpected effects are an important contribution of evaluation studies to our understanding of development phenomena' (Willoughby 1977: 30). A decade earlier, of course, Hirschman had already stressed the 'centrality of side effects' in project appraisal. Until recently, however, lending agencies have tended to take measures aimed at isolating projects and at creating controlled environments in which it is thought profitable to pretend to produce accuracy in social cost-benefit analysis (see further Chapter VII).

Executive Directors are generally reluctant to approve retroactive financing, and cost overruns also have to be argued carefully. Project authorities and recipient countries may also be unwilling to renegotiate loan agreements. If this happens, M & E units will be ineffective. After all, the Bank has itself resisted attempts to institute evaluation procedures of its own activities in the not too distant past. The Bank did not establish Operation Evaluation activities as a matter of course.[33] Strong American pressure to follow through on the Selden Amendment in the 1967 and 1973 Foreign Assistance Act was indispensable in this respect.

CONCLUSION

This review of lending for rural development has shown the complexity of issues that have to be faced. While the need for major reforms is recognized in many of the Bank's recent policy papers, powerful vested interests have often thwarted reforms in the past. Moreover, the character and functioning of international agencies make it unlikely that they can play a major role. Reorientation towards the poor means discrimination in shifting resources towards poor countries. Moreover, if a major shift in policies is a prerequisite for effective implementation of 'poor-oriented' programmes, the Bank will have to discriminate by nature of the political regime in power. It is self-evident that the Bank cannot take either course if it is not to lose the support of its near-global membership. In all likelihood, therefore, it will continue to lend to as wide a range of countries as possible, under a variety of political regimes.

The Bank has noted that 'in many countries, avoiding opposition from powerful and influential sections of the rural community is essential if the programme is not to be subverted from within' (*Rural Development* 1975: 40). It is to be expected, therefore, that rural development projects whose target group is the poorer segment of the community will be more strongly resisted than programmes which the rural elite can manipulate to their own advantage by controlling access to rural resources which are provided from outside. Under such conditions Bank-assisted programmes may well aggravate the plight of the rural poor, however well-intentioned they may be.

Virtually no country has a well thought-out rural strategy and it is therefore likely that many rural development efforts will take place in a context in which no major reforms will have been carried out *ex ante*, through existing institutional arrangements, and policy settings that remain by and large unchanged.

When the Bank began to support a rural development strategy based on increasing the productivity of small farmers using new and high yielding technologies, the results were already available of a global research project, undertaken by UNRISD, on the Social and Economic Implications of Large-scale Introduction of New Varieties of Foodgrain (UNRISD, 9 vols. 1971-74), directed by Andrew Pearse (see also Pearse 1977).

Studies had been undertaken in seven countries and 28 localities or area studies and one survey in Asia; in four countries, six locality studies and one survey in Africa; and in four countries in Latin America: 10 locality studies, a survey and various monographs (UNRISD 1974: Summary, 2).

The summary report notes that

... while those who are charged with guiding agriculture in the land-scarce countries in Asia continue to see the genetic-chemical based technology as the most important means of augmenting the productivity of the land, they have become apprehensive that certain tendencies which the use of the technology has fostered will become more pronounced. These tendencies lead toward the concentration of capital and land in the hands of richer farmers and service entrepreneurs; toward the concentration of investment in improved technology and productivity in certain physically and socially favoured zones; toward the introduction of labour-saving machinery; toward the dissolution of systems of rural livelihood and the consequent accelerated unsettlement, marginalization and proletarization of rural populations; towards a risk-fraught reliance on important inputs, sophisticated research, long-distance transport and worldmarket prices in providing for the daily food supplies of rural and urban population – in a world not yet free from disorders and catastrophes capable of rupturing the operations of these large-scale systems (Ibidem: 28).

The 1974-75 fertilizer scarcity underlined the seriousness of the increased vulnerability of the rural population to discontinuities in outside inputs.

With regard to the desirable reorientation of these unfavourable tendencies, the report also notes that

... in those countries in which large-scale modernizing agriculture has already made itself master of the lion's share of agricultural resources, situations of open and repressed conflicts are widely reported not only in the rural areas but increasingly from the cities as well. These countries are already restricted in their choice of policies on account of the political strength of the controllers of agricultural land and capital and the powerlessness of those who perform agricultural labour, whether small cultivators, tenants or landless labourers. A number of Latin American countries can be cited as examples of this situation (Ibidem: 29).

NOTES

1. Subsequently published under the title: *World Bank Operations, Sectoral Programs and Polities* (Baltimore 1972).

2. Some of these Sector Policy Papers of greatest direct relevance for a small farmer lending approach have been published in book form: *The Assault on World Poverty* (Baltimore 1975).

3. Baum (1970: 13) mentions a Bankwide share of 'problem projects' of 10% in 1970. These projects are watched with particular care and receive frequent supervisory visits.

4. Once the key references had been found, however, it was remarkable to see how closely the Bank's papers also adhered to them.

5. OED, Rural Development Projects: 'A Retrospective View of Bank Experience in Sub-Saharan Africa' (October 13, 1978, Report 2242).

6. The Bank's leading land tenancy specialist, Ladejinsky, has been largely ineffective in influencing India while stationed in the Bank's New Delhi Office between 1967-75 (see Walinsky 1977: 368).

7. These include studies by Clark, Dovring, Eckstein, Flores, Barbero, Shearer, Lindsey, Christensen, Ogura, Nasharty, Stipetic and Milosavlevic, Hong Cho, Ruthenberg, Cheung Chen, Dore, Saab, Warriner, Thiesenhusen, Cheung and Cline (see Adams 1969, 1973 for references).

8. For the political economy of the Kenya land transfer scheme see Leys 1975; Wasserman 1976, chapter 6; and Holtham & Hazlewood 1976, chapter 5, part I. Wasserman in particular had access to the personal papers of several of the authorities directly involved, as well as to various archives, although he was denied access to the World Bank Library in the Nairobi office (Wasserman 1976: 206 note 96). Several years ago, this project was thought to be in trouble with low Bank disbursements, payment arrears by settlers, and schemes that were perhaps no longer economically viable (Holtham & Hazlewood 1976: 109, 110, 122; Wasserman 1976: 156). The Kenya case is a suitable, if narrow, base for answering the questions asked at the beginning of this section.

9. The present author found very close links between officials of the Kenya government, the CDC, and the Bank, in connection with the smallholders tea projects in Kenya and Uganda. The same officials switched between organizations over time, and pushed for subsequent extension of earlier Bank lending. The build-up of relationships between the Bank and borrowers always proceeds by way of individuals. But it will be clear that in terms of project evaluation conflicting loyalties may occur.

10. Adams 1973: 137. See also the Selected Papers of Ladejinsky, one of the architects of US involvement in land reform in Japan (Walinsky 1977).

11. Such a strategy is analogous to that pursued by international mining companies (see Moran 1974).

12. See UN/FAO/ILO, 1966: *Progress in Land Reform*, Fourth Report, Ch. 2.

13. USAID: 'Guidelines on Project and Program Planning for Small Farmers Credit' (Circular: A 418, 1974, p. 7), cited in Lipton 1976: 545.

14. The data discussed here refer to all projects in which a minimum of 10% of the Bank loan was used for agricultural credit purposes. While this creates some inconsistency with some earlier Bank documents (e.g. *World Bank Operations*, 1972), the broader coverage provides a more accurate measure of the Bank's involvement (*Agricultural Credit* 1975: 23, footnote).

15. The details in the above paragraphs are taken from *Agricultural Credit* 1975: 10-11.

16. The details in these paragraphs are taken from Chambers 1969: 250-54.

17. See on this also the Policy Paper on *Forestry*, 1978: 17.

18. IBRD: *Appraisal of the Tea Factory Project* (Report 311a-KE, May 2, 1974).

19. The information, unless documented specifically, has been collected by the author while preparing the Project Performance Audits of the First Kenya and Uganda Tea Projects (Sec M74-132, March 5, 1974, and Sec M74-193, March 26, 1974).

20. IBRD: 'Appraisal of the Tea Factory Project' (May 2, 1974), 7.

21. Kenyatta's family was known to be among the largest 'tea farmers' in the country. The first African KTDA general manager was replaced by someone closer to the leading political power.

22. Project Performance Audit of First Kenya Tea Project, 1974: 1.

23. Two further loans went to Indonesia in 1971 and in 1973, for a total cost of $22.9 million.

24. IBRD: 'The International Tea Market' (December 20, 1972); 'Financing of Tea' (August 17, 1973); 'Performance Audit of First Kenya Tea Project' (March 5, 1974).

25. The decision not to lend for new tea plantings has caused some strain within the Bank, and in its relationship with Kenya. Within the Bank coordination between Regional and Central Staff was poor: Board presentation was blocked of a project providing further Bank financing for tea plantings, the appraisal report for which was almost complete. In Bank practice, a project is widely thought to be 'in the can' *before* the appraisal mission goes out, not *after* its return. One can imagine the annoyance in Kenya, when the Bank's Annual Report, published one month later, featured a tea-plucking scene on its cover, with tribal connotations, suggesting that the Bank had played a leading role in the development of Kenya smallholder tea. In view of the upcoming annual meeting in Nairobi, irritations were politically covered-up.

26. Reasons for the limited Bank leverage were that the Bank became involved only in 1964, whereas the pioneering stage of the programme (1960-64) had been backed by the Kenya government, the Commonwealth Development Corporation (CDC) and the German government. Moreover, the first IDA credit was partly cancelled because of lower-than-estimated KTDA cash needs and disagreement between Kenya and the Bank over alternative uses of funds outstanding. CDC had provided the main external management support during the initial difficult years, and not the Bank.

27. The National Advisory Council for International Monetary and Financial Policies, established in 1945, overseas the IFIs.

28. Nekby (1971) on CADU; Chambers & Belshaw (1973) on the Kenya Special Rural Development Programme.

29. IBRD: Kenya and Uganda Smallholder Tea Projects performance audits (March 1974).

30. For evaluations of India's community development experience see Lewis 1962; Mellor, Weaver, Lele and Simon 1968; Hunter 1970; Owens & Shaw 1972.

31. For a case study on Tanzania along these lines, see Van de Laar (1973) and on education in general, Coombs & Hallak (1972).

32. OED, Rural Development Projects: 'A retrospective view of Bank experience in Sub-Sahara Africa' (Report No. 2242 of October 13, 1978).

33. The first Chief of the Evaluation activities, at one time period, had to threaten to resign almost once every week to ward off pressure to undermine his autonomy in the evaluations.

VII

THE ORGANIZATION OF THE WORLD BANK

INTRODUCTION

The evolution of the World Bank can be summed up as a widening and deepening of its activities. The first has manifested itself in a constant broadening of the range of projects which the Bank has seen fit to finance. The deepening of activities means that the Bank has tended to make its projects more complex by including technical assistance whether or not requested to do so and, more generally, by undertaking institution-building activities in addition to the transfer of capital. The search for employment and income-distribution strategies for developing countries is likely to widen and deepen its lending activities even further through 'new style' projects. In addition, much technical assistance that is not directly project-related, mainly its economic missions, may be directed to the new concerns.

Re-orientation towards the poor of the policies of the World Bank and possibly of other donors, has implications at various levels. In Chapter V we have examined some of the issues relative to a possible and highly desirable reallocation of funds by country. In Chapter VI we discussed a number of project policy issues regarding the Bank's proposed strategy towards increasing the productivity of the small farmer. We shall now focus on a number of issues pertinent to the World Bank Group's own organization. By focusing on the organizational setting in which Bank decisions are made, some light may be shed on how the organizational environment contributes to the outcome of Bank activities, and also on whether it will be able to implement a broader set of new development concerns, with the major change that this will involve.

The issue of proper organization and of optimal delineation of Bank functions is related to two sets of problems. On the one hand there is the ongoing discussion on the reorganization of the UN system.[1] Although the organization and functioning of the World Bank has a bearing on the future structure of the UN system as a whole, it would be overly pretentious to view the 'desirable' role of the Bank from the perspective of the most desirable organization of that system.

On the other hand, and of more immediate concern to the Bank, is the

---

Footnotes to this chapter may be found on pp. 246-48.

current discussion on the General Capital Increase to supplement the selective capital increase proposed by the Executive Directors in May 1976. If, for instance, a doubling of the Bank's capitalization is approved, as last happened in 1959, are Bank activities likely to continue along the lines of the past nine years: a seven-fold increase in loan and credit amounts, an almost four-fold increase in operations and a nearly three-fold increase in professional staff? Is it conceivable that so large a World Bank may be considered no longer of a manageable size to effectively contribute to international development without major restructuring of its own organization? Such growth prospects for the Bank seem feasible. Developing countries have increasing need for capital, concentration on poorer countries requires extra funding, and it may be argued that the major reorganization of 1972 has prepared the ground for a continued and hopefully rapid expansion of Bank activities. The only previous major reorganization of the Bank was in 1952, and that supplied a structure that functioned for 20 years. Why, then, should the new structure not be adequate for the next 15 to 20 years?

Our task now, then, is to investigate some of the organizational issues that relate to the widening and deepening scope of Bank activities, and to explore whether some of those activities can be undertaken satisfactorily.

THE NATURE OF THE TASK; THE STRUCTURE OF THE ORGANIZATION

A foreign aid agency that is either national or international like the World Bank and the regional development banks, is very different to national money-spending bureaucracies.

The process of how development in LDCs can be made into a self-sustaining process is far from clear. Initial optimism regarding the possibilities of 'planning' this development has made way for increasing pessimism, or perhaps realism, as feedback becomes available on the unforeseen consequences and side effects of development policies as pursued over a wide spectrum. Economic growth often appears to go hand-in-hand with growing inequality, growing unemployment and growing political instability (Seers 1970; Ul Haq 1976).

The major intellectual approach to the study of development has been along the lines of 'modernization theory'. Many researchers have sought to determine which characteristics are common to rich and poor countries alike. Development policy planning was seen as the devising of mechanisms which would allow or induce the poor countries to 'catch up', to move from being 'underdeveloped' to 'developed' in an efficient manner. Poor countries were frequently said to have an 'advantage' in being latecomers to development, in view of the large stock of proven and transferable technical innovations that was assumed to exist in the most developed countries.

Central to the rationale for *donor agencies* (note the term), be they bilateral or multilateral like the World Bank, has been the concept of 'transfer'. It was thought desirable that poor countries should catch up with the rich countries. It followed that donor agencies had a role to play in the transfer of those attributes which 'modernization' theory had identified as lacking in the poor countries. If sufficient 'missing ingredients' could be transferred, with donor agencies acting as intermediaries, poor countries would presumably begin to resemble rich countries. Attention consequently focused on ways and means to increase the flow of capital to LDCs, to spread human skills through massive support for education, on efforts at 'institution building'; in short, on attempts to alleviate perceived shortages in all these areas.

Increasingly, however, it has been realized that the road to development is a venture into the unknown, requiring novel approaches, new ideas, new methods and new attitudes. The work of an aid agency involves not only 'doing things' but also 'learning', trying to understand why traditional and standard methods of problem-solving technologies often appear unsatisfactory. The root cause of the poor results can often be traced to inadequate diagnosis of the nature of the problem. This should therefore first be defined and clarified before alternative problem-solving techniques are applied. This raises complex issues for aid agency staff, as well as for the organizational structure of such agencies.

We have seen in Chapter IV that the World Bank is essentially staffed by 'foreigners', most of whom are citizens of the developed countries; LDC nationals, at least those recruited under the Young Professionals programme, have usually been educated in the west, and more specifically in the USA. Moreover, LDC nationals rotate between departments in the Bank just as much as Western staff; they too can expect to work for the greater part of their careers on countries which are culturally quite different from the one in which they were brought up. However, foreigners are not always efficient or effective in identifying problems in a context to which they are culturally alien.

Foster, in discussing the problems of the technical expert working in a culturally alien environment, notes:

There is no need to teach the average professional student to think first of identifying major problems and then working out solutions to these problems. The major problems are thought to be quite obvious; the need is to ameliorate, not to identify them. The professional knows the kinds of questions his society will ask of him and the job demands it will make upon him. Consequently, most professional training is designed in terms of programs rather than underlying problems (Foster 1962: 178-79).

An essential element of development assistance is not that the donor should define the needs of an LDC and subsequently transfer skills and methods with which to overcome those needs; it is often impossible to know what people in LDCs really want, which skills are really needed and what methods will work under different conditions. Uncertainty about the environment in which external inputs are introduced and ignorance about the reaction patterns that may evolve, require 'learning as a major output of technical assistance activity'.

Practitioners in development work have long been aware that unexpected side effects and consequences are bound to crop up whenever some course of action is suggested to policy makers. Since the early 1970s a growing flow of studies has attempted to document what 'went wrong' with past development policies and to analyse the causes of the discrepancy between expectation and realization. Both theorists and practitioners are forced to reassess their rationale and practices. In particular, agencies dispensing normative advice are forced to re-examine the premises, substance and consequences of their advice.

Adler (1972: 33-34), attempting an In-House *Dogmengeschichte* on The World Bank's Concept of Development, notes that in the 1940s and 1950s there were only a few studies whose aims were essentially descriptive and analytic and not normative. Rosenstein-Rodan, an Assistant Director of the Economics Department of the Bank in its formative years, 1946-52, and 'god-father' of the Economic Development Institute established in 1956, is said by Adler to have been 'instrumental in steering the Bank's scant staff away from the narrow aspect of specific lending operations towards broader issues of policy, not only of the Bank but of its member countries as well.' He was 'one of the very few staff members who had a clear idea of what economic development was all about. The impact of his ideas became an intangible long-term asset of the Bank' (Ibidem: 45).

The Bank gives technical assistance, provided such help is related to its past, present and future lending operations. The IBRD charter does not mention technical assistance, though the Article of Agreement V, Section 5(v) of IDA specifically authorizes it to give such assistance. It is interesting that the World Bank initially did not want to be identified with the broader technical assistance efforts being launched by the United Nations family (Mason & Asher 1973: 73).

Adler notes that 'in retrospect, there can be no doubt that in the early and mid-1960s the Bank's view of the development process came to reflect more and more the growing general recognition of analysts and policy makers of the complexity of the development process and the difficulties besetting it' (Adler 1972: 45). He concludes, *inter alia* that

the more social scientists probe, and the longer practitioners of development finance try to do the right thing to stimulate and accelerate economic development, the more complex the processes and problems appear to be. The attempts to understand and foster development have become more circumspect – to avoid the term sophisticated with its connotation of superiority. This does not mean that we know better; it only means that we are better aware of the limitations of our knowledge (Ibidem: 49).

The World Bank as an institution has always had to face the major problem of how to change its organizational structure and operational practices in response to changing perceptions of the character of its work.

Mason & Asher list a range of issues — not all of equal relevance — to show how slowly the Bank has responded to new insights. It 'required a good deal of outside criticism and pressure to persuade the Bank that the absorptive capacity of LDCs for external assistance could not be satisfied by a trickle of loans limited to the financing of the foreign exchange costs of specific projects.' The Bank's techniques of project appraisal were adopted 'long after they had become standard practice in the business world.' The use of shadow prices in project evaluation has come 'slowly and haltingly.' Various types of systems analysis applicable to related clusters of investment 'have only recently come into use.' Bank management has been 'reluctant to accept' the proposition that certain types of current expenditures can make as large a contribution to development as investment in capital equipment. The Bank was 'slow to break away' from its early devotion to capital infrastructure. Manpower analysis and techniques of manpower planning had 'developed extensively in the outside world before the Bank showed any great interest in human resource development.' It took several years of academic discussion of the difference between nominal and effective tariffs before the IBRD 'took a serious interest in the relation of these considerations to appropriate channels of industrialization.' The IBRD has 'only recently shown a concern for the effects of its lending policies on income distribution and through income distribution, on social development and political stability.' And now, after several years of public concern for the ecological consequences of economic expansion, the Bank is taking a 'somewhat belated interest' in the problem. In some ways the regional banks and various bilateral assistance programmes have been 'more venturesome and experimental in their lending programs than has the World Bank' (Mason & Asher 1973: 468-69).

One could go on: only since 1973 has the study of sociological and anthropological aspects been introduced as a regular part of project work, and it is only now being recognized by the Bank that this element is 'critical in many newer-style projects' (*Annual Report* 1977: 9).

By and large the Bank has also been very slow to organize its learning activities on the basis of its own experience. The Bank's self-proclaimed 'flexibility' on which it prides itself,[2] is less the result of its internal dynamics through organized feedback from its own experiences, than of continual, strong and sustained outside pressure. This situation has slowly begun to change for the better in the 1970s, although in several respects it has become more difficult in view of other developments that have taken place in the context in which the Bank has to function.

Willoughby notes that 'while the Bank is too large and multifacetted an organization for all the sources of most new policy initiatives to be pinpointed, it is clear that the reviews [of the Operations Evaluation unit] have produced the *main identifiable impact on changes in* Bank policy' (Willoughby 1977: 31; emphasis added). But the *ex post* project evaluation system has been in existence only since 1970, i.e. when the Bank had been concerned with development assistance for almost 25 years! And Israel notes as late as 1978 that 'the gathering of experience is becoming an increasingly important aspect of the Bank's work, in view of the experimental nature of the theory and the practice regarding many of the new-style projects' (Israel 1978: 28).

Although the uniqueness of the foreign aid agency's task has been recognized and is now understood, Tendler points out that the organizational environment that such a task requires has never been specified (Tendler 1975: 9-12). Nor has it been understood how the organization's inability to provide such an environment can contribute just as much to its ineffectiveness as can the pressures of outside interest groups, the insensitivity of the ethnocentric technician, and the restrictiveness of the legislative rules of the game, as embodied in its charter, by-laws and other guidelines.

The special nature of the foreign aid agency's task requires that it has the proper atmosphere in which to search without too much idea of what will result, to stray from tried and true solutions, and to struggle to escape from customary ways of thinking. If it is recognized that development knowledge is not simply a stock with transferable properties, the rationale for including technical assistance in the aid agency's task becomes less obvious than the commitment to transfer capital. Knowledge that is still to be learned cannot, by definition, be more abundant in one part of the world than in another (Ibidem: 11). There is thus apparently no clear basis for assuming that technical assistance and advice provided by the World Bank should be thought superior to that of other agencies, nor that it should play a leadership role in the international development effort, to which it has aspired with considerable success over the past decade.

National aid agencies and UN agencies specializing in technical assistance, however, *must* accept the notion of transfer of skills, with the implied assumption of superiority of their advice relative to knowledge and learning capacities in recipient countries, in order to justify to their financiers their continued existence as an organization. The World Bank and regional banks are under even greater pressure to maintain the appearance of superiority of their technical assistance as against that of the predominantly technical assistance-oriented agencies, because they have been entrusted by major financiers with the actual business of transferring capital, thus also implying their larger claim for funds. The difference between this outward image and the internal reality of such agencies gives rise to tension and contradiction. To the outside world an image of competence and self-assurance is necessary if the agency is to survive as an institution; internally, pervasive uncertainty prevails about the effects of whatever technical assistance is provided or of the approaches being tried out.

Adler, writing of the attitude of the Bank in the 1960s, mentions that 'in its public posture, the Bank continued to display self-assurance — that it knew the answers to the key questions of development' (Adler 1972: 45-46). Similarly, McNamara when he announced the Bank's rural strategy in 1973, did not pretend that the Bank 'knew all the answers', but it 'knew enough' to make a start.

If it is now accepted that innovation and learning should be the main characteristics of a development agency, organization theory should be examined for clues as to the type of organization that would be most likely to stimulate innovation and to generate feed-back systematically through learning. Specifically, from the literature on the 'management of innovation'[3] it may be inferrred that an organization in which problems and requirements for action arise which cannot be broken down and distributed among specialist roles within a clearly-defined hierarchy, is decentralized, with superior-subordinate demarcations blurred, access to superiors easy, and considerable responsibility assumed by subordinates (Tendler 1975: 12).

Whether an organization is flexible and in fact can learn from its collective experience depends not so much on the quality of the individuals who staff it as on the organization itself. The individual will not be good at development, no matter what his training, unless the organization is set up in a way that requires learning as an output (Ibidem: 11).

Mason & Asher note that 'over the years, the Bank has acquired a staff unique among the international agencies in terms of its professional competence (Mason & Asher 1973: 71). If one accepts this judgment, how is it that so much competence has made changes in Bank practices so difficult to effect? This makes it necessary for us to study organizational issues and forces which will either enhance or impede the creation of an organizational environment that is conducive to experimentation, so necessary for 'new style' Bank projects.

EVOLUTION OF THE BANK'S ORGANIZATIONAL STRUCTURE

The most characteristic feature of the World Bank is that it is predominantly based in Washington, where over 90 percent of the total staff is employed. The large-scale reorganization in 1972 had decentralization as its objective, but this proved to be decentralization in Washington and not towards the field.

The Bank was initially thought of primarily as a guarantee institution. After discarding this conception, the Bank saw itself as a series of loan windows to which projects for reconstruction and development would be presented for approval or disapproval. For the early reconstruction loans this image was not too far-fetched. Most early lending was in the form of programme loans with recipient countries deciding for themselves how the money should be used and thus involving little Bank scrutiny. For development lending this was too naïve. Initially there was little appreciation of the amount of field work that would be needed to facilitate the presentation of 'sound' projects, to make judgments as to their priority and to understand the economic, social and political settings in which projects would be left to flourish or wither. The volume of annual lending to any one country was not expected to be large enough to justify a resident mission in the borrowing country. Individual representatives were soon assigned to a few countries, but no arrangements were made for a regular 'foreign service' (Mason & Asher 1973: 72).

Once an agency is launched as a centralized institution, it tends to remain so. Key staff members develop a vested interest in the functions they perform and resist sharing them with field personnel. It becomes much more difficult to decide which functions can be decentralized. If, over time, an embryonic 'foreign service' is developed but service within it is not made essential to advancement on the career ladder, time so spent can easily become a handicap. Out of sight and without authority, the field personnel are also often out of mind when higher-level, more responsible jobs become available at headquarters. In this light, it is not surprising that Mason & Asher note that the Bank's record in selecting staff for foreign assignments is not one of uniform success (Ibidem: 743). But while they then argue that 'the selection process will need to be more rigorous' (Ibidem), they tend to overlook that even the 'best' people would be ineffective in the field if not given authority and not fitted into a proper promotions schedule upon their return to headquarters. For field staff to be effective the organization at headquarters should first be reconstructed, and this was never done.

Between 1952 and 1972 there were separate departments in Washington for 'project' and 'area' (country) work. The Technical Operations Department (later the Projects Department) was created with responsibility for assessing the economic, financial, and technical merits of projects proposed to the Bank for financing and for following the progress of projects financed by the Bank (King 1974; Mason & Asher 1973: 72-79). The Operations (later Area) Department was created 'to provide for more systematic and continuous contact between the Bank and its member countries.' Thirdly, an Economic Staff was maintained to advise the management and operational departments on general economic, financial, and investment problems of concern to the Bank, and to provide statistical services.

It is significant that the Central Economic Staff has never been a favourite of McCloy, Garner or Black and that its scope *was reduced* after 1952. At least until the mid-1960s, Economics was a small, undermanned department and no organized research programme existed (Mason & Asher 1973: 75, 467). Not until McNamara, following the recommendations of the Pearson Commission (1969: 214-20), did the Economic Staff begin to grow.

The Bank's management was not particularly hospitable to basic research as a function of its regular economic staff, but felt that the Economic Development Institute (EDI), established by and closely linked to the Bank, could become a leading centre for research on development (Mason & Asher 1973: 325). Since Eugene Black's departure, however, Bank presidents have shown little interest in the EDI (Ibidem: 329). The EDI invited outside lecturers to talk on a variety of general and more recent developments in development thinking.[4] Bank policies can be and are criticized but, note Mason & Asher (Ibidem: 331), it is doubtful whether many have been modified as a result, except for the use of cost-benefit analysis.

The most important operational effect of the 1952 structure was to separate responsibility for evaluating particular projects from that for judging the desirability or otherwise of lending to particular countries or borrowers and for determining the priority sectors in each country for such lending. In theory, this set-up prevented an inadequately-prepared project being pushed through the organization merely to satisfy the Bank's relations with a particular country, and, conversely, prevented a project from going through merely because it was fascinating.

Two coordination mechanisms were built into the 1952 reorganization. To resolve differences that might arise between Project and Area Departments a Staff Loan Committee was established, made up of the principal department heads and chaired by a Bank vice-president. As operational policy became fixed and standardized, actual work was done in lower level staff meetings typically of Project and Area Departments, General Council and selected staff mostly directly concerned with the project on hand. Similarly, an Economic Committee was established to ensure that economic work, including credit-worthiness, was of high quality, maintained consistent standards, and was coordinated with operational work. The Economic Committee was chaired by the Economic Advisor to the President.

While such an organizational set-up might work well on paper, it proved very difficult in practice. The relationship between Area Departments and Project Departments became the Bank's most difficult and pervasive organizational problem. Issues that strained relationships usually boiled down to matters of tactics and business judgment concerning conditions to be attached to proposed loans (Ibidem: 76).

Over the years, as its membership tripled and workload grew, the Bank expanded along the lines of the 1952 reorganization. Area Departments had increased from three to seven by 1972, and Projects Departments were organized into sectoral divisions, which became so large that they were re-established as separate departments. As a result, there were by 1972 eight sectoral projects departments: three − Agriculture, Public Utilities and Transportation − each staffed by over 100 professionals; three − Education, Industry and Special Projects − each with 30 to 50 professionals; and two − Population Planning and Tourism − each with less than 20 professionals. The Director of Projects, assisted by a small staff of Advisors, was thus responsible for the work of 534 professionals, fully a third of the Bank's entire professional staff (King 1974: 7).

A consequence of the separation of project and country work has been that much of the former is dominated by engineers and technical specialists. This is hardly surprising considering that many of the Bank's projects have a strong technical bias. Transportation and power projects, the mainstay of Bank Group lending through the 1950s, were obviously dominated by engineers. Who else would be capable of evaluating the highly technical engineering studies for a power generating plant, a railway, or a road? Diversification into agriculture and education in the early 1960s brought other groups of technical specialists into the Bank: soil, crop and cattle specialists, irrigation engineers, and architects and quantity surveyors to elaborate the design and costing of the schools which the Bank began to finance.

The technical bias of many Bank-financed projects is thus self-evident, but it does not mean that social sciences do not play a role. Financial and economic aspects, in particular, have been taken into account from the beginning, being studied in part by engineers who, through on-the-job methods, learned to look at such aspects as they rose to management ranks, in or outside the Bank, in their profession. Engineers acquired some of their economic knowledge also through formal education. Until 1967 no economist was ever employed in the technical division of the Bank that is concerned with appraising power projects (Mason & Asher 1973: 243). Among staff who were recruited under the Young Professionals Program, a substantial number of those with engineering or other technical backgrounds have done additional studies in business administration and management.

Among those with social science backgrounds, the only clearly identifiable professional group in the Bank staff are the economists (often as loan officers in Area Departments). A sprinkling of other social scientists may be found among bank staff, but their numbers are too small to enable any evaluation of their professional input in Bank work, with the exception perhaps of lawyers who play an important role.

The economist did not speak up in those early days about longer-range problems and broad policy questions of the Bank ... The gap was filled by the lawyer. It's extraordinary how in the early days the legal department produced broad concepts and ideas and suggestions, and gradually management began to expect the lawyers to have these ideas rather than the economists. It was not that we were excluded from contributing. We failed to contribute ideas (Harold Larsen, 'Oral History', 6-7, cited in Mason & Asher 1973: 75, note 20).

'Other' social scientists (i.e. non-economists) have been hired occasionally for specific projects or missions, but labour under the handicap that their services have only been used intermittently, at the discretion of those who hire them and not of the requirements of the project to be studied, and this has tended to limit severely their possible contribution to policy formation within the Bank.

With project departments dominated by engineers, the majority of economists in the Bank are to be found in the Area Departments and in the Central Economic Staff, dealing with creditworthiness analyses, general macro-economic issues, world market commodity price forecasts and fiscal perform-ance. The limited scope given to economic research has caused the Bank to be slow in picking up ideas and developments from outside. It is doubtful, there-fore, whether much of the wider concern about the social impact of projects that came to the fore in the 1960s could permeate into the actual work of project staff, particularly at the early design stage, because relatively few economists are institutionally embedded within the project departments.

In the early 1970s there were three principal reasons for changing the or-ganizational structure of the Bank. The growth of membership, particularly at the lower end of the development scale, increased awareness of the com-plexity of the development process and of the need for improved country economic work and better programming of Bank activities in the LDCs.

Project and area work showed increasing divergence and no individual could be held strictly accountable for the execution of the whole lending programme in any particular country. Departmental structures became more hierarchical and projects more complex. The pressure for a greater volume of lending in-creased markedly and rigidities and severe frictions developed between 'pro-jects' and 'areas', especially after the *one remaining institutional link* between those directly concerned with a project at the working level – the 'loan work-ing party', consisting of the country Loan Officer as chairman, with the country economist, projects staff, representatives of the Legal and the Treasurer's and other relevant staff – *was abolished* in September 1968 be-cause meetings became increasingly difficult to schedule (King 1974: 7).

Economists working in Area Departments thus lost the formal possibility for influencing the shape of projects from a social science perspective. Their effectiveness came to depend largely upon their success in establishing informal working relationships with projects staff, but this could create further tension because of hierarchical subordination to different project and area division chiefs.

In early 1972, McKinsey and Company, a management consulting firm, was called in to study the organization of the Bank.[5] Their central recommen-dation was that the Bank be reorganized along regional lines with five Regional Vice Presidents – reporting to a Senior Vice President Operations – respon-sible for the Bank's lending and technical assistance in the countries in their respective regions. Two Programme Departments responsible for 'area' work were created for each Region. At the same time, the Regions were made responsible for all project work in their countries. Most of the old Project Departments were also regionalized, each with sectoral divisions. Those pro-ject departments which were too small or too new to be effectively decentral-ized, were grouped under Central Projects. Conceptionally these units were considered, when working on a particular project, as working as subcontractors for the Regional Project Department concerned. Central Projects also was charged with responsibility for developing project policy, establishing project guidelines and standards, maintaining project quality and providing operational guidance and support. At the same time, a Development Policy staff was created out of Central Economics Staff and given broad responsibility for development policy, for setting standards and maintaining the quality of country economic work and country programming, for general economic work, for conducting research, and for computing activities.

This radical restructuring of the Bank's Washington-based operations had five major objectives:

— to handle more *efficiently* the 8% real increase in Bank lending planned for the 1974-78 period;
— to improve the quality of the Bank's programming and make it more *effective* by concentrating 'area' and 'project' work on the specific development problems of individual countries and regions;
— to facilitate a return to the *team work* approach that prevailed when the Bank was smaller;
— to increase the delegation of responsibility and provide greater *accountability*; and
— to provide borrowers with a single primary channel for communication instead of a multiplicity of Bank departments.

After 18 months experience with the new organization King, who had worked in Central Projects, felt that most of the objectives, with their stress on efficiency and accountability from which better quality was expected to result, were being achieved, without interrupting the flow of loan approvals. There was a considerable cost, however, in terms of staff morale.

Short term disruptions and dislocations did not affect its lending operations to an appreciable extent: 140 operations totalling $3 billion were approved in 1972 and 148 operations for $3.4 billion in 1973. This was an achievement, considering the considerable movement of personnel necessary — 1400 staff were moved over a long weekend in October — and the rudeness with which bodies were reassigned. Reid notes of this that the

method followed by the management of the Bank Group in making the changes in the structure of the administration and in transferring many officers from one post to another did not promise well for the future. Few officers were consulted adequately on the new structure required. Most officers who were moved, including many of the most senior, were simply given notice of their new posting a day or so in advance of the public announcement. The reorganization was carried out so impersonally and abrasively as greatly to lower morale throughout the whole professional staff (Reid 1973b: 183).

Closer working contacts were established between 'project' and 'area' staff during all phases of the project cycle, *particularly during field appraisal and the preparation of the appraisal report*.

Whilst the appraisal stage of the project cycle had received much attention in the reorganization discussion, King notes that 'it seems to take at least the same amount of time to get a project through the appraisal report cycle as before.' In explanation thereof, he notes: 'Project work is becoming increasingly complex as greater consideration is given to the employment effects of the project or its impact on income distribution or the environment. It may well be that savings resulting from the reorganization are offset by such extra work' (King 1974: 8).

The emphasis on project appraisal aspects reflects the response to customary general recommendations by various commissions that aid agencies ought to improve their project appraisal methods. Public agencies have reacted historically by generating new and improved methodologies: Little-Mirrlees while working in the OECD, Sen and Dasgupta working for UNIDO, and Squire-Van der Tak working in the World Bank.

Of course, better appraisal may help to clarify what is being done. But at that late stage in the project cycle the suggestion that a project should have been redesigned in view of appraisal results now judged to be undesirable, is counterproductive. It causes delays in Board presentation so that lending targets are not met. It causes irritation among project personnel who find that they have worked long hours in vain, which shows up as 'inefficiency' from the perspective of the bureaucracy; and it is unhelpful in that the project appraisor usually cannot provide specific suggestions as to what alternative choices should have been made at the early but crucial stages of project design and preparation.

Many Bank staff not surprisingly feel that the calculation of project rates of return is principally intended to put the 'icing on the cake' after all interesting decisions have been made. Insofar as Executive Directors need to be able to show that they have approved 'sound' and thus 'good' projects it is necessary to have a yardstick. Rates of return provide that yardstick, but they do not play much of a role in the selection from a range of fully worked-up alternative project proposals.

King, a lawyer by training (Harvard Law School 1948), puts his finger on a major weak spot of the whole 1972 reorganization exercise when he says:

Such new concepts as reaching the poorest elements of the population must be considered and they can be effectively integrated *only at the early stages of project design*. The structure and procedures which grew out of the reorganization study were largely aimed at improving the handling of the appraisal report cycle, the fulfilment of lending targets, and the process of getting projects to the Board for approval timely. This emphasis did not contribute to the development of procedures and methods for *more effective project generation and design*. And it is this phase of the project cycle which needs special attention if today's more complex project objectives are to be achieved (Ibidem: 34; emphasis added).

It is only fair to point out that the Sector Policy or Issues Papers that have been published since 1974 deal explicitly with issues of project design. While implementation along the lines advocated will be extremely difficult to achieve, their usefulness as policy documents would seem to be far greater than what can be gathered from recent developments in the formal theory of social cost-benefit analysis, which neglect the institutional environment in which such methods are to be used.[6]

EVOLUTION OF THE BANK'S ORGANIZATIONAL STYLE

The administrative style of the Bank in the pre-McNamara era has been described by Mason and Asher as unconventional and as particularly disturbing to those nationals of countries other than the United States who have worked in governments in which the responsibilities of the various administrative units are clearly understood and firmly respected. To these authors the Bank's style appears autocratic, quixotic and distressingly disorderly. The President's Council did not formulate policy, nor did any other group. What was not decided by the President tended to be left to the departments or divisions to arrange for themselves. As the Bank grew, considerable delegation was given in the Project and Area Departments. Roles at every level were loosely defined. The job classification system introduced by Vice President Garner in the late 1940s was never completed. Salaries were fixed without any clear or consistent relationship to formal titles. Individual initiative on the part of staff members was both expected and rewarded. By relying on people rather than procedures the Bank derived great advantage (Mason & Asher 1973: 72, 86).

If this is taken as a representative view of the Bank's style in earlier times, it would seem that it corresponds to an organizational structure which is appropriate for the management of innovation as discussed above where it was noted that an informal, loose organizational format may be conducive to innovation. Yet the lack of research and openness to new ideas and friction between 'project' and 'area' staff sharpened, suggesting that informality in Washington and within disciplinary groups was greater than that between groups. On the whole, then, the informality of its style, though necessary, was not sufficient to stimulate creativity. Classic is the judgement of George Woods, when he succeeded Black as Bank President: 'I never saw a more rigid institution — it is an institution, not a bank, why they call it a bank, I don't know (in Fatouros 1977: 67 note 35).

The expansion since 1968 has had far-reaching consequences for the Bank's operational style. The rapid increase of staff meant that the organization became too large to establish and maintain informal working-level contacts. It also led initially to a sharp reduction in the average level of staff experience in the complex procedures and investigative techniques used within the Bank, causing fear that the Bank was reducing the quality of its work standards. Ambitious lending targets put heavy pressure on project staff to rapidly gener-

ate a sufficient volume of projects; the normal time lapse between early identification and Board approval is on average two-and-a-half years. All this generated considerable pressure for a more systematic handling of planning and
policy making.

McNamara's most characteristic innovation has perhaps been in the field of
forward planning. The Bank has tried to establish five-year programmes, to
look ahead at what it should be doing, country by country, and to organize
itself for the job. Its work is being systematized and scheduled as never before
and designed to serve a broader clientele (Mason & Asher 1973: 101). Some of
the methods and practices adopted have been or are considered 'model' practices elsewhere. We shall review and analyse these 'tools' in this section and
discuss their consequences.

The country programming system

The planning system within the Bank may be seen as planning from the top
down. It reflects the Bank's conceptualization of planning for countries which
it introduced during the 1950s, and which led to the sponsoring of some 25
general economic survey missions during 1950-64, half of them in the first five
years.

The Bank's advocacy of programming was a significant institutional influence which contributed to acceptance by LDCs of the need for national
economic programmes in the immediate post-World War II years. Indeed, the
Bank stated in its Annual Report of 1955-56 that 'one of the most important
results of the comprehensive Bank missions is the influence they have exerted
in favour of a coordinated long-term approach to development problems. Often
the report represents the first attempt in a country to make a systematic
analysis of the economy as a whole and to project the development process
over a number of years.'

Underlying this early advocacy was the considerable external criticism of
the project approach to development lending, implying that the Bank did not
look at projects in a wider development context. The IBRD rooted its advocacy in a logical 'ideal' decision-model in which micro-units were to be designed and fitted together to form the required parts of a preconceived macro-
economic framework (Gold 1976: 17). Such a framework, it was assumed,
would enhance the likelihood that project and sectoral decisions would be
mutually reinforcing and consistent with specified development objectives.
Belief in the relevance of economic planning frameworks, which will flow from
macro via sectors to projects, has been widespread in much of the economic
planning literature of the 1950s and 1960s (Tinbergen 1967), and many development economists have been actively engaged for several decades producing
'multi-year and multi-level development plans'.

Although it is not a matter that can be reduced to simple demonstration, there is nowadays wide agreement that that practice of planning has generally failed to bring many of the benefits expected from it (Killick 1976; Healy 1972). Waterston's studies in the early 1960s of the 'lessons of experience', concluded that there have been many more failures than successes in the implementation of development plans (Waterston 1966: 293). Waterston also pointed out that

countries like Mexico ... have been able to establish and maintain high rates of growth over extended periods with no more formal planning arrangements than a public investment plan coordinated through their budgets, accompanied by policies and a few measures which established a favourable climate for private investors and influenced them to react in accord with government development objectives... Such countries can dispense, at least for a time, with comprehensive planning without seriously impairing their rate of growth (Ibidem: 90).

Ul Haq, for thirteen years associated with planning in Pakistan, review the 'seven sins of development planners': number games, excessive controls, investment illusion (a preoccupation with levels of investment, and less with its content and productivity), addiction to (shortlived) development fashions, divorce between planning and implementation, neglect of human resources, and a tendency to be mesmerized by high growth rates in GNP at the neglect of social justice (Ul Haq 1976: 12-26).

The disillusionment seems to apply in most parts of the Third World. Myrdal stated in *Asian Drama* (1968: 732) that 'planning can be considered a going concern only in India and Pakistan'; events since then have seen the disintegration of Pakistan as it then was and the publication of a plan in India which is widely thought to be quite unrealistic. The Organization of American States reported that it was 'repeatedly discovered that long-term plans were either not put into effect, or they were implemented officially for only a fraction of their time, or they were simply ignored at the moment of governmental decisions' (cited in Killick 1976: 163). The UN Economic Commission for Africa has stated that development plans 'had little, if any, impact on the overall development of [West African] countries, and can at best be taken as an expression of the desires of governments or the hopes of small groups of experts' (Ibidem). Moore's review of the first 15 published reports of Comprehensive Bank-sponsored general economic survey missions referred to them as 'the largest single collection of information existent on the problems and characteristics of underdeveloped economies,' though the author added that the reports were unsatisfactory as economic analysis and unsuitable as guides to development programmes (Moore 1958: 81).

Killick doubts whether plans have generated more useful signals for the future than would otherwise have been forthcoming; governments have rarely, in practice, reconciled private and social valuations except in a piecemeal manner. Seldom other than operational documents, plans have probably had only limited success in mobilizing resources or in coordinating economic policies (Killick 1976: 164). The picture that emerges from the studies of planning by Caiden & Wildavsky (1974) seems to support such a conclusion.

The Keynote Address by Dudley Seers to the 1969 Sussex Conference on The Crisis in Planning was entitled 'The Prevalence of Pseudo-Planning'. Not only have plans been deficient as documents in themselves (see Moore 1958; Seers 1970), but most economic planners have adopted a 'rational actor' model of politics which is a very poor model of the reality of politics and decision-making in developing and developed countries.[7]

Against this amassing evaluative evidence of plan failures, it is one of the great anomalies in the development of the Bank since the late 1960s that at a time when pseudo-planning has been discredited professionally and also in practice in many countries, use of this conceptual framework has materially increased within the Bank, without much effect on the allocation of its resources over countries or sectors, as will be shown below.

Country Program Papers (CPPs) are said to be

the principle instrument for defining the Bank Group's posture toward member countries and for orienting its activities in support of their development efforts. They are confidential internal documents, and are normally produced once a year for each potential borrowing member of the Group: if lending is envisaged the CPP includes a five-year Country Operations and Lending Program (Operational Memorandum, No. 1-12, August 16, 1971: 1).

The guidelines for the content of CPPs made it clear that fairly comprehensive coverage of relevant events in the country was expected, all within the confines of a 20-25 page paper. Shopping-around among staff members for suggestions as to what might be useful for management to be informed about, and to hedge against remarks that certain topics have not been adequately dealt with, quickly leads to a list of topics that require almost a fullfledged country economic report.

The section on *Country objectives* should cover the most important political, social and economic trends in the country in order to identify long-term socio-economic prospects against the background of past achievements, current developments and the government's development objectives. In addition to a selective analysis of macro-economic policies, pressing social problems should be spotlighted, such as maldistribution of income, unemployment, and regional disparities in development. In practice, this requires a fairly extensive macro-economic modelling exercise, whereby it has to be hoped that the Bank's macro-models yield roughly similar outcomes to those which may have formed the basis for projections made within the countries concerned.

A discussion of *external assistance* should include recent capital inflows and the prospects for the coming five years, including private direct investment. It should include an assessment of total external capital requirements, of its likely availability from major bilateral and multilateral sources, and of the creditworthiness of the country to service borrowing on conventional terms. Again, the data requirements for this part of a CPP are quite substantial, and require close consultation with major donors regarding their aid plans. It presupposes that they are willing to communicate to the Bank what the Bank is unwilling to communicate to its borrowers, namely the volume of its proposed lending.

The section on the *Bank/IDA lending programme* should lay out the Bank Group's strategy for the country in question, the status of the portfolio, the terms of lending proposed over the coming five years, Bank exposure in relation to the country's projected debt, and major policy issues such as country performance conditions, programme lending and local currency financing.

The next section should focus on the *sector distribution* of Bank activities, taking into account the country's own inter-sectoral priorities and the sector and project preference of other donors as well as of the Bank Group. Furthermore, each project or programme included should be discussed against the background of problems and policy issues within the sector concerned. Sector policy conditions for Bank lending should be brought out, and the impact of projects on the target group of the poor should be indicated.

A concluding section should summarize *major conclusions* and list *policy recommendations* for which management approval is sought (Ibidem: 2, and Annex 1; 1-12).

The whole process is initiated within the Regional Office which holds an informal meeting to discuss the broad outlines of the proposed paper. It is then the responsibility of the programme division chief to have the first draft written. In view of the vast amount of information required, a special country mission may sometimes have to be mounted to collect additional data. Thus, time demands on staff in the countries concerned may also be involved.

The draft CPP is reviewed within the Bank by representatives of other sections: Central Economic Staff, Central Projects, Programming and Budgeting Department most prominent among them, in three rounds: a working level review, a review by senior staff and, finally, a review by management. Excluding the time necessary for the first draft, the review cycle takes from six to eight weeks.

This brief description of the planning process shows that the production of CPPs is a highly labour-intensive process, calling for a vast amount of information and for a considerable amount of time, particularly, though not exclusively, of country economic staff. Where country division chiefs hold responsibility for more than one country, i.e. in about two-thirds of the total number of country programme divisions, most of the year may well be spent in preparing CPPs for each country consecutively, which in practice will mean that staff will be Washington-tied for most of the period.

There can be little doubt that, drawn up properly along the lines indicated, CPPs may be very useful as concise summings-up of a body of information pertaining to the Bank's perception of a country's problems and prospects and on the size and depth of its own involvement. It is clear, however, that their status as confidential internal documents may lead to apprehensions in aid-receiving countries as to their content and impact on Bank policy decisions. The reports may be feared to be inaccurate, biased or incomplete, and it should be obvious that countries may object to what they may see as 'central intelligence' that may negatively affect their country.

In reality, however, CPP usefulness for managerial decision-making purposes is severely restricted for a variety of reasons.

The requirement that CPPs be prepared annually for each of the 100-odd active borrowers has never been met. The sheer volume of documents to be processed is such that it could not be done, nor is it necessary. In many countries little happens that would, could or should lead to changes in Bank posture. In such cases CPPs would be repetitious and uninformative from one year to the next.

The requirement that a vast amount of information should be condensed into no more than 20-25 pages calls for excessive economy in words and a high degree of selectivity, and thus forces the paper to be so concise that many factors that would set a country apart from others simply cannot be treated. The extreme economy in words, however, does not mean that less work is required because the statistical work in connection with Annex tables showing macro-projections, debt projection, and socio-economic basic data still has to be done and updated. The introduction of computers into the Bank in the late 1960s greatly expanded these modelling and projection exercises.[8]

CPPs are not distributed to Executive Directors or outside parties. They are expected to be objective, honest and frank. Yet they are often less so in practice, basically for three types of reasons.

Area Departments are not always well-informed on up-to-date country material. Relying mostly on information generated through Bank channels, they may be ignorant of, or misinterpret, events reported in the media. The New York Times, the Washington Post or the major British papers sometimes give more and better information. Two examples will do. Firstly, the civil war between the Hutus and the Tutsis in Burundi in late 1972 reportedly cost the lives of perhaps three percent of the country's population in about two months. Only after this had been reported in the NYT could the Bank's Area Department be persuaded that tribal antagonism went deeper than an occasional killing in a bar fight, as was maintained in the review cycle of Burundi which was in progress at that very time.

Secondly, in CPPs for the early 1970s of several Sahel countries little could be deduced about the severity and consequences of the drought in the area which, as has become clear since, had lasted already for five years.

Government bureaucrats in the countries concerned rarely stray from their capital city, and are thus often uninformed of what is going on. Short-stay World Bank missions who, because of time pressure, have talks only with those capital-based officials, will inevitably receive misinformation. Only after conditions in the countryside had become desperate – the nomads with the remnants of their herds came into the towns – could the seriousness of the situation no longer be denied by the national authorities, and only then did the Sahel tragedy break into the open.

These examples of non- or misinformation should not be interpreted as attempts to lay blame on individuals. Rather, they are symptomatic and a structural characteristic of organizations which are predominantly located far away from the scene of action. The limited information available to the Bank's headquarters in Washington is sometimes, if not often, an unsatisfactory basis for decision making.[9]

In terms of the interpretation of country data for deciding on the size and 'blend' (i.e. the mix between IBRD and IDA where appropriate) of the country lending programme, the country economist as a professional economist is in an almost impossible position. When the issue was merely to decide on the volume of IBRD loans, the task of the country economist was to try to prove that that country was creditworthy for a certain amount. After IDA had become available in the 1960s, however, the desire was to show that countries were *not* creditworthy, so that they could qualify for IDA credits which were given on more favourable terms (Mason & Asher 1973: 401). Moreover, CPPs are widely seen by the Regions as lobbying documents for larger allocations. To the extent that most Bank divisions attempt to get larger allocations, because of the power and prestige that many staff-members attach to their association with large and active lending programmes, the CPPs become unreliable as a basis for management decision-making on the size of the allocations.

The notion that intersectoral priorities can be meaningfully derived from a 'comprehensive planning framework' is equally dubious. The actual sectoral distribution of proposed lending instead derives from a number of very practical commonsense considerations. From the Bank's point of view, the limited resources that are available should not and cannot be largely concentrated in one sector for many countries; this would not square with project staff availability in some sectors, and would present potential over-capacity problems in other project sectors, at least in the short run.

In small and poor countries where the Bank has a limited programme, it is quite a problem to find something suitable, given Bank project standards, and the question of choice among and within sectors does not arise. In larger and middle income countries it is advisable to do something in a variety of sectors in line with the diversification of Bank lending over other sectors than basic infrastructure. From the country's point of view, it would be irritating if foreign financing were to be made available for particular types of activities and not for others perhaps deemed by the country to be of equal or higher priority. Such a bias would also encourage inter-bureau rivalry in that particular agencies may have more access than others to foreign funds.

Other issues for management decisions cannot satisfactorily be dealt with in the framework of an individual CPP review. The core of the outcome of the CPP process is to obtain management approval to a basic table which shows amounts and numbers of operations by sector and by year and by type of financing. From this, an approved lending programme will result.

The individual CPP provides an authorization of what *may be done* in which sectors and when. But what *will be* done is a different matter. In terms of amounts, a change in the IDA allocation to one country will have immediate repercussions for compensatory changes in allocations to other countries, a constraint that is less binding for IBRD which has greater latitude in its level of lending. Often, dramatic escalations in estimated costs, not due to inflation, can be seen as project allocations are reviewed from year to year, implying that the shape and design of project ideas change a great deal between the initial notion and their eventual Board presentation. The severe rationing of IDA entails that cost increases may lead to simpler or altogether different project designs from those envisaged during the earlier stages of project identification and preparations. Revealing in this respect is the statement by R. Porter, of the British ODM:

it is a very rare situation for an aid agency to be confronted with an array of projects and asked which one it was going to pick. What was much more common was the case where one had to devote quite a lot of time and effort working with the recipient government in identifying and working out possible projects. This could be very time consuming and costly... It was an unusual case when a project was rejected after a large amount of time and energy had been spent on working it out ... the decision making is not so much a decision of whether or not to go ahead with a particular investment but rather whether or not it is worthwhile studying a particular proposal in order to turn it into an investment (Porter 1978: 234-35).

In terms of manpower allocation, a change in sector designation may lead to over-programming for the project division which is instructed to work on an extra project, while it may diminish the workload of the project division which 'loses' a project. While there is always some flexibility in staff time-use, the disturbances resulting from piecemeal decisions in respect of 15-20 countries in each region may be quick and sizeable, and generally will not cancel each other out because Bank-wide changes in sector-emphasis reinforce each other.[10] Decisions to change the timing of a project will have immediate consequences for the scheduling of missions to other countries in the region.

Whether project divisions will be able to handle the work at all depends not so much on what gets decided in the CPP review but on the administrative budget which controls the number of staff positions per department, whereby allowance should also be made for the fact that there are usually substantial recruitment lags for authorized positions. Moreover, staff turnover among Bank personnel has always been considerable.

The actual programming unit for the major operative Bank constraints is seldom an individual country, despite the Bank's claim that the CPP is the cornerstone of its planning process. In respect of IDA allocations, Executive Directors have stepped-in by instituting eligibility criteria and by direct allocation to the large recipients. Allocation of the remainder approximates a population-weighted allocation, adjusted for a slight small country bias. The Bank finds it extremely difficult to discriminate among eligible countries on the basis of the 'economic performance' criterion and the resulting allocation is fairly rigid. Variations in IBRD lending can be wider, yet some 20 countries account for 75 percent of IBRD lending over the past 15 years. Whenever sudden major changes in Bank lending have occurred (Indonesia and Egypt in recent years), they did not follow from *a priori* broad-based re-evaluation of the countries' economic prospects, but were rationalized by CPPs after the event.

The sectoral distribution of Bank Group activities is largely a function of short-term project staff availability and of past lending. Long-term sectoral emphasis does not depend upon individual country reviews. When, in 1969, McNamara felt that agriculture should be emphasized, he merely had to decide to hire more appropriate staff. Institution-building considerations in Bank lending tend to argue for long and continuous involvement through repeater loans in one way or another. If the Bank reacts excessively to short-term political or economic developments, which may not affect all sectors to the same degree, this will be counterproductive. It may find itself continuing to disburse on past commitments when it does not like the government of the day, or alternatively, unable to lend for lack of a project pipeline when the government changes for the better in the Bank's view.[11] Moreover, if and when major changes in Bank policy and posture are called for, a sensible way to bring them about is to reduce or increase the number and amounts of allocations over the last few years of the planning period rather than to make changes for the near years on projects for which preparation work is underway or commitments have been made. Such gradualism can better be accommodated through appropriate personnel policies.[12] The country programming concept thus rests on quite unsatisfactory assumptions about the cohesion between national, sectoral and project planning, while for most of the Bank's operational variables, individual countries are not the relevant planning units.[13]

In early 1974 the Bank chanced upon a simplified planning procedure. At that time management wished to review all operations and lending programmes in the light of the effects of the oil price increase and of the commodity boom of 1972-73. The timing of this review coincided with the budget cycle, and all relevant operational constraints could be taken into account simultaneously. Moreover, regional departments were given a freer hand to adjust their proposed programmes for individual countries. The resulting revised programmes were therefore more meaningful than the whole series of individual country reviews, and were constructed and approved in less than three weeks! Yet the shape of the programmes did not materially differ in most cases from what would have been approved taking the country-by-country approach.

Instead of drawing the conclusion, however, that this method of reviewing country programmes, if elevated to the *preferred* method, would free vast amounts of staff time that could be put to use on higher-priority activities, the Bank considered it as an aberration from existing procedures.

Whilst the Bank is predominantly a project lending agency, the central question for management ought to be how it can shape procedures and criteria to improve upon the quality of the projects that it finances. This crucial element is not satisfactorily dealt with in the CPP process, claimed to be the linchpin of the Bank's internal planning framework. The 1972 reorganization dealt mostly with the appraisal phase of designed projects. The CPP cycle covers a great deal of ground but does not deal with design criteria for better projects. Both the reorganization proposals and the central internal planning document therefore fail to come to grips with the central question in a project lending agency: how to generate better projects.

Manpower planning, and formalization of the staffing hierarchy:
rationale and effects

Another general feature of Bank work under McNamara has been the strenuous attempts to develop a system of manpower budgeting. Defining output of the programme departments by numbers of reports and studies produced, and defining project department work by staff time spent on new project preparation, supervision of ongoing projects and other activities, the Bank's Programming and Budgeting Department expected to be thus able to provide 'management tools' for forward planning.

The results have been of only limited significance for improving decision-making. The system can even prove to be harmful, for two basic reasons: firstly, the system improperly defines output; and secondly, the introduction and use of manpower coefficients for types of output as defined gives staff the wrong incentive. It discourages rather than encourages innovative behaviour, and thus will not help to make the Bank more responsive to the needs and tasks of an aid agency.

To plan Bank output by way of manpower coefficients assumes that it has control over most of the scheduling of work activities. This is rarely the case. Until the early 1960s the Bank's prestige in LDCs was such that it could send a mission after it had itself lined-up the staffing. At present, however, the LDCs more often than not let it be known that the timing proposed by the Bank does not suit internal operations. Postponements are then necessary and the staffing consequently disintegrates, particularly when such missions are fairly large − a prerequisite for broad-ranging country missions or in-depth sector missions − and count inter-agency and outside consultants among their members.

To make staff increasingly accountable for output after allocating only a normative time for the purpose, and to bring cases of 'overdue' output to the attention of management, introduces 'wrong' incentives for staff regardless of its professional capabilities. While there is an increasing need for greater care and more in-depth economic research on ongoing processes in LDCs, in interaction with policies pursued (and Bank sector policy documents show increased awareness of and sensitivity to the wider impact of its projects and policies as compared to the 1960s), the introduction of a severe time constraint on economic reporting tends to thwart that research. Moreover, responsible division chiefs attach priority to different types of work. In most cases, the immediate requirements of Board presentation of lending operations take preference over economic reporting and contemplative research. Country economic staff are then used primarily for project-related work, and country economic analyses are given lower priority within the country programme divisions. If, moreover, staff output is measured by the speed with which a 'product' is delivered, staff are strongly tempted to avoid anything that detracts from welltrodden paths; any deviant or more ambitious course of action introduces additional uncertainty and possible delays in completion dates, which look bad on staff records. This creates a highly tense working atmosphere, in which Senior staff must be willing to fight management to protect imaginative and potentially rewarding work, even at the risk that such efforts prove to have been in vain (which in itself could be a valid, though not spectacular, research finding), or that time budgets cannot be met. But such a position is hazardous for senior staff in their relationship with management. The prevailing work-environment entails that any novel approaches come about not *because* of the organizational style adopted but *in spite of it*. Departments which are relatively new and thus less 'organized' have an advantage over older and more established departments where precedent and established procedure are firmly entrenched. In this respect, the Agriculture and Rural Development Department is fairly well-off, but because 'new style' rural development projects are now the salient points of the Bank's publicity campaign to show the outside world that it can deliver on its promise to reorient its policies, time pressure on this department to 'deliver the projects' is even worse than elsewhere in the Bank and will tend to discourage innovation.

The drive to introduce manpower planning techniques could initially be seen as an attempt to bring order into what has been described as the informal, loose and unplanned character of Bank activities of an earlier time. It also fitted McNamara's very personal style of management. The setting-up of the Programming and Budgeting Department is analogous to his action on taking-over at the Pentagon in early 1961. In fact, several Pentagon hands came to the Bank with McNamara and introduced their techniques, as though the output of the organizations was comparable and amenable to standardization to a similar extent.[14]

Increasingly, however, the development of budgetary control techniques is pushed not in response to personal preferences of the Bank president, but in response to demands by the Board of Directors, led by the USA, for accountability in World Bank activities. While the World Bank was relatively small, Congressional (mostly hostile) attention was directed more towards USAID. During the 1970s the comparative sizes of the agencies changed, and Congressional interest has now shifted from the US bilateral programme to multilateral programmes and in particular to the World Bank, the largest and most vocal of the multilateral banks. The bureaucratization of Bank activities and the donor-inspired attempts to make the Bank accountable to its shareholders, will therefore continue in mutual reinforcement.

In 1976, data generated through earlier internal activities of the Programming and Budgeting Departments found their way into the presentation of the formal annual Administrative Budget. Fourteen output or activity categories were distinguished, accounted for by numbers of reports, man-years spent, and cost. In comparing forecasts and realizations, the Board increasingly uses these data to 'squeeze' more output out of staff; adherence to schedule is seen as highly desirable from a budgetary control point of view.

Formerly, the data base on which to control the organization was available only to management, but now it is also available to Board members and pressure on controlling IBRD activites has become independent of the person of the Bank president.

At this point one rather ominous development may be cited. From the 1978 *Financial and Operating Programme* and accompanying *Administrative Budgets* (May 16, 1977), it is evident that the Bank can now realize its 'output', number of loans, reports and the like, within very narrow margins of 'error' from plan targets almost 15 months earlier. It is also reported that the ratio of total lending cost to number of operations approved declined by 13 percent between 1973 and 1977, the explanation given being that a gradually diminishing amount of effort was devoted to lending work on projects which for various reasons never reach the stage of Board presentation. 'The reduction in this use of manpower suggests that nowadays staff efforts, particularly in the early stages of identification and preparation, are better focussed on projects which are *likely to materialize in due course as approved loans or credits*' (p. 14 emphasis added). Projects which promise smooth sailing through the Bank's hierarchy are not likely to be the experimental 'new style' projects which the analysis given in Chapter VI suggests are required. As King (1974) has noted, it is during the early stages of the project cycle that concerns about employment and income distribution can most adequately be considered. It seems, however, that Bank-wide practice is to economize on those early diagnosis and design stages of the project cycle, an economy invoked by the overriding concern for greater efficiency in IBRD lending to meet demands for external accountability of its activities.

A corollary of the bureaucratization tendencies within the Bank has been the introduction of a more hierarchically-structured staff as compared to the loosely-defined roles that characterized the early 1960s, when most operational staff had more or less direct knowledge of the projects under consideration.

The project hierarchy above the 'working level' consists at present of the following supervisory layers: section chief, division chief, assistant project director, project director, regional vice-president, loan committee. Parallel inputs are expected to come from programme staff at the corresponding levels, and also from Central Projects Advisory Staff.

The establishment of this hierarchy has led to additional supervision of the work done by staff at the 'working level', and to a major increase in the paper flow to enable supervisory roles to be realized. It may also lead to increased friction with developing countries.

While the Bank was small in size, a career service in the usual meaning of the term was difficult to implement. Hierarchically-defined job openings were limited, and vertical career opportunities were mainly a function of turnover statistics. The main incentive to staff performance had to be found in providing opportunities for interesting work that challenged the intellectual capacity of individuals. To maintain that challenge, lateral transfers were common, supplying new incentives to staff members to immerse themselves in issues confronting different countries. No onus was attached to lateral transfers in terms of bureaucratically-defined promotion or demotion, the quality of the work done was decisive, and salary advancement was not a function of the job hierarchy.

As the organization grew, formalization of the job structure became more of a necessity. Salary and career progressions are now increasingly tied to shifts from operative jobs to supervisory and managerial jobs. This tendency is reinforced through a progressive decline in mobility between headquarters and the field. Working-level staff tend to be young and therefore less constrained to travel. Older and more experienced staff encounter family constraints which make it less desirable for them to travel frequently to the countries on which they work.[15] Thus, there is strong pressure to find compensation through involvement in Headquarters intra-office routines.

While this trend towards establishing a more hierarchically-structured organization is to be expected in any growing bureaucracy, it can have very undesirable consequences for an agency such as the World Bank which attempts to widen the scope and depth of its activities in response to the increasing complexity of many of its activities. A particular type of people are now attracted to the Bank, namely, those who see their career more in terms of a hierarchical progression towards supervisory and managerial roles, with concomitant intra-office involvement. But the need for the Bank is to attract more scholarly types who are willing to cross disciplinary lines and who see the grappling with complex issues as their main task. Such complex issues do not lend themselves to segmentation and fragmentation, the essential division of labour characteristic of bureaucratic organization.

Various effects on the process of project generation and preparation should also be noted.

The hope that well-conceived, and well-prepared project applications would come cascading into headquarters, was dashed almost as soon as the Bank opened for business (Mason & Asher 1973: 73). During the 1950s, as we have seen, IBRD management argued against the SUNFED proposal on the grounds that it was not shortage of finance but of projects which proved the bottleneck in enlarging the flow of capital to LDCs.

The early emphasis on developing a national planning framework, however, had among its costs that 'it has often tied to a relatively unproductive agency economists who could have been better employed in budget bureaux, commerce ministries, finance corporations, and so on' (Killick 1976: 180). The deployment of these economists in project work might also have had greater pay-offs.

The shortage of projects persisted even after the Bank had emphasized for some time the desirability of national planning in the hope that this would lead to more and better project proposals. The 1964 Annual Report stated that the IBRD 'continued to place a high value on soundly conceived development programs.' Some pride in the Bank's institution-building efforts is reflected in the statement that 'the usefulness of development programs by now is generally recognized and hardly any developing country is without a plan.' The Report also noted, however, that 'there is still a shortage of well-conceived and well-prepared high priority projects available for financing.' This echoes a statement made in the Bank's 1948-49 Annual Report.

Formal responsibility for the preparation of projects belongs to the borrower and not to the Bank. This has been rigidly adhered to in the past to avoid a potential conflict of interest whereby the Bank had to appraise projects which it had helped to prepare. But this position has not been able to withstand the pressure of events. Baum has written: 'Experience has demonstrated that we do not get enough good projects to appraise unless we are involved intimately in their identification and preparation. Through better preparation, fewer projects are rejected at the appraisal stage, although the final version of the project may be quite different from its original conception' (Baum 1970: 6). In view of this persistent shortage of projects, President Woods believed that he should not borrow more than he did. McNamara started by borrowing much more than his predecessor and afterwards instructed the staff to find ways to spend the money. The increased availability of loanable funds has thus generated demand for more projects (and caused their 'bunching' in the last quarter of the fiscal year in board presentation). Throughout IBRD history, the primary concern of its lending activities has therefore been to generate projects and to influence, shape and control many stages of the project cycle. Various methods have been employed to this end. Some larger or more sophisticated borrowers are quite capable of preparing their own projects, particularly after first or second loans when they have become accustomed to IBRD requirements and procedures. If they do not have staff adequate for the purpose, they may have a regular relationship with a consulting firm for project preparation. In the absence of such a relationship, according to Baum, the Bank may urge the entity to get consultants to help prepare feasibility studies and guide it in the selection. Feasibility studies may be financed in various ways: by the borrower; out of the proceeds of an existing loan or credit (piggyback); occasionally by a Bank technical assistance grant or credit to facilitate preparation of a first project that will enable the Bank to make a first loan to a country in a particular sector. This technique was used successfully by the Resident Mission in Indonesia after 1968 in trying to build up a lending programme when IDA lending to Indonesia was initiated. It is also used in some of the poorer African countries which lack the money for such studies and, in the absence of well-prepared projects, cannot get Bank Group loans; more frequently, they receive a UNDP grant for which the Bank may act as Executing Agent.

When the Bank is concerned with the choice of consultants, it frequently also helps to shape the terms of reference of their work in order to ensure that the resulting design features are compatible with its preferred project arrangements. Diversification of Bank lending initially became possible when the Bank concluded cooperative agreements with other UN specialized agencies and had them prepare projects for its funding.

Adler notes (1971: 11) that 'in the last five years [1966-70], 25% of all loans were made to entities which had previously received at least one loan from the Bank Group, and a further 35% of the total were made to sectors which had previously received at least one Bank Group loan in that country. Thus the phenomenon that "one loan leads to another" through contacts that build up during appraisal and negotiation and lead to the extension of others, proves to be a major method by which the Bank builds its project pipelines.' There is no reason to suppose that this phenomenon has since ceased to exist. In fact, the shift in lending priorities, together with the hope that Bank projects 'new style' will set examples for countries and other donors to follow, makes it likely that the share of projects in whose preparation the Bank has been intimately involved has increased in the last few years.

The Bank's attempts to control the environment in which it operates extend further. If spending monies is a major criterion in judging agency performance, while staff resources are limited but public accountability is yet demanded, then it is rational to react by selecting fairly large capital-intensive projects which are organizationally economic. If such projects are beyond the institutional handling capacity of the local counterpart organization, there is pressure to make the loan conditional on the establishment of special project authorities, to be staffed by expatriates in most cases, accountable and reporting to the Bank. No amount of exhortation by analysts of aid agencies and of their practices that small, simple and labour-intensive solutions in project design should be sought, can overcome what the bureaucracy sees as a major purpose of its own activities: to quickly spend its budget allocations (see Tendler 1975). As an aid agency grows in terms of staff and budget it develops a bias against the design of small and simple projects. The fact that, notwithstanding the increasing severity of personnel and public accountability constraints, the search continues for alternative and simpler designs and features that are compatible with local institutional capabilities, more so in some parts of the Bank than in others, must be considered a major achievement. Such projects are unpredictable in their execution and more difficult for the Bank to influence and control.

The Bank's early involvement in the design stage of many projects which it subsequently finances means that the inputs of its staff at the lowest working levels are important. Organizations which characteristically have to rely on inputs at the 'working level' are relatively 'bottom heavy' because major inputs in project designs can be effectively introduced only at those levels, in conjunction with the developing country concerned.

Over the last decade the Bank has formalized its procedures and organizational style. It has established a pyramidal hierarchy and has consequently tended to become 'topheavy' in its organizational structure, with potentially detrimental effects on projects.

Countries which are capable of designing projects to their own full satisfaction, taking account of their national priorities and capabilities, would not take it kindly if various levels in the Bank project hierarchy were to suggest major changes to those projects when submitted, and would resist it as undue interference. If the Bank were to insist on such changes being made, e.g. the addition of 'poor-oriented' elements, the country concerned may well be driven to exploit other sources of foreign finance: export credits and Eurodollar borrowing which have become available in increasing volume to a widening range of countries. Additional layers within the Bank which tend to delay project processing may then prove irksome in that they provoke irritation, or may be counterproductive if countries decide to go elsewhere, perhaps leading to a shortfall on lending targets.

It may be argued that the Bank's project hierarchy is primarily useful for lending to countries which lack project planning capacity. To this end, one objective of the 1972 reorganization was to restore the teamwork between 'country' and 'project' departments which had broken down in 1968. At one level closer integration between Bank departments has been beneficial in that it made it possible to link country-general economic and project work within the Bank. At another level it tends to create additional problems and conflicts in Bank relations with prospective borrowers.

Two courses of action are feasible. Either Bank supervisors put considerable trust in the competence and judgement of the Bank project officer, in which case he will be supported and encouraged to continue his work. If, however, a supervisor acknowledges that many detailed project arrangements are beyond his powers of judgement because he has not been involved in direct interaction with country counterparts in the field, it is difficult for him to take responsibility for the work of the project officer, as required by his own place in the organizational hierarchy.

Alternatively, supervisors within the Bank as it were take over the initial project shape brought back by the project officers, reshape and remould it (sometimes beyond recognition), and send the project officer back to the country to re-sell the 'new design'. People involved locally may obviously be irritated by the modifications, putting the blame on the Bank project officer whose effectiveness is then likely to be undermined.

Under conditions of increasing bureaucratization the position of the project officer tends to be ambivalent: caught between the demands of national realities on the one hand, and those of the Bank's internal hierarchy on the other. He will be reluctant to innovate fearing a negative response by the Bank's supervisory hierarchy which, to compensate for knowledge of intimate country detail, must rely on precedent and standard Bank operating procedures, framed when the Bank was more conservative. On the other hand, the project officer will not want to alienate his counterparts in the country concerned, and under this dual pressure may well prefer to avoid taking any risks.

The consequence of Bank-LDC interplay about the shape of projects is likely to be less effective project design as more and more people, who have little to contribute, become involved in their shaping and reviewing. The project officer who, in interaction with local officials, nourishes and shapes a project idea into a viable design, makes a number of judgements on the basis of his assessment of the local context, his counterparts, and national institutions. In that interchange something is wrought in which local influence and commitment to implement is strong. When the project idea is brought back to Washington, however, the project officer has to nurse his project through many organizational levels, none of whose staff have been directly involved with those within the LDC who developed the project idea and are likely to be responsible for its subsequent execution and/or supervision. This is not to say that senior Bank staff are incompetent: on the contrary, they may be of high technical competence and may earlier have visited and thus 'know' the country in question. But when technical assistance, socio-economic impact and institutional aspects are of increasing importance, as in rural development and also in other projects, this is an insufficient basis on which to judge the nitty gritty of project aspects that are not specifically technical.

Over time, as more and more countries build up their project-preparation capacity, the gravity point in the interactive process of shaping a project must inevitably shift towards the LDCs, a point noted many years ago by Cairncross

(1959: 18-19). The LDCs will attempt to assert themselves and may prove less malleable to Bank wishes than in the past when they felt less secure. At the same time, decision making within the Bank may become more cohesive ('teamwork'), but this does not guarantee that the Bank-LDC dialogue will be smoother or more constructive.

Against the background of the Bank's pyramidal development and the increasing distance between the shapers and reviewers of projects, means have to be sought by which all this 'indirect labour' can have some impact. The 1972 reorganization prescribed that a brief 'Issues Paper' be prepared upon the appraisal mission's return from the field to identify major issues for resolution in advance of report drafting, to be followed by a 'Decision Memorandum' recording decisions reached at the 'Decision Meeting'. The extra work that this involves has added to the workload of project staff, explaining in part why the preliminary assessment of the reorganization could not find any speeding-up of the appraisal stage. Formerly, it was virtually impossible to suggest major changes after the draft appraisal report had been completed and loan negotiations were about to be finalized. It is not surprising now to read in the Bank's *Reorganization Assessment Report* (1974; 4) that the Central Project Staff

has had difficulty efficiently discharging its important quality assurance role, for while issues meetings have been widely viewed as rather late in the process for CPS to have a decisive impact on the quality of a project, the manpower has not been available to CPS to participate at an early stage.

King notes that 'in some cases there is a feeling that the CPS contribution is made at the wrong time, or in a highly technical or formalistic way without a real understanding of the problems the Region is facing' (King 1974: 34). But while King attributes this to a classic 'line vs. staff' problem that, in his view, need not be a serious one, it seems to us that it is a grave structural problem inherent in the distance between supervisory levels and the reality of conditions in LDCs.

The 'issues paper' is meant to enable 'indirect' Bank labour to perform its function; sector studies attempt to influence early project selection. The Bank began to experiment with such studies as comprehensive survey missions declined from the mid-1960s on. As the *Reorganization Assessment Report* has noted, however (p. 6), pressure to prepare projects for immediate presentation and the renewed emphasis on comprehensive reports has made it difficult to devote sufficient effort to detailed sector studies, whose preparation requires considerable expertise more generally to be found in project departments than in programme departments. Moreover, sector studies are only useful for influencing early project design choices if and when they cover sufficient ground in depth, which takes considerable time and money. Waterston finds that good sector studies 'are rarely carried out in less than a year or a year and a half'

(Waterston 1965: 321). The old conflict between the desire to launch concrete projects quickly and the desire to make the 'best' choice based on the fullest possible information, with resultant decision delays, is difficult to resolve. The micro-universe, as distinct from an analysis on the macro-level of an economy, is by no means easy to penetrate, and the toil and trouble required to do so have frequently been assumed non-existent by those intent on producing national plans or macro-oriented programmes (see Streeten & Lipton 1968: 7, 11; Hirschmann 1967: 23).

The same process of creating additional work to enable the various layers of the supervisory hierarchy to function also operates in the context of country economic reporting.

By the mid-1960s, less developed countries had become less interested in advice on overall policies and planning (Mason & Asher 1973: 333). A number were perfectly capable of producing their own surveys if they thought them useful. The Bank's practice of sending comprehensive country missions therefore declined. In 1966 the Bank stated that, while it would continue to send missions to its member countries, 'these missions are intended *primarily to improve the Bank Group's knowledge* of the development potental and problems of member countries' (*Annual Report* 1965-66: 19; emphasis added). To Gold, this seemed a sharp and unexplained departure from previous statements about the purposes of mission programmes as potential *action* instruments for both the Bank and the country involved (Gold 1976: 27). The renewed Bank interest in country economic reporting under McNamara, primarily to satisfy its internal bureaucratic information needs, puts considerable strain on the scarce local manpower in the countries concerned and is not necessarily welcomed.[16]

Growing realization of the complexity of the development process makes it *a priori* unlikely that short missions that have to write reports under severe time pressure on the basis of a few weeks' stay, can do much more than produce a useful and relatively up-to-date compilation of available data. To attempt more would require far greater depth in coverage, deeper involvement in policy options, and greater awareness of the social and economic implications of what would ultimately be recommended. It would call for more research, greater scholarship, more time, less pressure, and a much greater experience with the situation in a particular country than is commonly possessed by Bank mission staff. Insofar as such studies extend beyond the knowledge obtained by compiling material in the country in question, the Bank would be well advised to adopt an *open* publications distribution policy, rather than treating the majority of such studies as confidential internal documents.[17]

Draft economic reports made upon a mission's return are increasingly found unsatisfactory and attempts are now being made to have major issues papers prepared *before* the mission goes out. While this may lead to better reports, at least if the mission is able to find sufficient relevant material while in the country, issues papers will inevitably increase overall manpower requirements and may tend to prejudge the diagnosis of issues and solutions which the mission subsequently will find.

Finally, mention should be made of one aspect or consequence of the severe constraints which affect the Bank as an institution.

The focus on predictability of Board presentation and on 'efficiency' in early design stages, forces Bank staff to devise ways and means by which to escape from the excesses of its own manpower planning and budgetary control techniques. Two obvious strategies present themselves. One is the presentation of insufficiently- or inadequately-prepared projects, particularly those labelled 'new style', which are much less novel than is claimed or desired. 'Loose ends' which should have been investigated and resolved are presented, through lack of time, as problems for project management to solve after approval of the loan. Such hurried presentation increases the probability of major problems emerging in the future and, judging by the slowdown in disbursements, such problems are already being encountered.

A second strategem calls for means to bring a number of activities outside the purview of management and Board. One method is to include much larger amounts for research and studies in loan agreements rather than to make such studies beforehand. This tactic has been used by the Bank despite the fact that its own research activities have increased substantially since 1969.

The total amount of technical assistance included in IBRD loans and IDA credits in FY 1969 was $39.5 million, rising to $40.4 million in FY 1970 and $49.6 million in FY 1971 (Mason & Asher 1973: 316). In 1976 $218 million was included, and in 1977 $189 million (*Annual Report* 1977: 5). If these figures are related to the total for IBRD-IDA administrative expenses, all in current dollars, incorporated technical assistance equalled 70 percent of the total in 1969-71 but increased to slightly over 100 percent of the budget in 1976-77. In other words, the Bank has economized on its activities to some extent by pushing more technical assistance in its loans which is to be repaid by borrowers. It would be interesting to discover what precisely is hidden in the loan proposals, and whether the increase of the technical assistance item bears any relation to the worsened research climate in the Bank as a consequence of its evolving operational style. Unfortunately, however, no such study has been possible.

IS DECENTRALIZATION THE ANSWER?

Against the background of all these tensions and problems, it has to be asked whether further organizational growth of the World Bank along the lines of a headquarter-centered, increasingly top heavy institution, is a viable form of expansion for the 1980s.

Should some sort of decentralization not be contemplated? It should be remembered that in the past the Bank Group has not been very receptive to suggestions that it should alter its organizational structure. In answer to the Pearson Commission's recommendations the Bank agreed to do more of the things it was already doing, but resisted suggestions for changes in organizational matters, notably in respect of IDA and on collaboration with the IMF.[18] The 1972 reorganization was concerned only with decentralization in Washington, and the *Reorganization Assessment Report* (1974: 3) 'did not see the need for significant further structural changes beyond those already contemplated' (which related to minor further changes in the organization of the projects departments). Even the discussions on restructuring of the UN system do not appear to have yielded much more than promises of 'co-ordination'. Some degree of speculation is therefore inevitable in the following discussion, which may also be futile to some extent.

Decentralization may be seen in various ways: geographical, functional, or according to level of development of the various countries.

A foreign aid agency differs from a home-based government bureaucracy in that a major input into the programme of its activities must come from those outside it: recipient governments or other local borrower groups. The Bank has never been able to acquire sufficient financible projects without initiating its own activities in the development and shaping of proposals. The crucial input into the production of development assistance projects and programmes therefore has to be made by the bottom levels of the organization who can work in direct and close collaboration with local counterparts. Arguments that favour a shift from the 'top-heavy' structure in Washington to a 'bottom-heavy' one which emphasizes country-level missions will be reinforced as projects become more complex and more embedded in difficult institutional and social environments. Emphasis on resident country missions will also reduce the risk that necessary local inputs in project preparation and design are not forthcoming, preventing the agency from meeting its lending targets and weakening its position in negotiating larger allocations. Alternatively, it would continue to receive project designs that were unsatisfactory in respect of new policy orientations of the Bank and other donors.

Various reasons, however, make it unlikely that a major decentralization away from Washington will occur. The annual volume and frequency of Bank lending remains very small in many countries, and covers a range of sectors. A country mission staffed with the expertise to adequately cover those sectors may well be underutilized. Where the volume and frequency of Bank lending is large this danger of underutilization of staff may be small, but local project preparation capability is reasonably well-developed in many sectors in such countries, e.g. Brazil, Mexico, India, the Philippines. A Bank Resident Mission of any size may then well be resented on the grounds that the countries are perfectly capable of shaping projects as they themselves see fit without apparent tutelage.

Another argument against a significant decentralization of Bank staff is that friction may develop between the field and headquarters. Field staff will be closer to field conditions and local sensitivities, but may become alienated from headquarter's thinking.[19] Distrust may develop between staff in the field and those, usually of higher status and closer to authority, residing in Washington. Such conflicts will undoubtedly increase, but, as we have seen, considerable tensions have existed in the past and continue to exist since the 1972 reorganization. Not only is it difficult for differences of opinion to be avoided within Regional Offices and for Central Projects Advisory staff to provide more than non-trivial inputs in time to influence project designs, but severe friction also exists between regional staffs and the Development Policy Staff (DPS).

The DPS is, by a large margin, the most controversial operation in the Bank. Although the abilities of its members are highly respected throughout the Regions, the staff collectively is the object of widespread Regional criticism. The Regions do not consider DPS to be thought leaders or guardians of high standards of economic analysis; many in the Regions do not even think they should aspire to these roles. Generally, they resent the amount of staff resources made available to DPS. They consider DPS overly academic and feel that its resources could be employed far more fruitfully in Regional operations (*Reorganization Assessment Report* 1974: 4).

The benefits will have to be weighed between strengthening the internal cohesion of thinking and decision making in a highly centralized institution, and the cost of alienating collective Bank thinking from country opinions and local sensitivity. If country- and Bank-held opinions diverge, project design and implementation will suffer. As projects become more complex and enter sensitive areas, the adverse consequences of possible divergence will become more frequent and more serious.

The information base obtainable from a resident mission is likely to be superior to that gathered by a Washington-based and mostly desk-bound country officer. The fact that country mission staff tends to be short-term and may be transferred every two or three years is generally held to be a disadvantage: 'by the time they get to know the country, they disappear.' No doubt frequent transfers make it difficult to build a cumulative information base. On the other hand, the intensity and greater diversity of contacts which become possible when a relatively small resident mission immerses itself in the local developing country context are more promising than reliance on a few visits by country officers from Washington who, as a rule, are also transferred to other assignments within the Bank every few years.

Arguments that resident mission staff are likely to reside in upper-class residential areas and that this may negatively affect their effectiveness in working on 'poor-oriented' projects, are valid. On the other hand, this unfavourable demonstration effect is apparent in numerous visiting missions who operate from the best hotels in the capital city and demand, and usually obtain, special and costly facilities to make their short visits both more effective and more pleasant. Lal is caustic in this respect when he says:

I have seen agents of international agencies hectoring civil servants in at least one developing country about the need to reduce the incomes of people in the top decile of the
country. The implication ... is that this must include cuts in the inequitable income being
received by the civil servant being lectured to. A simple comparison, at least in India,
would, however, show that the high-level national civil servant being lectured to receives a
weekly income which is lower than the *daily allowance* of the international civil servant in
the country he is advising (Lal 1976: 33).

In any large organization, lower level staff, whether resident mission field
staff or headquarters-based flying staff, will be inclined to follow what Tendler
calls 'safe-for-all occasions, problem-avoiding behaviour' (1975: 25). As a
consequence, innovative and adaptive behaviour cannot thrive.

If the Bank's programme in a particular country is too small to warrant a
resident mission, this may be overcome by pooling the activities of the Bank
with those of other UN agencies. This was one of the objectives of the 1970
Consensus to organize activities under a country Resident Representative.
Experience with this system, however, has not been generally favourable
because the country is not a very useful planning unit for worldwide organizations, and because priorities and preferences of the participating organizations are non-congruent. Other UN specialized agencies are also very much
headquarters-centred, even though their proportion of total staff in the field is
larger than that of the Bank.

World Bank resident missions in developing countries increased from 14 to
24 between 1972 and 1977, and field staff from 27 in 1968 to 114 in 1977
(1978 Administrative Budget, Table 17). For the most part, missions are very
small, each with one or two professional staff who update country economic
information as it becomes available, and help to expedite paperwork between
the Bank and the country concerned. The fairly large India office does most
of the Bank's economic reporting on that country, India being too complex
to be X-rayed through short-term visiting missions.

The Eastern Africa (Nairobi) and Western Africa (Abidjan) Regional Missions are quite large and play a major role in project preparation work within
their region, particularly in respect of agricultural projects. They also carry out
most of the supervision of projects in the region.

The mission in Indonesia has enjoyed considerable latitude. Established in
1968 in order to develop quickly a lending programme in implementation of
the Bank's decision to mount a special effort in that country, its first director,
Bernard Bell, was given wide authority. Since his transfer in 1972, however,
subsequent directors have had far less authority and Washington pressure for
control has reasserted itself.

The proposal made by Reid regarding a major future reorganization of the
Bank deserves special attention. Reid considers that the 1972 reorganization
will make it easier to take the next step required to improve the structure of
the Bank: to transfer regional offices from Washington to regional headquarters, and to establish regional councils for each regional office in ac-

cordance with the provisions of section 10 of article V of the Articles of Agreement (Reid 1973b: 183). Section 10, which has not been used, reads as follows:

The Bank may establish regional offices and determine the location of, and the areas to be covered by a regional office. Each regional office shall be advised by a regional council representative of the entire area and selected in such a manner as the Bank may decide.

In Reid's view, the core of each regional office would be the staff of the regional office in Washington, and segments of the other (overhead and service) departments. He estimates that the size of the staff at headquarters could then probably be reduced by more than half (Ibidem: 184). A reduction in size of what in effect would become four-to-six regional banks under a World Bank umbrella would lessen the need for bureaucratization and might encourage more innovative behaviour.

The principal advantage of this move would be that the Bank Group staff directly concerned with a region would be living in that region, which should lead to better understanding of the special problems facing those responsible for regional policy making. Such increased understanding does not come automatically, however.[20]

In a career institution like the Bank, the pressure for conformity of thinking as a means to further and protect one's career is quite strong, particularly for those to whom alternatives at equivalent pay are not readily available, e.g. many staff from LDCs. Career service fosters an organization man, and in-house radicals, who might be necessary for the introduction of novel concepts or concerns, rarely stay for long.

The financial cost of decentralization would be quite high; housing, for instance, may be even more expensive than in Washington while educational allowances may also be higher. On the other hand, there may be offsetting factors: in the short run these would be found in reduced travel expenditure; in the longer run recruitment from within the region would reduce the need for special educational facilities for others. An added advantage of decentralization would be that as recruitment from within the region becomes easier, as is the experience elsewhere in other organizations, the geographical recruitment of Bank staff will improve.

Decentralization of the World Bank would force the Executive Directors to devise policy guidelines on the delegation of authority, which will in any case soon be necessary because of the sheer increase in loan proposals to be approved.

One suggestion would be that the Executive Directors should not approve individual loans but country operations and lending programmes. The discussion to which this would give rise would focus explicitly on issues discussed in Chapter V, and bring to the fore strong divisions between various categories of Bank members.

At present, EDs largely rubberstamp any loan proposals submitted to them. Not only do they not have the staff to review proposals but those from LDCs are primarily interested in getting as large a share as possible for their constituencies, while those from major creditor countries lack sufficient knowledge of the developing country to be able to review a loan proposal meaningfully. Moreover, all EDs are usually appointed for one term only and are therefore rarely well-informed.

EDs could focus on the overall size and shape of the lending programme, by region, country and sector for, say, a three-year planning period, coinciding with the IDA replenishment period. In between they might consider any necessary major adaptations to the planning figures. By making greater use of the Operations Evaluation Department, they could carry out their quality control function more effectively; thirdly, by focussing on Sector Policy Papers and other general policy issues they could still play a directing role for Bank activities. These three instruments in combination would seem to provide sufficient safeguards to protect the interests of the financiers and of the countries concerned.

All in all, it seems that Reid's proposal as discussed above has sufficient merit to be taken seriously. If no major reorganization of the World Bank should be possible, one other avenue remains open. The regional banks in Latin America, Africa and Asia should expand their activities relative to the World Bank, as discussed in Chapter V above.

NOTES

1. Its functioning as a non-system has been analysed by the Jackson report (1969) but little progress has been made since about steps to be taken to improve that functioning.
2. Adler 1972: 46; 'Policies and Operations' (June 1971), vii.
3. See, for instance, Downs 1966: Ch. 16; Thompson 1967; Burns & Stalker 1961; Lawrence & Lorsch 1968.
4. Tinbergen's book: *The Design of Development* (1958) resulted from such an association.
5. While that firm has acquired a reputation for assisting in the reorganization of large organizations, it might be asked whether its collective experience included many cases in which the essential function is to manage innovation. If not, it may perhaps unwittingly have slanted its advice towards a structure which did not do justice to the essential function of an 'aid agency'.
6. Repetto, writing of his experience in Pakistan wrote, 'Not only are shadow prices applied at the wrong end of the project planning process and by the wrong people, but they are also being applied to projects designed under an entirely different set of prices, the observed ones. By then it is too late to do much about the misallocation of resources. Even if directives are issued to the various agencies instructing them to use shadow prices in project design ... scarcities still do not impinge on the agencies' proclivity. (Repetto 1969: 157).
7. In the summing-up by Killick (1976: 171): 'Economists have adopted a "rational actor" model of politics. This would have us see governments as composed of public-spirited, knowledgeable, and role-oriented politicians; clear and united in their objectives; choosing those policies which will achieve optimal results for the national interest; willing

and able to go beyond a short-term point of view. Governments are stable, in largely un-differentiated societies, wielding a centralized concentration of power and a relatively un-questioned authority; generally capable of achieving the results they desire from a given policy decision. They are supported by public administrations with ready access to a very large volume of relevant information which can be produced efficiently. How political scientists might label such a regime is unclear but one is reminded of Wicksell's observation that "much of the discussion in fiscal theory proceeds on the implicit and unrecognized assumption that the society is ruled by a benevolent despot" – a paradoxical result to emerge from the liberal-individualist tradition of Western economics.'

8. The first Operational Memorandum was formulated in 1971; it was redrafted in 1973-74, and almost continually ever since. In 1978 a task force was formed to redraft the in-structions. While the objective of all these revisions has been simplification, in practice the data requirements for their preparation have continually increased!

9. The analogy with the war in Vietnam, realities in the field, and the data base for Pentagon and White House decision making comes to mind (see the Pentagon Papers).

10. In 1973 many proposed power projects were rejected by management. This led to over-capacity and low morale in the departments concerned. At the same time many agri-cultural projects had to be inserted, even though agricultural project staff was already overloaded.

11. The Bank's relation with Sri Lanka seems to reflect this stop-go attitude.

12. In March 1973, approval of the whole five-year operations and lending programme to Brazil was held up by management because it did not reveal enough 'poor-oriented' pro-jects. The Regional Office was instructed to re-submit an adjusted programme within six months which would reflect more 'impact on the poor'. This meant that project staff had to be withdrawn from work on other countries in order to 'find' poor-oriented projects in Brazil at short notice. Recent economic reports had found only very limited opportunities for such lending and these were heavily contested among competing donor organizations, all trying to shift their lending priorities simultaneously. Though the demand for a more balanced country programme can be understood in terms of external pressure, one can have doubts about projects and project standards that have to be generated in such a 'pressure cooking' atmosphere.

13. The view of planning as an effort to devise national strategies and sectoral strategies in order to derive notions of priority against which to measure the contributions of donor agencies in their generally small if not insignificant volume of resources, has been evident also within the UN. The UNDP, following the Consensus reached in the UN in 1970 (see Dubey 1977), has made strenuous efforts, largely through the Country Resident Rep-resentatives, to 'coordinate' and 'plan' the 'integration' of activities of other UN special-ized agencies so as to give proper weight to the 'balanced character' of their 'priority-ranked' activities. These efforts have mostly been in vain. The agencies still run their own show and many if not most World Bank missions notify or pay a courtesy visit to the UN Resident Representative only when they are already in the country. UNDP ineffectiveness in achieving substantive planning or active coordination is not necessarily to be regretted. If substantive planning were to be achieved, it would probably make it impossible to re-main flexible in the face of constant change which necessitates adaptation of existing plans. From the perspective of permitting continued flexibility, therefore, some loose form of coordination may well be preferable.

14. In addition, the Programming and Budgeting Department was staffed, in the early-1970s formation, by a group of fairly junior staff with limited or no Bank experience, some of whom had had no experience of working conditions in developing countries. Their sensitivity to the nature of the difficulties encountered by the Regions and Project Department was limited, yet they had the authority to impose a variety of 'tools for management use' on the organization.

15. Personnel regulations have been adopted by the Bank which set a *maximum* on the numbers of days that staff may travel on missions abroad.

16. 'We can render a unique service by becoming a highly informed and impartial source of precise and professional development reports – reports that are both current and com-prehensive. Our Country Economic Reports can and should become increasingly useful

tools to all organizations working in the field of development. Beginning this year, therefore, we will organize a regular annual mission to each major developing country to report in detail on economic and social progress and on the prospects for the future. These missions will investigate all major sectors of the economy, and will seek to determine priorities for both investment and pre-investment activities... They will provide an independent, objective, and wholly nonpartisan basis for evaluating progress in the Second Development Decade' (McNamara 1969: 22).

17. Other agencies are now tempted to send their own comprehensive missions, and much duplication in agency reports is the avoidable result.

18. See Memoranda to Executive Directors of December 11, 1969 and May 8, 1970.

19. See Tendler 1975: 23-36 for some of the problems which USAID encountered with a decentralized organizational approach.

20. Reid cites letters from officials in LDCs to the effect that those who spent many years abroad in international agencies have become so alienated from conditions in their *own* countries as to seriously reduce their usefulness.

VIII

CONCLUSIONS

In the 1960s, largely through the DAC, attempts were made to standardize donor procedures and criteria in matters of international development finance. Aid consortia were seen as means with which to forge a common position among donors in their dealings with developing countries, which at that time had little recourse to other sources of international finance. By the end of the decade the World Bank had taken a leading role in development lending, being the principal channel for the multilateral transfer of resources. World Bank influence was widened further through its chairing of numerous aid consortia. Its country economic reports served as major analytical papers which assessed the prospects of the country on whose behalf the consortium was formed, a practice that tended to reinforce the Bank's role when combined donor leverage was exerted on aid recipients.

This trend towards common front formation by donors has not continued during the 1970s. The shift in aid flow from bilateral to multilateral channels at first tended to strengthen the position of the Bank, but the trends of the 1960s were soon undermined and reversed.

A major feature of the 1970s has been that some countries have obtained access to international finance on an unprecedented scale. As the terms of IBRD loans hardened (1976) and the character of the Bank as a project-lending institution was given new emphasis (1977), implying long gestation periods and delayed disbursements, and as the new flow of programme loans became available from the Eurodollar market, some of the more developed LDCs were able to take a position of greater independence vis-à-vis the World Bank and its attempts to exert leverage on their internal policies. Development finance from new sources, notably OPEC, is now made available to countries according to preferences which do not necessarily coincide with those of the traditional providers of finance.

The malaise in ODA availability from DAC countries continued into the 1970s. IDA's significance as the most important ODA channel has weakened as the major regional development banks have established their 'soft loan' windows, and the FED's importance has increased. The institutional arrangements under which these ODA windows have been established ensure increased Third World influence in decisionmaking about their use. ODA from new sources, again mainly OPEC, has flowed through bilateral and newly-established regional channels rather than through IDA, and is directed mostly to the poorer Arab countries.

The slowness with which the World Bank has internationalized its staff, particularly at senior levels, together with attempts by the USA to reduce its financial participation while making sure that its nationals are brought in at senior levels from outside the organization, cannot but reinforce the image of the Bank as an essentially Western institution.

These trends towards diffusion of influence and the proliferation and attendant leverage of regional institutions as distinct from global institutions, are probably not directly related to the new poor-oriented lending policies of the IBRD and other bilateral donors. They reflect the increasing tendency towards differentiation and pluriformity of the development process. The shift in the policy intentions of some though not all major donors, to redirect their aid activities towards the poor has, however, a bearing upon the future of the World Bank as a near-global institution.

A focus on poor countries involves a focus on Southern Asia and Subsahara Africa (excl. South Africa). IBRD lending to large parts of Latin America should lose in emphasis and gradually be withdrawn. By the same token, a de-emphasis on lending to the two major socialist Bank member countries might be considered. Creditworthiness considerations inhibit a shift of IBRD lending to the very poorest countries, but a shift towards the lower end of the income range would make funds available to a set of countries which, on the whole, have less access to external resources than those in the upper range of middle income countries.

IDA funds have been allocated to the poorer countries since the late 1960s, a trend that continued into the 1970s. The upper eligibility limit for IDA is still a per capita income of around $550 per annum; the bulk of IDA resources, however, is at present allocated to countries whose average per capita income is less than half that amount. This implies a reduced future clientele for IDA, which is weakened as a world-wide institution.

The principal justification for a country re-allocation of IBRD funds is that it would add to the resources of those countries. Whether or not World Bank lending would be poor-oriented would need to be the subject of a separate decision. If the Bank were able to assess country policies in terms of their effects on the poor, a strong argument could be made that it focusses its lending on sectors in which it has acquired a comparative advantage.

In view of the fact that it is not generally possible for the Bank to pronounce on the effectiveness of public policy-making for the welfare of the poorer strata of a society, a focus on the poor will have to be judged by the type of projects that it chooses to finance. The Bank's approach to rural development has been analyzed in terms of its ability to carry out projects for the small farmers who, in the Bank's approach, are the major target group. We have seen that major problems are involved. Packages that meet a number of exacting demands in respect of productivity, acceptability and ecologically-sound land use, may not be widely available. In addition, our review of a number of comparative empirical studies regarding past approaches to the designing of small-farmers' projects has not led to any optimistic conclusions about the use of those approaches as models for the future. In many cases the initial distribution of productive assets and the characteristics of channels through which external inputs are provided and subsequent output is absorbed, tend to reinforce trends towards greater economic differentiation and social fragmentation in rural areas. If target-group approaches for population groups *within* countries are judged to be of limited effectiveness, the case for a reallocation *between* countries, with the Bank focussing on sectors of comparative advantage, is reinforced.

To the extent that continuation of past development trends is deemed undesirable in view of their side-effects regarding lack of employment creation and on income distribution, the case for a search for alternative policy sets and more experimental and novel project approaches is established.

The conventional approach to development, whether termed traditional, neo-classical, orthodox or economic, clashes with an alternative non-conventional, radical or political economy approach (Weaver & Jameson 1978). The 1970s have seen a proliferation of new approaches to development thinking which try to combine elements from these two major contending paradigms. While 'growth' is still an element in many such constructs, 'redistribution' receives increased attention. Accordingly, we find groups of theorists working on the following range of possibilities: Redistribution *with/from/ before* or *without* Growth. Whatever the merits of these theories, which are currently intensely debated, it is clear that they are suggestive of different strategies being offered to policymakers. While the World Bank is certainly active in this renewed academic debate, its claim to be able, in its country economic reporting, to provide a highly informed and impartial source of precise and professional development reports which should become increasingly useful tools to *all* organizations working in the field of development (McNamara 1969: 22), is an attempt to impose *its* views on how organizations should view development. In the current confused state of development theorizing, such claims are preposterous and untenable.

The search for experimental and novel project approaches is likely to be hampered in several respects. Countries which qualify only for IBRD loans will have to be convinced that they would be wise to contract hard-term foreign loans for projects which are difficult, experimental and high-risk ventures, under arrangements whereby all risks are born by the recipients and not by the Bank which initiated or supported such projects. While some IBRD clients have access to other foreign funds to cover their continuing needs for the type of projects which the Bank is no longer willing to finance, those which do not have that option and have to depend on assistance on concessionary terms, may be forced into high-risk ventures by external donors. There is a genuine fear that the donor-support base for ODA may erode further if the outcomes of induced ventures prove disappointing.

Disbursements on 'new-style' projects are slower than customary in Bank experience (*Annual Report* 1978) and are perhaps indicative of problems that have already been encountered. A backlash effect may well result, initiated by the many forces which, for various reasons, are hostile to aid programmes. Though the US Foreign Aid Act focussed on the need for US aid to reach the 'poor majority', a task force to the US State Department (Gordon 1977) has already concluded that it may be a wise policy for the World Bank to continue in sectors in which it has acquired a comparative advantage.

The search for more experimental project approaches is likely to be severely hampered by institutional characteristics of the Bank that have become more pronounced over the last decade. The growth in lending volume, the increasing bureaucratization of the Bank's staff structure and operational procedures, the persistent shortage of well-conceived project proposals, especially those expected to meet new design and impact criteria, and the increased need for external accountability and internal efficiency, are trends which are not conducive to innovation. On the contrary, they contribute to a work environment which induces widespread risk-avoiding behaviour of individuals. Moreover, attempts by the Bank to strengthen its control over the various stages of the project cycle and to re-establish cohesiveness of its own activities, may make it increasingly difficult to maintain a dialogue with recipient countries and may impede its creative and timely reaction to the dynamics of grass-roots organizations representing the target groups which the Bank tries to reach. Where self-help and local participation are essential preconditions for the success of sustained grass-roots development initiatives, a clash may arise with organizational demands that stress external reporting and accountability. Finally, the nature of an experimental project implies that one cannot really anticipate what will be required, as that has to be discovered once a start has been made in exploring actual needs. This has implications for the possibility of *ex ante* social cost-benefit analysis and project approval procedures which the Bank has yet to begin to appreciate.

BIBLIOGRAPHY

Adams, D.W. (1969): 'The Economics of Land Reform in Latin America and the Role of Aid Agencies' (Washington, Department of State, AID Discussion Paper 21; August).

—— (1970): 'Aid Agencies and Land Reform in Latin America: a Suggested Change in Policy', in: *Land Economics*, Vol. XLVI, No. 4, 423-34.

—— (1971): 'Agricultural Credit in Latin America; A Critical Review of External Funding Policy', in: *American Journal of Agricultural Economics*, Vol. 53, No. 2, 163-72.

—— (1973): 'The Economics of Land Reform', in: *Food Research Institute Studies in Agricultural Economics, Trade and Development*, Vol. XII, No. 2, 133-38.

—— (1978): 'Mobilizing Household Savings Through Rural Financial Markets', in: *Economic Development and Cultural Change*, Vol. 26, No. 3, 547-60.

Adams, D.W. & W. Coward Jr (1972): *Small Farmer Development Strategies: A Seminar Report* (New York: Agricultural Development Council).

Adelman, I. (1979): 'Redistribution Before Growth', in: *Development of Societies: The Next 25 Years* (The Hague, Martinus Nijhoff for the Institute of Social Studies), 160-76.

Adelman, I. & C.T. Morris (1971): 'An Anatomy of Income Distribution Patterns in Developing Countries', in: *Development Digest*, Vol. 9, No. 4, 24-37.

—— (1973): *Economic Growth and Social Equity in Developing Countries* (Stanford).

Adler, J.H. (1963): 'The Economic Development Institute of the World Bank', in: *The International Development Review*, Vol. V, No. 1.

—— (1966): 'What Have We Learned About Development?' in: *Finance and Development*, Vol. III, No. 3, 159-64.

—— (1971): 'Programming in the World Bank Group', in: Kaiser: *Planung VI* (Baden-Baden, Nomos Verlagsgesellschaft); also in: *Finance and Development*, Vol. 8, No. 2, 10-15.

—— (1972a): 'The World Bank's Concept of Development — An In-House Dogmengeschichte', in: J.N. Bhagwati & R.S. Eckaus (eds): *Development and Planning, Essays in Honour of Paul Rosenstein-Rodan* (London, Allen and Unwin).

—— (1972b): 'The Political Economy of Development With Social Justice' (Washington, October 7, mimeographed).

—— (1973): 'Development and Income Distribution', in: *Finance and Development*, Vol. 10, No. 3, 2-5; also in: *Weltwirtschaftlicher Archiv*, Band 108, Heft 3 (Tubingen, Mohr), 329-44.

Agency for International Development (1978): *Agricultural Development Policy Paper* (Washington DC, June).

—— (1978): 'A Strategy for a more Effective Bilateral Development Assistance Program' (Washington DC, AID Discussion Paper; March).

Ahluwalia, M.S. (1976a): 'Income Distribution and Development: Some Stylized Facts', in: *American Economic Review Papers and Proceedings* (May), 128-35.

—— (1976b): 'Inequality, Poverty and Development', in *Journal of Development Economics*, Vol. 3, No. 4, 307-42.

Ahmed, M. (1975): *The Economics of Non-Formal Education* (Praeger, New York).

Ahmed, M. & P.H. Coombs (eds) (1975): *Education for Rural Development: Case Studies For Planners* (New York, Praeger, for the World Bank and UNICEF).

Aluko, S.A. (1965): 'How Many Nigerians: An Analysis of Nigeria's Census Problems, 1901-1963', in: *The Journal of Modern African Studies*, Vol. III, No. 3, 371-92.

Asian Centre for Development Administration (1975): *Approaches to Rural Development in Asia: The South Asian Experience* (Kuala Lumpur), 3 Vols.

Asher, R.E. (1970): *Development Assistance in the Seventies, Alternatives for the United States* (Washington, The Brookings Institution).

—— (1971): 'Development Assistance in DDII', in: *International Organization*, Vol. 25, No. 1, 97-118.

Asher, R.E., et al (1957): *The United Nations and the Promotion of General Welfare* (Washington, The Brookings Institution).

Avramović, D. (1958): *Debt Servicing Capacity and Postwar Growth in International Indebtedness*, 1946-55 (Baltimore, Johns Hopkins for World Bank).

—— (1978): 'A Common Fund: Why and of What Kind?', in: *Journal of World Trade Law*, Vol. 12, No. 5, 375-408.

Avramović, D. & R. Gulhati (1960): *Debt Servicing Problems of Low-Income Countries 1956-58* (Baltimore, Johns Hopkins for World Bank).

Avramović, D., & Associates (1966): *Economic Growth and External Debt* (Baltimore, Johns Hopkins for World Bank).

Baer, W. (1976): 'The World Bank Group and the Process of Socio-Economic Development in the Third World', in: *World Development*, Vol. 2, No. 6, 1-10.

Baldwin, G.B. (1972): 'A Layman's Guide to Little/Mirrlees', in: *Finance and Development*, Vol. 9, No. 1, 16-21.

Bardhan, P.K. (1970): 'The Pattern of Income Distribution in India', in: T.N. Srinivasan & P.K. Bardhan (eds): *Poverty and Income Distribution in India* (Calcutta, Statistical Publishing Society), 103-38.

Barnaby, F. (1977): 'Arms and the Third World: the Background', in: *Development Dialogue*, No. 1, 18-30.

Barnett, T. (1977): *The Gezira Scheme; an Illusion of Development* (London, Frank Cass).

Barraclough, S. (1971): 'Farmers Organizations in Planning and Implementing Rural Development', in: Raanon Weitz (ed): *Rural Development in a Changing World* (Cambridge, Mass., MIT Press), 364-90.

—— (ed) (1973): *Agrarian Structures in Latin America; a Resumé of the CIDA Land Tenure Studies of Seven Latin American Countries* (Lexington, Lexington Books).

Barraclough, S.L. & A.L. Domike (1966): 'Agrarian Structure in Seven Latin American Countries', in: R. Stavenhagen (ed): *Agrarian Problems and Peasant Movements in Latin America* (New York, Anchor Books, Doubleday & Co., 1970), 41-97.

Basch, A. (1949): 'International Bank for Reconstruction and Development, 1944-1949: A Review', in: *International Conciliation*, No. 445 (Carnegy Endowment for International Peace; January), 791-827.

Baum, W.C. (1970): 'The Project Cycle', in: *Finance and Development*, Vol. 7, No. 2, 2-13.

Beckerman, W. (1977): 'Some Reflections on "Redistribution With Growth"', in: *World Development*, Vol. 5, No. 8, 665-76.

Beckman, B. (1976): *Organizing the Farmers: Cocoa Politics and National Development in Ghana* (Uppsala, Scandinavian Institute of African Studies).

Benor, D. & J.Q. Harrison (1977): *Agricultural Extension. The Training and Visit System* (Washington, World Bank; May).

Berlin, L.H. (1967): 'A New Agricultural Strategy in Latin America', in: *International Development Review* (September).

Bernstein, H. (1971): 'Modernization Theory and the Sociological Study of Development', in: *Journal of Development Studies*, Vol. 7, No. 2, 141-60.

Berteling, J. (1971): 'Totstandkoming Internationale Strategie DD-2', in: *Internationale Samenwerking*, Cahier No. 7 (The Hague, NOVIB).

Beyen, J.W. (1949): *Money in a Maelstrom*, Chapter X: 'The Bretton Woods Agreements' (New York, MacMillan).

Bhagwati, J.N. (1970): 'Amount and Sharing of Aid' (Washington, DC, Overseas Development Council, Monograph No. 2).

Bhagwati, J.N. & R.S. Eckaus (eds) (1970): *Foreign Aid: Selected Readings* (Harmondsworth Penguin Modern Economics Readings).

Bibliographic Information Bulletin on Selected National Experiences in Integrated Development of Predominantly Rural Areas (United Nations Secretariat, ESA/SDHA/Misc. 15, March 1976).

Bird, R.M. & L.H. de Wulf (1973): 'Taxation and Income Distribution in Latin America: a Critical Review of Empirical Studies', in: *IMF Staff Papers*, Vol. 20, No. 3, 639-82.

Bitterman, H.J. (1971): 'Negotiation of the Articles of Agreement of the International Bank for Reconstruction and Development', in: *The International Lawyer*, Vol. 5, No. 1, 59-88.

Black, E.R. (1971): 'Development Revisited', in: *The Virginia Quarterly Review*, Vol. 47, No. 1, 1-17.

Blaug, M. (1972): *An Introduction to the Economics of Education* (Harmondsworth, Penguin).

Bleicher, S.A. (1970): 'UN vs IBRD: a Dilemma of Functionalism', in: *International Organization*, Vol. XXIV, No. 1, 31-47.

Bose, S. (1974): 'The Comilla Co-operative Approach and the Prospects for Broad-Based Green Revolution in Bangladesh', in: *World Development*, Vol. 2, No. 8, 21-28.

Boserup, E. (1970): *Woman's Role in Economic Development* (London, Allen & Unwin).

Brown, L.R. (1970): *Seeds of Change: The Green Revolution in the 1970s* (New York, Praeger).

—— (1972): *World Without Borders* (New York, Random House).

Bruce, C. (1976): 'Social Cost-Benefit Analysis: A Guide for Country and Project Economists to the Derivation and Application of Economic and Social Accounting Prices' (World Bank Staff Working Paper No. 239; August).

Bruton, H.J. (1969): 'The Two Gap Approach to Aid and Development: Comment', in: *American Economic Review*, Vol. 59, No. 3, 439-46.

Buchanan, J.M. & G. Tullock (1962): *The Calculus of Consent* (Ann Arbor, University of Michigan Press).

Bunting, A.H. (ed) (1970): *Change in Agriculture* (London, Ducksworth).

Burns, T. & G.M. Stalker (1961): *The Management of Innovation* (London, Tavistock).

Byres, T.J. (ed) (1972): *Foreign Resources and Economic Development: A Symposium on the Report of the Pearson Commission* (London, Frank Cass).

Caiden, N. & A. Wildavsky (1974): *Planning and Budgeting in Poor Countries* (New York, Wiley).

Cairncross, A. (1959): 'The International Bank for Reconstruction and Development' (*Essays in International Finance, No. 33*; International Finance Section, Princeton University; March).

—— (1976): 'The Limitations of Shadow Rates', in: A. Cairncross & M. Puri (eds): *Employment, Income Distribution and Development Strategy: Problems of the Developing Countries. Essays in Honour of Hans Singer* (London, MacMillan).

Carlin, A. (1967): 'Project versus Program Aid: From the Donor's Viewpoint', in: *Economic Journal*, Vol. 77, 48-58.

Carter, N.G. (1973): 'A Handbook of Exported Values of Structural Characteristics' (World Bank, June; mimeographed).

Cavanagh, R.W. (1965): 'The Financial Structure of the World Bank', in: *Finance and Development*, Vol. II, No. 4, 217-22.

Chadenet, B. & J.A. King Jr (1972): 'What is "a World Bank Project"?', in: *Finance and Development*, Vol. 9, No. 3, 2-12.

Chambers, R. (1969): *Settlement Schemes in Tropical Africa* (New York, Praeger).

Chambers, R. & D. Belshaw (1973): *Managing Rural Development: Lessons and Methods from Eastern Africa* (Sussex, Institute of Development Studies).

Chenery, H.B., M.S. Ahluwalia, C.L.G. Bell, J.H. Duloy, R. Jolly (1974): *Redistribution with Growth* (London, Oxford University Press, for the World Bank and the Institute of Development Studies, University of Sussex).

Chenery, H.B. (1971): 'Growth and Structural Change', in: *Finance and Development*, Vol. 8, No. 3, 16-27.

Chenery, H.B. & N.G. Carter (1973): 'Foreign Assistance and Development Performance 1960-1970', in: *American Economic Review*, Vol. LXIII, No. 2, 459-68.

Chenery, H.B. & M. Strout (1966): 'Foreign Assistance and Economic Development', in: *American Economic Review*, Vol. LVI.

Chenery, H.B. & M. Syrquin (1975): *Patterns of Development 1950-70* (Oxford University Press).

'Chile and the World Bank' (1976) in: *Inter-American Economic Affairs*, Vol. 30, No. 2, 81-91.

Clay, L.D. (Chairman, Committee to Strengthen the Security of the Free World) (1963): 'The Scope and Distribution of US Military and Economic Assistance Programs' (Washington DC, Department of State, March).

Cliffe, L., et al (1968): 'An Interim Report on the Evaluation of Agricultural Extension' (Dar es Salaam, Rural Development Paper No. 5, University College).

Clifford, J. (1966): 'The Tying of Aid and the Problem of "Local Costs"', in: *The Journal of Development Studies*, Vol. 2, No. 2, 153-73.

Cline, W.R. & N.P. Sargen (1975): 'Performance Criteria and Multilateral Aid Allocation', in: *World Development*, Vol. 3, No. 6, 383-91.

Co-financing (1976): *Review of World Bank Activities* (December).

Cole, G.D.H. (1944): *A Century of Co-operation* (Manchester, Cooperative Union).

Collier, W., et al (1975): 'Tebasan System, High Yielding Varieties and Rural Change: an Example in Java', in: *Prisma, Indonesian Journal of Social and Economic Affairs*, Vol. I, No. 1, 17-31.

Collins, J.D. (1976): 'The Clandestine Movement of Groundnuts Across the Niger-Nigeria Boundary', in: *Canadian Journal of African Studies*, Vol. 10, No. 2, 259-78.

Committee for Economic Development (1969): 'Assisting Development in Low-Income Countries: Priorities for US Government Policy. A Statement on National Policy by the Research and Policy Committee' (New York, September).

Congressional Research Service (CRS): Library of Congress; see: Weaver et al, 1978.

Coombs, P.H. with M. Ahmed (1974): *Attacking Rural Poverty. How Non-Formal Education Can Help* (Baltimore, Johns Hopkins, for IBRD).

Coombs, P.H. & J. Hallak (1972): *Managing Educational Costs* (New York, Oxford University Press).

Cron, F.W. (1975): 'A Review of Highway Design Practices in Developing Countries' (World Bank, May).

Dalrymple, D.G. (1974a): *Development and Spread of High Yielding Varieties of Wheat and Rice in the Less Developed Nations* (US, Department of Agriculture).

—— (1974b): 'The Green Revolution, Past and Prospects' (Washington, USAID).

—— (1976): *Development and Spread of High-Yielding Varieties of Wheat and Rice in the Less Developed Countries* (US, Department of Agriculture in Cooperation with USAID; Foreign Agricultural Economic Report No. 95).

Dasgupta, B. (1977): *Agrarian Change and the New Technology in India* (Geneva, UNRISD).

Deboeck, G.J. (1978): 'Monitoring and Evaluation of Rural Development Projects: an Early Assessment of World Bank Experiences' (Paper prepared for the OECD Workshop on Experiences with Information Systems for Rural Development Projects, Paris, March 20-22).

The Declaration of Cocoyoc (1974) (Cocoyoc, Mexico).

Deely, R.E. (1966): 'World Bank Bonds in the World's Capital Markets', in: *Finance and Development*, Vol. III, No. 3, 179-85.

Diaz Alejandro, C.F. (1976): 'International Markets for Exhaustible Resources, Less Developed Countries and Transnational Corporations' (Yale University Economic Growth Centre, Centre Discussion Paper No. 256).

Diebold, P.B. (1966): 'How Planners Should View Land Reform', in: *Development Digest* (October).

Dorner, P. (1972): *Land Reform and Economic Development* (Harmondsworth, Penguin Modern Economic Texts).

Downs, A. (1966): *Inside Bureaucracy* (Boston, Little, Brown & Co.).

Dubey, M. (1977): 'The Future of the United Nations Development Programme', in: *Development Dialogue*, No. 1, 85-99.

Edelman, J.A. & H.B. Chenery (1977): 'Aid and Income Distribution', in: J.N. Bhagwati (ed): *The New International Economic Order: The North-South Debate* (Cambridge, Mass. MIT Press), 27-49.

Eisen, H. & J. White (1975): 'What Can a Country Do to Get More Aid?', in: *Bulletin of the Institute of Development Studies*, Vol. 6, No. 4, 65-84.

Eke, I. 1966): 'Population of Nigeria 1952-65', in: *Nigerian Journal of Economic and Social Studies*, Vol. VII, 289-310.

Faber, M. & D. Seers (eds) (1972): *The Crisis in Planning* (London, Sussex University Press, 2 Vols).

Falcon, W.P. (1970): 'The Green Revolution: Generations of Problems', in: *American Journal of Agricultural Economics*, Vol. 52, No. 5, 698-710.

Feder, E. (1970): 'Counterreform', in: R. Stavenhagen (ed): *Agrarian Problems and Peasant Movements in Latin America* (New York, Anchor Books, Doubleday & Co), 173-225.

Fei, J.C.H. & G. Ranis (1968): 'Foreign Assistance and Economic Development: Comment', in: *American Economic Review*, Vol. 58.

'Financing of Land Reform Programmes, Compensation Payments' (1966): in UN/FAO/ILO: *Progress in Land Reform* (Fourth Report; New York, United Nations).

'Food for a Growing World Population' (1976; Amsterdam, Free University, Economic and Social Institute).

'Foreign Aid: Evading the Control of Congress' (1977) in: *International Policy Report* (Vol. 3, No. 1; Washington DC, Center for International Policy).

Foster, G.M. (1962): *Traditional Culture and the Impact of Technological Change* (New York, Harper & Row).

Frank, C.R., Jr & W.R. Cline (1969): 'Debt Servicing and Foreign Assistance: an Analysis of Problems and Prospects in Less Developed Countries' (Department of State, Agency for International Development, Discussion Paper No. 19).

Freebairn, D.K. (1973): 'Income Disparities in the Agricultural Sector: Regional and Institutional Stresses', in: T. Poleman & D.K. Freebairn (eds): *Food, Population and Employment: The Impact of the Green Revolution* (New York, Praeger, for Cornell University), 97-119.

Friedman, E. (1978): 'The World Bank's Energy Activities' (Washington, World Bank, May).

Friedman, I.S. (1974): 'Review of Mason & Asher, *The World Bank Since Bretton Woods*', in: *Finance and Development*, Vol. II, No. 1, 36-37.

Gaitskell, A. (1959): *Gezira: A Story of Development in the Sudan* (London, Faber).

General Accounting Office (1973): 'More Effective US Participation Needed in World Bank and International Development Association' (Washington, B-161470).

Ghai, D.P., et al (1977): *The Basic Needs Approach to Development. Some Issues Regarding Concepts and Methodology* (Geneva, ILO).

Gittinger, J.P. (1972): *Economic Analysis of Agricultural Projects* (Baltimore, Johns Hopkins).

Gold, J. (1970): *Special Drawing Rights, Character and Use* (IMF Pamphlet Series, No. 13).

Gold, S.S. (1976): 'The Shifting Emphasis on Macro- and Micro-Levels in Development Planning, The IBRD Experience, 1946-1973', in: *Journal of Developing Areas*, Vol. 11, No. 1, 13-38.

Gordon, L.E., et al (1977): *An Assessment of Development Assistance Strategies* (Washington, The Brookings Institution; mimeographed; Interim Report submitted to the Department of State).

Gordon, R.A. (1976): 'Rigor and Relevance in a Changing Institutional Setting', in: *American Economic Review*, Vol. 66, No. 1, 1-14.

Gotsch, C.H. (1972): 'Technical Change and the Distribution of Income in Rural Areas', in: *American Journal of Agricultural Economics*, Vol. 5, No. 2, 326-41.

Griffin, K. (1976): *Land Concentration and Rural Poverty* (London, MacMillan).

Gulhati, R.I. (1972): 'The Question of India's External Debt', in: *India Quarterly*, Vol. XXVIII, No. 1, 2-11.

Gulhati, R.I. & W. Diamond (1973): 'Some Reflections on the World Bank's Experience with Development Finance Companies', in: *Economic and Political Weekly*, 'Review of Management', Vol. VIII, No. 23, M 47-56.

Haan, R.L. (1971): *An Inquiry into the Monetary Aspects of a Link Between Special Drawing Rights and Development Finance* (Leyden, Stenfert Kroese).

Habermeier, W. (1973): *Operations and Transactions in SDRs. The First Basic Period* (IMF Pamphlet Series, No. 17).

Hadwen, J.G. & J. Kaufman (1960): *How United Nations Decisions Are Made* (Leyden, Sijthoff).

Halberstam, D. (1973): *The Best and the Brightest* (New York, Fawcett Edition).

Haq, M. ul (1967): 'Tied Credits – A Quantitative Analysis', in: J.H. Adler (ed): *Capital Movements and Economic Development; Proceedings of a Conference of the IAE* (London, MacMillan).

—— (1972): 'The Crisis in Development Strategies' (Paper for the International Development Conference, April 19-21, 1972; Washington DC), mimeographed.

—— (1976): *The Poverty Curtain: Choices for the Third World* (New York, Columbia University Press).

Harberger, A.C. (1968): *Survey on Literature on Cost-Benefit Analysis: Evaluation of Industrial Projects* (New York, UNIDO).

Hawkins, E.K. (1970): *The Principles of Development Aid* (Harmondsworth, Penguin Books).

Hayami, Y. & V.W. Ruttan (1971): *Agricultural Development: An International Perspective* (Baltimore, Johns Hopkins).

Hayter, T. (1971): *Aid as Imperialism* (Harmondsworth, Penguin Books).

Hazzard, S. (1973): *Defeat of an Ideal. A Study of the Self-Destruction of the United Nations* (London, MacMillan).

Healey, J.M. (1971): *The Economics of Aid* (London, Routledge & Kegan Paul).

Heilbroner, R.L. (1974): *An Inquiry into the Human Prospect* (New York, Norton).

Helleiner, G.K. (ed) (1976): *A World Divided: the Less Developed Countries in the International Economy* (Cambridge, Cambridge University Press).

Henderson, P.D. (1968): 'Investment Criteria for Public Enterprises', in: R. Turvey (ed): *Public Enterprise* (Harmondsworth, Penguin Modern Economic Readings).

—— (1971): 'The Distribution of Official Development Assistance Commitments by Recipient Countries and by Sources', in: *Bulletin of the Oxford University Institute of Economics and Statistics*, Vol. 33, No. 1.

Herdt, R.W., A. Te & R. Barker (1978): 'The Prospects for Asian Rice Production' (Los Baños).

Hicks, N.L. (1976): 'A Model of Trade and Growth for the Developing World', in: *European Economic Review*, Vol. 7, No. 3, 239-55.

Hicks, N.L., et al (1975): *The SIMLINK Model of Trade and Growth for the Developing World* (IBRD Staff Working Papers No. 220).

Hirschman, A.O. (1967): *Development Projects Observed* (Washington DC, The Brookings Institution).

—— (1970): *Exit, Voice and Loyalty* (Cambridge Mass., Harvard University Press).

—— (1973): 'The Changing Tolerance for Income Inequality in the Course of Economic Development', in: *Quarterly Journal of Economics*, Vol. LXXXVII, No. 4 (November).

Hirschman, A.O. & R.M. Bird (1968): 'Foreign Aid – a critique and a proposal' (*Essays in International Finance*, No. 69, International Finance Section, Princeton).

Holsen, J. & J. Waelbroeck (1976): 'LDC Balance of Payments Policies and the International Monetary System' (World Bank Staff Working Paper No. 226).

Holtham, G. & A. Hazlewood (1976): *Aid and Inequality in Kenya: British Development Assistance to Kenya* (London, Croom Helm in association with the Overseas Development Institute).

Hopkins, M.J.D. & H. Scolnik: 'Basic Needs, Growth and Redistribution: a quantitative approach', in: Tripartite World Conference on Employment Income Distribution and Social Progress and the International Division of Labour: *Background Papers*, Vol. 1, 9-50.

Hornstein, R.A. (1977): 'Cofinancing of Bank and IDA Projects', in: *Finance and Development*, Vol. 14, No. 2, 36-39.

Howard, J.B., et al (1977): *The Impact of International Organizations on Legal and Institutional Change in the Developing Countries* (New York, International Legal Center).

Howe, J.W., et al (1975): *The US and World Development Agenda for Action* (New York, Praeger, for the Overseas Development Council).

Hughes, H. (ed) (1973): *Prospects for Partnership. Industrialization and Trade Policies in the 1970s*, Seminar held at IBRD, October 5-6, 1972 (Baltimore, Johns Hopkins).

Hunter, G. (1970): *The Administration of Agricultural Development: Lessons From India* (London, Oxford University Press).

—— (1973): 'Agricultural Administration and Institutions', in: *Food Research Institute in Agricultural Economics, Trade and Development*, Vol. XII, No. 3, 233-51.

Hunter, G., A.H. Bunting & A. Bottrall (eds) (1976): *Policy and Practice in Rural Development* (London, Croom Helm with ODI).

Huntington, S.P. (1970-71): 'Aid: For What and For Whom?', in: *Foreign Policy*, No. 1 (Winter 1970-71); and No. 2 (Spring 1971).

International Cooperative Alliance (1967): *Report of the ICA Commission on Cooperative Principles* (London).

ILO (1971): *Matching Employment Opportunities and Expectations: a report on Ceylon* (Geneva).

—— (1972): *Employment, Incomes and Equality: a Strategy for Increasing Productive Employment in Kenya* (Geneva).

—— (1976): *Background Papers*, Vol. I: *Basic Needs and National Employment Strategies*; Vol. II: *International Strategies for Employment*.

—— (1976): *Employment, Growth and Basic Needs: a One-World Problem* (Report of the Director-General of the International Labour Office, Geneva).

—— (1977): *Poverty and Landlessness in Rural Asia* (Geneva).

Isenman, P. (1976): 'Biases in Aid Allocations Against Poorer and Larger Countries', in: *World Development*, Vol. 4, No. 8, 631-41.

Islam, N. (1978): *Development Strategy of Bangladesh* (Oxford, Pergamon Press).

Israel, A. (1978): 'Toward Better Project Implementation', in: *Finance and Development*, Vol. 15, No. 1, 27-30.

Jackson, Sir R. (1969): *A Study of the Capacity of the United Nations Development System* (Geneva, UN).

Jain, S. (1975): *Size Distribution of Income: a Compilation of Data* (Baltimore, Johns Hopkins).

Jencks, C. (1975): *Inequality* (Harmondsworth, Penguin Books).

Johnston, B.F. (1970): 'Agriculture and Structural Transformation in Developing Countries: A Survey of Research', in: *Journal of Economic Literature*, Vol. 8, No. 2, 369-404.

Johnston, B.F. & P. Kilby (1975): *Agriculture and Structural Transformation. Economic Strategies in Late-Developing Countries* (New York, Oxford University Press).

Johri, C.K. & S.M. Pandey (1978); 'Dimensions of Poverty and Incomes Policy', in: *Indian Journal of Industrial Relations*, Vol. 14, No. 1, 1-44.

Jones, N.G. (1967): 'Disbursing World Bank Loans', in: *Finance and Development*, Vol. IV, No. 1, 51-55.

Joshi, V. (1970): 'Saving and Foreign Exchange Constraints', in: P. Streeten (ed): *Unfashionable Economics (Essays in Honour of Lord Balogh)* (London, Weidenfeld & Nicolson), 111-33.

Kamarck, A.M. (1967): 'The Financial Experience of Lenders and Investors', in: J.H. Adler (ed): *Capital Movements and Economic Development* (London, MacMillan), 71-128.

—— (1970): 'The Appraisal of Country Economic Performance', in: *Economic Development and Cultural Change*, Vol. 18, No. 2, 153-65.

—— (1971): ' "Capital" and "Investment" in Developing Countries', in: *Finance and Development*, Vol. 8, No. 2, 2-9.

—— (1972): 'The Allocation of Aid by the World Bank Group', in: *Finance and Development*, Vol. 9, No. 3, 22-29.

Khan, A.M. (1972): *Tour of Twenty Thanas* (Comilla, BARD).
—— (1974): 'Reflections on the Comilla Rural Development Projects' (Overseas Liaison Committee, Paper No. 3, American Council on Education).
Khan, O. & J. Hexner (1976): *Poverty Oriented Rural Development and the UN System* (New York, for the Administrative Committee on Coordination).
Killick, T. (1976): 'The Possibilities of Development Planning', in: *Oxford Economic Papers*, Vol. 28, No. 2, 161-84.
King, J.A. (1967): *Economic Development Projects and their Appraisal: Cases and Principles from the Experience of the World Bank* (Baltimore, Johns Hopkins, for IBRD).
—— (1972): 'The World Bank, Project Lending and Cooperatives', in: *Finance and Development*, Vol. 9, No. 1, 30-35.
—— (1974): 'Reorganizing the World Bank', in: *Finance and Development*, Vol. 11, No. 1, 5-8, 34.
Klein, T.M. (1973): 'Economic Aid Through Debt Relief', in: *Finance and Development*, Vol. 10, No. 3, 17-20, 34.
Knorr, K. (1948): 'The Bretton Woods Institutions in Transition', in: *International Organization*, Vol. II, No. 1, 19-38.
Koenig, N. (1967): 'The Technical Assistance and Preinvestment Activities of the World Bank', in: *Finance and Development*, Vol. IV, No. 3, 202-208.
Kolko, G. (1975): 'The United States Effort to Mobilise World Bank Aid to Saigon', in: *Journal of Contemporary Asia*, Vol. 5, No. 1, 42-52.
Kravis, I.B., A. Heston & R. Summers (1978): *International Comparisons of Real Product and Purchasing Power* (Baltimore, Johns Hopkins).
Kravis, I.B., Z. Kenessey, A. Heston & R. Summers (1975): *A System of International Comparisons of Gross Product and Purchasing Power* (Baltimore, Johns Hopkins).
Kuznets, S. (1955): 'Economic Growth and Income Inequality', in: *American Economic Review*, Vol. 45, 1-27.
—— (1963): 'Quantitative Aspects of the Economic Growth of Nations: Distribution of Income by Size', in: *Economic Development and Cultural Change*, Part 2, Vol. 11, No. 2, 1-80.
—— (1972): 'Problems in Comparing Recent Growth Rates for Developed and Less Developed Countries', in: *Economic Development and Cultural Change*, Vol. 20, No. 2, 185-209.
van de Laar, A.J.M. (1970): *Report of an Evaluation Survey of University Level Manpower Supply and Demand in Selected African Countries* (Addis Ababa, UN Economic Commission for Africa; E/CN.14/WP.6/32).
—— (1971): 'Education and Employment in Anglophone Africa', in: *Kroniek van Afrika*, No. 4, 230-43.
—— (1973): 'Toward a Manpower Planning Strategy in Tanzania', in: L. Cliffe & J.S. Saul (eds): *Socialism in Tanzania*, Vol. II, *Policies* (Dar es Salaam), 224-46.
—— (1975): 'The Young Professionals Programme of the World Bank: an Analysis of an Elite Group', in: *Development and Change*, Vol. VI, No. 3, 5-26.
—— (1976a): 'The World Bank: Which Way?', in: *Development and Change*, Vol. 7, No. 1, 67-97.
—— (1976b): 'The International Development Association' (ISS *Occasional Paper*, No. 56).
—— (1976c): 'The World Bank and the World's Poor', in: *World Development*, Vol. 4, Nos. 10-11, 837-51.
Lachman, A.E. (1968): *The Local Currency Proceeds of Foreign Aid* (Paris, OECD Development Centre).
Ladejinsky, W. (1970): 'Ironies of India's Green Revolution', in: *Foreign Affairs*, Vol. 48, No. 4, 758-68.
Lal, D. (1974): *Methods of Project Analysis: a Review* (Baltimore and London, Johns Hopkins for the World Bank).
—— (1976): 'Distribution and Development: A Review Article', in: *World Development*, Vol. 4, No. 9, 725-38.
Lawrence, P.R. & J.W. Lorsch (1967): *Organization and Environment: Managing Differentiation and Integration* (Boston, Harvard University Graduate School of Business Administration).

Lele, U. (1975): *The Design of Rural Development, Lessons from Africa* (Baltimore, Johns Hopkins for the World Bank).

Lewis, J.P. (1962): *Crisis in India* (Washington, Brookings Institution).

Lewis, J.P. & I. Kapur (eds) (1973): *The World Bank Group, Multilateral Aid and the 1970s* (Lexington, Lexington Books, DC Heath & Co.).

Leys, C. (1975a): 'The Politics of Redistribution With Growth', in: *IDS Bulletin*, Vol. 7, No. 2, 4-8.

—— (1975b): *Underdevelopment in Kenya: The Political Economy of Neo-Colonialism* (London, Heinemann).

Lindblom, C.E. (1973): 'The Science of "Muddling Through"', in: *Public Administration Review* (Spring 1959), Reprinted in A. Fuladi (ed): *A Reader in Planning Theory* (Pergamon Press).

Lipson, C.H. (1976): 'Corporate Preferences and Public Policies: Foreign Aid Sanctions and Investment Protection', in: *World Politics*, Vol. XXVIII, No. 3, 396-421.

Lipton, M. (1974): 'Towards a Theory of Land Reform', in: D. Lehman (ed): *Agrarian Reform and Agrarian Reformism* (London, Faber & Faber).

—— (1976): 'Agricultural Finance and Rural Credit in Poor Countries', in: *World Development*, Vol. 4, No. 7, 543-53.

—— (1979): 'The Technology, The System and The Poor: the Case of the New Cereal Varieties', in: *Development of Societies: The Next 25 Years* (The Hague, Martinus Nijhoff for the Institute of Social Studies), 121-35.

Lipton, M. & J. Firn (1975): *The Erosion of a Relationship. India and Britain Since 1960* (London, Oxford University Press).

Little, I.M.D. & J.M. Clifford (1965): *International Aid* (London, Allen & Unwin).

Little, I.M.D. & J.A. Mirrlees (1974): *Manual of Industrial Project Analysis in Developing Countries*, Vol. II, *Social Cost-Benefit Analysis* (Paris, OECD Development Centre, 1968). A revised version published as *Project Appraisal and Planning for Developing Countries* (London, Heinemann, 1974).

Little, I.M.D., T. Scitovsky & M. Scott (1970): *Industry and Trade in Some Developing Countries: a Comparative Study* (London, Oxford University Press, for OECD).

Long, C.D. (Chairman) (1978): *Hearings* (House of Representatives, 95th Congress, 2nd Session, Part 1).

Maddison, A. (1965): *Foreign Skills and Technical Assistance in Economic Development* (Paris, OECD, Development Centre Studies).

Marris, R. (1970): 'Can We Measure the Need for Development Assistance?', in: *Economic Journal*, Vol. 80, 650-67.

Marx, K. & F. Engels (1967 ed): *The Communist Manifesto*, With an Introduction by A.J.P. Taylor (Harmondsworth, Penguin Books).

Mason, E.S. (1960): 'Foreign Money We Can't Spend', in: *The Atlantic Monthly*.

—— (1966): *Economic Development in India and Pakistan* (Harvard University Centre for International Affairs, Occasional Papers in International Affairs, No. 13).

Mason, E.S., et al (1960): 'The Problem of Excess Accumulation of US-owned Local Currencies' (Findings and recommendations submitted to the Under-Secretary of State, Washington).

Mason, E.S. & R.E. Asher (1973): *The World Bank Since Bretton Woods* (Washington, The Brookings Institution).

Mathur, K. (1975): 'Administrative Institutions, Political Capacity and India's Strategy For Rural Development', in: *Approaches to Rural Development in Asia: the South Asian Experience*, Vol. III (Kuala Lumpur, Asian Centre for Development Administration).

Maynard, G. (1973): 'Special Drawing Rights and Development Aid', in: *The Journal of Development Studies*, Vol. 9, No. 4, 518-43.

McCloy, J.J. (1949): 'The Lesson of the World Bank', in: *Foreign Affairs*, Vol. 27, No. 4, 551-60.

McInerney, J.P. & G.F. Donaldson (1975): 'The Consequences of Farm Tractors in Pakistan' (World Bank, Development Economics Department, Bank Staff Working Paper No. 210).

McKitterick, W.T. & B. Jenkins Middleton (1972): *The Bankers of the Rich and the Bankers of the Poor; the Role of Export Credit in Development Finance* (Washington, Overseas Development Council).

McNamara, R.S. (1969): *Address to the Board of Governors* (Washington, September 29).

—— (1973a): *Address to the Board of Governors* (Nairobi, September 24).

—— (1973b): *One Hundred Countries, Two Billion People* (New York, Praeger).

—— (1976): *Address to the Board of Governors* (Manila, October 4).

—— (1977): *A Proposal to Reach a Break-through in the Development Cooperation* (Address on the occasion of receiving the World Affairs Council Christian A. Herter Memorial Award, Boston, January 4).

—— (1978): *Address to the Board of Governors* (Washington, September 25).

Measures for the Economic Development of Underdeveloped Countries (1951) (New York, UN Department of Economic Affairs).

Mellor, J.W. (1976): *The New Economics of Growth: A Strategy for India and the Developing World* (Ithaca & London, Cornell University Press).

Mellor, J.W., T.F. Weaver, U.J. Lele & S.R. Simon (1968): *Developing Rural India: Plan and Practice* (Ithaca, Cornell University Press).

Mensah, J.H. (1973): 'Some Unpleasant Truths About Debt and Development', in: *Development Dialogue*, No. 1, 3-16.

Merriam, J.E. (1977): 'Banging the Bank Around', in: *Bank Notes of the World Bank* (April).

Mikesell, R.F. (1968): *The Economics of Foreign Aid* (Chicago, Aldine Publishing Co.).

Mikesell, R.F. & J.E. Zinser (1973): 'The Nature of the Savings Function in Developing Countries', in: *Journal of Economic Literature*, Vol. XI, No. 1, 1-26.

Ministry of Overseas Development (1975): 'Overseas Development: The Changing Emphasis in British Aid Policies: More Help to the Poorest' (London, HMSO).

Montgomery, J.D. (1972): 'Allocation of Authority in Land Reform Programs: a Comparative Study of Administrative Processes and Outputs', in: *Administrative Science Quarterly*, Vol. 17, No. 1, 62-75.

Montrie, C. (1973): 'The Organization and Functions of Foreign Aid', and A.O. Hirschman: 'Reply to Mr. Montrie', in: *Economic Development and Cultural Change*, Vol. 21, No. 4, Part I, 697-716.

Moore, F.T. (1960): 'The World Bank and its Economic Missions', in: *The Review of Economics and Statistics*, Vol. XLII, 81-93.

Moran, T.H. (1973): 'Transnational Strategies of Protection and Defence by Multinational Corporations: spreading the risk and raising the cost for nationalization in natural resources', in: *International Organization*, Vol. 27, No. 2, 273-87.

—— (1974): *Multinational Corporations and the Politics of Dependence: Copper in Chile* (Princeton University Press).

Morgan Stanley & Co. & The First Boston Corporation (1973): *World Bank, International Bank for Reconstruction and Development: A Financial Appraisal* (New York).

Morgenstern, O. (1963): *On the Accuracy of Economic Observations* (Princeton University Press).

Morris, J. (1963): *The Road to Huddersfield. A Journey to Five Continents* (New York, Pantheon).

Morss, E.R., J.K. Hatch, D.R. Mickelwait & C.F. Sweet (1976): *Strategies for Small Farmer Development: An Empirical Study of Rural Development Projects in The Gambia, Ghana, Kenya, Lesotho, Nigeria, Bolivia, Colombia, Mexico, Paraguay and Peru* (Boulder, Westview Press Inc.).

Muda Study (1975): Vol. I text; Vol. II Statistical Tables (Rome, FAO/World Bank Cooperative Program).

Myrdal, G. (1968): *Asian Drama*, 3 Vols (Harmondsworth, Penguin).

—— (1970): *The Challenge of World Poverty. A World Anti-Poverty Program in Outline* (Harmondsworth, Penguin).

Nafziger, E.W. (1976): 'A Critique of Development Economics in the US', in: *Journal of Development Studies*, Vol. 13, No. 1, 18-34.

National Planning Association (1969): *A New Conception of U.S. Foreign Aid* (Washington, DC, Special Report No. 64).

Nekby, B. (1971): *CADU: An Ethiopian Experiment in Developing Peasant Farming* (Stockholm, Prisma Publishers).

Nelson, M. (1973): *The Development of Tropical Lands: Policy Issues in Latin America* (Baltimore, Johns Hopkins, for Resources for the Future Inc.)

Netherlands Economic Institute (1961): *The Need for Pre-investment Activities in the Newly-Developing Countries* (Rotterdam).

Nieuwenhuize, J., et al (1974): *Investeringen van de Wereldbank in de landbouw, en haar 'strijd' tegen de armoede in Malawi* (Wageningen, De Uitbuyt).

Niskanen, W.A. (1968): 'Non-Market Decision Making: The Peculiar Economics of Bureaucracy', in: *American Economic Review*, Vol. 58, No. 2, 293-305.

Nixon, R.M. (1970): *Foreign Assistance for the 'Seventies'* (Message to Congress, 15 September).

Nsekela, A.J. (1977): 'De Wereldbank en de Nieuwe Internationale Economische Orde', in: *Internationale Samenwerking*, Vol. 10, No. 8, 350-56; also in: *Development Dialogue* (1977) No. 1, 75-84.

OECD (Annual): *Development Assistance: Efforts and Policies of the Members of the Development Assistance Committee* (Paris).

—— (Annual): *Development Co-operation* (Paris).

—— (1967): *The Flow of Financial Resources to Less Developed Countries 1961-65* (Paris).

—— (1973): *Performance Compendium – Consolidated Results of Analytical Work on Economic and Social Performance of Developing Countries* (Paris).

Ohlin, G. (1966): *Foreign Aid Policies Reconsidered* (Paris, OECD).

—— (1976): 'Debts, Development and Default', in: G.K. Helleiner (ed): *A World Divided. The Less Developed Countries in the International Economy* (Cambridge University Press).

Oliver, R.W. (1971): *Early Plans for a World Bank* (Princeton Studies in International Finance No. 29).

—— (1975): *International Economic Cooperation and the World Bank* (London, MacMillan).

Olson Jr, M. (1968): *The Logic of Collective Action: Public Goods and the Theory of Groups* (New York, Schocken Books).

'An Overall Evaluation of the Special Rural Development Programme 1972' (Nairobi, IDS, Occasional Paper No. 8).

Owens, E. & R. Shaw (1972): *Development Reconsidered* (Lexington, Mass.).

Palmer, I. (1976): *The New Rice in Asia: Conclusions from four country studies* (Geneva, UNRISD).

Park, Y.S. (1973): 'The Link Between Special Drawing Rights and Development Finance', *Essays in International Finance*, No. 100 (Princeton University, International Finance Section).

Paukert, F. (1973): 'Income Distribution at Different Levels of Development: a Survey of Evidence', in: *International Labour Review*, Vol. 108, Nos 2-3, 97-125.

Pearse, A. (1970): 'Agrarian Change Trends in Latin America', in: R. Stavenhagen (ed): *Agrarian Problems and Peasant Movements in Latin America* (New York, Anchor Books, Doubleday & Co), 11-41.

—— (1977): 'Technology and Peasant Production: Reflections on a Global Study', in: *Development and Change*, Vol. 8, No. 2, 125-59.

Pearson, L.B. (Chairman) (1969): *Partners in Development. Report of the Commission on International Development* (London, Pall Mall).

Perkins, D. (Chairman, President's General Advisory Committee on Foreign Assistance Programs) (1968): *Development Assistance in the New Administration* (Washington, USAID).

Perroux, F. (1961): *L'économie de XXème Siècle* (Paris, Press Universitaire).

Peterson, R.A. (Chairman, Task Force on International Development) (1970): 'US Foreign Assistance in the 1970s: a New Approach', Report to the President (Washington, US Government Printing Office).

Pincus, J. (1965): *Economic Aid and International Cost Sharing* (Baltimore, Johns Hopkins).

Please, S. & L.E. Christoffersen (1969): *Value-Linking of Financial Contracts* (IBRD, Economic Staff Papers).

Poleman, T.T. (1973): 'Food and Population in Historical Perspective', Chapter 1 in: T.T. Poleman & D.K. Freebairn (1973), 3-18.

Poleman, T.T. & D.K. Freebairn (eds) (1973): *Food, Population and Employment. The Impact of the Green Revolution* (New York, Praeger for Cornell).

Prest, A.R. & R. Turvey (1966): 'Cost-Benefit Analysis', in: *Surveys of Economic Theory*, Vol. III (London, MacMillan).

Proceedings and Documents of the United Nations Monetary and Financial Conference, Bretton Woods (1944) (Washington, U.S. Government Printer).

Prosterman, R.L. (1966): 'Land Reform in Latin America: How to Have a Revolution Without a Revolution', in: *Washington Law Review* (October), 189-211.

Pyatt, G. & E. Thorbecke (1976): *Planning Techniques for a Better Future* (Geneva, ILO).

Rahim, S.A. (1972): *A Comparison of Comilla and Chandina Thanas* (Comilla, BARD).

Raper, A.F. (1970): *Rural Development in Action* (Ithaca, Cornell University Press).

Raup, P.M. (1967): 'Land Reform and Agricultural Development', in: Y.M. Southworth & B.F. Johnston (eds): *Agricultural Development and Economic Growth* (Ithaca, Cornell University Press).

Reid, E. (1965): *The Future of the World Bank. An Essay* (Washington, IBRD).

—— (1973a): 'McNamara's World Bank', in: *Foreign Affairs*, Vol. 51, No. 4, 794-810.

—— (1973b): *Strengthening the World Bank* (Chicago, The Adlai Stevenson Institute).

Repetto, R.C. (1969): 'Economic Aspects of Irrigation Project Design in East Pakistan', *Economic Development Report* No. 123 (Cambridge, Mass., Harvard University).

Rice, A.E. (ed) (1972): *International Development. Development Targets for the 70's: Jobs and Justice.* 12th World Conference of the Society for International Development, Ottawa (May) (New York, Oceana Publications).

Rice, E.B. (1974): *Extension in the Andes: An Evaluation of Official U.S. Assistance to Agricultural Extension Services in Central and South America* (Cambridge and London, The MIT Press).

Richards, P. (1976): 'Poverty, Unemployment and Underemployment', in: ILO: *Tripartite World Conference on Employment, Income Distribution and Social Progress and the International Division of Labour.* Background papers, Vol. I, *Basic Needs and National Employment Strategies* (Geneva).

Ripman, H.B. (1973): 'Project Supervision', in: *Finance and Development*, Vol. 10, No. 2, 14-18.

Rockefeller, N.A. (1969): *The Rockefeller Report on the Americas. The Official Report of a United States Presidential Mission for the Western Hemisphere* (Chicago, Quadrangle Books).

Rogers, E.M., J.R. Ashcroft & N.G. Röling (1970): *Diffusion of Innovations in Brazil, Nigeria and India* (East Lansing, Michigan State University).

Rondinelli, D.A. & K. Ruddle (1976): *Urban Functions in Rural Development: an Analysis of Integrated Spatial Development Policy,* for Office of Urban Development, Technical Assistance Bureau, AID, US Department of State (New York, Syracuse).

Rosenstein-Rodan, P.N. (1961): 'International Aid for Underdeveloped Countries', in: *The Review of Economics and Statistics*, Vol. 43, No. 2, 107-38.

—— (1969): 'Criteria for Evaluation of National Development Effort', in: *Journal of Development Planning*, No. 1, 1-13.

Rostow, W.W. (1952): *The Process of Economic Growth* (New York, Oxford University Press).

Rostow, W.W. (ed) (1963): *The Economics of Take-Off into Sustained Growth* (London, MacMillan).

Rotberg, E.H. (1976): *The World Bank: A Financial Appraisal* (Washington, World Bank).

Ruttan, V.W. (1975): 'Integrated Rural Development Programs: A Skeptical Perspective', in: *International Development Review*, Vol. XVII, No. 4, 9-16.

Ruttan, V.W. & Y. Hayami (1972): 'Strategies for Agricultural Development', in: *Food Research Institute Studies in Agricultural Economics, Trade and Development*, Vol. XI, No. 2, 129-48.

Sacchetti, U. (1973): 'Financial Aspects of Development Institutions', in: *Economic Notes* (Montedei Paschi di Siena Bank) Vol. 2, No. 1, 19-50.

Sachs, I. (1964): *Patterns of Public Sector in Underdeveloped Economies* (Bombay, Asia Publishing House).

Sanford, J. (1977): 'US Policy and the Multilateral Banks: Politicization and Effectiveness' (Staff Report to the Sub-Committee on Foreign Assistance of the Committee on Foreign Relations, US Senate; Washington, US Government Printing Office).

Schultz, T.W. (1951): 'A Framework for Land Economics – The Long View', in: *Journal of Farm Economics*, Vol. 33, 204-15.

Schumpeter, J.A. (1963): *History of Economic Analysis* (New York, Oxford University Press).

Seers, D. (1962): 'Why Visiting Economists Fail', in: *Journal of Political Economy*, Vol. LXX, No. 4, 325-38.

—— (1963): 'The Limitations of the Special Case', in: *Institute of Economics and Statistics Bulletin*, Vol. 25, No. 2, 77-98.

—— (1970): *The Meaning of Development* (Geneva, International Institute for Labour Studies).

—— (1976): 'The Political Economy of National Accountancy', in: A. Cairncross & M. Puri (eds): *Employment, Income Distribution and Development Strategy: Problems of the Developing Countries. Essays in Honour of H.W. Singer* (London, MacMillan).

Sewell, J.P. (1966): *Functionalism and World Politics* (New Jersey, Princeton University Press).

Shanin, T. (ed) (1971): *Peasants and Peasant Societies* (Harmondsworth, Penguin Modern Sociology Readings).

Shaw, R. d'A. (1970): *Jobs and Agricultural Development* (Washington, Overseas Development Council, Monograph No. 3).

Shultz, G.P., Secretary of the Treasury (1973): 'Statement Before the Sub-Committee on International Finance of the Banking and Currency Committee of the House of Representatives on Replenishment of the International Development Association and of the Asian Development Bank' (Washington).

Siffin, W.J. (1972): 'The Institution Building Perspective: Properties, Problems and Promise', in: D. Woods Thomas et al: *Institution Building: A Model for Applied Social Change* (Cambridge, Mass.,Schenkman).

Simmons, J. (1976): 'Retention of Cognitive Skills Acquired in Primary School', in: *Comparative Education Review*, Vol. 20, No. 1, 79-93.

Sinaga, R. & W.L. Collier (1975): 'Social and Regional Implications of Agricultural Development Policy', in: *Prisma, Indonesian Journal of Social and Economic Affairs*, Vol. I, No. 2, 24-36.

Singer, H.W. (1965): 'External Aid: For Plans or Projects?', in: *Economic Journal*, Vol. 75, 539-45.

Speight, J.F. (1973): 'Community Development Theory and Practice: A Machiavellian Perspective', in: *Rural Sociology*, Vol. 38, No. 4, 477-90.

Spring Review of Small Farmer Credit (1973), 20 Vols. February-June (Washington, USAID).

Squire, L. & H.G. van der Tak (1975): *Economic Analysis of Projects* (Baltimore, Johns Hopkins for World Bank).

Srinivasan, T.N. (1972): The State of Development Economics (mimeographed), 25.

Srinivasan, T.N. & P.K. Bardhan (eds) (1974): *Poverty and Income Distribution in India* (Calcutta, Statistical Publishing Society).

Stevens, R.D. (1974): 'Three Rural Development Models for Small-Farm Agricultural Areas in Low-Income Countries', in: *The Journal of Developing Areas*, Vol. 8, No. 3, 409-20.

Stewart, F. & P. Streeten (1976): 'New Strategies for Development: Poverty, Income Distribution and Growth', in: *Oxford Economic Papers*, Vol. 28, No. 3, 381-405.

Stolper, W. (1966): *Planning Without Facts* (Cambridge, Mass.).

Streeten, P. (1972): *The Frontiers of Development Theory* (London, MacMillan).

Streeten, P. & M. Lipton (1968): 'Two Types of Planning', in: P. Streeten & M. Lipton (eds): *The Crisis of Indian Planning* (Oxford University Press).

Streeten, P. & M. ul Haq (1977): 'International Implications for Donor Countries and Agencies of Meeting Basic Human Needs' (Washington, World Bank *Basic Needs Paper No. 3*).

Strout, A.M. & P.G. Clark (1969): *Aid, Performance, Self-Help and Need* (Department of State, Agency for International Development AID Discussion Paper No. 20).

Strijker, R.E. (1979): 'The World Bank and Agricultural Development: Food Production and Rural Poverty', in: *World Development*, Vol. 7, No. 3, 325-36.

Taubman, P.J. & T. Wales (1975): 'Education as an Investment and a Screening Device', in: F.Th. Juster (ed): *Education, Income and Human Behaviour* (New York, Carnegie Commission on Higher Education/BNER Report, McGraw Hill).

Taylor, K.W. (1970): 'The Pre-Investment Function in the International Development System', in: *International Development Review*, Vol. 12, No. 2, 2-10.

Tendler, J. (1975): *Inside Foreign Aid* (Baltimore, Johns Hopkins).

Thompson, J.D. (1967): *Organizations in Action: Social Science Bases of Administrative Theory* (New York, McGraw Hill).

Thompson, J.D. (ed) (1966): *Approaches to Organizational Design* (University of Pittsburgh Press).

Thorbecke, E. (1973): 'The Employment Problem: a Critical Evaluation of Four ILO Comprehensive Country Reports', in: *International Labour Review*, Vol. 107, No. 5, 393-423.

Thurow, L.C. (1975): 'Education and Economic Equality', in: *The Public Interest*, No. 28 (Summer 1972). Reprinted in: D.M. Levine & M.J. Bane (eds): *The 'Inequality' Controversy, Schooling and Distributive Justice* (New York, Basic Books).

Tims, W. (1968): *Analytical Techniques for Development Planning. A Case Study of Pakistan's Third Five-Year Plan, 1965-1970* (Karachi, Pakistan Institute of Development Economics).

—— (1975): 'The Developing Countries', in: E.R. Fried & C.L. Schultz (eds): *Higher Oil Prices and the World Economy; The Adjustment Problem* (Washington, The Brookings Institution), 169-95).

—— (1977): 'De Schuldenpositie van de Ontwikkelingslanden', in: *Economisch Statistische Bulletin*, Rotterdam (6 July; 10 August, 28 September), 644-46, 758-61, 936-40.

Tinbergen, J. (1967): *Development Planning* (London, World University Library).

—— (Chairman, Committee for Development Planning) (1970): *Towards Accelerated Development. Proposals for the Second United Nations Development Decade* (Tinbergen Report) (New York, UN).

Tinbergen, J., et al (1976): *Reshaping the International Order* (Amsterdam, North Holland).

Turner, H.A. & D.A.S. Jackson (1970): 'On the Determination of the General Wage Level – A World Analysis; or "Unlimited Labour Forever"', in: *Economic Journal*, Vol. LXXX, 827-49.

UN (1973): *Multinational Corporations in World Development* (New York, ST/ECA/190).

UNCTAD (1979): 'Some Aspects of the Impact of Inflation on the Debt Burden of Developing Countries', in: *World Development*, Vol. 7, No. 2.

UNIDO (1972): *Guidelines for Project Evaluation* (New York).

The United States and the Multilateral Development Banks (1974). Prepared for the Committee on Foreign Affairs by the Foreign Affairs Division, Congressional Research Service, Library of Congress (Washington, US Government Printing Office).

United States Foreign Aid in Action: a Case Study (1966). Submitted to the Sub-Committee on Foreign Aid Expenditure of the Committee on Government Operations (Washington, US Senate).

The United States and the Third World. A Discussion Paper (1976) (Washington, Department of State Publications 8863).

UNRISD (1969-75): *Rural Cooperatives and Related Institutions as Agents of Planned Change* (Geneva, 8 Volumes).

—— (1971-74): *The Social and Economic Implications of Large-Scale Introduction of New Varieties of Food Grain – Summary of Conclusions of a Global Research Project* (Geneva, 8 Volumes).

Uphoff, N.T. & M.J. Esman (1974): *Local Organization for Rural Development: Analysis of The Asian Experience* (Ithaca, New York, Cornell University Centre for International Studies).

USAID (1963): *Principles of Foreign Economic Assistance*. USAID Program Coordination Staff (Washington).

Vibert, F. (1977): 'The Process of Replenishing IDA Finances', in: *Finance and Development*, Vol. 14, No. 3, 25-27, 40.

Vinson, F.M. (1946): 'After the Savannah Conference', in: *Foreign Affairs*, Vol. 24, No. 4, 622-32.

de Vries, B.A. (1972): 'Unemployment and Poverty – What Remedies Are Feasible', in: *Finance and Development*, Vol. 9, No. 1, 10-15.

—— (1973): 'The Plight of Small Countries', in: *Finance and Development*, Vol. 10, No. 3, 6-8, 34.

van Wagenen, R.W. (1972): 'Training as an Element in Bank Group Projects', in: *Finance and Development*, Vol. 9, No. 3, 34-39.

Walinsky, L.J. (ed) (1977): *Agrarian Reform as Unfinished Business. The Selected Papers of Wolf Ladejinsky* (Oxford University Press for the World Bank).

Wall, D. (1973): *The Charity of Nations: the Political Economy of Foreign Aid* (London, MacMillan).

Wallerstein, I. (1971): 'The Range of Choice: Constraints on the Policies of Governments of Contemporary African Independent States', Chapter 2 in: M.E. Lofchie (ed): *The State of the Nations, Constraints on Development in Independent Africa* (Berkeley, University of California Press), 19-33.

—— (1973): 'The State and Social Transformation', in: H. Bernstein (ed): *Underdevelopment and Development. The Third World Today* (Harmondsworth, Penguin), 277-83.

Ward, B., et al (1971): *The Widening Gap: Development in the 1970s* (New York, Columbia University Press).

Warriner, D. (1960): *Land Reform in Principle and Practice* (Oxford University Press).

Wasserman, G. (1976): *Politics of Decolonization. Kenya Europeans and the Land Issue 1960-1965* (Cambridge, Cambridge University Press).

Waterston, A. (1976): *Development Planning: Lessons of Experience, 1965* (4th Edition, Baltimore, Johns Hopkins).

Weaver, J.H. (1965): *The International Development Association: a New Approach to Foreign Aid* (New York, Praeger).

Weaver, J., et al (1978): 'An Assessment of the Effectiveness of the World Bank and the Inter-American Development Bank in Aiding the Poor', in: *Hearings before a Sub-Committee of the Committee on Appropriations* (Chairman, C. Long), House of Representatives, 95th Congress, Second Session (Washington, Government Printing Office).

Weaver, J.H. & K.P. Jameson (1978): 'Economic Development: Competing Paradigms – Competing Parables' (USAID Development Studies Program, *Occasional Paper* No. 3, January).

Weckstein, R.S. (1972): 'Shadow Prices and Project Evaluation in Less-Developed Countries', in: *Economic Development and Cultural Change*, Vol. 20, No. 3, 474-95.

'De Wereldbank, aanzet tot analyse', in: *NESBIC Bulletin*, Vol. 6, Nos 8-9, 1-41.

Wharton Jr, C.R. (1969): 'The Green Revolution: Cornucopia or Pandora's Box?', in: *Foreign Affairs*, Vol. 47, No. 3, 464-76.

'What Now – Another Development' (1975) (Uppsala, Dag Hammerskjöld Foundation).

White, J. (1967): *Pledged to Development: A Study of International Consortia and the Strategy of Aid* (London, Overseas Development Institute).

—— (1970): *Regional Development Banks* (London, Overseas Development Institute).

—— (1974): *The Politics of Foreign Aid* (London, The Bodley Head).

—— (1976a): 'The Evaluation Of Aid Offers', in: *Development and Change*, Vol. 7, No. 3, 233-48.

—— (1976b): 'International Agencies: the Case for Proliferation', in: G.K. Helleiner (ed): *A World Divided. The Less Developed Countries in the International Economy* (Cambridge University Press), 275-93.

de Wilde, J.C., et al (1967): *Experiences with Agricultural Development in Tropical Africa*, Vol. I The Synthesis; Vol. II Case Studies (Baltimore, Johns Hopkins for World Bank).

Williams, J.H. (1967): 'International Bank for Reconstruction and Development' (Paper delivered to the Fourth Maxwell Institute on the United Nations, Bretton Woods, 27 August-September 1 (February 28, 1968; mimeographed).

Willoughby, C. (1977): 'Ex Post Project Evaluation – the Bank's Experience', in: *Finance and Development*, Vol. 14, No. 1, 29-31.

Wilson, J.Q. (1966): 'Innovation in Organization: Notes Towards a Theory', in: J.D. Thompson (ed): *Approaches to Organizational Design* (Pittsburgh, University of Pittsburgh Press), 193-218.

World Bank Publications
—— *Issues Paper*
    'Agricultural Land Settlement' (January 1978).
—— *Papers*
    'Agricultural Credit' (August 1974).
    'Land Reform' (July 1974).
    'Rural Electrification' (October 1975).
    'Rural Enterprise and Non-farm Employment' (January 1978).
    'Sites and Services Projects' (April 1974).
    'Village Water Supply' (March 1976).
—— *Reports*
    'Agricultural Credit' (May 1, 1974; No. 436).
    'Land Reform' (May 2, 1974; No. 440).
—— *Sector Policy Papers*
    'Agricultural Credit' (May 1975).
    'Development Finance Companies' (April 1976).
    'Employment and Development of Small Enterprises' (February 1978)
    'Forestry' (February 1978).
    'Health' (March 1975).
    'Housing' (May 1975).
    'Land Reform' (May 1975).
    'Rural Development' (February 1975).
    'Urban Transport' (May 1975).
—— *Sector Working Paper*
    'Education' (December 1974).
—— *Staff Working Paper*
    'The Economic Analysis of Rural Road Projects' (August 1976, No. 241).
—— *Annual Reports* (Various years)
—— (1978): 'Annual Review of Project Performance Audit Results' (November).
—— (1975): *The Assault on World Poverty* (Baltimore, Johns Hopkins for the World Bank).
—— *Atlas* (Various years)
—— (1972): 'Bank Operations in Colombia: An Evaluation' (Programming and Budgeting Department, Operations Evaluation Division, Report No. Z-18, Washington, May 25, 1972).
—— (1954): *The International Bank for Reconstruction and Development 1946-1953* (Baltimore, Johns Hopkins).
—— (1961): '1946-1961 Fifteenth Anniversary Edition', in: *International Bank Notes*, Vol. 15, No. 6 (IBRD Personnel Division) (June), 4-27.
—— (1977): 'IDA. International Development Association' (April).
—— (1978): 'IDA. International Development Association' (April).
—— *Operations Evaluation Department*
—— (1979): 'Rural Development Projects: A Retrospective View of Bank Experience in Sub-Saharan Africa' (Report No. 2242, October 13).
—— (1976): 'Operation Evaluations. World Bank Standards and Procedures' (Washington, June).

—— (1971): 'Policies and Operations, IBRD, IDA and IFC' (Washington, June).
—— (1974): 'Policies and Operations. The World Bank Group' (Washington, September).
—— (1970): 'Possible Improvements in Techniques of Lending. A Study Prepared by the Staff of the World Bank, requested by UNCTAD' (Washington, April).
—— (1977): 'Prospects for Developing Countries 1978-85' (Washington, November).
—— (1977): 'The External Debt of Developing Countries' (Appendix I to 'Prospects for Developing Countries 1978-85', Washington, November).
—— *Questions and Answers.* World Bank and IDA (March 1976, January 1974, September 1971).
—— (1975): Research Program: *Abstracts of Current Studies* (October).
—— (1968): 'Some Aspects of the Economic Philosophy of the World Bank' (Rio de Janeiro, September).
—— (1973): *Summary Proceedings of the 1973 Annual Meeting of Governors IBRD/IDA/ IFC, Nairobi, September 24-28* (Washington, December).
—— (1972): *World Bank Operations. Sectoral Program and Policies* (Baltimore, Johns Hopkins for IBRD).
—— (1978): *World Development Report* (August).
Young, J.P. (1950): 'Developing Plans for an International Monetary Fund and a World Bank', in: *US Department of State Bulletin*, Vol. XXIII, No. 592, 778-90.
Yudelman, M. (1966): *Agricultural Development in Latin America: Current Status and Prospects* (Washington, Inter-American Development Bank).
—— (1976a): 'The World Bank and Rural Development', in: G. Hunter, A.H. Bunting & A. Bottrall (eds): *Policy and Practice in Rural Development* (London, Croom Helm for ODI), 21-29.
—— (1976b): 'The Role of Agriculture in Integrated Rural Development Projects: the Experience of the World Bank', in: *Sociologia Ruralis*, Vol. XVI, No. 4, 308-325.
—— (1977): 'Integrated Rural Development Projects: the Bank's Experience', in: *Finance and Development*, Vol. 14, No. 1, 15-18.

QUEEN MARY
COLLEGE
LIBRARY

WITHDRAWN
FROM STOCK
QMUL LIBRARY